The Reminiscences Of
Admiral Arthur D. Struble
U.S. Navy (Retired)

Interviewed By
John T. Mason Jr.

U.S. Naval Institute • Annapolis, Maryland

Copyright © 2011

Preface

The heart of this memoir deals with amphibious warfare, a specialty in which Admiral Struble had a great deal of experience. In the 1930s, he was involved in an experimental landing exercise when he was on the staff of a battleship division commander. Doctrine and expertise in the amphibious warfare developed steadily in the 1930s and became a hallmark of U.S. success in World War II—in North Africa, the Mediterranean theater, the continent of Europe, and in the island-hopping campaign against Japanese strongholds in the Pacific. He was chief of staff to operational commander Rear Admiral Allen Kirk for the U.S. portion of the huge D-Day landings at Normandy, France, in June 1944. Afterward he was soon on his way to the Pacific, where he was operational commander himself for a series of assaults in the Philippine Islands. He thus had the rare distinction of flag-officer service in amphibious warfare in both Europe and the Pacific.

In the postwar period, Struble commanded the entire amphibious force of the U.S. Pacific Fleet as doctrine continued to develop. The need to employ that knowledge came sooner than expected. At the outbreak of the Korean War, Struble was Commander of the Seventh Fleet and was on-scene commander for the historic landing at Inchon, South Korea, in September 1950 and the one at Wonsan, North Korea, the following month. As a result, Struble devoted the lion's share of his recollections in this oral history to amphibious events. In both World War II and Korea he had frequent contact with General of the Army Douglas MacArthur and thus was in position to offer informed assessments when interviewed.

In addition, Admiral Struble's memories illuminate many other phases of his career—presented from the perspective of a generation now gone, those who entered the naval service prior to World War I. Through his words one learns of a Navy far different from that of the present time, particularly in the capability of its ships and equipment. Thus we can be grateful to Dr. John T. Mason Jr., the founder of the Naval Institute's oral history program, for conducting the interviews when his subject was available.

For some reason, the project stalled prior to completion. Apparently additional interviews were intended to cover the remainder of the admiral's life but were not done. Nor did Admiral Struble provide inputs to the transcripts of the interviews that were. The oral history was still unfinished when Dr. Mason retired in 1982, and Admiral Struble died the following year. For a number of reasons, the history remained idle for many years. Since then, I have done minor editing on the transcript and added footnotes and an index for the benefit of readers. Ms. Ann Hassinger formatted and printed the resulting version. Ms. Janis Jorgensen of the Naval Institute staff has coordinated the printing and binding of the finished product.

In completing this volume, the Naval Institute expresses its gratitude to the Tawani Foundation and the Pritzker Military Library of Chicago for their generous financial support of the oral history program that produced this memoir.

Paul Stillwell
U.S. Naval Institute
January 2011

ADMIRAL ARTHUR DEWEY STRUBLE
UNITED STATES NAVY (RETIRED)

Arthur Dewey Struble was born in Portland, Oregon, on 28 June 1894, son of Walter Burr and Hannah Wadsworth (Fairchild) Struble. He attended Lincoln High School in Portland before his appointment to the U.S. Naval Academy, Annapolis, Maryland, from the Second District of Oregon in 1911. As a midshipman he played lacrosse and soccer. Graduated and commissioned ensign on 5 June 1915, he progressed in rank to that of vice admiral, to date from 26 April 1948. On 1 July 1956 he was transferred to the retired list of the U.S. Navy and was advanced to the rank of admiral on the basis of combat awards.

Following graduation from the Naval Academy in 1915, he served consecutively in the USS South Dakota, USS St. Louis, and USS Glacier until September 1917. After assisting in fitting out the USS Stevens at Quincy, Massachusetts, he joined that destroyer as engineer officer upon her commissioning on 24 May 1918. In October 1919 he reported as executive officer on board the USS Shubrick and as such participated in the Haitian campaign. He latter commanded that vessel and in April 1920 transferred to the USS Meyer, in which he had duty as executive officer until September 1921.

He was an instructor in the Department of Marine Engineering and Naval Construction at the Naval Academy until June 1923, when he joined the USS California. From October 1925 until September 1927 he served successively as aide and flag lieutenant on the staff of Commander Battleship Divisions, Battle Fleet, and Commander Battle Fleet.

In October 1927 he was assigned to the Office of Naval Communications, Office of the Chief of Naval Operations, Navy Department, Washington, D.C., where he remained until May 1930, and the following two years he had duty on the staff of Commander Battleship Division Three as aide and flag secretary. In June 1932 he reported as gunnery officer on board the USS New York, and in June 1933 was detached for a two-year tour of duty as district communication officer, Twelfth Naval District, San Francisco, California.

He reported in June 1935 aboard the USS Portland and served as her first lieutenant and damage control officer until June 1936. He then joined the staff of Commander Cruisers, Scouting Force, as damage control officer, and on being detached from that assignment a year later, was attached to the Central Division, Office of the Chief of Naval Operations, Navy Department.

He joined the USS Arizona in June 1940 and served as executive officer until January 1941, when he assumed command of the USS Trenton. He was in command of that vessel, cruising in the Southeast Pacific, upon the outbreak of World War II, and until May 1942.

Struble was assigned to the Office of the Chief of Naval Operations, Navy Department, as Director of the Central Division. For this duty he received a letter of commendation with authorization to wear the Commendation Ribbon from the Secretary of the Navy. In November 1943 he reported a chief of staff and aide to Commander Task Force 122, 12th Fleet. "For exceptionally meritorious conduct as Chief of Staff to the Western Naval Task Force previous to and during the amphibious assault on the enemy German-held coast of Normandy commencing June 6, 1944 . . . " he was awarded the Legion of Merit with authorization to wear the Combat "V."

In August 1944 he was assigned duty as Commander Group Two, Seventh Amphibious Force (redesignated in October of that year as Amphibious Group Nine, Seventh Amphibious Force). While serving in that command he directed the initial landings at the entrance to Leyte Gulf, then commanded the assault landings at Ormoc Bay, and the successful amphibious assault on Mindoro. On 29 January 1945 his force successfully put the 11th Army Corps ashore in the San Narciso Area at Zambales, northwest of Subic Bay. Forces under him captured Subic Bay, Mariveles, and Corregidor. He later conducted numerous landings in the Central Visayas.

As Commander Amphibious Group Nine, Struble was awarded a gold star in lieu of a second Legion of Merit (with combat "V") "For exceptionally meritorious conduct . . . in action against enemy Japanese forces in the Philippine Islands, from November 17 to December 8, 1944 . . . " and a gold star in lieu of a third Legion of Merit (with combat "V") for outstanding services " . . . in action against enemy Japanese forces in the Philippine Islands, from December 8, 1944 to January 2, 1945. . . "

The Distinguished Service Medal was awarded for services ". . . in the Philippine Islands Area from January to August 15, 1945. As Attack Group Commander, [he] demonstrated brilliant leadership and resourcefulness in the tactical execution of operational plans for the amphibious landings at Zambales, Bataan, and Corregidor on the Island of Luzon; on the Islands of Negros and Panay; and at Macajalar Bay on the Island of Mindanao. His sound judgment in the preparation of assault plans, his tact in coordinating the joint operations of the Allied Military Forces, and his professional skill in the discharge of his duties were major factors in the success of the Philippine Islands operation and in the ultimate regaining of complete control in the Southwest Pacific Area . . ."

He was also awarded the Distinguished Service Medal by the Army for "distinguished service to the Government in a position of great responsibility from 30 August to 17 November 1944 as an Amphibious Attack Group Commander during operations against enemy Japanese Forces in the Philippine Islands during the liberation of that area from Japanese domination . . . ."

In September 1945, after the capitulation of the Japanese, he assumed command of Minecraft Pacific Fleet, in which duty he was responsible for clearing the mines in the Western Pacific. He received a letter of commendation with authorization to wear the Commendation Ribbon from the Secretary of the Navy for services in this assignment from 30 August 1945 to 1 June 1946. He transferred to command of Amphibious Force Pacific Fleet in June 1946. Elements of the forces under his command, together with an Army infantry division, an Army engineer brigade, and Army, Navy, and Marine Corps aircraft, participated in the first full-scale peacetime amphibious training exercises, held in late November and early December 1946. These exercises were conducted off the coast of Southern California and were brought to a successful conclusion on 14 December 1946.

In April 1948 Struble was detached from command of Amphibious Force, U.S. Pacific Fleet and assumed duty as Deputy Chief of Naval Operations (Operations), Navy Department, Washington, D.C. In that capacity he was the Naval Deputy on the Joint Chiefs of Staff. He remained in that assignment until May 1950, when he became Commander Seventh Fleet. In July 1950 he commanded the initial Korean War carrier operations in the Yellow Sea and the Sea of Japan. He was responsible for preparing the U.S. plans and for the conduct of operations in connection with the security of Taiwan.

On 24 August 1950, he commenced the preparation of the joint operation plan for the Inchon invasion. He commanded the force of 261 ships of the United Nations forces, plus the U.S. Tenth Corps, consisting of the First Marine Division and the Seventh U.S. Army division for that invasion. On 15 September, this force carried out a highly successful amphibious assault against Inchon, Korea, under difficult hydrographic conditions. The assault and landings were successfully completed, and the occupation of this area by United Nations forces turned the tide in Korea and forced the withdrawal of North Korean forces from South Korea.

About one month later, he commanded a large landing at Wonsan, Korea. Later in the year his forces furnished close air support and gun support for the U.N. troops operating in North Korea, for the now-famous evacuation of the First Marine Division from the Chosin Reservoir area and for the redeployment of the Tenth Corps from Hungnam.

Until 28 March 1951, when he was detached from the command, the Seventh Fleet continued in support of the U.N. operations in Korea, providing gunfire and close air support in addition to bombardment and air interdiction missions against the enemy's transportation system in North Korea.

For heroism against an armed enemy during the period of 15 September to 19 October 1950, he was awarded the Distinguished Service Cross by the Department of the Army. The citation follows:

"Vice Admiral Arthur D. Struble . . . United States Navy distinguished himself by extraordinary heroism in action against an armed enemy of the United States during the period of 15 September to 19 October 1950. Serving as Commander of the SEVENTH Fleet, he was personally responsible for the execution of all the fleet's activities against the North Korean aggressor. As a direct result of his bold execution of plans in smashing enemy shore defenses and providing close air coverage, the spectacular Inchon invasion, one of the most difficult ever attempted because of extreme tides, was brilliantly effected with minimum loss of landing forces. [His] personal bravery, in evidence at all times, was particularly notable during the mine-sweeping operations at Wonsan. There, over a prolonged period, he personally supervised the work of eliminating this navigational menace, acquiring firsthand knowledge to insure success of the operations and to encourage the mine-sweeping group by his presence. Through his conspicuous courage and daring execution of brilliant tactical naval operations, Admiral Struble made an invaluable contribution to the cause of the United Nations in Korea, and reflects great credit on himself and the military service. . . "

He was also awarded a gold star in lieu of the second Distinguished Service Medal for "exceptionally meritorious service . . . a Commander United States SEVENTH Fleet during operations against enemy aggressor forces in Korea from June 27, 1950 to January 1, 1951 . . . " The citation further states: "Thoroughly understanding the unusual military situation confronting our armies, Vice Admiral Struble quickly and skillfully planned for the most effect employment of large Naval surface and air forces. He established and maintained a schedule of air strikes and shore bombardment against the enemy which served in a great measure to relieve the pressure being exerted against friendly ground forces. As Commander of the principal Naval forces afloat in the Far East, he vigorously executed the broad Naval phases of the Inchon and Wonsan operation, carried out with marked success despite extreme difficulties imposed by treacherous current and tidal conditions as well as mine-obstructed waters in the target area. . . ."

Detached from command of the Seventh Fleet, he reported on 28 March 1951 as Commander First Fleet. He served as such until 24 March 1952, and then proceeded to duty with the Joint Chiefs of Staff, Washington, D.C.

On 14 May 1952 he became the United States Naval Representative on the Military Staff Committee of the United Nations, and on 1 July 1953 assumed the duties of chairman of the U.S. Military Delegation to the Military Staff Committee of the United Nations. On 1 June 1955 he reported as Commander Eastern Sea Frontier and Commander Atlantic Reserve Fleet, and continued to serve in his latter assignment at the United Nations headquarters. On 1 July 1956 he was transferred to the retired list of the U.S. Navy.

In addition to the Navy Distinguished Service Medal with gold star, the Army Distinguished Service Cross and Distinguished Service Medal, the Legion of Merit with two gold stars, and the Commendation Ribbon with bronze star, Admiral Struble received the Mexican Service Medal; the World War I Victory Medal, Destroyer Clasp; the Haitian Campaign Medal; American Defense Service Medal, Fleet Clasp; American Campaign Medal; European-African-Middle Eastern Campaign Medal with one star; Asiatic-Pacific Campaign Medal with silver star (five engagements); the World War II Victory Medal; Navy Occupation Service Medal; United Nations Service Medal; and the Philippine Liberation Ribbon with two stars.

He was also awarded the Legion d'Honneur, Rank of Officer, and the Croix de Guerre with Palm from the government of France; the Royal Order of the Phoenix, High Commandeur, awarded by the government of Greece; Commander of the Order of Leopold with Palm; the Croix de Guerre with Palm, from the government of Belgium; and the Order of Military Merit Silver Star from Korea.

Admiral Struble was married to the former Hazel L. Ralston of Portland, Oregon; she died in April 1962. They were the parents of three children: Commander Arthur D. Struble Jr., U.S. Navy (Retired); Mrs. Nancy Struble Wilhite; and Mrs. Elizabeth Struble Wilson. Admiral Struble died 1 May 1983; he was survived by his second wife, Margaret.

Deed of Gift

The U.S. Naval Institute is hereby authorized to make available to individuals, libraries, and other repositories of its choosing the transcripts and/or tape recordings of 12 oral history interviews concerning the life and naval career of the late Admiral Arthur D. Struble, U.S. Navy (Retired). The Naval Institute may also, at its discretion, use the material in electronic/digital format, including posting on the Internet. The interviews were recorded on 25 May 1976, 28 May 1976, 10 June 1976, 18 June 1976, 23 June 1976, 10 December 1976, 15 December 1976, 6 January 1977, 13 January 1977, 19 January 1977, 27 January 1977, and 3 February 1977 in collaboration with Dr. John T. Mason for the U.S. Naval Institute.

The undersigned does hereby release and assign to the U.S. Naval Institute the rights and title to these interviews, with the following exceptions. The undersigned retains the right to use the material for his own purposes, as he sees fit. The undersigned reserves the right to publish all or parts of the oral history as well as material drawn from it. The copyright in both the oral and transcribed versions shall be held jointly by the undersigned and the U.S. Naval Institute. The tape recordings of the interviews are and will remain the property of the U.S. Naval Institute.

Signed and sealed this 7 day of APRIL 2003.

Arthur D. Struble, Jr., for the estate of
Admiral Arthur D. Struble, USN (Ret.)

Interview Number 1 with Admiral Arthur D. Struble, U.S. Navy (Retired)
Place: Admiral Struble's Home, Chevy Chase, Maryland
Date: Tuesday, 25 May 1976
Interviewer: John T. Mason, Jr.

John T. Mason, Jr.: Admiral, this is a great day. This is something I have been looking forward to for—well, since 1971, I guess, when you first said that you might do an oral biography. Now we have arrived at the day when you are going to begin.

Would you begin in the proper way with a biography by telling me the date and place of your birth and then something about your father and mother?

Admiral Struble: I was born in Portland, Oregon, on June 28, 1894. My father had come out to Oregon with his father shortly after—a couple of years, maybe—after the Civil War. He had been in the Civil War from Ohio. Then two or three years after the Civil War he decided to go out to the Oregon country.

John T. Mason, Jr.: The land of opportunity it was then.

Admiral Struble: The land of opportunity, you might say.

John T. Mason, Jr.: What was his business? What did he do?

Admiral Struble: My grandfather was a lawyer and was a lawyer in the city of Portland and twice ran for one of the county or city offices and held some local office for a while—a very fine old white-haired gentleman in my memory, a very fine person. My father, however, had gone into the meat business early in his life and was with the Union Meat Company, which was a large supply house in Portland.

My mother's family lived in northern New York—I would say 100 miles or so north of New York City—on a farm. He apparently had a pretty good-sized farm, possibly was slightly interested in politics. His name was Fairchild. Some time, I suppose I would say in the 1870s, he was offered the appointment to be head of the Indian reservations in Oregon country. The Oregon country doesn't mean just the state of Oregon now, but it meant the area that is now the state of Oregon, now the state of Washington, and part of Idaho.

John T. Mason, Jr.: It was the whole Northwest.

Admiral Struble: Well, it was the Northwest, yes. So he went out, and at the same time that he was in Oregon he lived, of course, on one of the Indian reservations about 30 miles or so south of where Portland is today. His wife was a small, little, tiny, I would say, Englishwoman, because she was quite dainty.

My mother at that time was 14 years of age when they went west. She loved to ride horses, and her father, in handling the Indian reservations, was expected to visit all the reservations in his area twice a year, which, of course, he had to do by horseback. His wife was not interested in horseback riding, but his 14-year-old daughter was. So she became his companion on these trips through the Northwest to visit the Indian tribes. Actually, when I was a boy she could speak about 20 or more Indian dialects perfectly.

John T. Mason, Jr.: Remarkable! As a young girl she picked them up very readily.

Admiral Struble: Oh yes, as she went around with her father. Now, at that time I was the youngest, and I suppose the time I am talking about, which would have been about 1908, for example, Mother was in the 60s, I guess. I remember one day in particular we were down on the Columbia River, and there were a group of about 20 Indians gathered together. She kind of held up her hand, and the children—I being the youngest—all stopped. She stood and looked, I remember, for two or three minutes and then walked over and spoke to them in their own dialect. As you know, all the Indian dialects of all these different Indian tribes were slightly different. They could talk to each other, but there were differences. She spoke in their own language. Of course, they were bowled over.

John T. Mason, Jr.: I guess they would be.

Admiral Struble: Well, this was an interesting thing about her. She was a very fine person. I grew up in Portland and went to Ladd Grammar School and then to Portland High School, which later became known as Lincoln High School. We had a second high school on the east side of the river which was named Washington High School. So the two big high schools in Portland were Washington and Lincoln.

John T. Mason, Jr.: Did you take to riding, too, as a youngster?

Admiral Struble: No, I was more inclined to be good in mathematics. I did very well in physics and very well in chemistry.

John T. Mason, Jr.: I meant did you take up horseback riding?

Admiral Struble: No, actually, in my life I rode very little.

John T. Mason, Jr.: You were the studious type then.

Admiral Struble: No, it was simply because by the time I grew up, I grew up as a city boy. When we were very young, probably before I was born, some of my older brothers had ridden horseback on the farm that we had east of Portland for a while.

John T. Mason, Jr.: I see.

Admiral Struble: The older children were gone from the household. As a matter of fact, in the last six years of my life in Portland I was the only child at home.

John T. Mason, Jr.: How many children were there in the family?

Admiral Struble: Five—one girl and four boys.

John T. Mason, Jr.: When did you get the idea that you would like to go to the Naval Academy?

Admiral Struble: Well, that is rather interesting. In the year 1908 my father and mother took me down to the mouth of the Columbia River. There is the Washington beach that goes north from the Columbia, and there is the Oregon beach that goes south at the entrance to the Columbia River. Actually we used to go on the Washington side of the river, the north side, every summer. The family would pick up and go down for two or three months and pick up and come home again.

But in 1908, in about March, as I would remember—but it was before we usually went down there for vacation—they took me down to the mouth of the Columbia River. And we saw the Great White Fleet pass the mouth of the Columbia River, going north to Puget Sound.[*] It had stopped at San Francisco; the next stop was Seattle. Of course, Portland people were mad as hell that they didn't come into the Columbia River. But, actually, the Columbia River at that time would not have been a particularly suitable spot for the fleet to have come in and tried to anchor in. It's a big river. It's one of the two big rivers of the country, but it wasn't too suitable for handling the fleet. Now a big ship can come in, and pretty good-sized ships can come up to Portland.

John T. Mason, Jr.: But this intrigued you?

Admiral Struble: Well, I was interested but immediately dropped it and had no further thought of Annapolis. I decided to go either to the University of Oregon, which was a possibility, or possibly go to Berkeley or Stanford because they were in California, and they apparently had more prestige than Oregon.[†] I had a couple of friends, older boys, that had gone south. One in particular was at Berkeley, and he persuaded me that I ought to go to Berkeley.

---

[*] Between December 1907 and February 1909, a fleet of 16 battleships sailed around the world as a demonstration of U.S. naval power. Because U.S. warships of the period typically had white-painted hulls, the ships were known collectively as the Great White Fleet.
[†] Berkeley is the site of the University of California; Stanford University is in Stanford, California.

So I had planned to go to Berkeley and probably take an engineering course. But out of a clear blue sky in May of 1911, it was announced in the paper that some boy who had been given an appointment to Annapolis had fallen out, and the congressman in Washington was going to have a special examination for about three hours on Saturday morning. And the boy who stood high in that would get the nomination.

So just being a little bit competitive, I went down for the fun of taking the exam.

John T. Mason, Jr.: But no advance notice, really?

Admiral Struble: Oh no, there was no advance notice on this thing. The boy that was supposed to go in June had fallen out, so he had to make his appointment. I have forgotten how many boys there were. I don't think there were over a half a dozen or eight assembled and took a little three-hour exam that the superintendent of schools in Portland had prepared to test us out. I apparently tested high on that one and was told I could have the appointment.

But I still hadn't made up my mind. My father got mad and said, "You better make up your mind." He called my older brother, who was down in Washington. He was 1908, so he was seven years ahead of me.*

John T. Mason, Jr.: Washington, D.C.?

Admiral Struble: Yes, he was at George Washington University taking an advanced course in ordnance that the college had intended to start and put on as a regular thing—a postgraduate course. He was taking that. He got on the phone and gave me hell.

John T. Mason, Jr.: Had he gone to Annapolis?

Admiral Struble: Oh yes, he had gone and graduated in 1908, so he was seven years ahead of me. Now actually after the Mexican incidents of 1914—he was down in

---

* Ensign George W. Struble, USN. He had stood fourth of the 201 graduates of the Naval Academy's class of 1908. He resigned his commission in October 1914 as a lieutenant (junior grade).

Veracruz—he came home, and he resigned from the Navy and went to work for Bethlehem Steel and became their ordnance expert.*

So I came pretty much at the last minute.

John T. Mason, Jr.: It took a little pressure to get you here.

Admiral Struble: Well, I hadn't made up my mind. I had kind of made up my mind to do something different. I wasn't going to be jumped around too quick. However, I came east and took the exam and passed and went into Annapolis. I guess I entered about the end of June 1911.

John T. Mason, Jr.: Well, that was a great occasion. You passed the physical exam with flying colors, I take it.

Admiral Struble: The only possible trouble was that I was just at the ragged edge on height. I was five-foot-two, and that was the lowest you could—and I was just at that. I remember I was very small. I weighed 96 pounds.

John T. Mason, Jr.: Well, indeed you were small.

Admiral Struble: So, of course, at the Naval Academy the upperclassmen considered me always as a kid. For some reason a youngster like myself gets lots of attention from the upperclassmen who feel it's their duty to bring them up right.

John T. Mason, Jr.: He becomes something of a mascot.

Admiral Struble: Well, yes. As you've heard stories about hazing and everything, they sometimes did have a few cases of hazing that weren't good at the Naval Academy. But

---

* In April 1914 a U.S. Navy paymaster was detained ashore in Veracruz, Mexico. Rear Admiral Henry T. Mayo, USN, demanded an apology and amends. The situation worsened when a German ship approached with guns and ammunition for the Mexican government. The result was that a landing force of U.S. Marines and sailors went ashore at Veracruz on 21 April and fought a series of gun battles with Mexicans.

on the whole, it was somewhat [unclear] and not generally really spiteful, and therefore I never thought it was bad. I guess I was a little bit flip as a youngster. I was quick on the trigger with talking, so I received lots of favorable attention from the upper class, who thought it was up to them to bring me up right.

I never regretted it. I stood on my head many times, and I told stories and did all sorts of things.

John T. Mason, Jr.: And got under the table?

Admiral Struble: Oh yes, I was put under the table a number of times. I don't know if I should tell you one of my really famous stories on that or not.

John T. Mason, Jr.: Yes, you should.

Admiral Struble: Well, we used to march into the mess hall and be seated at the table. We sat down in chairs, and underneath the seat of the chair is a little bit of wire mesh and a place to put your hat. You were supposed, when you came into the mess, to turn your hat over and put the top down underneath your chair so that when dinner was over and you would rise and march out, you would reach under and put your cap on and march out of the mess hall.

So everybody's white hat was underneath their chairs, including the upper class too. At each end of the long table there would be a couple of first classmen.* Then there'd be a few second classmen, and then there'd be a few third classmen. And then in the center on each side there'd be maybe four or five plebes on each side of each table. The upperclassmen—the first classmen very much, the second classmen a fair amount, and the third classmen—were not encouraged to talk to the plebes too much at the table. Although they were permitted to, they were kind of young themselves and were not supposed to talk to them.

---

* Naval Academy midshipmen compared with their civilian counterparts as follows: plebe, freshman; third classman, sophomore; second classman, junior; first classman, senior.

John T. Mason, Jr.: They were in the process of emerging.

Admiral Struble: So that night there was some talk going on which, of course, the midshipmen all were interested in. Something was said, and I kind of grinned at some statement that was made. Of course, the typical Naval Academy reply at that time was to, "Take that grin off your face." So I was addressed by one of the upperclassmen, and I don't remember what I said back, but it was a little bit of a flip statement back.

And this man said to me, "Mister, get under the table." Of course, that happened a certain amount. Plebes that were told to get under the table, got under the table. They had to obey, and we did. And, in all honesty, I've got to say that maybe my reply had been a little flip.

So I was down under the table. As soon as I got down below and under the table, the first classman that had apparently sent me under the table told a couple of plebes sitting on each side of me at the table, "Fix up his plate and send it down below to him. We don't want to starve him." So my plate was sent down below to me under the table so I could get something to eat.

Well, I've forgotten what it was we had for dinner that night, but I hadn't been too interested in it anyway. But I ate a little bit more. I was wondering what the dessert was going to be and had hopes. Well, it seems that the dessert was one of these kind of squishy things that nobody wanted. So the plebes were told to pass the dessert down to me—kind of a meringue. It hadn't been popular and still wasn't popular with the midshipmen.

I had gotten a plate of it down below to me when one first classman said, "I don't want mine, so I'll give it to the kid." He sent it down the table to the midshipmen that were sitting, but it was passed down to me. Pretty soon I had about 10 or 12 plates of dessert passed down. I was sitting down below the table with all these plates of dessert when I thought, "Mmm. Look at those hats." So I went over, and I deposited desserts in the hats of a large number of the upperclassmen at the table.

Well, pretty soon—a couple or three of four or five minutes—the order came to stand up from the table. The command was to rise, where everybody stands up. And the march-out, and in due order they start marching out of the mess hall. I had not been able to resist temptation. With this rise, march-out, I realized that this wasn't going to be so good. So I had already removed my hat, and I had edged my chair at the table out a little bit. So when the rise came, I crawled right out and shoved my chair out of the way and got three or four feet away from the table. So at the march-out, I was off down the row and joined the company ahead of me marching out. So I got out of the mess hall all right.

But, of course, that didn't prevent the aftermath. The two boys in each room were supposed to study for two hours from 7:30 to 9:30. At 9:30 the study hall would be over, and from 9:30 to 10:00, we could walk around the halls. You could visit people. You could also go up to the bathroom and so forth. Some of the rooms had bathrooms but some didn't. So you would go to the bathroom and that sort of thing, and then at 10:00 o'clock, bang-o, in your rooms and lights out and go to bed.

Well, in that 9:30 period that night I received a large amount of attention in my room. A few of the upperclassmen had decided to pay me some attention, and I was invited to visit their rooms the next night at 9:30. They would like to discuss some of these problems with me. So I went through a little bit of what was known by the midshipmen as being run. "Running" was a smaller adaptation of the word "hazing."

The first class by that time had frowned on some of the methods of old hazing and weren't permitting it. But a plebe was still expected to report in an upperclassman's room at 9:30 if he was told to. He might be told to stand on his head, or he might do some pushups, or he might be told to tell some stories, or they might have a little bit of other things. In my opinion, as far as I was concerned, except for one or two very scattered cases, it didn't bother me, and I think maybe it didn't harm at all in being brought up at the Naval Academy that way. Occasionally an upperclassman maybe would get a little off his own balance and be a little unnecessarily bad about handling his part of it. But on the whole I didn't think it was a bad thing.

John T. Mason, Jr.: On this particular occasion, what kind of punishment was meted out to you?

Admiral Struble: Oh, I got a little more punishment than usual after that pie business, and I think maybe I deserved it.

John T. Mason, Jr.: You mean perhaps, the broom. Did you get the broom or something like that?

Admiral Struble: No, I was stood on my head. They often would stand you on your head. Your head would be on this wooden floor so you would have to push up with your hands; otherwise, it got kind of bad on the top of your head. And I was kind of bad, and I got a certain amount of that for a week or ten days after this one incident I told you about. I had been fresh, and I don't think it hurt me.

John T. Mason, Jr.: But they had invited it by putting this temptation before you—giving you all the deserts.

Admiral Struble: Yes, they put the temptation in my way, but I had certainly used it.

John T. Mason, Jr.: How did you take to the regimented life?

Admiral Struble: I adapted myself to it easily. I didn't mind running errands and doing some of this hazing business at all. In my experience, it was only once or twice some of the upper class, you might say, got a little mean. On two of those occasions that I can remember now, on both occasions another upperclassman stepped in very soon and stopped it himself by persuading the other upperclassman, "Now wait, George, you've gone far enough." There were some cases that probably weren't good, but on the whole it wasn't too bad.

John T. Mason, Jr.: In that time you were confined to the Naval Academy, most all the time with very little freedom.

Admiral Struble: Oh, of course, the plebes got very little freedom, so in a way some of this attention by upperclassmen, if they didn't overdo it, was of interest—to hear them talk and hear what they said and everything else, even though you were being hazed a bit.

John T. Mason, Jr.: It was a kind of entertainment.

Admiral Struble: Well, it was a change for you. Of course, when I was a plebe, we were only allowed out in town very occasionally, as it were, and we were kept pretty much in the academy for eight months solid.

John T. Mason, Jr.: Did you go back to Oregon on leave periods?

Admiral Struble: I went twice to Oregon during my summer's leave, on the train back and forth. But my first class year, instead of going back to Oregon, a number of first classmen—there must have been about five or six of us—took out the Naval Academy yacht called the Robert Setter, which first class midshipmen were permitted to take out for the month of September on their own throughout the Chesapeake Bay. And five or six of us, as new first classmen, took the Robert Setter out from Annapolis and cruised all over Chesapeake Bay, ending up with a final splurge in Baltimore at the yacht club there, which was really a lot of fun. Then back to Annapolis, having spent our September leave sailing the Robert Setter all over the Chesapeake.

John T. Mason, Jr.: Unsupervised?

Admiral Struble: No, there was a chief boatswain's mate, an old-timer, a splendid old boy, a splendid sailor, who went with us. But he was kind of supervisory. He normally let us run the boat completely. When we left Baltimore, I think we made probably as fast a trip in the Robert Setter to Annapolis that has ever been made. We left the Baltimore Yacht Club about 7:00 o'clock in the morning. When we got out into the bay, we had a real wonderful wind going down the bay, quite strong. We went down from Baltimore to Annapolis in the Robert Setter with our lee rail under the water, just heeled way over and making knots.

John T. Mason, Jr.: How big was she, the Robert Setter?

Arthur D. Struble, Interview #1 (5/25/76) – Page 12

Admiral Struble: The <u>Robert Setter</u> was a one-masted yacht that had been presented to the Naval Academy. She was a good boat; she was fast. We made a very quick trip to Annapolis. I would have thought, maybe, we were turning out 14 knots.

John T. Mason, Jr.: What about your classes at the academy, the course of study? You had no problem at all with it, did you?

Admiral Struble: Well, yes. My problem was with the Spanish and French.

John T. Mason, Jr.: Which one did you choose?

Admiral Struble: I took Spanish. I was not good at it; I was always just skinning by. Otherwise, I had no problem.

John T. Mason, Jr.: You had no problem with math or anything like that.

Admiral Struble: No, I was very good in math, and so forth—gunnery and marine engineering. I generally was a pretty good student.

John T. Mason, Jr.: You didn't inherit your mother's facility for language, because she must have had it.

Admiral Struble: No, I didn't. I got into trouble when I went into the Naval Academy, the plebe summer. I had a case of flu or something, and went over to the hospital for about two weeks in early September. During the month of September, the plebes took a preliminary month's course in either French or Spanish, whichever they were going to take from the professors at the academy. I missed that early training. I had gone over to the hospital, and I took the language book with me, and I tried to learn some Spanish myself sitting over there in bed for about two weeks. The result was that when I came back from the hospital I was inclined to—I had looked at this book, and it said, "Si, senor." And instead of saying "Si, senor," which is, of course, what it should have been pronounced, I looked at it and called it "sigh sayner." I read the book a lot at the hospital, and I talked to myself, which I read and I got accustomed to saying some of these very poor things. When I came over to Spanish class and came out with "sigh, sayner," the Spanish prof busted me that month, and I, from then on, had a hard time in Spanish. But I did manage to just get by.

John T. Mason, Jr.: You were too early to benefit by the Berlitz method.

Admiral Struble: That's right.

John T. Mason, Jr.: Well, tell me about the summer cruises.

Admiral Struble: The first cruise we went on the Massachusetts, which was a typical old midshipmen's cruise.* All the three classes were on the Massachusetts: the first class, second class, and youngsters.

John T. Mason, Jr.: On an old coal-burner.

Admiral Struble: The Massachusetts was an old-timer, yes. She was a very, very old battleship. It was a good ship for midshipmen's cruises. It was splendid to have the first and second class on board because they could take care of you better. They knew the ropes. So a few first classmen and a few second classmen could do an awful lot on a midshipman's cruise to keep discipline and everything. It wasn't as good from the standpoint of technical learning, or maybe discipline, as the fleet cruise we took the following summer when we were parceled out—all three classes—to big, modern battleships in the Atlantic fleet. That was the best cruise, because we learned more about the ship; we had better discipline, because there weren't too many of us.

---

* USS Massachusetts was commissioned in 1896 and took part in the Spanish-American War in 1898. She was 351 feet long, 69 feet in the beam, and had a standard displacement of 10,288 tons. She had four 13-inch guns, eight 8-inch, four 6-inch, and six torpedo tubes. She was decommissioned for the last time in 1919, later scuttled off Florida.

John T. Mason, Jr.: They were just operational ships, were they not?

Admiral Struble: Operational ships, and we learned a lot.

John T. Mason, Jr.: Now that was somewhat of a departure from the norm?

Admiral Struble: That was a departure from the normal that we had gotten accustomed to. On the plebe cruise that we took, due to the fact that we didn't have enough people, there was nothing between us on the Massachusetts cruise but a few officers and under officers. It was bad training for the plebes, and we weren't brought up properly on the Massachusetts, as we were when we were split up in a number of ships in the Atlantic Fleet, and there were both first and second class over the plebes. That was a much better cruise.

My final cruise, we were on a cruise to Europe with all three classes present. Of course, by that time I was a first classman. That, I think, was an excellent cruise from that point of view—good for the midshipmen, except that while we were over in the Mediterranean, the Idaho was sold to the Greeks, the battleship we were on.[*] That was because World War I was in prospect, and the Greeks were feeling very much their lack of navy, so they wanted to buy an old battleship from the United States. The United States was willing to sell them the Idaho. So instead of going up to London and Paris with the other two battleships that were in the practice cruise squadron, the battleship that I was on stayed down at Nice for about two or three weeks while an old battleship was put into commission in a hurry and came over and took us off the Idaho, at which time I was at the ceremony when we officially transferred the Idaho to the Greek flag.[†]

She was, of course, a pretty good ship for them in the eastern Mediterranean, because she had more gun power than anything in the . . .

---

[*] USS Idaho was commissioned in April 1908. She was 382 feet long, 77 feet in the beam, and displaced 13,000 tons. She had four 12-inch guns, eight 8-inch, eight 7-inch, and two torpedo tubes. She was decommissioned at Villefranche, France, on 30 July 1914 and turned over to the Greek Navy. She became the coastal defense ship Kilkis.

[†] For more on this cruise see the Naval Institute oral history of Vice Admiral John L. McCrea, USN (Ret.). McCrea and Struble were Naval Academy classmates and were shipmates in the Idaho in 1914.

John T. Mason, Jr.: What did she have, 14-inch guns?

Admiral Struble: Oh, 12-inch. But, boy, she was flying the gunnery trophy of the Atlantic Fleet. The year before she had had the best battle practice among all the battleships. So she was a fine ship, relative to what was in the Mediterranean. The Greeks, therefore, had a bigger ship than the Turks had, which was an important thing.

John T. Mason, Jr.: You were at the ceremony when it was turned over.

Admiral Struble: Oh, yes, we had a formal ceremony in the harbor there.

John T. Mason, Jr.: In Paris? Did you take it over there?

Admiral Struble: Oh, no, in Nice, France. A Greek transport—a civilian ship—came in with the Greek crew to be on board. They came over and visited us the day before the official transfer. We showed them around the ship and everything. Then the next day we hauled the flag down, turned it over to them, and we all left.

    We immediately went to this old battleship—I've forgotten her name now—that had come over.[*] We went on board her and sailed the next morning to return to the United States. So we never did see the Idaho, except we witnessed the hoisting of the Greek flag the next morning. We transferred the ship, not really to the Greeks, but through a civilian intermediary. Of course, there was no doubt who was getting it.

John T. Mason, Jr.: In these cruises on the old battleship, did you get involved in the coaling process?

Admiral Struble: Oh, certainly. Oh, yes. We learned the coaling process very thoroughly.

---

[*] Naval Academy records indicate that Struble and his shipmates transferred from the Idaho to the battleship Maine for the return to the United States.

John T. Mason, Jr.: What about you, as the kid, so to speak?

Admiral Struble: Oh, yes. The kid always got plenty. But one of the things I remember, I learned at that time, which the upperclassmen pointed out to us, they said, "Now, don't forget, coaling ship is not just to be done by the sailors. When we coal ship in the fleet, the battleships, the junior officers in the division go down and personally supervise on the barge handling the coal." The division officers who were by this time, say, lieutenants—they didn't go down on the barge, but the younger officers in the battleship's crew put on their old dungarees and got just as dirty as the men.

I first coaled ship as an ensign out in San Francisco Harbor. Believe me, I was down in the barge and understood what it was all about.

John T. Mason, Jr.: Quite a colorful process it was.

Admiral Struble: It was. Boy, you got dirty as hell before it was over. However, there was no doubt in the Navy at that time, that that was a matter of honor for the younger officers to be down on the coal barge, not just standing up on deck supervising in their better uniforms.

John T. Mason, Jr.: As a result of the cruises, did any of the midshipmen decide this was not for them?

Admiral Struble: I would say yes. Some of them petered out of the Naval Academy, because maybe the cruises weren't what they expected them to be. I think that's possible.

John T. Mason, Jr.: Back at the academy, what was your role in athletics?

Admiral Struble: Well, I played class lacrosse and soccer. I played a little class soccer as a first classman. I played class lacrosse a longer period. But when you got to be first class, it was hard to man these class teams, because all the good people in the business had gone to the varsity by that time or quit. So the class soccer team was having a very difficult time just having enough members to scout a team. So I played a little class lacrosse first-class year just so there would be one or two substitutes for about the 13 that were left still playing at that time. I was never really a soccer player, except I wasn't too bad. In a way, lacrosse was quite a bit like soccer. I mean, a lot of running and all that.

John T. Mason, Jr.: It was a little bit more strenuous perhaps than soccer, isn't it?

Admiral Struble: I think yes, because in lacrosse when you hit the ball, you are expected to go down the field at full speed. And, of course, it is very important, because if you don't get down fast enough, the players on the other side of the field, and maybe some of those behind you, come up and break it up. Probably at those times, there'd be maybe only one fellow between you and the other fellow's goal, which is, of course, very much to your advantage when you try to make a goal yourself.

John T. Mason, Jr.: Yes. In retrospect, what is your estimation of the course of study at the academy?

Admiral Struble: I thought the general course of study was very good. I think it was suitable for becoming an officer, but I think, definitely, it could be improved, as I am sure it has been in certain ways. I think the engineering at times was a little bit too much the old boiler, and so forth, and I'm sure it's improved. In fact, when I went back as an instructor, we were already improving the steam engineering courses then.
    I think it was a pretty good, all-around education for the purpose.

John T. Mason, Jr.: And with great stress on leadership.

Admiral Struble: Yes. You were able to talk to, and understand fairly intelligently, graduates of other colleges whom we would meet as time went on, if you had done well at the Naval Academy.

John T. Mason, Jr.: Yes. Incidentally, what was your class standing at the academy?

Admiral Struble: I guess about eight or nine, maybe.* It should have been better.

John T. Mason, Jr.: Well, that's pretty good, isn't it?

Admiral Struble: Yes, but I fiddled the last two years when I shouldn't have, because that's when the marks count the most.

John T. Mason, Jr.: Were you tempted to become a naval constructor or anything like that?†

Admiral Struble: No. I was advised to be a naval constructor, but turned it down. I thought of it pretty seriously for a while, but in the meantime, I had gone to sea on a destroyer in World War I at Queenstown, and I decided this handling a ship with everything was pretty good stuff.

John T. Mason, Jr.: Admiral, when you were at the Naval Academy, I think you told me off tape that some of the midshipmen were becoming interested in naval aviation, which was certainly in its early stages at that time. Can you recall anything pertaining to that?

Admiral Struble: There was always a number of officers from about the time I graduated who did become interested early in aviation, and I think they assisted in the development of it. I think the fact that they had gone to the Naval Academy and/or West Point, if they were in the area before they went into aviation, it was a very good thing, because you then did have young aviators who, while they were young in aviation and all that, they had had a good military background and, therefore, their effect on military aviation was, on the whole, going to be very good.

---

* Struble stood number 12 of the 179 graduates in the Naval Academy class of 1915.
† The custom of the time was for the men at the top of each class at the Naval Academy to take postgraduate education in naval construction or marine engineering. There were, of course, exceptions.

Now, the Army early adopted the idea of having the aviation very much under the Army. I believe that at times it wasn't as good for aviation as it would have been, probably, if they had adopted a broader view initially about aviation. Now, when we finally got the third service in aviation, we then had developed a certain amount of in-fighting between the three services, which wasn't good, never will be good, and at the time, we have avoided it quite a bit.* But there is always going to be a certain amount of a recurring problem.

Some of the Air Force have had the idea that the Air Force is the only thing, and, therefore, the Air Force should get all the money. Well, of course, this, I think, has got to be met by all three services having a much broader view of our job.

John T. Mason, Jr.: Well, Vietnam itself has taught us that this is the case. We certainly learned that the bombing, by itself, is not the solution.

Admiral Struble: Well, I had a classmate who was quite an aviator, named Cooper. He was quite a brilliant man from Florida, left the Navy, became one of the early aviators in France, and then went on to become an aviator in Poland after World War I and helped the Polish a lot with their problems they had after World War I. Cooper then returned to the United States Air Force in time to be out in the Southwest Pacific in World War II. He's a man who has had quite a career.†

John T. Mason, Jr.: How fascinating!

Admiral Struble: He was quite a friend, and he was not in the same company, but in the next company to me at the Naval Academy. I knew him all four years here at the Naval Academy. He was a very remarkable person.

John T. Mason, Jr.: Oh, I see. Tell me about your first flight, which happened shortly after you graduated from the Naval Academy.

---

* In 1947 the previous U.S. Army Air Forces became a separate service, the U.S. Air Force.
† Brigadier General Merian C. Cooper, USAF (Ret.), who left the Naval Academy prior to graduation.

Arthur D. Struble, Interview #1 (5/25/76) -- Page 20

Admiral Struble: Well, I would think it happened probably in the spring of 1915. The Glacier was stopped in San Diego going north and south.* We would usually spend a week or two weeks off of San Diego, then go up to San Francisco and load and make another trip down to the Mexican west coast.

During this time I met a young Army cavalry officer, who was in the cavalry at Calexico, California, about 30 miles or so east of San Diego. He became interested in aviation and was permitted to fly and obtained permission then from the Navy at North Island to keep up his flight knowledge by once a month taking a flight around San Diego from the North Island field.† So he said to me one day, "Why don't you come over? You're Navy, you don't have any trouble getting around North Island, and I'll take you up for a flight. Nobody will know you're not supposed to do it."

So I went over one day, one Saturday morning, and we took off the north field and had a nice flight over San Diego. That was my first flight in an aircraft with an Army cavalry officer, who had still not yet joined aviation in the Army, but had gotten his training for flying.

John T. Mason, Jr.: Did this tempt you in any way to be serious about aviation?

Admiral Struble: No, it just made me realize the importance of aviation, but I was so solid on handling ships at that time. On the old Glacier, I was the third officer in the ship on board, and I stood a lot of watches and I handled the ship quite a bit, and I was learning and liking to be in that business.

John T. Mason, Jr.: The Glacier a cruiser, was she?

Admiral Struble: No, the Glacier was a supply ship. I had been ordered to a cruiser when I left the Naval Academy, but then the cruiser, which was then in Honolulu, was

---
* USS Glacier was a stores ship that supplied Navy ships with food and other provisions.
† North Island Naval Air Station is on the end of the Coronado peninsula, across the harbor from San Diego.

ordered back to Mare Island for repairs.* So my orders to the Maryland, which was one of our armored cruisers, were canceled. Then an officer was needed on the supply ship in a hell of a hurry, and I went over to her.

It was very independent duty for a youngster like me. I missed all of the life that the average ensign gets when he goes to a battleship or a cruiser and goes through being in the lowest mess on the ship, and is brought up, you might say, on board ship. I missed all that, because on the Glacier I was a fairly important officer. And I gained quite a knowledge of the west coast of Mexico, which I think was interesting. Then we went through the canal down into Rio just before we entered the war.† Down there, we had the job of also meeting all the merchant ships that came into Rio to see if we could get news about German subs in the Atlantic, which eventually arrived there.

John T. Mason, Jr.: When you were with the Glacier and making these trips down the west coast of Mexico, what was the purpose of that?

Admiral Struble: We had a large number of small gunboats up and down the west coast of Mexico, and they had to be fueled and provisioned.

John T. Mason, Jr.: And they were there for what reason?

Admiral Struble: Well, we were having trouble in a large number of places with the Mexicans. As you remember, a little later in '16, the Mexicans even came up to the border in force. Do you remember the Yakui Valley Indian raids and everything going on?

John T. Mason, Jr.: That was the heyday of Pancho Villa, wasn't it?‡

Admiral Struble: It was. That's why we had cavalry in Calexico.

---

* Mare Island Navy Yard, Vallejo, California.
† Rio de Janeiro, Brazil.
‡ Francisco "Pancho" Villa was a Mexican cattle thief, bandit, and revolutionary leader. In March 1916 he and his men raided Columbus, New Mexico, killing 16 and partly burning the town. He was pursued by U.S. troops under General John Pershing.

Arthur D. Struble, Interview #1 (5/25/76) -- Page 22

John T. Mason, Jr.: I see.

Admiral Struble: But I learned a lot of seamanship and a lot of that kind of thing. But I did lose the influence that new ensigns get on board a big ship when they first go with a cruiser or battleship, which I think is probably good for them.

John T. Mason, Jr.: And none of your classmates were with you on the Glacier?

Admiral Struble: Oh, no. The captain was a lieutenant commander, the executive officer was a lieutenant, and I was an ensign. The other watch officers on the Glacier, when we went to sea, were boatswains or chief boatswains. Of course, I was senior to them, so I went on board as the senior watch officer. But it gave me a very excellent experience in navigation and everything that I never would have gotten on a cruiser.

John T. Mason, Jr.: And important to your future career with the amphibious forces.

Admiral Struble: Well, it happened that I later got into that, yes. But you got a lot of small boat experience as a young ensign because of this loading and unloading. I mean, you didn't always unload in order, so I learned quite a bit of seamanship as a young ensign, more probably than I would have had had I gone to a cruiser.

John T. Mason, Jr.: Can you recall any experiences along the Mexican coast and any brushes with the Mexican guerrilla types?

Admiral Struble: Well, during this Yakui Valley Indian raid off of Topolobampo and also over at Guaymas—at Guaymas there was a railroad station on the railroad that came down from the United States, and there were a number of Americans and similar people located. When the Yakui Valley Indian raids started to break things up in 1916, the Glacier was sent up into Guaymas to be the ship that would evacuate the local Americans, if needed.

John T. Mason, Jr.: What were they, ranchers and that sort of thing?

Admiral Struble: No, they were railroad people working for the railroad. Things had gotten pretty bad at that time, and we were ordered to remain there, anchored, simply to take on board American citizens.

One day the captain sent for me and said, "You are to go over and pay a call on the consulate. There seems to be some new information." And he said, "I think under the circumstances, you had better wear a sidearm."

So I went down below, and I thought, "Oh, boy, this sounds like business." So I put on my better uniform and put on my .45 and belt, and so forth, and came up on the deck. The captain looked at me and said, "Who the hell told you to wear that gun?"

I said, "Why, you did, sir."

"No, I didn't." He said, "I told you to wear a sidearm. Get that gun out of your belt and get down there and get your sword."

So I wore my formal sword ashore.

John T. Mason, Jr.: This was a diplomatic call you were making.

Admiral Struble: I was making a diplomatic call. I went in to shore to this central city landing place—Mexicans standing around and obviously antagonistic, but no particular show of force. So I got out of the boat and I told them to lay off well clear of the beach until they saw me. Then I said, "You know, there is outside of town about a mile and a half to the eastward, another landing spot. I may want you to come there when you come back, but if I do I'll try to signal some way from the beach to you."

John T. Mason, Jr.: Were you anticipating some difficulty, perhaps?

Admiral Struble: Well, I thought I might have a problem. So I started up the main street of the city street, along the sidewalk. There were all these Mexicans, generally from, say,

16 to 24, lounging around. As I would walk past, they would spit on the sidewalk behind me—not in front of me but behind me.

I thought it over. I wasn't sure what I should do if they started spitting in front of me, but I decided that their spitting behind me wasn't my business. So I walked all the way up the main street, about six blocks, and then was met by a Mexican who obviously was friendly, who said, "Oh, you are from the ship."

And I said, "Yes."

He said, "I will show you how to get to the consulate."

So we turned left at the next block, went over a block or two to the consul's house. So I described to the consul what I had done, and he said, "I think you were very smart." He said, "If you had gotten something started, you would have just gotten into trouble and overwhelmed. So you were smart not to get into it."

So then the problem was discussed how we could accommodate so many people. The ship was there and we could bring in boats and pick them up and so forth. The consul said, "Well, this landing east of town is very unfrequented, and there's nobody who lives around there, so that's the place where we'll undoubtedly bring refugees, and you can pick them up there and take them to the ship. It's shorter and better for the ship in every way."

He said, "We've decided that the thing is getting bad and by late afternoon, or certainly tomorrow morning—but I think by late afternoon—we'll commence to have people arriving whom you can take out to the ships." So I told him we could take 100 easily. He said, "Boy, we're going to have more than that."

I said, "I don't know about that. Well, we'll get you on board." So a couple hours later I was driven by the consul's wife in a horse and buggy outside the city to the other dock, where I was met. In the meantime, one of the consul's men had gone down to the dock and waved them back to the ship, and they came in later to the other dock and picked me up and took me back to the ship.

The upshot was that they wanted, if they could, as many as 250 to 300 spaces for people. We didn't realize the number of people who were filtering in through parts of the country that were going to need a place to come to. Inside the inner harbor of Guaymas there was, as I remember, a German three-masted merchant ship that had been tied up there for eight months, unable to move. So the captain and the boatswain had been discussing the matter, and they decided to go in that night and cut her out and bring her over alongside the Glacier where we were outside of the port for half or three-quarters of a mile.

John T. Mason, Jr.: She had a German crew on board, didn't she?

Admiral Struble: No. It was vacant, nobody on the ship.

John T. Mason, Jr.: Oh, I see.

Admiral Struble: But she had a chain down to the bottom anchor. So I thought I would get to go on that trip, but the captain said, "No, I think the boatswain can handle this probably just as well, or maybe better than you can, so you can stay on the ship."

So that night the boatswain went in and cut the anchor. We had the captain's barge, which was a small steamboat, tow this merchant ship out, and we put her alongside the Glacier. Then we had plenty of room to store people. We had, I guess, eventually, maybe 250 people that came from ashore on the ship. Eventually the Yakui Valley Indian raids stopped, and the problem smoothed out a bit. We then offered to take back to the United States anybody that wanted to go. However, things came to be very normal around Guaymas, and most of the people went ashore.

John T. Mason, Jr.: How long a period did you have them on board?

Admiral Struble: I suppose we had them there for ten days.

John T. Mason, Jr.: My! And what about the food supply?

Admiral Struble: Well, the Glacier was a supply ship, you know. So we could handle that part of the problem naturally.

John T. Mason, Jr.: What about the people that were on the German ship? What kind of accommodations did they have?

Admiral Struble: Oh, they were just snaked out laying on deck. Down below there were a certain amount of rooms. They were allowed to live anywhere on the ship they wanted to. It was pretty good accommodations for people having to come to a place like that.

John T. Mason, Jr.: And the Mexicans could at least not get at them.

Admiral Struble: That's right. We were able to supply plenty of food, and everybody was cheerful. Most of them were determined to go back to their jobs and their homes as soon as it appeared that it was safe, and when it was, they did. A certain number, some of the older people, maybe, who were only down there kind of visiting or something, a certain number of the older people decided they would like to stay on the <u>Glacier</u> and we sailed. We eventually picked up more people in Topolobampo and some more people in Guaymas, also in Mazatlan, and took them all back to the United States.

John T. Mason, Jr.: You said you also had a story about Mazatlan.

Admiral Struble: Well, I'm not sure whether this was before or after the one I just told you, but I don't think it's important. We had the same situation. The consul was maintaining his status ashore. Of course, this was a bigger harbor, a bigger place, a bigger city. Mobs up to as many as a 100 or 200 or more were always around the dock area. Whether they were going to be friendly or not, you didn't know.

There was a small gunboat stationed offshore at Mazatlan. The captain of the gunboat maintained communications with the American consulate by sending in a boat from the ship with a young officer, who would step out on the dock. Then the consul's carriage would meet him, and he would be taken up town and brought back. Then the ship's boat would come in and pick him up and take him back to the gunboat. That way the captain of the gunboat would get the news of what was going on from the consul and would be able to send the news back to the Navy Department.

Well, the day we got in there had been quite a performance. The young officer from the ship that had been sent in, of course, would be a young ensign. In this case he was Scrappy Kessing, a man from the class of 1914, a year ahead of me.* As he went in in the boat, he told the coxswain, "You know, it looks to me like this crowd is getting a little more unruly. So you go in very slowly to the dock." There were no Mexicans on the immediate end of the pier then, but as they approached to go alongside and put this officer ashore, some of them started strolling out to the dock. He had already told the coxswain, "The moment I step out of the boat, you're to go back out about 40 or 50 feet and not come back in until I tell you to, because I don't want the Mexicans to take charge of it."

Well, he was very smart. The boat was hauled off and the Mexicans said, "Oh, no, keep both." The boat, in the meantime, had hauled off far enough so they couldn't get it. But they did have the officer.

John T. Mason, Jr.: As hostage.

Admiral Struble: As hostage, which, in effect, they were saying, "Well, the general wants to talk to you." And Kessing insisted that he was there to visit the American consul, which he was entitled to do. The Mexicans then apparently told him, "Well, you'll have to go see the general first."

Now, of course, Kessing knew that maybe he was going to see the consul, or maybe he wouldn't. But, of course, there wasn't anything else he could do but go with them. So they took him up to the fort, and, as might have been anticipated, they put him in the jug there. He was going to have to wait until the general returned, because the general would want to talk to him. The general was outside the city somewhere.

Well, apparently the news spread to the consul. The consul was also out on the outskirts of the city investigating, I guess, the same thing the general was—what the hell was going on outside. But the consul's wife was a very courageous woman. I think maybe she was Spanish, and she could speak Mexican thoroughly. She went down then to the fort to see the captain. She knew the captain personally. Then she found out he

---

* Ensign Oliver O. Kessing, USN.

wasn't there. Then she told the number-two man she understood that an American ship's officer had been held. "Well," said she, "I want to talk to him."

He said, "I'm sorry. The general wants to talk to him, and, therefore, I've got to hold this man for the general to talk to."

She kept arguing with this number-two officer. She finally got the number-two man pretty worried about whether he better hold this officer or not. In the meantime, the Mexicans had him behind iron doors.

John T. Mason, Jr.: There's nothing worse than a Mexican prison, I'll tell you.

Admiral Struble: And the Mexicans were coming out and spitting and pointing guns in, and all that kind of harassment. However, this woman was very courageous, and she kept arguing, and they finally turned Kessing loose to her custody. She put him in the carriage and drove downtown, and arrangements were made for the boat to come in and for him to get into the boat and back out. So it was a very unhappy thing for quite a while. However, he did get back out to the ship. Of course, regular calls with the consul were then dispensed with while this thing was at its height.

Now, as the boat came in for Kessing, the Mexicans again stood back a little bit, but Kessing had the coxswain properly primed to come in slowly and be ready to go back in a hurry if he had to. He said, "The moment you see I can jump for the boat, you get under way and head back." And that's what he had to do. Then the mob started coming out on the dock, but, in the meantime, he made it safely back to the ship.

So that's an interesting story about the courage of this Spanish woman, who was the consul's wife.

John T. Mason, Jr.: And also indicative of the atmosphere that prevailed.

Admiral Struble: Oh, the atmosphere that prevailed was very bad.

John T. Mason, Jr.: Tell me about that very brief period you were on the station ship in San Francisco before you were assigned to the Glacier.

Admiral Struble: What happened was that there were three of us who stood a watch in three on the station ship in command. The station ship was used for the purpose of handling people going to and from the Asiatic and duties of that sort around San Francisco Bay.

John T. Mason, Jr.: It was kind of a floating hotel, was it?

Admiral Struble: Well, a kind of floating hotel for people coming and going. I had to stand a watch in three—in other words, every third day I would stay on the ship 24 hours. The other times you had to be there for all working hours. Of course, in the other evenings, there was a big World's Fair in San Francisco and you had a good time seeing the city of San Francisco, which was a very interesting and a very pleasant place.*

Actually, I found out that my ensign's salary was giving out, just paying my taxicab bills going up and down in town. Finally, after about two months of luxurious living, I got mad one night and went back to the ship and sent a message to the Navy Department. I said I was a brand-new young ensign, and I thought I ought to have more active duty than I had. In about two or three days, I was ordered to the <u>Glacier</u> for duty, which regularly went from San Francisco to San Diego to the Mexican west coast ports, often down into Nicaragua.

Actually, I enjoyed the duty because it was very interesting having top watch on ship at sea. I was assistant navigator and did a lot of the navigation for the navigator, who was also the executive officer of the ship and responsible for her, more or less, complete running. I think I learned a lot of practical navigation, which often young ensigns don't get for two or three or four years in their normal life. They get some, but not quite as much, probably, as I had.

John T. Mason, Jr.: You said you got down the coast as far as Nicaragua. Were there activities there too?

---

* The Panama-Pacific International Exposition was held at San Francisco from 20 February through 4 December 1915 and drew more than 18 million people. The Panama Canal had first opened for traffic 15 August 1914.

Admiral Struble: Yes. We had problems in both Mexico and in Nicaragua. We often had gunboats stationed permanently in various harbors off the west coast.

John T. Mason, Jr.: What were the gunboats like? I mean, how big a ship was it?

Admiral Struble: The gunboat was a ship with anywhere from a 100 to 160, maybe, in the crew. She was possibly of a little greater tonnage than a destroyer, much shorter—it was wider, it was slower, but was more of a good-sized boat. She had a number of small guns on board. A destroyer was long and narrow.

John T. Mason, Jr.: Yes. This was all a part of our national policy, this policing of the areas in Central America and Mexico?

Admiral Struble: Well, it was in those countries where our relations weren't entirely happy. We were having problems on the Mexican west coast, and at times we had problems on the Nicaraguan coast. Yet we had merchant ships trying to go in and out and everything. So it was just a question of handling a problem as it occurred.

We left San Francisco in the early part of 1917, presumably headed for the Mexican west coast, but actually we went to Panama, went through the canal under sealed orders—if you've ever heard about sealed orders.

John T. Mason, Jr.: Oh, yes indeed.

Admiral Struble: I never will forget—about 80 or 90 miles east of Panama, when the captain opened his sealed orders, we found out we were headed for Rio de Janeiro, where we were assembling a cruiser division and certain American shipping. The purpose was to find out what was going on in the South Atlantic, right close at hand from American ships. Because we were then anticipating that we were going to get into the World War.

John T. Mason, Jr.: I suppose this was a move that was comparable to what we called the neutrality patrol in World War II, before we actually got into it.

Admiral Struble: Yes. It could have been considered so.

John T. Mason, Jr.: It was an alert state.

Admiral Struble: That's right. Now the duty in Rio, of course, was very pleasant and very interesting, but at times it was very active because my job was to use the only small boat we had on the Glacier, which was the captain's barge. From early dawn until darkness in the evening I, as any young ensign on the ship, was supposed to visit every ship that came in the Rio harbor and find out if the captain had any information.

John T. Mason, Jr.: You were a kind of intelligence officer then?

Admiral Struble: Well, in a way. I would meet these incoming ships, and they would slow down. They'd throw us a line, and I would go up over a ladder on board and go up on deck, talk to the captain for five or ten minutes and thank him, and then leave and meet another ship. It was very active duty in a way—I mean, you were very active carrying it out. And, of course, the captain didn't have his gig anymore when I was out doing that kind of stuff.

John T. Mason, Jr.: And you were trying to find out about the location of German submarines?

Admiral Struble: We were trying to get any possible information we could from these ships of anything they had seen, which would indicate the presence of German submarines, including merchant ships, which might be supplying them.

John T. Mason, Jr.: I see. Mother ships.

Admiral Struble: Mother ships for them, in effect. So that was the way we got a lot of our information in those days, from ships that came into the harbor. Anybody sailing south of the equator was bound to be headed for Rio, probably, so you got a lot of information from ship captains.

By the way, I was personally directed by the captain of my ship to report the information I got to the vice admiral commanding the Brazilian ships in the harbor. We kept them informed, also, with any information we got. I would go to his flagship and report to him, and he had me come in personally to tell him, which was interesting.

John T. Mason, Jr.: How was your Portuguese at this point?

Admiral Struble: Not very good, but he could speak good English. Actually he was a very fine person, very splendid naval officer. He was very nice to me, because after I had paid regular calls on him for a time, he invited me one evening to go to the opera in Rio de Janeiro. I had the pleasure that night of listening to Caruso sing for the first time in South America.*

That happened in about, I'll say June, maybe, of 1917.

John T. Mason, Jr.: That was an occasion!

Admiral Struble: That was an occasion.

John T. Mason, Jr.: Did the Germans operate raider ships in the South Atlantic, in addition to their submarines?

Admiral Struble: They did, but generally on the other side rather than on ours. There were only very few raiders that I remember hearing of on the Brazilian, Argentine coast. But there were more, I think, over on the African coast.

---

* Enrico Caruso, an Italian tenor, was one of the most prominent operatic singers of the era.

John T. Mason, Jr.: The information you gleaned from these merchant ships was utilized by Washington too?

Admiral Struble: Yes. Washington would get the information, and we were, of course, attempting to get any information of any suspicious vessel that we felt would be worthwhile sending the American cruisers out to investigate. We had no small light ship like small cruisers or anything, so one of the armored cruisers would have to go if there was anything that needed to be investigated. That, of course, was the purpose of trying to get the information.

John T. Mason, Jr.: How long were you down in Rio?

Admiral Struble: I was offered a job on one of these big armored cruisers. But from my point of view, I felt that they were going to just be stuck there for the rest of the war, and I felt that I wanted to get back up to the United States. So I asked for orders to the United States, and eventually, about July or August, was sent home on a merchant ship and went to the fuel oil testing plant in Philadelphia to learn how to burn fuel oil.* Then I was sent up to Quincy, Massachusetts, to become chief engineer of a new destroyer when it went into commission.

John T. Mason, Jr.: What was the attitude in the fleet at that stage, this anticipation of getting involved in World War I?

Admiral Struble: We all thought it was coming. I would say all the American officers down there were sure it was coming. You had that feeling.

John T. Mason, Jr.: You were telling off the tape about the fuel oil testing plant in Philadelphia where you had to go before you went to Quincy.

---

* The destroyers that went into service before then were equipped to burn coal rather than oil, so Struble was being trained in the new technology.

Admiral Struble: The fuel oil testing plant was a plant that was equipped to teach you all of the information about burning oil at sea in a destroyer, the kind of equipment you would have, and the manner in which you could burn it best, because, of course, it was quite a change from what we had had previously.

John T. Mason, Jr.: Yes, quite a new technique.

Admiral Struble: That's right. A new technique. Therefore, all the new destroyer engineers were sent through that fuel oil testing plant and given a very thorough course with quite a bit of knowledge on the subject. Naturally on board ship you had an old experienced man in the engineering department, who had been at sea many times in destroyers. But he might not necessarily be as experienced in the new views about burning fuel oil, which you should have absorbed at this fuel oil testing plant. I think the course lasted about a month. It was a very thorough course and very excellent, and was very valuable from my point of view.

John T. Mason, Jr.: You might tell me at this point—it would be logical—was the fleet experimenting with fueling at sea?

Admiral Struble: We had done, I believe, some experimenting in connection with fueling destroyers. But I wouldn't have any knowledge of it, because we sure didn't do it in South America or on the West Coast.

John T. Mason, Jr.: You had to go into a port.

Admiral Struble: Well, no. I think it was being developed in the bigger fleet in the east. They were hardly capable of crossing on the fuel they carried.

John T. Mason, Jr.: They were short-legged then.

Admiral Struble: Very short-legged. So fueling at sea has become an important subject.

John T. Mason, Jr.: It was an inevitable development.

Admiral Struble: Yes. Later, I was operating out of Queenstown. We'd operate out on about half of our fuel going out and still have the other half to operate on coming in. So we didn't really need normally to fuel. But at the height of the time we were going the farthest out to sea to meet the convoys, we didn't have any too much fuel for the purpose.

John T. Mason, Jr.: And for the convoy, did you have the same system in World War I that we had in World War II at the mid-ocean point where the destroyers from the other side took over?

Admiral Struble: No, we didn't have any destroyers coming over until we joined us. They had no destroyers with the ships out of the United States. We were only conducting this on the east side of the Atlantic.

John T. Mason, Jr.: I see. We can go on to Quincy now to the fitting out of the Stevens.* You say the Stevens was one of a new class of destroyer.

Admiral Struble: She was one of the new flush-deck destroyers. They were a little bigger; they were theoretically a little faster. We were supposed to get up to 35 knots. Actually, I think the Bath boat eventually established the record. It got up to 39 or 38«.

John T. Mason, Jr.: How long a period were you there when she was fitting out?

Admiral Struble: Well, I went there, I would say, in September. In December, I was allowed to go back to Portland for ten days at Christmas time, during which period I got married.

---

* USS Stevens (later DD-86), a Wickes-class destroyer, was commissioned 24 May 1918. She had a standard displacement of 1,284 tons, was 314 feet long, and 31 feet in the beam. Her top speed was 34.5 knots. She was armed with four 4-inch guns, two 3-inch guns, and 12 21-inch torpedo tubes.

John T. Mason, Jr.: How did you manage to carry on a courtship during this very active period at sea?

Admiral Struble: Well, I had really been engaged when I left San Francisco on the Glacier to go around to Rio.

John T. Mason, Jr.: Oh, you had.

Admiral Struble: Yes. I brought my wife back with me, and as I remember, we left Quincy to go to the war in June of 1918. We went over to Queenstown, Ireland. We were there until the peace was declared in late 1918.

John T. Mason, Jr.: When you went over to Queenstown, were you engaged in any convoying during that period?

Admiral Struble: We went over as part of a convoy, and thereafter in the Queenstown destroyers, we would either leave Queenstown and pick up the convoy and take it out to sea, or we would leave Queenstown and go to sea and pick up a convoy and bring it in. Often we'd pick up a convoy, bring it in, refuel, take one out, and then come back to Queenstown. We were, of course, at Queenstown when the battleship scare came up, and the battleships came over to the west coast of Ireland—Bantry Bay, I believe it was called. And we joined the battleships at Bantry Bay. There was a thought afloat at that time that the whole German outfit might come out for a last stand. Our battleships were sent over to join up with the British for that purpose. But the whole thing, as I remember, went flat and the whole thing stopped before we got those battleships out of Bantry Bay. In other words, the war was over.[*]

John T. Mason, Jr.: It was a very dull period for battleships, actually.

Admiral Struble: Yes.

---

[*] World War I lasted until an armistice was achieved on 11 November 1918.

John T. Mason, Jr.: During this period when you were escorting convoys and going out to meet them and what have you, did you have any brush with the German submarines?

Admiral Struble: No, I can't say that we really did. We had a couple of apparent close, maybe, possibilities, but nothing really.

John T. Mason, Jr.: What kind of equipment did your destroyer have for getting in contact with German submarines?

Admiral Struble: I would say our apparatus was very modest, and you can't say it wasn't of any value, but it was not at all effective like things are today.

John T. Mason, Jr.: It certainly wasn't a sonar.

Admiral Struble: Well, it was the early stuff, and everybody was having trouble operating the machinery to some extent, and it wasn't producing much. No, we didn't have much.

John T. Mason, Jr.: Did you have antiaircraft guns of any sort? Any protection from attack from the air?

Admiral Struble: As I remember, we had one or two little 3-inchers of some sort that were supposed to be of some value against an aircraft, but it was very minor. There was practically no—we never discussed it or worked on it.

John T. Mason, Jr.: Which indicates the fact that there wasn't much danger there.

Admiral Struble: That's right. No, there was no doubt about it. The biggest thing we did—we're talking broadly now—was we were keeping the German subs down and out of the way, a certain amount. They were much more dangerous to us, I presume, out in the center of the Atlantic where they might pick up a ship and nail it than they were close in, where they then commenced to be fairly vulnerable themselves.

John T. Mason, Jr.: They were the hunted rather than the hunters.

Admiral Struble: Now, the submarines that they had near England were, I would say, operating to stay away from us and only to come up if they had a chance to get a merchant ship. They operated against the ships going north, as well as the ships going the regular route across to Liverpool.

When I went over to go to London in World War II, I went across the Atlantic a ways, and then we went north and up into Scotland. Well, we hadn't started to do that in World War I much. I don't mean to say that no ships ever did go that way, but we weren't trying to do it particularly in World War I. We didn't need to.

But in World War II there were plenty of German subs under the waters of the Atlantic such that you went about halfway over, before you really knew which way they were going to go. You had a destination, but you were quite likely to have it altered halfway over, and that was because the Navy Department at that time was keeping very good track of where the German subs were. If they had an important convoy at sea and about halfway over, and it looked like they were congregating on the southern leg, you might say, they'd send them north, or they could turn around and do it vice versa. If they thought the German subs were going north—this is now in World War II—then they would change the convoy halfway over and let her go straight in.

John T. Mason, Jr.: That's the intelligence . . .

Admiral Struble: They would plan on the intelligence as it developed. Now, when we had them down off Florida, we knew they were there. We lost a hell of a lot of ships, but we couldn't do too much about it. We didn't do too much about it for a long time. For a long time we had problems.

John T. Mason, Jr.: You certainly did. Well, now, in World War II, I know that the Germans had also speedboats, the E-boats, operating in the channel and various other places. Did they have anything comparable in World War I? Any motorboats of any type?

Admiral Struble: No. The Queenstown outfit was a very good destroyer outfit, and they did keep the subs away pretty damn well. The Brest outfit was the same thing, quite good, similar. They operated out of Brest, France. They weren't able to go quite as far at sea as we could, because we were a certain amount to the westward of them from our home base. Mick Carney, by the way, was at Brest.*

John T. Mason, Jr.: The Queenstown operation was fruitful in that it held off German submarines rather than that it destroyed any.

Admiral Struble: Oh, yes, very definitely. And by the way, it was very interesting duty. We traveled, of course, at night without lights. So you were convoying close aboard these big ships at night in the dark. You had to be a good watch officer.

John T. Mason, Jr.: And a good navigator as well.

Admiral Struble: We learned a lot about handling destroyers and all that.

John T. Mason, Jr.: What sort of shore leave did you have when you were stationed at Queenstown?

Admiral Struble: When we were stationed at Queenstown, we could go ashore into a little city there. There was nothing there. On the other side from where the little city was, there was an old golf course, so you could go ashore and play a little golf. There

---

* Ensign Robert B. Carney, USN, later an admiral and Chief of Naval Operations from 1953 to 1955. Admiral Carney's oral history is in the Columbia University collection.

Arthur D. Struble, Interview #1 (5/25/76) – Page 40

were a few Irish girls over there. They'd give you some sort of a bit to eat maybe, after you had played golf a little, and you could get a drink usually. So that was our exercise.

We had trouble with the boys. Right above Queenstown, there's an Irish city, but at the end of the war when we started to let the sailors go up there on leave, why, that was bad news. The local boys and the sailors didn't mix, because the girls—which is something we always do—they always look for the strangers in the sailor boy's uniform, and then the local boys want to fight. And, of course, the local boys get together, and one or two sailors are out with a couple of girls, and the local boys as a crowd jump them.

So one day the boys going up from the destroyer force, all got together, and they kept together, and they cleaned up on the city boys by military methods.

John T. Mason, Jr.: In union there is strength.

Admiral Struble: So from then on, they were barred from going up there anymore. And even an officer like myself, when I had to go to London, once, I had to stay on the train and couldn't get off in that city. I've forgotten the name of the little city now. But it's right above Queenstown.

Well, the Stevens went back to Boston after the armistice. I had about a year of duty around Boston, and I was in command of her for a while because the captain left. Then I was ordered to go to the Shubrick.* I was changed to the Shubrick because she was coming to the Pacific, and I had gone down to Haiti. I went into Haiti in the Shubrick, and we delivered a lot of small money down there in 1920, because there was a temporary shortage of small change.

John T. Mason, Jr.: When you say small money, do you mean silver?

Admiral Struble: Yes. We took all of this out of New York in a very hurried trip and went down there. There was a kind of money crisis down there. We took all the small

---

* USS Shubrick (later DD-268) was commissioned 3 July 1919. She had a standard displacement of 1,215 tons, was 314 feet long, and 31 feet in the beam. Her top speed was 34.7 knots. She was armed with four 4-inch guns, one 3-inch gun, and 12 21-inch torpedo tubes.

money for the New York bank down there and delivered it. We then were out of fuel and ran over to Guantanamo going on next to nothing.*

The captain said, "The chief engineer says we had better not go. We don't have enough oil."

I said, "Captain, I've been looking for oil today around here. We're not going to get any here. We're not going to get any water here. So I'm all for going to Guantanamo, and I think we'll make it."

John T. Mason, Jr.: You were in Port-au-Prince?

Admiral Struble: Port-au-Prince, yes.

John T. Mason, Jr.: Well, the U.S. was in occupation of Haiti at that time, wasn't it?

Admiral Struble: Oh, no. This was after the war. One of the big New York banks was trying to keep that place on its feet and had asked the Navy to have a boat take this down just as quickly as possible, to relieve a hell of a nasty money problem that was coming up. The government undertook to transport the bank's money to Port-au-Prince as a government gesture to meet the problem. It couldn't be handled. It would have been a week before it got down there in the normal civilian transportation. There wasn't any air in those days.

---

* Guantanamo Bay, on the south coast of Cuba, near the eastern end of the island, for many years provided a fleet anchorage and training area for U.S. Navy ships.

Arthur D. Struble, Interview #2 (5/28/76) – Page 42

Interview Number 2 with Admiral Arthur D. Struble, U.S. Navy (Retired)
Place: Admiral Struble's Home, Chevy Chase, Maryland
Date: Friday, 28 May 1976
Interviewer: John T. Mason, Jr.

John T. Mason, Jr.: On this beautiful spring morning, let us resume your story. Last time we left the Shubrick in Guantanamo. You had been to Haiti, and you came on to Guantanamo. You want to take her from there?

Admiral Struble: Shortly after arrival in Guantanamo, the Shubrick sailed for Jamaica and stopped in Jamaica, then through the Panama Canal and up to San Diego on the western coast of the United States.

John T. Mason, Jr.: Sir, you might comment on the value of the Panama Canal at that time to our fleet units since it's so much the topic of conversation in this day.[*]

Admiral Struble: Well, of course, the Panama Canal is a very important matter to the Navy of the United States in order to be able to transfer ships promptly from one ocean to the other ocean. It gives us a much better command of the sea on each side, when we know we can count on the Panama Canal.

John T. Mason, Jr.: Now, at the beginning of the '20s, I take it that all of our naval ships were able to traverse the canal without any difficulty.

Admiral Struble: Yes, and later the canal was altered sufficiently so the larger carriers went through very successfully. In my opinion, it's a very important naval matter to maintain and control the Panama Canal. Our experience, particularly with small countries, is that sometimes they get very jealous of what they think are their rights.

---

[*] In 1977 the United States and Panama signed a treaty that resulted in the transfer of the Canal Zone to Panama in 1979 and the canal itself to Panama on 31 December 1999.

They can cause very considerable trouble if we accept the idea that they will cooperate with us, because when some of the small countries of that character don't want to cooperate, they don't cooperate. I think we'd be very foolish to give up any of our clear-cut rights for the operation of the canal.

Now, the country concerned receives very good return from, let me say, an American-controlled and -operated canal, for its own benefit financially. I don't believe today that there is anything that we do, hardly, that is bad for that local country, except the possible idea that if the local politician feels that it isn't commensurate with his dignity for it to be that way. Except for that one fact, I do not believe that the Panamanians have anything to stand on. We have treated them well, and we should hold the control we have.

John T. Mason, Jr.: How vulnerable is the canal to sabotage and that sort of thing?

Admiral Struble: Well, the canal would be susceptible to a foreign strike, of course. As regards its protection from such foreign strike, there is no comparing the defense that America would have and be prepared for, as compared to what the local country might be prepared for. Actually, we would have a much greater knowledge of what kind of raid might be attempted on the canal. I think we'd be much more able to repel it.

Now I think we've just got to reach some arrangement in which the local pride of the country concerned is reasonably satisfied and then stick to that kind of agreement.

John T. Mason, Jr.: In the case of many of our smaller neighbors, their pride seems to be worn on the sleeve most of the time, doesn't it?

Admiral Struble: Well, I don't think that's out of the way because that's bound to happen, and that's been our trouble all the way along working with these Central and South American countries, is trying to solve the problem of their local pride and yet step in and do things for them.

For instance, in Peru we developed for quite a while a very fine arrangement to help the Peruvians out. But so often some question of local pride then destroys the effect of it. Of course, it is true that once you get into a small South American country that way, there is always the chance that your local business connections may not prove to be the best for our political relations with that country. Now, that's a point that we in the government cannot exactly control.

John T. Mason, Jr.: No. You're thinking, perhaps, of mining operations where we take so much out.

Admiral Struble: Well, all of those things, you see, the government doesn't really control those or anything. Those are handled between the commercial company and the country concerned. But our government gets the blame for it if the relationship isn't satisfactory.

John T. Mason, Jr.: Exactly. Well, I'm sorry to divert you like that.

Admiral Struble: Well, I think we've got that covered reasonably.

John T. Mason, Jr.: Yes. Now we are again on the <u>Shubrick</u> going to San Diego.

John T. Mason, Jr.: Admiral Struble: I would say that at that time in our life we had a destroyer force that, just having been through our experience in World War I and our experience with German submarines, put us in a position where we went into a period of advancement in destroyer operations that was splendid. We had an excellent destroyer force that improved and improved thereafter. We were well trained; we were better organized; we were more capable to act as a formidable unit. That was due to a number of peacetime years of advancement and gain that had come out of our experience in World War I.

John T. Mason, Jr.: And I suppose one of the important elements was the personnel, the men who had fought in World War I.

Admiral Struble: That's right. The young lieutenants who were in World War I were advancing in rank and knowledge, and our destroyer force became an excellent operating organization. In addition to that, the battleships also improved very extensively because of their relations. Do you want me to go ahead with that right now?

John T. Mason, Jr.: Yes, you say that.

Admiral Struble: The battleship people had realized how important battleship action might be, and, therefore, their attention to gunnery and their attention to the use of small floatplanes on battleships for gunnery spotting purposes and everything, clearly showed our advancement and improvement in what our battle force would have been able to do had it been called on to do it. There is no doubt in my mind that the battleship force of, say, 1925, that made this big fleet cruise from California to Australia, and picked up a considerable amount of the Atlantic Fleet as it passed Panama, was probably the most powerful organization, certainly in the world afloat at that time, and the best trained and the most capable.

I remember when we arrived off Sydney, Australia, and went through the heads and in the beautiful big harbor. As we entered, we sent our planes from the battleships in ahead of us through the entrance and made quite an impressive show. The banks of the entrance on either side were just jammed with Australians who had come to see it. The show was well put on, but it was a demonstration of the fact that we had learned a lot in World War I and were taking practical operational advantage of it in our training.

John T. Mason, Jr.: That's very interesting, sir. In terms of new ideas that were gleaned from our experience in World War I being incorporated in new ship designs, this didn't work with battleships very much, because they didn't build any new ones.

Admiral Struble: Of course, it did affect the design of new ships a certain amount, yes, because from then on anything that we built was bound to be gauged to be up to date as regards the air menace, both on your side and on the other fellow's side. In other words, both offensively and protectively, you tried to take those things into account. But it was

Arthur D. Struble, Interview #2 (5/28/76) – Page 46

true we already had a large battleship fleet. We were not going to have very many new, modern additions made to that battleship fleet because of the expense, and because the older ships had generally been modified and were still the most offensive number-one battleship force in the world. So we didn't have to build too many new battleships.

John T. Mason, Jr.: And actually we didn't, did we, until the North Carolina came along?*

Admiral Struble: We did not try to build many battleships, because we knew that it would be smarter to start developing carriers, and that was also going to be expensive. In fact, the aircraft carriers that we built during this period were very valuable in World War II. The carriers had a lot to do with a number of our actions in the Pacific.

John T. Mason, Jr.: Yes, indeed.

Admiral Struble: And they performed very admirably. In fact, they disrupted any idea of the Japanese going too far afield with their naval forces. That was one of the developments in World War II. Of course, it was very sad that the fleet got caught in Pearl Harbor and that we got heavily bombed.† At the time when World War II was started by the Japanese attack, we suffered a lot of heavy losses, which you are always liable to have by a surprise attack coming in on you. But if there was any type of ship which would take the brunt of that attack and be less valuable to us for the next two or three years, it was the battleship.

We needed the carriers; we needed the cruisers; we needed the small, faster ships, but we didn't need the battleships for another two or three years. During that period, we

---

* Because of the Washington naval disarmament treaty of 1922, no U.S. battleships were commissioned between the West Virginia (BB-48) in 1923 and the North Carolina (BB-55) in 1941.
† In late November 1941, the Imperial Japanese Navy dispatched from the Kurile Islands in the North Pacific a task force built around six aircraft carriers. A force of some 350 fighters, dive-bombers, and torpedo planes attacked U.S. military installations on the island of Oahu, Hawaii, on Sunday, 7 December 1941. The principal focus of attack was the collection of American warships at the naval base at Pearl Harbor. All eight battleships in port at the time were either sunk or damaged. The U.S. Congress declared war on Japan the following day.

got them home, we got them repaired, and they were out in the Far East when we needed them, and we hadn't needed them in between.

John T. Mason, Jr.: That's a very interesting point to make.

Admiral Struble: Well, you could see the situation.

John T. Mason, Jr.: Oh, yes, if the Japanese in some way had been able to concentrate on our carriers, few carriers, and destroyed them at Pearl Harbor . . .

Admiral Struble: That would have been much better for them and much worse for us.

John T. Mason, Jr.: It would have been devastating for us, wouldn't it?

Admiral Struble: Yes. You know, we go from this to a certain amount of political discussion of this thing. Roosevelt has been criticized for keeping the fleet, as you know, in Honolulu.[*] The moving of our American fleet from our West Coast out to Honolulu was, of course, primarily a political maneuver. Now, Roosevelt was entirely right in that matter. He moved it out there, and it stopped the Japanese tentatively from some ideas they may have had.

John T. Mason, Jr.: That was really waving a big stick, wasn't it?

Admiral Struble: It was waving a big stick, and temporarily it kept the Japanese out of the problem. However, after a certain amount of time, they decided that they could take a good crack at the American battle fleet. At that time, the American naval officer commanding the fleet was a very fine man, J. O. Richardson.[†] He was in favor of having the battleships withdraw to California and not remain in too advanced a position. From the military point of view he was entirely right. The battleships were of no need and

---

[*] Franklin D. Roosevelt was President of the United States from 4 March 1933 to 12 April 1945.
[†] Admiral James O. Richardson, USN, served as Commander in Chief U.S. Fleet from 6 January 1940 to 1 February 1941.

value in Honolulu Harbor, and from a strictly naval-military point of view, we shouldn't have had them out there, maybe. We should have only had light forces. So as a professional naval officer, I think he was entirely correct.

However, in handling a government and handling a war, there are two parts to it. One of it is the professional military part, and the other is the professional political part of it. Now on that score, I don't believe that Roosevelt kept those battleships out there just as bait to bring the Japanese over at all. But I think he was trying to keep them out of the thing, and he thought that was just as good a way as we had to do. In other words, politically, he felt that keeping the battleships out there in Honolulu was very important, not only worldwide, but maybe in its effect on Japan. So that I do not criticize Roosevelt necessarily for deciding to override the experience of his very capable, splendid naval officer in the matter.

John T. Mason, Jr.: And indeed dismissing him.

Admiral Struble: Well, I would not connect that with the matter. I think if J. O. put up this tremendous job of arguing this with the President and told him what he thought, I think that the time for a new military boss had arrived then. In other words, to remove that antagonism that did exist between the military and the political at that moment and put a new man in. It would have been very fine had he kept him, because I think J. O. was a fine man and would have done a fine job. But possibly, under those circumstances, maybe from the political viewpoint, the time had arrived. So I'm not as critical on that as some naval and military people may be. I think it might have been all right for him to send out a new man.[*]

Now, actually, Pearl Harbor was a tremendous success for the Japanese apparently, but in the war as it then resulted, we had our light forces out there for a while and did all that was necessary. The carriers were capable of handling the Japanese advancement. As you know, in one action later, the carriers assisted in a very tough stand against the Japanese, and we turned them around. They only got so far across the

---

[*] Richardson's replacement was Admiral Husband E. Kimmel, USN, who served as Commander in Chief Pacific Fleet until 17 December 1941. He was removed shortly after the Pearl Harbor debacle.

Pacific from their side when they had to quit advancing. So we gained our point militarily. Do you follow me?

John T. Mason, Jr.: Yes, indeed, I do. You're talking about Midway.*

Admiral Struble: Yes, sure.

John T. Mason, Jr.: Well, shall we go back to the Shubrick now?

Admiral Struble: All right. Boy, what a big drop! She joined the forces in San Diego. Certainly the destroyer forces in San Diego, with their training and everything, developed in the next two or three years in a hurry to be a most capable, effective force that had advanced in the destroyer knowledge and training very much in the next 10 or 15 years. They were, of course, part of the fleet that went to Australia in 1925. That was, I think, the summation I have for the destroyer service. I enjoyed it very much. I had command of a destroyer as a lieutenant at that time, and it was a fine command and certainly taught me a lot of seamanship and a lot of other things in a hurry.

John T. Mason, Jr.: Well, you stayed with her until the next year, 1920, and you then took over another destroyer.

Admiral Struble: Well, yes. That happens, of course, in the destroyer force often. One goes out of commission and goes into the Navy yard for overhaul or something and then you're transferred to another one. That doesn't really mean anything.

John T. Mason, Jr.: I see.

---

* From 4 to 6 June 1942, U.S. and Japanese naval forces fought a battle northwest of Midway Island in the Pacific. After Japanese bombers had struck the island, carrier-based U.S. dive-bombers attacked and sank the Japanese carriers Hiryu, Soryu, Kaga, and Akagi and the cruiser Mikuma. U.S. ships lost were the carrier Yorktown (CV-5) and the destroyer Hammann (DD-412). The battle was both a tactical and strategic victory for U.S. forces.

Admiral Struble: I'd say after that destroyer experience, my next job was to go to the Naval Academy.

John T. Mason, Jr.: Yes. Was this something that you wanted to do?

Admiral Struble: Well, I realized that it was time to go ashore for a tour. I kind of thought that the Naval Academy would be an excellent place to go, and I'm very glad I went. I think going to the Naval Academy and reviewing in your own mind, as a reasonably young officer, your experience at the Naval Academy in how the midshipmen might be better trained is a good thing. You're going to get more of those ideas at the Naval Academy from the younger officers who come back as new instructors. They aren't going to be able to tell the people at the Naval Academy how to run it and how the change should be made, but they are capable of saying this way of handling the midshipmen isn't giving them the experience they ought to have. The change is going to have to be accomplished by the older, more experienced officers at the Naval Academy. You are going to have to take some of the faculty who get a little hidebound and move them around a little bit, but you are going to get better training, and we certainly got it after that.

We improved the Naval Academy by virtue of a whole lot of the younger people who came back to the Naval Academy for duty and had been through the war, and they could point out why better training was better.

John T. Mason, Jr.: I suppose in one way, for you as a person coming back to the Naval Academy then, was like going to postgraduate school, where it gave you a chance to draw on your brief period of experience with the fleet and focus.

Admiral Struble: Well, actually, I had thought of going to postgraduate instruction about the time I was leaving the Naval Academy, and possibly going into the construction department as a professional by going to Boston to teach and all that and being in the Construction Corps of the Navy. I was almost on the verge of doing that.

John T. Mason, Jr.: That's when you were offered the opportunity to be a naval constructor?

Admiral Struble: No, it was after I came back after the war from Queenstown that the question came up. But then I was told that if I went into naval construction, I would have to go in junior to everybody else who was already in the corps. Of course, I said no, I didn't want to do that, because I would have lost altogether too much seniority. In the meantime, anyway, I think I had decided I probably wanted to stay in the line in the Navy.

John T. Mason, Jr.: You liked the operational side of things.

Admiral Struble: I decided I liked the operational side.

John T. Mason, Jr.: Tell me about some of your experiences when you were there at the academy as an instructor in the Department of Marine Engineering. What were some of the innovative ideas you may have had?

Admiral Struble: I think that it was clear that steam engineering had made tremendous advances, and they were going to advance more. I had found that out by virtue of being an engineering officer on a new destroyer which was different from an old destroyer. There was no doubt that already the senior people in engineering at the Naval Academy realized that the whole Department of Engineering needed to be redone in order to get into the advancement that was going to occur in ship propulsion and all that. And they did it. I don't think I deserve any credit for that.

John T. Mason, Jr.: But it happened at that time.

Admiral Struble: Oh, yes. That was when the Naval Academy recognized very clearly the necessity of getting ahead with our engineering training. I don't think I can say who the individuals were that should be given credit. I don't think I should try to get into that, because I don't believe I know it.

John T. Mason, Jr.: You were saying off tape that J. O. Richardson was the head of the Department of Marine Engineering when you were there.*

Admiral Struble: Yes, as I remember, he was the head of the Department of Marine Engineering at that time. He would have been much more responsible than any of the rest of us for that improvement.

John T. Mason, Jr.: Now, the diesel was coming in with great force, was it not?

Admiral Struble: Yes. Of course, it had its place, but it was a different place. The diesel wasn't going to be the big engine of the future for certain ships, but it was for others.

John T. Mason, Jr.: The submarine, for instance.

Admiral Struble: Yes. Now, of course, the submarine force made tremendous advances because of its war experience. There is no doubt of that.

When I left the Naval Academy in 1923, there were a number of my class that, like I, were lieutenants, and we were instructors. I think all of my class were going to be ordered to submarines when they left the Naval Academy. We had kept too many older officers in submarines too long. While they had enjoyed it and had been happy staying in the submarines, it wasn't good for the submarine force. So they decided to take all of the lieutenants of my time at the Naval Academy and send them to submarine instruction, and then submarine duty.

There was a very fine man in my class who wanted to go to battleships. He went over to Washington to see the officer who assigned people to duty afloat and said, "Look, I don't see why I should have to go into submarines. There are an awful lot of people

---

* As a commander, Richardson was a department head at the Naval Academy from 1919 to 1922.

who want to go into submarines, and I don't happen to want to. I'd like to go into a battleship. Why should I have to go to submarines?"

The detail officer said, "Well, we need 40 good officers there in a hurry. These officers are just about the right age. They are capable of commanding submarines as regards their age and the war experience and so forth. The only thing is they don't know submarines. So if we put them all now in training for submarines, we'll have a large number of good submarine commanders of the proper age, and so forth, to meet the problem. So that's why I'm doing it."

Well, he was justified in his approach. That was a good reason for his doing it.

So this fellow said, "Well, it seems to me you're making a mistake here. Suppose a man in my class that's down there now has never been on a battleship, and you are going to force him to go into submarines."

The detail officer said, "If you can name anybody that hasn't been on a battleship that's in this group, I'll cancel his orders to submarines."

McCormick said, "I know Struble hasn't been on a battleship."*

So the detailer said, "Well, he'll go."

So I was the only man in my class that was ordered to battleships; at that time; all the others were ordered to submarines. I don't think it was a very smart decision, but I must say I appreciated it. The California was a battleship, but it was also the flagship of the Pacific Fleet, and I'm sure I learned a hell of a lot on the California.†

John T. Mason, Jr.: Indeed, it was customary when men graduated from the academy to put them on battleships first, wasn't it?

Admiral Struble: It was, and I had been ordered to a big ship. But due to a quirk, I had started out in small ships. The detail officer said right away, "Hell, he's had too much

---

* Lieutenant Lynde D. McCormick, USN, who had stood second in the class of 1915. He later became a four-star admiral.
† USS California (BB-44) was commissioned 10 August 1921. She had a standard displacement of 32,000 tons, was 624 feet long and 97 feet in the beam. Her top speed was 21 knots. She was armed with 12 14-inch guns, 14 5-inch guns, and two 21-inch torpedo tubes. She was later sunk during the attack on Pearl Harbor in December 1941 and subsequently refloated, modernized, and returned to service.

small ship duty anyway. It's a good thing for him to go to battleships." This is just one of the quirks that occur.

John T. Mason, Jr.: Just one of the little happenstances. Tell me, did you take to teaching at the academy? Is that something you liked to do?

Admiral Struble: Well, you see, I had been chief engineer on a destroyer, and I had been a chief engineer in World War I. I also was a deck officer, you understand. I stood my regular watch on that destroyer when I was chief engineer, when I was over in Queenstown. So I had a lot of destroyer experience. I had had just as much experience handling a destroyer as a lieutenant as the other boys did on the ship. But my main assignment on the destroyer was to be a chief engineer instead of being a deck officer.

John T. Mason, Jr.: And in being in these various capacities, you did do a certain amount of teaching. My point was . . .

Admiral Struble: Well, yes, when it came to teaching at the Naval Academy, I'm sure that a certain amount of teaching I did was good, because I was able to find out how it led to practical experience in matters. I said I also thought that it was a very smart thing, for any naval officer, to have a couple of years' tour in connection with engineering at sea, even though he was only interested in the line and gunnery part of the thing, because I felt my engineering experience had been valuable to me. I never went back to engineering again, but as the captain of a ship, when I went down below in the engine room, I knew my way around. When the chief engineer came up to kick about a boiler problem, I knew a little bit about it.

John T. Mason, Jr.: Tell me about some other aspect of life at the Naval Academy when you were there. Were you married at that time?

Admiral Struble: I was married.

John T. Mason, Jr.: That's something you neglected to tell me—when you were married.

Admiral Struble: Well, I was married in San Diego when I had command of this destroyer after World War I. I had a boy born in San Diego in December and then went to the Naval Academy in July or August. Then I had a daughter born when we were in Annapolis.

John T. Mason, Jr.: And I expect the other lieutenants were in somewhat similar circumstances.

Admiral Struble: Somewhat similar situation. The duty was very pleasant. The Naval Academy is an interesting place to be. I think maybe it's a good thing for you in your understanding of young officers and everything, maybe, to have had a tour of duty as an instructor. I would recommend to any youngster that it's good to have a tour, because I think it's training for them. I saw no use in going back to the Naval Academy further and didn't. I don't think that going back just because it's a pretty nice spot to live is advantageous for a naval career.

John T. Mason, Jr.: But some men did go back and back and back.

Admiral Struble: Oh, a lot of men found it very pleasant, and their wives loved it, so they go back and back. I don't think that's good for a naval career. You get too Naval Academy-minded. Then, of course, there are many other more important jobs in the Navy Department, which are connected with your future if you get to high command. It's very important for you to know how the Navy Department functions, what the various sections of it are, and what they do. It puts you in a better position when you are a captain of a ship somewhere and some incident breaks. Your experience in the Navy Department for a couple of tours of duty would be more valuable to you in background on what to do than additional tours at the Naval Academy.

John T. Mason, Jr.: But that causes me to ask you, sir, about that aspect of things. How important was the thought of future advancement in your plans for duty? And was it to the fore?

Admiral Struble: I can tell you a good yarn about that, but I'll tell it to you at the time that I left the California, the fleet flagship, in '27 to go ashore. There is a good yarn I'm going to tell you then, and it will tie in better after the discussion of my duty in the California.

John T. Mason, Jr.: Yes. So you joined her in 1923.

Admiral Struble: And I was assigned as communications officer, which was a new assignment in the Battle Fleet, because we had to coordinate the visual signaling with the radio signaling, and its being a part of communications and having what we called a communication department on the ship which controlled both the radio and the visual end and everything. It meant that the handling of communications got together. The message that comes by a visual signal is just the same thing as a message that comes by radio in its being handled—who it's routed to, who's responsible for it. So this was the start of communications.

John T. Mason, Jr.: It was a watershed time then for communications.

Admiral Struble: That's right. So I became communications officer on the California, which was a fine job. You automatically became kind of a captain's personal aide, because he was the man you sent for all the time. "I understand that Admiral So-and-so sent a message over here."
    And you'd say, "Yes, sir."
    "Well, where is the message?"
    "Well, a copy was sent to you, but the copy for action was sent to the commander, because I thought he would handle it for this reason."

"Oh," he said. "All right." Which was a means of coordinating communications in the ship. So, therefore, as the younger officer, it was a rather important job. You were working directly with the captain and with the executive officer of the ship quite a bit.

John T. Mason, Jr.: And the California remained in the Pacific, did she?

John T. Mason, Jr.: Admiral Struble: Well, the battleships were then engaged in very heavy postwar training, and the improvement in battleship operations and everything really gained an awful lot. The fleet maneuvers that were held from that time on were much better than we had held previously, more practical. In Southern California, there was the distinct advantage of good weather conditions and everything for training. Also, the fact that every summer the whole fleet would go north up to Puget Sound and make a cruise on the fleet north, enhance training and knowledge a lot. We'd have about two months up in the northwest and then come south again. All of this was conducive to good seamanship and training and knowledge with the forces that was far better than we had had before World War I.

John T. Mason, Jr.: Did you engage in war games of any sort?

John T. Mason, Jr.: Admiral Struble: We generally had two big war games every year: one in the spring which would be held down in the Panama area, and the Atlantic Fleet would generally come down and engage in it; and then one in the early spring and another one in the early fall where the Pacific Fleet would have a maneuver of its own in the Pacific but involving all types of ships and aviation.

John T. Mason, Jr.: Whom did you envision as the potential enemy at that time?

Admiral Struble: Well, of course, always at that time the advance of the Japanese in this business was remarkable, and we couldn't help but recognize that it was there. But we also had a tendency to remain oriented a little bit towards Europe because of our recent experience. So while I guess Japan was in the back of our minds quite a bit as a potential threat, you were always thinking of your European experience too.

John T. Mason, Jr.: And it was the battleship era, was it not? The carriers were beginning to come in.

Admiral Struble: The carriers were beginning. But you see what my idea had been by the time we got out to Honolulu on the matter, which I explained.

John T. Mason, Jr.: Yes. If you could focus, say, on 1925 or thereabouts 1926, what was the attitude in the fleet towards aviation as such?

Admiral Struble: On the whole, I think it was very good. There were some of the younger line people and some of the older line people who probably didn't accept aviation too quickly and too easily. But I think most of the clearer-minded officers, let's say, were recognizing that it was going to be a very important factor in the future and were attempting to enhance it.

John T. Mason, Jr.: I remember a man like Admiral J. J. Ballentine told me that when he wanted to go into aviation, his superior officers did everything they could to dissuade him from this dead-end street.[*]

Admiral Struble: Well, he's talking about a period that's just a little bit earlier, I think.

John T. Mason, Jr.: This was about 1921 when he went into training.

Admiral Struble: Well, you see, that was immediately after the war. Now, these things that I've described to you didn't happen overnight. They went on for a period through the '20s. There was still lots of antagonism toward aviation, because the naval aviators wanted to command everything in sight that they could, you might say. And a lot of

---

[*] Admiral John J. Ballentine, USN (Ret.), whose oral history is in the Columbia University collection.

people realized that they still weren't the top ship commanders that the regular line officers were, I mean in training and knowledge. Because the time that they spent in aviation didn't make them good sailors and navigators. Do you see what I mean?

John T. Mason, Jr.: Yes.

Admiral Struble: That transition was bound to take 20 years or so to happen.

John T. Mason, Jr.: And accompanying it, of course, was the development of new planes and new plane design.

Admiral Struble: Exactly. That's right. All of that was a part of the plane picture. But the naval officer at the start of World War II who was, maybe, quite a good aviator had been in aviation more or less since World War I—in other words, about 20 years. The naval aviator of that period who was captain of a big ship was relatively nowhere as good a seaman as a comparable line officer. Now, that's just a fact.

Now, some of them, like Ernie King who was a captain at that time and a very good naval officer—smart and everything—I would not say my remarks applied to him.* They applied to some of those who were not quite as acute as he was.

John T. Mason, Jr.: Well, he wasn't essentially a flier anyway.

Admiral Struble: No. But he had been one of the earlier people in aviation, because he was a hell of a smart man and a good naval officer and a good seaman. He had been put in command because they felt he would recognize and handle the new subject. I think the other people who were then in aviation resented having old line officers command them. But, of course, it was sound at first.

---

* Captain Ernest J. King, USN, went through flight training at Pensacola, Florida; he received his wings as a naval aviator in May 1927, when he was 48 years old. Later, as a four-star admiral, he served as Chief of Naval Operations from 26 March 1942 to 15 December 1945 and as Commander in Chief U.S. Fleet from 20 December 1941 to 2 September 1945; he was promoted to the rank of fleet admiral in December 1944.

John T. Mason, Jr.: I've been told that the Navy in its wisdom wanted to upgrade aviation as an arm of the service, and, therefore, sent some of these older men like King to take training to give the aviation the kind of status it didn't have up until that point.

Admiral Struble: Well, I think that's true. I think the problem was recognized by a number of older people, and they went into it. I think it was a very good thing. But a young captain commanding a carrier at that time, even though he had spent quite a reasonable amount of time in aviation, wasn't really the man to command forces or anything. He might or might not be a good ship captain. He had had practically no training in handling forces. So you had a carrier with a captain on it, and he wanted to run the force. It wasn't usually a good thing. A man like King could and did.

John T. Mason, Jr.: Now, when you joined the fleet on the California in '23, this was a time when we were thinking in terms of treaty limitations on the fleet, and the opportunities for advancement were beginning to be less than they had been. What was the status of morale as a result of all this?

Admiral Struble: Well, in the period for five or six or seven years after—let's say around '20—there was a period there when a number of naval officers, I think, at time were discouraged and unhappy about the future in the Navy. However, I am inclined to believe that the advancement in our training was constantly bringing up the fact that new things were in the offing. I think that encouraged a lot of people to decide this was all right, this was going to be a good career.

John T. Mason, Jr.: Now, that was your own experience.

Admiral Struble: That was my own experience, yes.

John T. Mason, Jr.: You had no temptation then to get out.

Admiral Struble: No, I did not. I had a temptation occur to me when I went to the California as communications officer on her for a couple of years. It meant that I had a job close to the captain and kind of became the captain's aide. I mean, he wanted to call me his aide; he wasn't entitled to have an aide, really. A captain doesn't have one; an admiral does, but a captain doesn't.

We had lots of maneuvers in the fleet in those days. At the maneuvers, all the officers have jobs around the ship in connection with the guns and everything else. Up on the bridge, the navigator had always been the officer who took the conn—that means the officer of the deck, handling the wheel and the engines and everything. The captain of the ship would go up and sit in a chair on the bridge. He might personally handle the ship all the time, particularly if he liked to. But if he did, he wasn't the best captain for the ship and the crew, because nobody would get any training but the captain.

Now, most captains would conn the ships out of harbor themselves. Once a ship was at sea the captain would turn it over to the subordinate. Then he would sit on the stool and watch him perform, and say he could have done better this way or that. Now, that kind of captain was better for both the ship and the Navy, because he was training people.

So when I went to the California, the captain very early made me, as the communication officer, the officer of the deck at general quarters, which is the time when everybody goes to their battle stations and gets ready to fight. Well, that has always been the proverbial job of the navigator, and you might wonder why he did it. But the reason was that on the California, there was the big staff of the admiral commanding the fleet, and the staff and the admiral were constantly wanting to know from the ship's navigator where we were and what course he thought they ought to lay to head for so-and-so and so forth. In other words, the staff and admiral had a tendency to use the navigator on the California as the staff navigator too. So the navigator, entering and leaving port and during maneuvers, was always very busy with the staff.

This particular captain that I was with decided to make me the ship handler at general quarters and leave the navigator free so that if the admiral wanted to say, "Hey, come down and show me your chart on this," why, the navigator could leave the bridge and go down and talk to the admiral, and things would go on as normal.

Arthur D. Struble, Interview #2 (5/28/76) -- Page 62

So, actually, as a young lieutenant I got an awful lot of good practice and training in handling a battleship, because I handled it for the captain. In maneuvers it got to the point where he never would conn, which was very pleasant. It was good experience for me.

John T. Mason, Jr.: This was a deterrent if you ever had thought of getting out. I mean, you were doing something that was vital.

Admiral Struble: Yes. Well, you realized you were getting a lot of very fine training.

John T. Mason, Jr.: You say you met Nimitz on the California.

Admiral Struble: Well, Nimitz was the operations and planning officer for the commander in chief of the fleet.[*] As such, of course, he was a very important officer in the fleet plans for exercises and operations, and all that sort of thing. There was no doubt in my mind that Nimitz was a very fine influence on the good training and the good planning and everything that went on during that period. They took the fleet to Australia. Robison was fleet commander; Nimitz was tactical officer.[†]

John T. Mason, Jr.: I see. Well now, before we hear about that trip to Australia in some detail, tell me about the thinking again in terms of morale on board. Tell me about the role of athletics in maintaining interest among the enlisted men, and that sort of thing.

Admiral Struble: There were fine fleet schedules for athletic training. Ashore in San Pedro, there was an excellent area, and everything was done, more or less, that could be done to keep fleet athletics on a good, high level—lots of football games, lots of training. Younger men and younger officers were constantly engaged in various types of athletics.

---

[*] Commander Chester W. Nimitz, USN. As an admiral Nimitz was Commander in Chief Pacific Fleet during World War II. The Naval Institute oral history collection contains a number of specialized interviews regarding Admiral Nimitz.
[†] Admiral Samuel S. Robison, USN, Commander Battle Fleet, 1923-25.

John T. Mason, Jr.: In competition?

Admiral Struble: In competition. I think Admiral Robison, and I'm sure that Chester Nimitz's influence was very strong and very good.

John T. Mason, Jr.: Did you get embroiled in athletics yourself?

Admiral Struble: No, I was too busy, I guess. I had a very busy job when I was on the California. I got in a tiny bit of golf myself, but it was very poor work.

John T. Mason, Jr.: Well, now you might tell me about that grand tour to Australia in the fleet. What was the purpose of it?

Admiral Struble: The purpose was to go on an extended cruise, which would strain the limits of capabilities of fuel and all other things of that sort, and develop knowledge about how to make a long cruise if you had to, such as maybe go across the ocean. But you would have lots of exercises. We had constant gunnery exercises, constant tactical exercises, and constant air operations in the fleet on the way to Australia and on the way back.

John T. Mason, Jr.: How many ships approximately were involved in this hegira?

Admiral Struble: I suppose at the maximum we probably got up to 150.

John T. Mason, Jr.: Well, the logistics of that operation were quite considerable.

Admiral Struble: Oh, yes, we were also straining the logistics people too. It was a very good cruise. It was also a good cruise to take us out into the Asiatic area, and it was a good thing for us to get acquainted with the Australians, because 20 years later we were certainly going to be helping them and operating with them.

Arthur D. Struble, Interview #2 (5/28/76) – Page 64

John T. Mason, Jr.: So it had some political overtones as well?

Admiral Struble: Oh, it had lots of good political overtones. It was a fine cruise and a useful cruise. And out of that came advanced air training and improvement. Out of that came—not in the '20s I would say, but in the '30s—out of it came the advancement in the amphibious forces, which was started in the fleet in Rear Admiral Pringle commanding a division.* He had the first kind of an amphibious operation with the Army up in San Francisco Bay.

John T. Mason, Jr.: And that was approximately when?

Admiral Struble: That was in the early '30s. I had been in the <u>California</u>, and I had been ashore in the Navy Department. I came back and was on Rear Admiral Pringle's staff as his senior aide and so forth.

John T. Mason, Jr.: You say that the inception of the idea was during this fleet maneuver to Australia.

Admiral Struble: Well, not the inception of the idea. The recognition that all kinds of operation might be going on, and we ought to be training for them. It had not yet developed into what I would call the amphibious angle—that was '25. In the early '30s, it started to develop into the amphibious thing because of the Marines. A Marine officer who was one of the staff officers in the fleet and later went ashore in San Diego where he was a commanding officer of troops, was constantly bringing up this—we ought to be learning more about landing troops.

Now he's written a book on that subject, I am sure, and he was very instrumental in it. Due to the fact that everybody was alert in the fleet, the Marines had been training at handling troops in and out of boats for landing. We finally had a landing up in San

---

* In the early 1930s Struble served as flag secretary for Rear Admiral Joel R. P. Pringle, USN, Commander Battleship Division Three.

Francisco Harbor in the early '30s from this battleship division. The troops were taken in and attempted to land.

John T. Mason, Jr.: I would think, sir, that there would have been ideas as you went down to Australia, made that long trip, of the need for perfecting techniques of landing on islands, because you passed so many.

Admiral Struble: That's right. The people that were in that business, which is primarily the Marines—all of them who were on that cruise got to thinking about it. The captains of the naval ships hadn't yet gotten around to thinking about it, but the Marines were thinking about it. Their staff officer in the fleet command in the late '20s was the man that, as a Marine, had fomented movement into shore down in southern California. He and the Marines had been doing a lot of landing and everything. He, of course, saw it as being a very excellent Marine adjunct for future wars, so he wanted the Marines to be the amphibious people.

Now, you see, you can't have real amphibious people without getting the Navy into it, although the troops are going to be landed to fight ashore. So there's no doubt about it that we took a couple of big motor sailers from <u>Tennessee</u> around to this Army post and landed them for the general's benefit, and one of my best stories is on that.

John T. Mason, Jr.: The story about Presidio in San Francisco Bay.

Admiral Struble: In the early '30s, a battleship division under Rear Admiral Pringle went up to San Francisco with the fleet Marine officer for the purpose of having some trial landing experience from naval ships on a beachhead. The beach at the Presidio, which is just inside the harbor, is an excellent spot, so it was decided to have the training at the Presidio. The Presidio sent out troops to the battleship division. They were then put into large motor sailers and taken around by water to land on the beach at the Presidio.

The boats, of course, were standard Navy boats. They weren't really designed for landing, and they were really a little large for the purpose. There was a large crowd gathered on the beach at the Presidio, including the Army general, who was in command of Presidio. As the motor sailer moved in on the beach, she got into about four feet of water when, due to the heavy loading of the boat, she stopped about 16 feet short of the beach. The beach was fairly steep. The young lieutenant in command of the Army troops standing in the bow of the motor launch realized that the launch had stopped and wasn't going to go any further. He had on a big, what I would call Spanish-American War sombrero. He took a look toward the beach, took a look aft at the crew, and decided he had to do something. So he said, "Men, follow me." And he leaped over the bow of the motor launch.

Well, we had about five to six feet of water by that time under the bow of the motor launch, and he went into the water and went underneath. His hat kind of floated away on the water. He came up for air and he was able to swim into the beach, but the landing became, of course, a terrible fiasco.

As Admiral Pringle's aide, I was ashore on the beach standing with the admiral, witnessing this trial. And I immediately said, "Oh, General, this has gone to pot, and I'll take the responsibility for the Navy. We made a bum boat landing here for you, and I'm wondering if we can't schedule it for tomorrow or the next day again, and do a good job." The general agreed.

So we later came back. The boat coxswain the next time was an experienced man who knew his business, and we rammed the boat up on the beach the way it should have been on the first day. So eventually we learned something about landing troops. We all realized simply from the mistake we had first made that we surely needed a lot of training. It was really the start of the amphibious business, for which I must give great credit to the Marines.

John T. Mason, Jr.: That's a fine story too.

Admiral Struble: Is that all right?

John T. Mason, Jr.: Yes, indeed. Tell me, when the fleet went down to Australia, did you have any cooperation from the Royal Navy units? Were any of them accompanying you?

Admiral Struble: No. It was the Australian Navy. No, I think that wouldn't have been a good thing, and I don't think the British would have wanted to have done it, because the first visit of the American fleet to Australia had to be handled by the Australians, I am sure. Not that the English weren't quite willing to help us in every way, but I am sure they recognized the value of having the—and, as I remember, we did run into a certain number of British officers ashore. They were there, but there was no British fleet present.

John T. Mason, Jr.: No. Did any new ideas come into being on fueling at sea as a result of this long trip?

Admiral Struble: Fueling at sea, of course, had been pushed because, I would say, of our World War I experience rather than by the fleet cruise. But the fleet cruise opened people's eyes to certain things and undoubtedly made us realize that a lot of the new training, which we had gone in for after World War I, was very worthwhile.

John T. Mason, Jr.: In your job as communications officer you must have had a terrific workout on this trip.

Admiral Struble: Well, that is true. It was a very interesting cruise from that standpoint of view, and, of course, we had a tremendous message problem once we got to Australia to handle everything that was coming back and forth from the shore.

John T. Mason, Jr.: You said that the idea was to stretch the fleet to the limit of its capabilities, and I would think that it stretched you to the limit.

Admiral Struble: Well, it was a cruise that did much for naval interest and so forth in its people. The Australians, by virtue of having seen us for quite a while and having had a lot of contact with us, were not hesitant in the slightest when World War II broke, asking us to come down there.

John T. Mason, Jr.: How long did you stay in Sydney Harbor?

Admiral Struble: We spent about two weeks and then went to Auckland and were about two weeks or more in Auckland. All of the fleet by turn, were allowed to go up to Rotorua when we were in Auckland, which is, of course, quite a spot.

John T. Mason, Jr.: Yes. So there were some scenic sidelines as well.

Admiral Struble: Oh, yes, the people in the fleet got a chance, both in Australia and also in New Zealand, to take trips by train somewhere and really see something. I think it was a very invigorating thing—good thing.

John T. Mason, Jr.: Let's resume your story and tell me about stepping up to the fleet when you became aide and flag lieutenant on the staff of the battleship division commander. You left the California.

Admiral Struble: I left the California and went over as aide to the vice admiral of the battleships.

John T. Mason, Jr.: This was in October of '25.

Admiral Struble: Yes. Admiral Richard H. Jackson had command of the battleships for a year, and then became the commander of the Pacific Fleet for a year.[*] Of course, this was very interesting duty. During that period, we made a cruise to the East Coast and up to New York.

John T. Mason, Jr.: You took the whole fleet?

---

[*] Admiral Richard H. Jackson, USN, Commander Battle Fleet, 1926-27.

Admiral Struble: We took the whole Pacific Fleet through the canal and had maneuvers with the Atlantic Fleet in the Cuban area, and then went on up to New York and had stops in both New York and Newport.

John T. Mason, Jr.: Did anything significant happen en route? I mean, going through the canal or the maneuvers in the Caribbean?

Admiral Struble: No. They were very interesting; they were good maneuvers; they were well-designed, because this time you had kind of two fleets playing against each other, so that it provided better maneuvers in some ways than we had had by ourselves in the Pacific where we'd have to divide into two fleets in order to have two forces operating against each other, which wasn't generally good for training. But the training on the fleet cruise was very good around Guantanamo.

John T. Mason, Jr.: Were planes beginning to have a greater significance?

Admiral Struble: They were increasing in significance every year.

John T. Mason, Jr.: In what sense, sir?

Admiral Struble: Well, after you had operated a while, you found out that an airplane could do this for you. Then you had to turn around and persuade the aviators that this would be their job to do this for us rather than they defending their own job with the airplanes, which was to go shoot the enemy. In other words, you had to approach and work out the cooperation that was needed to help you rather than the fact that they were out to do their own shooting.

John T. Mason, Jr.: I take it then that they didn't always think of it as doing operations.

Admiral Struble: Well, in those early days we really did have a tendency to think that the battleship can do better if we have this. The aviator whose planes you now want to run and operate—he has ideas about what he might do to hit some enemy battleships, you see. So that did still exist.

John T. Mason, Jr.: What role did the seaplane play?

Admiral Struble: The seaplane was valuable, because it could operate at considerable distances from shore establishments and didn't need to be operated from ships. That was the part that the seaplane had. The ability to land on the water was a safety factor for it. It also gave the seaplane an opportunity to land and look around inside a bay, or maybe go to a bay and land and be available to take off when it would be desirable for the accomplishment of its mission, which might be when it got a radio report that battleships were approaching from the south, say. In the meantime, they wouldn't have been flying around up in the air using the gas. They could have been resting on the water someplace to take off at the right time, to accomplish their mission.

    Cooperation is really the seat of most of these situations. You always have a situation where you have the straightforward fight, which would go ahead in our talk, really, to the time when you get to the place where the small carriers were sent into the Sulu Sea and the Japs diverted their air flight then, which was very good for us as we were going to Mindoro.[*]

John T. Mason, Jr.: Yes. On this early occasion, with the fleet going through the canal, did you have a seaplane tender accompanying the fleet?

Admiral Struble: Yes, we had what was known as AirPac with us, which was about two old, small carriers, as I remember.[†]

John T. Mason, Jr.: That's about all the fleet had.

Admiral Struble: Well, yes, that was the whole thing. It was very small at that time.

---

[*] This is a reference to operations in the Philippines late in World War II.
[†] AirPac was the name of the type command in later years. In the late 1920s it was known officially as Aircraft Squadrons Battle Fleet.

John T. Mason, Jr.: After maneuvers in the Caribbean, you say you went on up to New York, and there's a very interesting event you want to relate during your stay in New York and just before you went up to Newport.

Admiral Struble: We were due to leave New York on a Friday. On Thursday Admiral Jackson sent for me and said, "Be ready tomorrow morning early. I want to take the official car and drive out on Long Island. I understand that there are about three boys out there that are going to try to fly the Atlantic to Paris. I'd like to go over and look at them in their planes."

So the next morning, the admiral and I left early and inspected the three different flights that were going over for the first flight of the twin-engine, good-sized engine, still quite large and well equipped. And the third plane, when we came to it, was a rather small, little modest plane that had flown in from San Diego.

John T. Mason, Jr.: Was this part of a contest or what? Were they competing with each other?

Admiral Struble: They were competing with each other in that nobody had yet flown to Paris from New York. I believe there was a prize for the first man that flew the Atlantic to Paris from New York. So that was the reason the planes had probably assembled pretty much simultaneously. It was obviously chosen as the period that would be favorable to such a flight. It was the time of year when the winds would be favorable for such a flight.

Now, Lindbergh's plane was very interesting to me.*

John T. Mason, Jr.: His was the small plane.

---

* Charles A. Lindbergh became a national hero when he made the first solo flight across the Atlantic Ocean in May 1927. The light cruiser Memphis (CL-13) brought Lindbergh and his plane back to the United States, arriving at the Washington Navy Yard on 11 June.

Admiral Struble: Because his was the small plane. He sat in his seat. He had nothing beneath him but a board so he couldn't see down. He had two side windows out of which he could look to right or left, but he had no way of really seeing in front of him. He had decided to cut a small place in the wood underneath him and put in a piece of glass so that if, in flying the Atlantic, he had to come down close to the water, he could see the waves underneath him as he went down toward the ocean. He would never have vision ahead except that he had a little mirror on each side that he could adjust to get a little sight ahead. I asked about his supplies. He had, he hoped, enough to make Paris, and the morning of the flight he would come down and get a cup of coffee and a sandwich at Mame's, and then probably ask her to make a sandwich for him, which he would take with him for his food on the flight.

John T. Mason, Jr.: That was the local hot dog stand, wasn't it?

Admiral Struble: The local hot dog stand. Actually, the next morning, as the fleet stood out of New York, we realized that he had taken off that morning for Paris and was on his way. So it became quite an interesting thing to realize that we had been there the day before.

John T. Mason, Jr.: You reported to me a certain conversation you had with Lindbergh and the admiral had with him, one charming note.

Admiral Struble: Oh, yes. During the conversation Lindbergh was very polite with the admiral. He asked the admiral if he had any friends in Paris, because he himself didn't have any and he wondered if the admiral knew somebody that he knew. Admiral Jackson said, "Well, no, I don't know that I know anybody right now in Paris. I'm sorry I didn't look it up before I came over."

John T. Mason, Jr.: Admiral, I think at this point, since you mentioned Jackson in connection with the visit to Long Island, and Colonel Lindbergh, that perhaps it would be well for you to give an account of Jackson as a person, as an officer.

Admiral Struble: Well, he was a short, small man, very strong, very capable. He was certainly one who could make a sound decision quickly, and was, also, always thoughtful about the future.

John T. Mason, Jr.: What do you mean by that?

Admiral Struble: I mean that he was always looking ahead to what ought to be done next. He was a very remarkable man. I had the feeling that I learned an awful lot, and it was a privilege to serve with him.

John T. Mason, Jr.: His decisions at the moment would take the long-range point of view into consideration.

Admiral Struble: Always. Also, he had plenty of nerve for problems. I never will forget the time we were bringing the Battle Fleet out of San Francisco Harbor. There was an unusually heavy westerly wind, and the rollers were just rolling in the Golden Gate. Now, at San Francisco Harbor entrance, the western approach is just a straight roll into the harbor. There is, as you go partway out of the harbor, an additional way out of the harbor that curves to the north. It's deeper than the main channel and has a little more protection from the waves, and, therefore, is a better channel to use for a big ship with heavy rollers directly against her.

So on the way out, he increased the fleet's speed from 12 to 15, and decided to go out the north channel rather than the main ship channel, which I don't believe had ever been done before and was quite unusual. However, he was in the lead ship, the <u>West Virginia</u>, and we took her out the north channel very successfully in this very heavy weather.

I think there are few admirals that I know that would have made such a quick but clearheaded decision on a tactical matter, you might say, that had to be done right away.

John T. Mason, Jr.: Obviously he had great confidence in his decisions.

Admiral Struble: He had entire confidence in his decisions, yes.

John T. Mason, Jr.: How does a man acquire that ability? You had it too. How does a man acquire it?

Admiral Struble: Well, I suppose a man acquires that from learning all he had about each individual thing that he is doing at the time he does it. If you are handling a ship, you learn how to handle her the best possible, to take every opportunity to learn anything you can about her. And Jackson had done that. He had no hesitation in deciding to make this decision on that occasion.

John T. Mason, Jr.: What was the occasion of the visit to Newport with the fleet and Jackson?

Admiral Struble: We were on our way home then. It was just simply a stop. It's a naval area, and it was just a place to go in and stay there, and then depart for the West Coast.

John T. Mason, Jr.: You said that you got to be very close to Admiral Jackson because of his own personal situation. His wife had died, and he brought his niece out to be his hostess.

Admiral Struble: And, of course, my wife, therefore, became very good friends and was with her quite a bit, which meant that I knew the admiral in a much more close and personal way than I normally would have. He was a very fine man and a man of very considerable decision.

John T. Mason, Jr.: How much did he know about the individual ships in his fleet? How much attention did he pay to them? And how much inspection did he indulge in?

Admiral Struble: He probably got around talking to the division commanders and such officers more than most admirals did. He made a point of going around and talking to them. He had a very keen sense of duty, very keen. I think that he was not as outgoing a character in any way as we usually had in the fleet. Neither as Rodman, or anywhere near as much as Hughes and so forth.*

John T. Mason, Jr.: He was more introspective.

Admiral Struble: Yes, he was.

John T. Mason, Jr.: What would you say were some of the things you actually learned from him because of your close relationship, not only serving with him but knowing him as a man? What were some of the lessons that, perhaps, you learned from this unique individual?

Admiral Struble: I think I learned from him, very much the idea of being thoughtful and thinking over, and possibly discussing various different courses of action or various individuals with whom you might be meeting in advance and having settled yourself reasonably well on what you might attempt to accomplish in your conversation. I think he did that very much. I think he was very thoughtful of what he was going to try to accomplish if he could, in talking to somebody.

John T. Mason, Jr.: I suppose one could see in your own experience later on, the application of this principal in terms of amphibious landing. I mean, the careful consideration of the various points of view before an operation took place?

Admiral Struble: Well, I think that I learned that from him. His number-two man, who was J. R. P. Pringle and a very wonderful admiral and a very capable admiral, was very outgoing. He had more ability in meeting people and talking with them and getting them

---

* Admiral Hugh Rodman, USN, was Commander in Chief Pacific Fleet, 1919-21; Admiral Charles F. Hughes, USN, was Commander Battle Fleet, 1925-26, and Commander in Chief U.S. Fleet, 1926-27.

opened up than Jackson did. That was the source of his success, which was very marked also. I felt that I was very fortunate in having been associated with both of those men.

John T. Mason, Jr.: To see two different approaches.

Admiral Struble: To see two different approaches and to recognize that we had two very fine people there. Actually, in my respect for our senior admirals out in the Pacific, it was great. Nimitz, who proved to be a very capable man, was at that time a commander on the California. He was the senior man in plans and operations for his admiral. He undoubtedly was one of our best later—steady, reliable, thoughtful. You couldn't have a better man. And we had him at the right time.

John T. Mason, Jr.: Well, this idea you express about Jackson showing concern for other people and their points of view and so forth, impresses me as something that isn't universal with military people.

Admiral Struble: Well, of course it's very easy in the military life. You have so many things going on that just go ahead with the business without always, maybe, striving to get all the information you could. People are different. All of these admirals that you mentioned are all a little different, all have their high spots. Most of those we've talked about were generally very capable.
    Admiral Hughes was quite a different type, but he was still a very capable officer.

Interview Number 3 with Admiral Arthur D. Struble, U.S. Navy (Retired)
Place: Admiral Struble's Home, Chevy Chase, Maryland
Date: Thursday, 10 June 1976
Interviewer: John T. Mason, Jr.

John T. Mason, Jr.: Well, sir, we resume your very interesting story this morning, and you were back with the fleet in San Pedro with Admiral Jackson. You got word that you were wanted in Washington. Will you take up the story at that point, sir?

Admiral Struble: Well, I had previously talked to the captain of a battleship who was going down to San Diego, to take charge of the training station there and to train new cadets. He had asked me to go down with him as the drill officer, and in that capacity I would get a nice set of quarters. This looked very good to my wife, to whom I had already explained this, and who was, of course, very interested in it. I thought it would be a very nice, fine, interesting naval tour of duty.

John T. Mason, Jr.: I assume it would have been for two years.

Admiral Struble: Yes, it would have been a two-year assignment. However, Admiral Charles Hughes, who had previously been in command of the fleet, had gone to Washington as the CNO, and at this time he sent out a message from Washington that he wanted me to come east to be the officer in charge of the code and signal section in Washington.* I explained this to Admiral Jackson and said, "Now, how do I tell Admiral Hughes no?"

He said, "My God! You're not going to tell him no, are you? He's offered you a very fine job. If you want to be a real naval officer, you better get back there and take it."

So I excused myself from Admiral Jackson's presence, went around in my room and thought it over for about five minutes, and decided to go to Washington.

---

* Admiral Charles F. Hughes, USN, served as Chief of Naval Operations from 14 November 1927 to 17 September 1930.

John T. Mason, Jr.: The career won.

Admiral Struble: The career won. The code and signal section proved to be a very interesting assignment.

John T. Mason, Jr.: What was its state when you went there?

Admiral Struble: Well, at the time they had just completed breaking a part of the Japanese code.

John T. Mason, Jr.: It was the diplomatic code?

Admiral Struble: I guess I'd call it a diplomatic-military code, because I think it kind of was both. I think both the Japanese State Department and Navy Department used the thing with each other. The story is not about the code, because, of course, in a year or two, maybe, the code was changed, and it started all over again—from our point of view of conducting intelligence.

But the interesting part of the thing for me was that in designing our own signals and in considering our own code, we had to recognize that the other man was probably just as capable of doing something like that as we were. Therefore, it was very important that in our code business, we didn't let a code run too long. So that if it were broken, it would be a continuous source of intelligence to the other side.

John T. Mason, Jr.: And when a change was made, it was made a complete change, was it not?

Admiral Struble: Yes. You made a change that separated it from the previous situation, which, of course, I think was a very important lesson for all of us to learn. We had been changing our codes a reasonable amount before that, but we certainly understood from then on that it was important to do it more often.

John T. Mason, Jr.: How frequently would that be?

Admiral Struble: It would depend upon what the code was and how it was used, I guess.

John T. Mason, Jr.: I see—what sort of messages went out.

Admiral Struble: Yes. But we really jerked up our own security quite a bit at that time because of this situation. The code and signal section also prepared the visual codes—flag signals and all that sort of thing. It was a very interesting assignment, and, actually, I was kept on for three years in Washington.

John T. Mason, Jr.: So you were there from 1927 until—

Admiral Struble: Until about 1930. It was a very pleasant and interesting three years.

John T. Mason, Jr.: And in that period of time, of course, Japan was noticeably developing as a future adversary.

Admiral Struble: That's right, as a possible adversary, and developing a much broader navy. Both facts kind of go together, you see, from the standpoint of what our problem was.

John T. Mason, Jr.: What was your particular job in that area, in that section?

Admiral Struble: Well, we had a radio section and a visual section. We prepared the codebooks for the Navy in connection with signals and that sort of thing, so that we had quite a bit to do with highly secret messages. In our capacity we were the one section in the Navy Department which could release a very secret message—which we occasionally did as a matter of business—to, say, a fleet command on a very secret matter that concerned secret codes. So it was something that you had to handle very carefully and thoughtfully.

John T. Mason, Jr.: How closely did you work with ONI?[*]

Admiral Struble: This was the part of the performance in which we came in very close contact with ONI. If ONI wanted to send a very secret message to their representative, let's say, out in the Asiatic, for instance—

John T. Mason, Jr.: You mean a naval attaché.

Admiral Struble: Or even maybe a top officer on the admiral's staff. They wouldn't turn that message in to ONI up above; they would bring that to us. The coding would be secretly done by the officer that was in charge of that coding section down in my bailiwick. Then it would personally go up to the central office and go out. That ensured that a lot of people didn't see it going and coming.

John T. Mason, Jr.: I see. A very limited distribution.

Admiral Struble: Well, in other words, as the head of the code and signal section, I had a limited authority to release a message in code that was already coded. Otherwise, any message that went to the communications system to go around the world somewhere and be decoded, was coded or decoded up in the big communications center. This little extra center we had down below was a very small thing and was naturally more easily kept very secret to one or two people.

John T. Mason, Jr.: Now, we had a contingent of Japanese language students in Tokyo in that period, and continuing on, young naval officers who were learning to master the Japanese language. When they came back, were they for the most part absorbed into communications?

---

[*] ONI—Office of Naval Intelligence.

Admiral Struble: No, I would say that they continued in intelligence. They were staff for intelligence and continued. This code part of it is a different matter, really, from intelligence. It does become intelligence when you solve something.

John T. Mason, Jr.: It certainly did in World War II.

Admiral Struble: But it's a different matter entirely than intelligence in the normal application.

John T. Mason, Jr.: Were any of the men who later were famous in terms of codes and deciphering—were they in the organization at that time? People like Safford?

Admiral Struble: Most all of those people had gone through this at some time.

John T. Mason, Jr.: Safford and Rochefort.*

Admiral Struble: I remember Safford and Rochefort, but I don't know that I know any others. I was only there for a short time.

John T. Mason, Jr.: Wenger was another.†

Admiral Struble: Yes, Wenger was with me.

John T. Mason, Jr.: Was war plans in being in the Navy Department at that time? And if the Division of War Plans was in being, what relationship did that have to codes and communications?

---

* Lieutenant Commander Laurance F, Safford, USN; Lieutenant Joseph J. Rochefort, USN. The oral history of Rochefort, who retired as a captain, is in the Naval Institute collection.
† Lieutenant (junior grade) Joseph N. Wenger, USN.

Admiral Struble: There was a war plans section that was working on war plans and primarily working on the preparation of our own war plan. Therefore, while they would like to know anything they could about what somebody else was doing so that they could use that knowledge to prepare our plans, they primarily had no connection with the intelligence on the subject, except such intelligence as the intelligence section gave to them.

We had a kind of different connection between communications and intelligence in that we jointly were working on foreign codes, so, therefore, we temporarily worked closely with intelligence to assist them, as well as to assist ourselves in our preparation of naval codes and ciphers. In other words, we had to protect our codes and ciphers, if we could, from what we were trying to do to somebody else's code and ciphers.

John T. Mason, Jr.: What sort of a sharing of information did you have with the Royal Navy, with the British?

Admiral Struble: At this time, which is in '27 to '30, we had practically no connection in that area.

John T. Mason, Jr.: After that three-year stint in Washington with codes and communication, you went back to the fleet, and you went to the commander of the Battleship Division Number Three as aide. And in what other capacity were you there?

Admiral Struble: Flag secretary.

John T. Mason, Jr.: Who was the commander of the third division of battleships?

Admiral Struble: Admiral Pringle, a very well-known, very capable officer in our Navy. Admiral Pringle had previously been chief of staff to Admiral Jackson when Jackson had the fleet. Pringle also had been president of the Naval War College.* He was a very, very thoughtful, splendid naval officer. Two years of experience with Pringle, in my opinion, was one of the most valuable assets I ever had.

John T. Mason, Jr.: Would you elaborate upon that? In what sense?

Admiral Struble: The admiral had a tendency at times to gather one, or two, or three of the staff together, and he would analyze a war problem we were conducting, or a situation that existed, and point out to us how we could study it and learn something from it, and how we could use it in future operations ourselves. He was very clearheaded, very thoughtful. Experience with him, in my opinion, was especially valuable to a younger officer. I felt that I was very privileged to have been able to serve with him for a couple of years. He was a very fine man.

Unfortunately, he developed a medical problem and was unable to finish out his naval career. I'm sure that he would have been Chief of Naval Operations if his health had not prevented it.

John T. Mason, Jr.: He retired on disability, did he?

Admiral Struble: Well, yes, and he died shortly.†

John T. Mason, Jr.: It's interesting as you mention these various tours of duty and the men, the interchange of positions would indicate the family nature of the Navy at that time.

Admiral Struble: Yes. I think there was a tendency for the young officer who was ordered to some flag officer's staff to learn a considerable amount of valuable experience from that senior officer. Now, by virtue of that job, he became himself a little more

---

* Rear Admiral Joel R. P. Pringle, USN, served as president of the Naval War College from 19 September 1927 to 31 May 1930. Pringle Hall at the war college is named in his honor, as was the destroyer Pringle (DD-477), commissioned in September 1942.
† Admiral Pringle died 25 September 1932.

prominent than he might otherwise have been, because of his experience with this well-known senior officer. Therefore, the next time you went to sea, you might be offered a very good job which would keep you in the top line of command thought, and so forth, part of the Navy, which is of importance.

For instance, my friend, Mick Carney, is a good example of that.[*] He undoubtedly had a number of continuing jobs connected with admirals in high command. It was both valuable to that admiral to have Carney, but it was also very valuable to Carney to have had that experience.

John T. Mason, Jr.: Yes, and one could go on and cite other men. Nimitz also had that experience.

Admiral Struble: Oh, of course, certainly. Nimitz had been the operations officer for the first admiral that I mentioned on the California.

John T. Mason, Jr.: Yes. What I was underscoring was the small, family-like nature of the Navy in that time.

Admiral Struble: To some extent. Yet I believe those senior officers didn't often call people back simply because they had become old family friends. They were called back because the officer concerned felt they had a capacity in something they could use.

John T. Mason, Jr.: And he had gotten to know them.

Admiral Struble: Yes, he had gotten to know them and, of course, felt that he could trust him more than he might someone he had never seen before. That would be normal.

John T. Mason, Jr.: Yes. Well, tell me about some of the operations of the battleship division in that two-year period of 1930-32.

---

[*] Lieutenant Commander Robert B. Carney, USN. Carney, who graduated from the Naval Academy a year behind Struble, eventually became an admiral and served as Chief of Naval Operations from 1953 to 1955. His oral history is in the Columbia University collection.

Admiral Struble: I think there was one operation there that was very, very important—withal the fact that it was a failure—in that it represented the future. Battleship Division Three, which Admiral Pringle had, was sent up to San Francisco about halfway during that tour to make a landing out at the Army post at the Presidio. In other words, something in the line of an amphibious landing, but we hadn't yet gotten around to using the term "amphibious landing" much.

However, the Marines at that period had foreseen and were strong for joint efforts with the Navy to land Marines on the beach here or there for military purposes. I think that the Marines deserve very great credit for pushing this idea which eventually became the amphibious landing. Now, there were some of us in the Navy who thought it offered something. As a matter of fact, I myself felt that this did offer something for the future, but our first experience was a terrible failure.

We had a great big 50-foot heavy motor launch which I guess drew almost three and a half to four feet of water, heavily loaded down with maybe as many as 100 Army troops with the captain in command from the Army. We took them around to the Presidio beach, and before a number of observers, including the general and others, we brought them in to this landing on the beach as if we were landing troops. They were troops. They were Army, and they had their big sombreros on, and they had their guns.

The place where we came in which we had not really known or used before was rather steep, we thought. Actually, it was not as steep as we thought, and therefore this heavily loaded 50-foot motor launch with a lot of men in it and therefore heavy, grounded some 15 feet offshore from the beach itself. Actually, the water, I guess, was as much as six feet deep at the bow of the boat.

However, the Army captain wasn't to be deterred. He stood up in the bow of the boat with his hat on and said, "Follow me, men," and jumped in. Well, the water was over six feet, and he went down under, and his hat floated away on the top of the water. A lot of the men who followed him in, of course, had similar experiences. So the landing really was a very unhappy thing.

I was standing over on the beach as Admiral Pringle's representative. He was ill and had been unable to go to the landing that day. I was standing over there to watch the landing as soon as it happened. I said, "Oh, General, this is a flop. This thing is going to be no good. We've got to do it again in a couple of days and we'll do a lot better job."

The general agreed that it had been quite a flop, and we'd better do it again. So a couple of days later we went over with a much lighter, better boat for the purpose. Less people in the boat so we could ram up on the beach more, and we did recoup a little of the losses we made that previous day. We did make the situation still easily arguable that this was a good idea and we ought to go after it. Fortunately, the Marines did keep after this amphibious landing idea very heavily. In the next World War, the reasonable amount of knowledge we had developed—which was not too much—was, of course, very valuable.

John T. Mason, Jr.: Let me ask, sir, what practice the fleet had prior to that time in terms of landing parties?

Admiral Struble: Previously it had been a question of sending a landing party ashore. Generally we had gone to a pier or something where you could land in a normal fashion. Now, of course, if you were gong to go in to a beach, you might take a heavily loaded motor launch in, not in to the beach but offshore and have a smaller boat take the people from the motor launch in to where they could run the lighter boat practically up on the beach. I mean, people wouldn't have to have more than 10 or 12 inches of water to go through to get ashore. Of course, the dryer you get your troops ashore, the better. I mean, they are capable of carrying on better than if they have gotten heavily wet down on the way in.

John T. Mason, Jr.: Did we have any knowledge of landing operations on the part of other fleets, such as the British and the Japanese? Were they engaged in experiments with amphibious landings?

Admiral Struble: My knowledge would lead me to suspect that we had practically no knowledge of foreigners engaged in this business, and I question that there was very much of that type of activity going on abroad. I think probably our Marines, who could see a great value to them in this matter, were the ones that were the active element that was pushing it at that time.

John T. Mason, Jr.: I know that a few years after this—probably in '32 or '34 or something like that—Walter Ansel, who later became a rear admiral and landed in North Africa, was sent down to Quantico to spend a period of time with the Marines to learn from them and to contribute to their efforts at amphibious operations.*

Admiral Struble: Well, you see, this would just follow what happened.

John T. Mason, Jr.: Yes.

Admiral Struble: These Marines were good people; they could see the value of this, and they kept working on it. So they got a naval officer down to Quantico, and that's where they were able to develop a number of the ideas that might someday come to fruition. Actually, I think it's too bad we didn't have almost in some way a Marine contingent to land at Normandy, simply because the Marines had done an awful lot of that art. Of course, the landing at Normandy was primarily the landing of Army troops.†

John T. Mason, Jr.: Yes, and by that time the British had done a lot and had a lot of experience too.

Admiral Struble: The British had done a certain amount too. Well, I presume they had had a fair amount of experience.

John T. Mason, Jr.: Later on, perhaps, you will talk about their experiment at Dieppe.

---

* Lieutenant Commander Walter C. Ansel, USN. The oral history of Ansel, who retired as a rear admiral, is in the Naval Institute collection.
† Later in the oral history Admiral Struble discussed the Allied landing at Normandy, France, during World War II.

Arthur D. Struble, Interview #3 (6/10/76) – Page 88

Admiral Struble: Well, a little bit of that, although I'm not an expert on Dieppe. I can discuss Normandy.

John T. Mason, Jr.: I know you can. Well, what else happened during that two-year period with the battleships?

Admiral Struble: Well, I would say that the battleship gunnery reached a very high point in its accuracy.

John T. Mason, Jr.: What did you have at that point, 14-inch guns?

Admiral Struble: I guess we were still in the 14-inch period. But the development of the use of air spotting and all that had gone ahead very measurably, as well as the amphibious business. After this period that I mentioned, which was the early '30s, the training in both of those factors went ahead quite rapidly.

John T. Mason, Jr.: I expect this was the time when Admiral Reeves became commander in chief.*

Admiral Struble: Well, part of the period that I have just discussed, talking about when Pringle went to sea as division commander, Reeves was the first commander of the air forces in the Pacific.† In other words, the air force had now gotten out to the point where they were established as a kind of separate command in the fleet, and therefore their usefulness and value was constantly on the increase. Reeves was quite heavily engaged in it and connected with it.

John T. Mason, Jr.: And he was aided and abetted in the effort by the fact that we were beginning to get new, improved types of planes.

---

* Admiral Joseph M. Reeves, USN, served as Commander in Chief U.S. Fleet from 15 June 1934 to 24 June 1936.
† In 1930-31 Rear Admiral Reeves was Commander Carriers Battle Fleet. Earlier, 1925-29, in essentially the same role, Reeves's title was Commander Aircraft Squadrons Battle Fleet.

Admiral Struble: Well, yes, of course. Naturally, in the aviation field the equipment was going ahead by leaps and bounds. You didn't have that same leap and bound increase in naval ships, though, because they would be gone for a lone time and had been improved over long periods of time.

John T. Mason, Jr.: Yes, and in that particular period, '30 to '32, we were going through a bad Depression, and the fleet was suffering as a result.

Admiral Struble: That's true. We were still held very much to our own battleship fleet. However, I think it's just as well to recognize that the Navy did go in for some little carriers and did go ahead with some advances in aviation, which I think is important. In other words, the carriers were then on their way. We were having carriers in fleet exercises in the period from the '30s to the '40s very much out in the Pacific. We were constantly working on that problem, and I think to our advantage.

John T. Mason, Jr.: Turning for the moment to the effects of the Depression and the limitations in the fleet, were you handicapped in your exercises because of restrictions on the use of live ammunition and that kind of thing?

Admiral Struble: Well, not so much on the ammunition part, but much more on the fuel part. You see, a big exercise can burn an awful lot of valuable fuel. I would say that we were held up more on that score rather than on the ammunition.

John T. Mason, Jr.: There was another restraint, was there not, in terms of reduction in pay and that kind of thing? Wasn't that the time of the 15% reduction?

Admiral Struble: I ought to remember it, but I don't. Either way, one of the advances that was made in that period which we haven't mentioned was the heavy cruisers that were brought into the fleet.

John T. Mason, Jr.: Oh, yes.

Admiral Struble: So we did have some new Navy ships. We had the heavy cruisers brought in. They were our first heavy cruisers, about 8,000 to 10,000 tons and very well armed.

John T. Mason, Jr.: And what did they have, 8-inch guns?

Admiral Struble: They had 8-inch. They were very valuable heavy ships. They had quite a bit of duty later in the South Pacific. Without them the early Jap advances toward Australia would have gone a lot farther. So our heavies were valuable, but we were just developing them in that period before 1940.

John T. Mason, Jr.: When the heavy cruiser began to come in, was there any thought that it was a threat to the battleship?

Admiral Struble: Not too much. Although we realized that the heavy cruisers were going to be valuable, and that therefore we would have to have some of them even if it meant decreasing slightly the size of the battle fleet. Our battle fleet really was big enough at that time to handle any job we had, so it really didn't need to increase. Of course, a battle fleet under those conditions would need to be kept modern, and the so-called battle cruiser was eventually going to come out. As you know, the Germans were building a battle cruiser.

John T. Mason, Jr.: The British had some.

Admiral Struble: Yes, so the battle cruiser was being experimented with a little, I would say, at that time. But we went in for a certain number of heavy cruisers, and they were very valuable because of their much better speed than the battleship. That, I think, is the important factor there, the fact that they had pretty heavy gun power, but they had the speed. They were definitely very valuable in the Southwest Pacific, when the Japanese were on their way to Australia.

John T. Mason, Jr.: Well, now, what use did the battleships make of Pearl Harbor and the naval facilities there in this 1930-32 period that you were with the battleships in the Pacific?

Admiral Struble: We generally made one cruise to Pearl Harbor every year and had fleet exercises and everything. It was a very good place for you to get an aviation exercise with the fleet. So we had our fleet exercises and tried to advance in our techniques very much during that period of '32 to '40, plus by going to Pearl Harbor and having exercises over there and having them combined—cruisers, destroyers, and such heavy cruisers as there were at that last part of it just before Pearl Harbor. That was a valuable training ground. It always has been and always will be for the Navy.

John T. Mason, Jr.: What do you remember of the facilities in Pearl Harbor in the 1930s—'31, '32?

Admiral Struble: They could handle the biggest ships and dock them and repair. They could handle the biggest thing we had and do it well. I think they had only one dock that would take one of the great big fellows, but you could accomplish your repairs in peacetime satisfactorily. You might have to wait a little.

John T. Mason, Jr.: In June of 1932 you left the Battleship Division Three staff and you went as the gunnery officer on the battleship New York.* Now, she was also in the Pacific, was she?

---

* USS New York (BB-34) was commissioned 15 April 1914. She had a standard displacement of 27,000 tons, was 573 feet long, and 95 feet in the beam. Her top speed was 21 knots. She was armed with ten 14-inch guns, 16 5-inch guns, and eight 3-inch guns. She was eventually decommissioned in 1946 after service in World War II.

Arthur D. Struble, Interview #3 (6/10/76) – Page 92

Admiral Struble: She was in the Pacific. I was happy to go to the New York as gunnery officer, because I had had so much staff duty that I wanted to have some of the practical duty.

John T. Mason, Jr.: You were getting typed as a staff officer, were you?

Admiral Struble: Typed as a staff officer. I had a very happy year as gunnery officer of the New York. The New York was a very happy battleship. She was one of the old-timers, but she was one of the best of the old-timers. Actually, that year the New York won the long-range battle practice business with all the new battleships.

John T. Mason, Jr.: Would you focus on battle practice?

Admiral Struble: Well, once a year we would have a long-range practice for each battleship which would go down the range. The target would be at quite long range, and you would have an opportunity to open fire and fire for about a minute or two, heavy salvos at the target, and then the time limit was up. Airplanes would have registered your shots, and the ship that got the most hits and so forth would win the long-range battle practice.

John T. Mason, Jr.: You talk of long range. What was the range?

Admiral Struble: In the case of each battleship it would vary a little. The newer battleships had to fire a little bit farther because their guns were longer. In the case of the New York, as I remember, we opened up to about 18,000 yards. We had a very good battle practice, and it was really a top battleship.

John T. Mason, Jr.: You got the E.

Admiral Struble: No, we didn't get the E.* The E is for all-around proficiency, not just the one battle practice. One of the modern battleships with the much more modern antiaircraft equipment got a hell of a high mark in the antiaircraft department. On the New York we had the old, old antiaircraft material, and we got a very low mark. Another battleship averaged higher and got the E.

John T. Mason, Jr.: That must be in a sense dispiriting, because—

Admiral Struble: Oh, no, no. That's the way things are. You can't make a competition between a ship like the New York and a modern battleship which was built several years later. The new equipment, if it's properly handled, is probably going to make the better score. I think the important point from our point of view was at the long-range practice we beat some of the big fellows, the new ones.

John T. Mason, Jr.: Did the New York have planes on board and catapults?

Admiral Struble: We had a couple of planes on board and catapults, just like the big ships.

John T. Mason, Jr.: And those planes were used primarily for what purpose?

Admiral Struble: Spotting. They would fly in the air overhead, and they would spot and tell you where your first salvo landed and attempt to correct it for you so the next one would hit. So it was a combination at that time of some airplane spotting assistance and main battery gun power to properly direct it.

John T. Mason, Jr.: How were the aviators treated on board the New York? Did they stand watches and that kind of thing?

---

* An "E," for excellence, is generally awarded to a ship or component of a ship as a result of top performance in competition with other ships during a given time period.

Arthur D. Struble, Interview #3 (6/10/76) -- Page 94

Admiral Struble: No. Although there was a policy, which I think was very sound, of trying to give the aviators a certain amount of navigational and that type of ship experience while they were on board if it could be done, but as I remember it was never required. In other words, it wasn't made an additional thing they had to do. It was more a question of giving them the opportunity of learning something, if conditions permitted, which would be valuable experience for them. Now, I imagine that the aviators were happy in some ships and not so happy in others. But I think on the New York we treated them very well.

John T. Mason, Jr.: And had an appreciation for their efforts.

Admiral Struble: Yes, that's right.

John T. Mason, Jr.: I would think that would determine whether they were happy or not.

Admiral Struble: Yes, I think so too. That's the way most things like that work out.

John T. Mason, Jr.: Well, now you said you did get involved with the earthquake.

Admiral Struble: We were up in Seattle at the navy yard under overhaul at the time of the earthquake.* My wife and two children were down at Long Beach, and that's where the earthquake was. When it got very bad, she had taken the two children out of town a ways to a big golf course there that seemed to be a safe spot. A number of wives and others were there. Then she remembered she wanted to telephone about something. I've forgotten now what the reason was she wanted to telephone. But she got this other lady to take her two children and she went in town to get that woman's husband who was on the fire department so that she could make this one message up to Bremerton to let me know where she was.

---

* The earthquake at 5:54 on the afternoon of 10 March 1933 at Long Beach was one of a series in the southern California area; 58 people were killed in Long Beach.

Well, while she was gone, the second thing, the tidal wave, started. That started about in the late afternoon. Immediately there was this hip-hip-hoorah and all the streets and roads were crowded with people. The cry was "Take to the hills, the tidal wave is coming!"

So this woman had had her two children and had our two children. She had a mother living in Pasadena, so she got in the car and decided to go to Pasadena. Hazel wasn't there, so she couldn't do anything for her. My wife got back out there, and the whole area where everybody had been was empty. So she just had to spend the next six or eight hours in a more or less perfect hell worrying and wondering. But eventually she got in communication with the woman in Pasadena and went up there and found her children. They all came back about a day later.

John T. Mason, Jr.: I take it that the area they had evacuated wasn't covered by the tidal wave, was it?

Admiral Struble: No, no tidal wave finally. That was just a scare. That part of Long Beach where we lived was in good shape. But when I heard of this on the radio up in Bremerton—that the children of Lieutenant Commander Struble were at the house of So-and-so in Pasadena but that Mrs. Struble wasn't there—I got permission from the captain to take some leave in a hurry, which was reasonable. I went over to Seattle and flew down the next day and got there about 7:00 o'clock at night. I found that my family were all right, but I had enough leave so that I could get in the car and help drive them north and just leave the house at Long Beach the way it was.

John T. Mason, Jr.: Was the <u>New York</u> obliged to participate in various festivals along the coast?

Admiral Struble: Yes, we had been at a very big festival in Santa Barbara. [Unclear section] represented the Navy ashore at that time. Santa Barbara had always liked them to have one big ship in for their big spring festival, and the <u>New York</u> had been chosen that year to go up. It was very interesting from the festival point of view. The governor of California was always down there for it. The Navy always tried to meet those kind of problems, which was a good thing to let the Navy become known to the people of the country.

John T. Mason, Jr.: Did the crew generally like that kind of duty?

Admiral Struble: Well, it was generally a nice interlude for a couple of days. We got to a different port, we saw different people. They saw the party [unclear] the show that went on there. It was an interesting part of naval experience. I think it was good for the Navy to become known to the people of the country. It think it was always good for those people in the crew who hadn't been around very much. It gave them a little chance to kind of see the world, even if it was only in their own country.

John T. Mason, Jr.: What part did organized athletics play in the life of the New York?

Admiral Struble: Well, in peacetime, the New York had one excellent baseball team, as I remember, and they competed very favorably with the bigger, newer battleships on that score. I think athletics, which was at that time being developed quite a bit in the fleet, was an excellent thing for the men. It gave the men something to do. A certain number of them played. A large number of them enjoyed going over to see the ball games and hollering for their ship's team.

So any military organization can well afford to have that kind of a get-together because it produces just what you may later need—the willingness, the knowledge of how to cooperate and work together.

John T. Mason, Jr.: And the team spirit.

Admiral Struble: And the team spirit—oh, yes.

John T. Mason, Jr.: I suppose it does a great deal for morale too—a happy ship.

Admiral Struble: Why, it makes the ship happier, that's right. Even if they don't win the local championship if they had a pretty good team and they played well, they are still very happy. If they lost, most of them are determined to go out and do better next year, so it's all for the good.

John T. Mason, Jr.: In retrospect, what would you say your duty as gunnery officer on the New York contributed to your development as a naval officer?

Admiral Struble: It was very valuable in getting me away from the staff duty, if only temporarily, and letting me see the effects of staff from the other end of the line. In other words, appreciating the staff did well when they did one thing and didn't do well at another. You would appreciate how it affected you on the ship. You also realized that if naval ships were going to be good, the ship itself had to be a very sound instrument and had to be supported. Therefore, when you later got to higher command, you were able to appreciate the problems of making that ship work well. I think that under those conditions, you are a better senior officer later with a knowledge of how to handle the problem which you could remember having seen years before when you were on the New York.

John T. Mason, Jr.: This was then another facet—

Admiral Struble: Another facet of the very fine experience to be head of a department of a battleship, in my opinion. And the experience was almost as good on the New York in every way it was on the biggest and newest battleship they had.

John T. Mason, Jr.: Now, was this assignment a part of your own wisdom or was it something that the Bureau of Navigation . . . ?*

Admiral Struble: Well, in this case, having been with Admiral Pringle a couple of years on the staff, I had very much made the point of view that I wanted to be gunnery officer

---

* The Bureau of Navigation made officer assignments to various duties in the years prior to World War II.

of a battleship. I didn't try to say I had to have one of the big new ones. And I didn't get one the big new ones, but I was still very happy.

John T. Mason, Jr.: In June of 1933 you were assigned to duty as district communications officer for the 12th Naval District at San Francisco. Was this something that you sought?

Admiral Struble: I had been in communications when I was in the naval code and signal section. Communications felt that I was a communicator rather than being a gunnery man or rather than being an engineering man.

John T. Mason, Jr.: They put their tag on you.

Admiral Struble: They felt that they had a little tag on me. So they wanted me to go to the 12th Naval District. I thought maybe that would be an interesting, satisfactory experience, so I said yes.

John T. Mason, Jr.: You didn't object to the label of communicator then?

Admiral Struble: No, I had been in communications before, so I realized that it was going to improve a lot and be a very important part of the Navy. I thought that it would do me no harm to get some of that part of communications when my previous part had been quite restricted to codes and ciphers.

So I went there very willingly and had a very pleasant tour of duty and saw how naval districts operated and saw some of their good points and some of their bad points. So I think I might have gained more by trying to go to Washington, but I'm not so sure that I would have. I got plenty of Washington duty. I knew my way around Washington pretty well.

John T. Mason, Jr.: Talk a little about your duties as communications officer of the 12th District. Particularly, what was the job?

Admiral Struble: You were a little more important than you might have been at some other place because you were the eastern end of the transpacific radio system. You communicated all the way out to Manila and so forth, as well as Pearl Harbor. But we worked, of course, directly into the Philippines from San Francisco.

So we did have an important communications system that was a part of what I will call the Pacific communications system which was going to be, if it were developed well, and if it grew, it was going to be important if we needed it later—which we did after Pearl Harbor.

It was a part of a system. It wasn't just being connected with the local 12th Naval District office and having it. I don't think I would have wanted to go the 12th Naval District just to have had some of the other jobs. But the fact that you would then learn how the communications and how the command systems worked and all that made it a more attractive thing to me.

John T. Mason, Jr.: Did the Navy make much use of some of the islands in the Pacific for their communications facility?

Admiral Struble: We hadn't developed it then as much as we commenced to realize we would maybe need later. But we were commencing to think in those terms. This was the importance of San Francisco. It was very much a part of the Pacific communications system.

John T. Mason, Jr.: Where were your offices located?

Admiral Struble: They were located downtown in San Francisco, and they were just as good as if they had been located out where the radio station was. You don't have to be at the station. We had a position downtown very close to waterfront. It was very convenient for fleet naval ships when they came in to contact us and for us to contact them. Part of our naval district duty, of course, was being able to assist the ships that came into the San Francisco Bay.

John T. Mason, Jr.: What kind of relationship did you have with the Coast Guard?

Admiral Struble: We had quite good relations with the Coast Guard, and they were important because they also were out where we had a station north of San Francisco, and they were able to cooperate with us as well for our good as we at times cooperated with them a little. They were on the other side of the bridge. We were on the south side of the bridge; they were on the north side of the bridge on the coastline.

Now, of course, we were also at the place where the ferries came from Oakland, which is the east and west thing. This is just a matter of communications.

John T. Mason, Jr.: I see. Did you have anything to do with the weather ships?

Admiral Struble: No.

John T. Mason, Jr.: That was strictly Coast Guard.

Admiral Struble: Well, we, of course, often functioned to help out the system in communications. But we did not have any Coast Guard ships under us. They generally were related to their own Coast Guard stations which handled them. On the other hand, we did have a man out at the Coast Guard station just outside the entrance to San Francisco Harbor to assist and help them from the naval viewpoint. That was bit of local cooperation we went through, which didn't amount to too much. I mean, it was not a large amount. But we did have a Navy man out on the Coast Guard station that is right outside the entrance to San Francisco Bay.

John T. Mason, Jr.: Did you have quarters in San Francisco?

Admiral Struble: Oh, no, no.

John T. Mason, Jr.: Where did your family live?

Admiral Struble: They were just down south of San Francisco in what's called San Mateo. It's one of the little parts of San Francisco to the south. It was a very nice place to live, very pleasant.

One of the better parts of it was at that time the road coming up from the south came into San Francisco fairly close to the naval headquarters, and you could go home from work better than if you lived in the other part of San Francisco. You see what I mean? It was a good place for your local travel where you were working.

John T. Mason, Jr.: An easy egress from—

Admiral Struble: That's right. Particularly if you could get out five minutes ahead of most of the stores around there, and you usually could, why, you'd be on your way south in no time at all. In just a few blocks you were south and out of the city.

John T. Mason, Jr.: I can appreciate that.

Admiral Struble: Ah, yes. If you happened to live over in Sausalito and you could get a half an hour's start, you could get across the bridge going to Sausalito. If you were over in Oakland, then you really had to get away good and early because you were in the middle of it. It was a mess at that time.

John T. Mason, Jr.: Again in retrospect, what did you learn from this particular assignment as communications officer?

Admiral Struble: I think I commenced to recognize the value of the Navy's broad Pacific communications system which, of course, the station in San Francisco was the mainstay on the continent for that system. By the time I left San Francisco I realized that we needed to improve our whole broad Pacific communications system, because if we ever started to operate large numbers of force, which might some day be necessary, we would be a number-one broad Pacific system.

John T. Mason, Jr.: And that served you in good stead when you had naval commands in the Pacific.

Admiral Struble: Well, yes, but I mean the main idea was to back the improvement in the big Pacific communications system so that if and when the ships needed it, it would be there. And, of course, at that time, communications were on the advance and improvement in their type of apparatus, like a large number of things.

John T. Mason, Jr.: What, for instance, was coming in?

Admiral Struble: You mean what specific thing?

John T. Mason, Jr.: Yes.

Admiral Struble: I don't think I'll try to get into the details. I was not in it that much, but I did realize that we improved our system every time we set up a good station at some island that was strategically located out there. In addition to the one place that we had, we previously had San Francisco, Guam, and Manila. But we could use a number of more and better stations if we could have them out there also and I think this was the trend toward getting them.

John T. Mason, Jr.: What relationship, what kind of cooperation did you have with the commercial communication lines---the Western Union and that sort of thing?

Admiral Struble: We very rarely had any contact with them, but they were satisfactory. We used them for a little of our local distribution, and generally we made a point of knowing them and getting along well with them because at times of something coming up and creating a little bit of a temporary emergency they could be very helpful. So it paid you to know them and be able to talk to an individual. As in all things, if you can talk to an individual under those circumstances, you can get things done a lot better than if you had to call and ask to I speak to the head man. Maybe you can't talk to him and maybe the person that you do finally reach isn't in tune with you very well and doesn't understand how he might be able to help you. But if you know a man beforehand, then he will be useful.

Where did I go from San Francisco?

John T. Mason, Jr.: In June of 1935 you went aboard the Portland as first lieutenant and damage control officer. Would you talk about the Portland and damage control facilities and techniques in the fleet at that time?

Admiral Struble: I was very happy to go to the Portland.* She was one of the new cruisers.

John T. Mason, Jr.: She was a heavy cruiser, wasn't she?

Admiral Struble: Yes. And she was one of the new cruisers that had been built with a certain amount of damage control in mind in case of action. In other words, in her construction they had tried to consider what would be the best way to take care of the ship if she gets a certain amount of heavy gun action. Is the ship then designed best to handle it over the way they have always built ships previously? They found out that they could improve the interior building of the ship a considerable amount so that it would be easier to repair it in case of damage.

John T. Mason, Jr.: What caused this new input of knowledge into the design of the Portland and her sisters?

Admiral Struble: Well, the fact that having drawn our attention to new ideas in ships and shipbuilding and airplanes and everything else, we had finally gotten around to study this

---

* USS Portland (CA-33) was commissioned 23 February 1933. She had a standard displacement of 9,950 tons, was 610 feet long, and 66 feet in the beam. Her top speed was 32.7 knots. She was armed with nine 8-inch guns and eight 5-inch guns. She was eventually decommissioned in 1946 after service in World War II.

one angle which was damage control. So the Portland, I would say, was the first type of ship that was designed with a better damage control arrangement than we had ever had before. In other words, it was thought about before the ship was built; it wasn't thought about afterwards—now that we've gotten the ship, where do we want to put this or that so in case we have damage we can repair it? But to design the ship beforehand with that in view.

And that was, therefore, the time when the damage control was new. The first lieutenant had always been the first lieutenant, but the first lieutenant and damage control officer became the new name because this was a ship on which there was a real damage control arrangement.

So we then started in to develop a useful employment of what I would call new damage control ideas.

John T. Mason, Jr.: What were some of these ideas as you saw them incorporated on the Portland?

Admiral Struble: Well, I think probably one of the most particularly interesting things was that they arranged for a place low down, more or less toward the rear of the ship, way down in the bottoms almost, where the first lieutenant would be located with adequate communication all over the ship. This was done in case they are in action and are hit by gunfire, maybe the captain on the bridge had been knocked down. This fellow down below in there isn't knocked out; he's got communication everywhere, and he's now in a situation where he's able to decide what to do and how the ship should do it. He's not only well located in the safest possible spot not to be hit by the damage, but he has had communication arrangements made for him in the ship so that he can talk all over the ship—to the bow or the stern, here and there, and so forth.

John T. Mason, Jr.: It sounds almost like an auxiliary CO.*

---

*CO—commanding officer.

Admiral Struble: Well, yes, you could call it that. Of course, who knows? The commanding officer of a ship is always the senior officer that's left alive—if he knows it. But the temporary man who might start issuing orders and doing this and doing that would have been the first lieutenant, who would have started what we call the damage control plan. It might be that he was the senior one left. Now, if he were the senior one left, he'd have to decide when it was time for him to leave the spot where he was located and go up on the bridge or whatever is left and try to run the ship, in which case he'd leave his assistant down below. Normally, he'd probably stay where he was, and the senior line officer left alive up above would temporarily assume command up on top. This was not designed and wasn't intended to fight the command principle but to do it with it.

John T. Mason, Jr.: Yes. Now had you personally given any thought to the importance of damage control before you took this job?

Admiral Struble: The only thought I had ever given to the problem was it had become talked about and everything. I thought to myself that damage control officer of one of the new ships sounded like a good job, because it was something they don't know anything about; it's new. So I was willing to take it and learn it.

John T. Mason, Jr.: As it developed, these new techniques that were incorporated into the Portland and the others, did they pay off?

Admiral Struble: In some cases, yes. Of course, we didn't necessarily foresee what might happen. Although I think it was a good idea, and I think probably it turned out useful in a large number of cases.

We had some pretty heavy actions among those types of ships out in the Southwest Pacific, and that's why I believe that the arrangements we made were very desirable. We were more minded to what to do when something happened, and we all knew that you had to get on the job and do something when something happened, but we hadn't exactly figured it out. This made it a one-man study, a one-man job that he took over. The people in between him and the captain who were senior to him were not senior to him in the damage control business except for the one that became captain.

But that command part of it—I don't want to stress that too much as being highly important either, because I don't think there's any doubt in cases like that everybody all works together. They realize they've got to. In a thing like that, a lot of people on the ship might not know who is alive and who is the commanding officer for a long time. But hopefully there is some fellow existing on the ship who is at the point where he can best handle it. And he will start doing it right away. If somebody else that is senior to him shows up at that spot then he becomes the captain.

John T. Mason, Jr.: What authority did you have, and what of your time was involved in enforcing some of the damage control rules on the crew?

Admiral Struble: We had at least one drill a week. We tried to indoctrinate the people in what they were supposed to do and where they were supposed to be. At the drill, we would try to presume the maybe-accident to see how it would work out. There was a certain amount of training. It undoubtedly would have been and was, I think, useful knowledge that we were developing. I'm sure that some of the ships that got hit in the Southwest Pacific probably came out a little bit better because they had had a certain amount of that type of training, and a certain amount of that type of thoughtfulness had been put into the matter beforehand.

John T. Mason, Jr.: Yes. That brings to mind something. One officer that was involved in a very precarious operation of saving a ship out in the Pacific told me that the real contributing factor to his ability to save the ship was his foresight before they sailed from the States in taking on board various bits of equipment that he envisioned as supplementary to the damage control effort on board ship—rope and things of that sort.[*] So he took a lot of that along and this is what came—

---

[*] See the Naval Institute oral history of Rear Admiral George H. Miller, USN (Ret.).

Admiral Struble: Yes, who knows but what it was the damage control idea that spiked him to think about this. I think it was a useful and a helpful thing and just what you've said is undoubtedly true. Of course, ships kind of stock themselves in general terms. Most ships have a certain required stocking in various parts of the ship and all that, but if, as you go around the ship and inspect and you're inspecting it for cleanliness and is it up to snuff and everything, but you all of a sudden say to yourself, a 50-foot coil of so-and-so rope would be very useful in this compartment in case of trouble. And then you can order it and get it probably from the navy yard. You had a certain amount of money, and you could probably do it almost entirely on your own. If you thought it was a good idea, at the next division conference when four or five ships' people were together you might tell the other people about it.

John T. Mason, Jr.: I brought it up because I wondered if this was a general practice or if it was exceptional in his case that he had this foresight to do this.

Admiral Struble: There have been a hell of a lot of our people that at times have been foresighted, and they've done very well. A man that tells you something like that is very honest. He thought of that, he did it, and it proved useful. So it just shows that the system is working. Now, that doesn't show that every ship in the fleet had it because they possibly didn't. He thought of something that was a little unusual, so he thought he'd try it out. He may later broadcast that idea, and it might have become a must on ships in the future to have this and that.

Of course, one of our problems with the ships is that you can eventually get the damned ship overloaded too heavily, and then you have to get someone to figure what he ought to get rid of. I mean, this is true. You see what I mean, don't you?

John T. Mason, Jr.: Yes.

Admiral Struble: It works good right away, but then sometimes if you get too much stuff on board you've got to decide what you're going to get rid of.

Arthur D. Struble, Interview #3 (6/10/76) – Page 108

John T. Mason, Jr.: I understand that this was the eternal problem of the Ship Characteristics Board.

Admiral Struble: Well, of course, it was. You always had the arguments on the Ship Characteristics Board, "Why can't we have that? We need it."

And somebody else will say, "Gee, we need this other new thing more." Well, those are the things to discuss, evaluate, and you eventually try to have one.

John T. Mason, Jr.: Yes. Well, up this point we've been talking of the Portland and your duty on the Portland as though she were stationary. But where did she operate?

Admiral Struble: She operated with the Pacific Fleet. She operated north in the springtime. She operated generally sometime in the fall over in the Hawaiian area. And if it was a fortunate year, why, she would go down to the Panama Canal and go through the canal and go up on the East Coast. We didn't go around to the East Coast every year; it was a little bit expensive. So we went around probably every two or three years. On those years we always operated at Panama.

Previous to that, a number of years earlier, we had always gone to Panama every year. But in the latter periods, we sometimes only went to the canal every other year. We generally tried to have the Atlantic Fleet come down at the same time to Panama. We generally tried to have it come through the canal and be on the Pacific side so that as we approached Panama we could have a joint exercise with her defending Panama. I mean, all of those were practical problems in getting the most out of the oil you were expending.

John T. Mason, Jr.: Yes. Did the Portland carry planes?

Admiral Struble: Oh, yes, sure. We had planes. We had a catapult of our own. We had a nice boom that we swung out to lift them out of the water; we'd pick it up—bang, bang. We had, at that time, modern equipment for the purpose of catapulting a plane and for the purpose of picking it up.

John T. Mason, Jr.: Did you have a contingent of Marines on board too?

Admiral Struble: No. I guess we had a couple of Marines, but we had no real contingent. If we had had a contingent it would have meant that we had enough to be a slight military force to put ashore, so we didn't have that. But we did have a couple, as I remember.

But they had the airplane thing. Well, we'd go south, and we could have exercises and send a plane up in the air, have it approach the ship, which was interesting for our gunnery department to see if they could pick it up and get ahold of it and all of that. It was interesting experience for the pilot to get up in the air. There would be an island maybe sometimes 20 or 30 miles away, and he wouldn't necessarily be told where it was. He would maybe be told to see if he could find it.

I mean, we had a lot of good exercises that we were able to have for ships proceeding independently or maybe just one or two in company and that sort of stuff. We were commencing to realize the value of using all of our oil usefully if we could. We could get some exercise out of it at the same time that we made passage of her.

Now, we were getting to be a much more thoughtful, much more far-looking Navy than we had been. Of course, these cruises to Australia and places like that could bring out ideas for you to think about, not necessarily about the Australians or something, but then you might say, "Why couldn't we teach them something." And you'd try to, which we did when we went there in '25. We cooperated with them very much.

There's no doubt about the fact that our '25 cruise was valuable to us when we went to war out there in the Southwest Pacific because from the start, whammo, the Australians and the Americans were close together and cooperated beautifully. You were kind of feeling each other out.

John T. Mason, Jr.: You didn't have time for that anyway.

Admiral Struble: Oh, you didn't have time but, boy, believe me lots of times in these situations we've been in, we've wasted a lot of time that way—feeling each other out and trying to get together. But, hell, we were there long enough on the '25 cruise so that we got to know each other and we kind of trusted each other. The people that were youngsters and got drunk in '25 were the people that were up in position of more authority when we got into the real war. That's good stuff, no doubt about it. You don't spend time in preliminaries.

John T. Mason, Jr.: This middle period in the '30s represented a time of real progress in the Navy, didn't it?

Admiral Struble: Oh yes, I think it did. I think we learned a lot during that period. I think we became much more proficient and better.

John T. Mason, Jr.: Can you analyze the incentives for this?

Admiral Struble: Well, we had a lot of young active people who were interested in a career; it looked like it was a good career to them. They wanted to improve it. That's what happened. People like Mick Carney and myself—we were almost the same time; I was a year ahead of him. We were always trying to think of a good idea to improve things. I happened to mention him because he and I were together, and we knew each other very well. We were always competing with each other.

John T. Mason, Jr.: That's always a stimulant.

Admiral Struble: Well, of course, it's a stimulant. If Mick had a ship, nothing could be happier for me than if I did better than he did.

John T. Mason, Jr.: You were only on the Portland for a year, I guess, from June '35 to June '36.

Admiral Struble: That's right.

John T. Mason, Jr.: And then you joined the staff of the Commander Cruisers, Scouting Force.

Admiral Struble: You see, there's what happens to you. Once you've been a staff man such as you are always sure to be if you're on the Commander Battleships staff, you're always a little bit in demand to go to another staff.

Well, my personal idea was that I didn't object to that too much, but I wasn't going to be just a staff man. If I went to another staff, I wasn't interested in returning to the same old one that I had been on before. This fellow had been promoted and I would have a bigger job. Well, that I don't think is necessarily good for you. So when I left the Portland, the new man that had been made Commander Cruisers wanted me. He said, "Look, you've had a year of this damage control stuff and have learned something about it. None of us know much about it now. I want you to come over to the staff as damage control officer to see if you can keep up the interest and make things go better."

Well, as I thought it over, that wasn't illogical. In other words, we didn't have any trained damage control officers yet in heavy cruisers.

John T. Mason, Jr.: And you were in a sense a trained damage control officer.

Admiral Struble: I was as well trained as anybody was by that time.

John T. Mason, Jr.: And also you were a staff officer so it was logical for you.

Admiral Struble: I had been on a staff and had a lot of staff duty all right. There was no doubt of that. I did know staff pretty well. The thing was that I did know the damage control duties. Then I was put in charge of the C&R funds. Well, I think I was one of the first fellows maybe. I don't know.

John T. Mason, Jr.: Put in charge of what?

Admiral Struble: Construction and repair funds. There's a Bureau of Engineering and a Bureau of Construction and Repair. C&R are the people that build the ships. The engineers are the ones that put in the machinery, and both have large amounts of money available they needed for repairs. When I got the damage control job, I automatically became the C&R man, which put me in charge of the C&R funds. The C&R professionals were horrified that a line officer was controlling their funds.

John T. Mason, Jr.: What would they amount to in a cruiser like that?

Admiral Struble: It was just a case really of doing this job. A trained C&R man would have done it better than I did. But if we are going to send a heavy cruiser up to Bremerton for two months for repair, it's a question of whether I would give them $400,000 or $200,000 for these repairs.* The money wasn't there indefinitely. You were limited in the amount you had to use. So you would try to figure out whether this ship that was going up there needed a certain amount of money. And you'd know something about the C&R department because you had been head of it previously on the Portland. So you'd go looking over your cruiser and say, "It would be very nice for you to have this $400,000, but $300,000 is all I can give you. I think this and this and this. All these are number one things that you've got to do first. After you've been there a while maybe, if you've got the real problems all done and you need another $50,000 or something, send me a message. I won't guarantee I'll give it to you, but maybe I will."

That's the way I handled the job. I tried to make the amount of money I had last me a year and do the job for all the ships that would be going.

John T. Mason, Jr.: Now, in connection with your damage control assignment on the staff, you must have found a great inequality in the equipment in the various cruisers, or were they all new cruisers?

Admiral Struble: This was the new heavy cruiser force. So we were a new force started. We had no old cruisers with us.

---

* Puget Sound Navy Yard, Bremerton, Washington.

John T. Mason, Jr.: So you were uniform.

Admiral Struble: Not necessarily. The ships were not completely uniform. But they were new cruisers based on the fact that none of them was much over about two years old. So they were all new ships. They were roughly the same size. However, the new ones that came just as I left the job were a little bigger but definitely heavier and had more gun power. So a slightly different approach was going to be needed to handle them. However, they were big, heavy cruisers even if they did have a little more gun power than the earlier ones. Whether they would prove to be better gun ships, we didn't necessarily know. But it was worth trying it out to see if with a little more gun power we couldn't make a better, stronger fighting ship.

Now, I was not in the Southwest Pacific. I didn't go through that part of the campaign, so I can't say that I've ever found out which was the better fighter or which functioned better.

But they really got into a couple of messes with the Japs. They really had pretty tough stuff on their hands. Usually the Japs were more and therefore had more gun power with them. The first time they hit us, they certainly gave us a pretty bad treatment.

John T. Mason, Jr.: They certainly did. One other question in regard to your C&R hat with the cruisers—where were they largely repaired?

Admiral Struble: They were mostly repaired at Bremerton, but they might go to Mare Island from where we were on the West Coast. As far as I'm concerned, I believe both yards were very good. So I never tried to manipulate. Of course, both of the yards would have been glad if we gave them all our business because they needed the business. But I tried to work between the two.

There was a fleet constructor also who could give me instructions which would tell me what to do. He could always send me a message and say cancel so-and-so at Bremerton, shift her for October overhaul to Mare Island. All he had to do was send me an order and I would do it—unless there was a hell of a good reason that I'd go over and talk to him about. But if he didn't give me that order, I would have made my own mind up before that.

But the navy yard overhaul has got to be done by the fleet constructor man, because he's the one who has to handle casualties when they occur. So if something happens and he sends some ship into a yard where it wasn't expected because this is the place he thinks she ought to go, he may have to take one ship previously scheduled out of that yard and send it to the other one. So it's quite logical and reasonable.

I enjoyed that tour a little because on the heavy cruiser staff the admiral had his chief of staff, his gunnery officer, and me dine with him. I mean, we ate in his cabin. The ship was a little crowded and he kind of liked to have company with him anyway. So we ate in the captain's cabin—the three of us—which made it interesting because he would often be discussing things and talking it over.

John T. Mason, Jr.: You were talking off tape about these messing conferences when you discussed the use of the cruisers and perhaps use of them in a new sense that they were new and more capable instruments of warfare. Just tell me about what you planned for the next fleet exercise, what you anticipated should be done.

Admiral Struble: When the new fleet exercise was coming up with a new type of ship, the heavy cruiser and so forth, I felt that in our new exercises we should try to develop the heavy cruiser as a weapon that would be usefully employed to attack. It had speed, and it had fairly good gun power. We had never had that type of ship in the fleet exercises before, so I thought that we ought to go after some dashing types of employment rather that simply protecting the larger ships until the proper time for the big battle occurred.

John T. Mason, Jr.: Did you meet with a consensus of opinion on the part of these other officers and the admiral?

Admiral Struble: Well, one of the officers agreed with me, one disagreed a little, and one disagreed a little more. They weren't sure that we wanted to take this fine new instrument and necessarily operate it on its own off on a separate mission from the main body before we had even gotten together in a fight. My attitude was we might be able to use her in some action earlier which maybe would prove very valuable. One of my ideas I would say was to put them up ahead against the destroyer scouting line. These new cruisers were pretty fast ships, and if you ran into a destroyer scouting line, they could go down the line and shoot up as many destroyers as you could and make a big hole in their destroyer scouting line, which would immediately be disconcerting and maybe valuable to the further handling of the exercise, from your point of view.

John T. Mason, Jr.: Was this achieved? I mean, was this idea implemented?

Admiral Struble: Only partially, not quite the way I wanted, but a part of it was accomplished in the next exercise.

John T. Mason, Jr.: Well, that's gratifying.

Interview Number 4 with Admiral Arthur D. Struble, U.S. Navy (Retired)
Place: Admiral Struble's Home, Chevy Chase, Maryland
Date: Friday, 18 June 1976
Interviewer: John T. Mason, Jr.

John T. Mason, Jr.: Admiral, it's good to see you today. I believe we are going to begin with an account of the year 1937 when you went to the Central Division of the Chief of Naval Operations in the Navy Department in Washington. Tell me about that Central Division. What was the scope of its activity?

Admiral Struble: The Central Division was an office in the front corridor. In the center you had the Chief of Naval Operations's office. Next to that was the Vice Chief of Naval Operations's office—he being the number-two man to the CNO.[*] Next to that was this fairly decent sized office with a couple of rooms in which there were four officers who were called the Central Division. They were kind of senior staff officers who each had a specified billet. They were to assist the Vice Chief in handling a large number of different types of jobs, and particularly the rush jobs.

The job that I had, I thought, proved to be most interesting. It was liaison with State Department. There were other parts of it, but that was the basic and important part. In all of our relations then with the State Department that came up in the Navy Department, I would be the officer that went over to consult with the various office heads or department heads over in the State Department and discuss this State-Navy problem originally. Often after having had a discussion or two, I would accompany the senior officer from the Navy Department, sometimes the Chief of Naval Operations or sometimes the Vice Chief, over to the State Department for his final discussion on this subject with one of the senior people in State. So eventually you get over into the diplomatic side of the picture and our relations on that level around the world, which was a very interesting subject to be in.

---

[*] At the time the official title was Assistant Chief of Naval Operations.

John T. Mason, Jr.: Did you sometimes meet with representatives of the Army as well?

Admiral Struble: We used to discuss with the Army, either by phone or by visit, some of our trips to the State Department that we felt they should know about. There were some of the problems that we had that concerned both of us very much, such as people over in China and things of that sort. Occasionally, we would jointly go over to the State Department to discuss a problem with State. But I would say that most of our business was Navy direct with State.

John T. Mason, Jr.: Can you give me some illustrations of the sort of thing you did do?

Admiral Struble: At that time there were a number of problems developing with our personnel who were out in China. We had personnel in China to support and try to help the Chinese government and to help and support their efforts in handling their own problems. We weren't handling the problems; we were only attempting to support. Actually at that time we had American gunboats up some of the rivers.

The American gunboats, of course, were over there for the purpose of protecting American interests, particularly personnel, in case local squabbles started. It was our position at that time in the Central Division to keep in close contact with State. On the occasion of difficulty with one of the gunboats up the river, we would then go to our operations office in the Navy Department which issued orders to fleets and to distant places. We would counsel them then as to what kind of order ought to go out to this group of gunboats, we'll say, on one of the rivers—how it ought to be phrased and what we should avoid in the orders. There were things to avoid, you see.

John T. Mason, Jr.: I think it was at that time that we had the sinking of the Panay on the Yangtze.*

---

* On 12 December 1937 the Yangtze River gunboat USS Panay (PR-5) was attacked and sunk by Japanese aircraft near Nanking, China. Two crew members were killed and 43 wounded. Japan claimed it had made an error in identification and paid an indemnity for the incident.

Admiral Struble: That's right. The handling of the sinking of the Panay was done by the Central Division that I just mentioned. In this specific case, I was the representative for the Navy Department. I had a number of visits with the State Department on that subject and I would say had at least two high-level discussions in which either the Vice Chief or the Chief of Naval Operations himself went over. In other words, the final conference that was held on that Panay business in which we agreed with State as to what the diplomatic position of the United States would be was conducted at a meeting at which the Chief of Naval Operations was present. I, who had been following it for two or three months, was there as his assistant.

John T. Mason, Jr.: We looked upon that as a very serious incident, did we not?

Admiral Struble: Yes, we did. There were some parts of it that could have become very serious, and you were commencing in a way maybe to set precedents that might be used elsewhere in the world again. So you always had that sort of problem with a decision of that character to be sure that your decision, which might look fine from that standpoint right now, would be reasonably consistent with something you might want to do over in the Mediterranean. You had to always keep your eye on what you call the diplomatic position the world around.

Of course, that's what the State Department tries to do, very much. The fact is that's their business.

John T. Mason, Jr.: At the same time, we had what was called the Shanghai Incident when the Japanese were attacking the Chinese forces around Shanghai.

Admiral Struble: Well, of course, as you probably realize, there were incidents, some minor, some a little more important, that were often happening in the Asiatic area. That kind of kept that a little bit of a place where there was often liable to be one problem or another.

John T. Mason, Jr.: Who was Chief of Naval Operations, Admiral Leahy?

Admiral Struble: I guess it was Leahy, and he was succeeded by Stark.*

John T. Mason, Jr.: What else did you do in the Central Division besides the liaison with the State Department?

Admiral Struble: There were a large number of problems that would come up often, we'll say, with important people or an important head of another government department somewhere, who is interested in a specific thing because it involved him in his own business. He would first phone to the Secretary of the Navy or the Assistant Secretary, whomever he might know, and say, "Look, this is causing us a hell of a lot of problems. What can you do to help us?"

The Secretary's office would generally send it right over to the CNO's office, and it was then deposited in the Central Division to deal with the matter and see what it was about. In other words, there were all sorts of sometimes fairly small problems that were temporarily important maybe to an important man in another department. Why they might be important to him could be any one of a number of reasons.

John T. Mason, Jr.: Can you think of an illustration of that?

Admiral Struble: I can think of one thing that's an illustration. Right after we got in World War II we had a French battleship enter New York with its crew. At that time, there were two sets of French.

John T. Mason, Jr.: The Free French and the other.

Admiral Struble: That's right. The Vichy French.† This battleship was Vichy French.

---

* The CNO at the time of the Panay incident was Admiral William D. Leahy, USN; Admiral Harold R. Stark, USN, succeeded him in August 1939.
† Vichy, a resort town in south-central France, became the site of a French government on 1 July 1940 after most of the nation had been occupied by Germans shortly before. The new state of Vichy France governed the one-third of the country the Germans did not occupy. The new government existed officially until the summer of 1944 but actually had little power after November 1942, when Germans occupied the remainder of France.

John T. Mason, Jr.: That was the Richelieu, wasn't it?

Admiral Struble: That's right. She came into New York Harbor and had a crew on board.* The other French who were then in New York also were running a number of small ships from England over to the northeast part of the United States with their crews on board. Of course, they were fighting the Vichy French still. This was before they had finally agreed to get together. So they started to proselyte the sailors off the Richelieu to join their Free French Navy.

Here we had a big new battleship in New York. We were spending American money and quite a bit to fix her up and put on the final touches that she needed and send her to sea in the Atlantic to fly the flag of France as a French battleship and in good shape. Of course, she wasn't going to be worth anything if she didn't have a crew. If all her crew was proselyted ashore to join the Free French Navy, why, it would get nowhere.

So to endeavor to stop this proselyting, I got ahold of the Free French representative in Washington and said, "You will have to stop this. We realize that you and the Vichy French are not going to be joint comrades and friends yet, but you can't be fighting each other because that is hurting our war effort. This battleship should go to sea and should fly the flag of France across the Atlantic, should be worth something. The money we are spending to try to fix it up is lost if you are going to get the crew off the ship."

Well, he wouldn't agree that they would stop. He said Mr. De Gaulle wouldn't permit it.† Of course, he didn't know whether Mr. de Gaulle would permit it or not and probably de Gaulle hadn't ever had the problem put up to him. In any event, from his point of view, there wasn't anything he could do about it.

So in this case, I applied to our legal department in the United States Government and said, "These sailors are only permitted to come ashore from the ship in Brooklyn Navy Yard over to New York on the basis of just temporary leave periods. They have to

---

* The 35,000-ton French battleship Richelieu was completed at Brest in early 1940. When France collapsed in the spring of 1940, the ship was ordered to Dakar, French West Africa, where she was subjected to British attacks. In early 1943, following Allied landings in Northwest Africa, the ship was sent to the New York Navy Yard for repairs and enhancement of her combat systems. After that was completed, she operated as part of the Royal Navy.
† General Charles de Gaulle was the leader of the Free French government in exile.

return to their ship. They are not allowed to leave the ship and go somewhere else in the United States."

He said, "Of course, that's definitely the rule and law."

I said then, "Will you persuade the necessary legal talent in New York to break up this practice of proselyting these people off the ship?" Boy, he went right into that. He backed it up with New York. They caught a number of the boys that had come ashore on leave that had gone to this place where the Free French were. They were giving them a lecture, and they were having a good time. Sure, they would all join up. So they were all arrested and taken back to the ship and there was quite a big to-do about it.

About two days later we had a tremendous formal presentation from de Gaulle against this action. However, we stuck to our guns on the American side, and the Free French were forced to stop that bad practice. Now, some time later—I don't know the exact timing—the French question petered out, and we commenced to be able to bring these two together. We were still doing business for quite some time with two sides in the French government, but they were getting closer together and weren't fighting each other as much.

John T. Mason, Jr.: Yes, with advent of Darlan in North Africa.*

Admiral Struble: Now, our object was acting in this situation as a kind of intermediary. I imagine there were lots of people in the United States who were for the Vichy French, and I imagine there were a large number that were for the Free French. But we had a war going on, and we had to try and get those two to make some reasonable arrangements with each other without either one of them giving up what they felt was their own right to represent France.

John T. Mason, Jr.: And particularly since we could use the battleship.

---

* Admiral Jean Francois Darlan was Commander in Chief of the French Navy until the French surrender in 1940. He became Minister of Marine for the Vichy regime and had dealings with both the Allied and Axis powers. In November 1942, after the allied invasion, he became political head of French North Africa. He was assassinated in December 1942.

Arthur D. Struble, Interview #4 (6/18/76) – Page 122

Admiral Struble: Well, we could use the battleship, but we also were very happy to have Free French help in a lot of places too. We really wanted both sides to help us. Until they settled their own dispute, we never tried to influence either one of these two sides on who ought to be the final one in charge of France. We didn't get into that French fight in the slightest.

John T. Mason, Jr.: No, that's like getting mixed up in a family dispute.

Admiral Struble: That's right. That was a very interesting proposition.

John T. Mason, Jr.: In the Central Division, did you maintain any kind of liaison with the White House?

Admiral Struble: A reasonable amount, and if we did I was the one that went over. My job in the Central Division, which you see was with State, would mean that I would go over to the White House. For instance, in World War II Leahy was acting as assistant to the President in the White House.*

John T. Mason, Jr.: Yes, and he was his chief of staff.

Admiral Struble: Well, I was the man who went over from the Central Division to talk to Admiral Leahy at the White House.

John T. Mason, Jr.: But this was in the second tour of duty.

Admiral Struble: This was the second tour of duty. I'm afraid we are getting the two tours mixed up.

John T. Mason, Jr.: That's all right.

---

* Admiral Leahy retired in 1939 following his term as Chief of Naval Operations. In 1940 he became ambassador to Vichy France, and in 1941 he became Chief of Staff to the Commander in Chief, President Roosevelt.

Admiral Struble: That's really true. What I just said was really applicable to the war part of the situation.

John T. Mason, Jr.: When we come to that time I will again ask you about the visits to Leahy.

Admiral Struble: I should have tried to figure out the case earlier. I don't think we want to go into that further, do you?

John T. Mason, Jr.: I want to ask you what happened to the Central Division, because they don't have that kind of division now, do they?

Admiral Struble: In effect, they have a replacement for it, but I don't believe they necessarily use the same name anymore. You realize now that we are talking about 27 years, and since then the whole naval operations organization in the Navy Department would probably have at least two to three big changes in its organization to meet the new needs of other government departments as well as their own.

John T. Mason, Jr.: Well, being in the Central Division was just that in terms of your contacts and all the rest of it. It was interesting in that sense, wasn't it?

Admiral Struble: Very much.

John T. Mason, Jr.: You were a kind of right-hand man to the CNO and his deputy.

Admiral Struble: Yes. While we normally did most of our work after discussion with the deputy, generally when it was necessary for a more senior man to go to the State Department with me for a final discussion, maybe on the Secretary of State level, the CNO usually went on those occasions. But you did more of your daily business with the Vice CNO.

John T. Mason, Jr.: Did the Central Division have anything to do with congressional people?

Admiral Struble: Yes. There were a certain number of contacts with Congress that were made by the Secretary of the Navy's office themselves. But when things that got over into the real combat part of the Navy were brought up, that would be put into the Central Division, which then would talk to maybe Naval Intelligence or maybe the Fleet Operations, and it would be handled by the CNO rather than by the Secretary's office.

The Secretary's office tried to keep in political business but not in naval business, if I could make a distinction.

John T. Mason, Jr.: Yes. You must have had a close relationship then with ONI.

Admiral Struble: Oh, yes. We had quite a close relationship. The fact is sometimes I felt that they should maybe go over to the State Department and be the representative for this thing. Then, of course, that would just be taken into the Vice Chief, and he decided which he wanted. He usually chose to have us from the Central Division go in order to keep an intelligence man from going over there and being party to a conference with which he might know something that he couldn't really afford to tell and shouldn't.

There is a disadvantage in having an intelligence man be the representative for a political consultation.

John T. Mason, Jr.: It puts him on the spot, doesn't it?

Admiral Struble: It's no good. He should be the adviser to the man that does it, like he's the adviser to an ambassador, you see. He doesn't have to tell the ambassador everything he knows. He's got to give him a clear, straight picture, but he doesn't have to tell him where he got the information. Then the ambassador can't tell where he got the information because he doesn't know it. But he can say, "I think so and so." It's all in the art of diplomacy and so forth.

There was no doubt in my mind that the Central Division at that time was very effective in its ability to have good relations and prompt action from senior officers in other government departments and better than we had ever had before because you could get in and talk to a senior officer in another department quickly. He would know that you could commit the CNO, which you were able to do, and you could therefore get a joint Navy-State Department solution, for instance, accomplished in much less than if you handled it in the normal way.

John T. Mason, Jr.: That's a very concise statement. I'm glad to have that. There's one other thought that comes to my mind, and that is perhaps because you had close dealings with ONI in the pre-World War II period, you might say something about its status as a division in the Navy. How was ONI looked upon by the operational part of the Navy?

Admiral Struble: I think the Navy operational people appreciated the information that intelligence often obtained. I think possibly some of the operational people resented the fact that ONI wouldn't often tell them what was going on, you might say, and kind of keep them up to date on lots of things.

Well, in some cases the intelligence that ONI had should not have received very wide distribution. Intelligence in the long run is only good as long as you keep it limited to a few people. The moment more and more people know what the intelligence is, the less valuable it often becomes. For instance, if Japan gets an inkling that we know something, they are going to change their way of doing things, and therefore you will defeat your own purpose if you have some really secret intelligence and start giving it too wide a distribution.

John T. Mason, Jr.: I was thinking of various statements that I have heard in the past that ONI in that pre-World War II period was largely thought of as a kind of repository of information, a collector of monographs on this subject or that subject and it had that aspect toward a library effect.

Admiral Struble: Well, of course, that was part of its duties, to produce broad knowledge about various places and things. Some ONI people maybe had a tendency to flaunt this, "I can't tell you. You shouldn't know that." Of course, that's just liking waving a red flag in a bull's face. The operational people, of course, resent any of that sort of thing very much—the idea that they can't be trusted with the information. But if you have some information and you're not going to use it, there's no use broadcasting it to a lot of people because some of the people that get it won't necessarily appreciate why it shouldn't go any further and pretty soon it leaks out.

John T. Mason, Jr.: I made the statement off tape that the other side of the coin is that if you have some intelligence and you don't give it to the operational people who would be able to use it, then what is the value of the intelligence itself?

Admiral Struble: Well, the way that works out from a practical point of view is this: you have, let's say, a bit of intelligence information. How positive it is you may not yet know, but you are getting very much in the frame of mind where you think you have gotten ahold of something. If you give that to a lot of the operational people, the information that you are nosing around in that direction may lead—but also the information is not yet positive enough to necessarily take into account operation. In other words, you shouldn't really count on it in making a specific operational change that might be something. Now, that information goes in to the Naval Intelligence head. He may well come up and decide to talk to the Vice Chief of Naval Operations about this thing, and he undoubtedly counsels the Vice Chief of Naval Operations, "We don't think this thing should get out at all. We don't think we ought to try to use it. It hasn't reached the point yet where it should be used."

Then the Vice CNO could call a member of the Central Division in and say, "Get over to State and investigate this subject and see what you can find out." In order for you to do that intelligently, he had to trust to you the ONI information. However, you are a specialist—you should have been well trained and capable and so forth. You go over to State Department, and you nose around in the department over there that you have got to talk to that is concerned in this and you find out what they think.

Apparently State has a certain amount of this same knowledge, and they aren't interested at all in having any discussion of it all. You come back with your own mind made up, and you then have the course of action that the Vice Chief of Naval Operations can call in Naval Intelligence and say, "This is what we think you ought to do about it."

That doesn't detract from the Director of Naval Intelligence in the slightest way. It's just a means of accomplishing this purpose of best use of operating with each other.

John T. Mason, Jr.: In the Central Division at this time did you have a good working arrangement with Stanley Hornbeck?*

Admiral Struble: Oh, yes. I knew Stanley very well. We had a lot of relations with him, because I would say 60% of our business with State was with Stanley Hornbeck or his office.

John T. Mason, Jr.: Because of his office on the Far East.

Admiral Struble: Yes.

John T. Mason, Jr.: What was your estimate of him?

Admiral Struble: He was a very capable, smart man. We didn't always agree on the best solution, but I felt he was a very capable, very strong man.

John T. Mason, Jr.: Do you recall what his general attitude was toward the developing situation in the Far East with Japan?

Admiral Struble: He was, of course, very interested in the relationship of the two sides of the Chinese problem as we got closer and farther along. I'm getting two terms of this thing mixed up together a little bit here. The first term which we are talking about and

---

* Dr. Stanley K. Hornbeck served from 1928 to 1937 as chief of the Division of Far Eastern Affairs in the State Department. From 1937 to 1944 he was special adviser on political matters to Secretary of State Cordell Hull.

Arthur D. Struble, Interview #4 (6/18/76) -- Page 128

the second term came after we entered the war. After we entered the war, the relationship of the two Chinese vis-à-vis Japan, of course, had a much more important meaning.

John T. Mason, Jr.: Oh, yes, yes.

Admiral Struble: That I assume is the period you are trying to display interest in now, talking about Hornbeck. I forget whether Hornbeck was still there with me.

John T. Mason, Jr.: I think during this period also we saw the Japanese establish that new state in Manchuria—Manchukuo. Was that a part of your problem?

Admiral Struble: Well, a little, but not really the important thing from my point of view. I think the important thing from our point of view was possibly what would be the effect on China and what would be the resultant action of China on that matter.

John T. Mason, Jr.: Well, perhaps we should go on then to your next sea duty which began in June of 1940, when you went as executive officer on the Arizona.*

Admiral Struble: That's right. I had been offered command of a noncombatant ship when I went to sea that time, but strongly objected and said I would prefer to go as executive officer of a battleship, which is number two, you see, rather than command a big ship and everything, but it would be noncombatant.

John T. Mason, Jr.: What was that, an oiler?

Admiral Struble: No, it was going to be one of the big transports that goes from San Francisco to the Far East. It would have been interesting in one way, because you would have maintained somewhat of a relationship with the Far East.

---

* USS Arizona (BB-39) was commissioned 17 October 1916. Following modernization in the early 1930s she had a standard displacement of 34,200 tons, was 608 feet long and 106 feet in the beam. Her top speed was 21.2 knots. She was armed with 12 14-inch guns and 12 5-inch guns. The ship was lost to Japanese attack at Pearl Harbor in 1941.

John T. Mason, Jr.: And also would have met many of the important officials going there.

Admiral Struble: Well, yes. It would have been an opportunity for that sort of thing, but in my opinion I had already made up my own mind that the war was coming. Therefore, I wanted to be in a combatant ship, and I wanted a command. So at the moment not being able to get command of a combatant ship, I went as executive officer of the Arizona, which was very interesting and it was a very fine job. At the end of about six months I was selected for promotion to captain. The moment that I was selected for captain I was immediately ordered to command the Trenton, even though I remained a commander for maybe another six or eight months.

John T. Mason, Jr.: Tell me about the six months on the Arizona. Who was the skipper of the Arizona?

Admiral Struble: Harold Train was the skipper of the Arizona—a fine man.* In my opinion we had a very fine crew in the Arizona. We were part of the force then out in Honolulu, and we had regular maneuvers. I would say that our efficiency in the fleet at that time was very good. It reached quite a fine level.

John T. Mason, Jr.: What was the state of the alertness of the fleet being in Honolulu at that time?

Admiral Struble: Well, of course, the fleet was really out in Honolulu as a political gesture. There was no doubt about it that the President had determined that this we should do—put the fleet in Honolulu as a clear indication to Japan that we recognized that her course of action was very important, whatever it might prove to be. In other

---

* Captain Harold C. Train, USN, commanded the battleship Arizona (BB-39) from 3 February 1940 to 3 February 1941. The oral history of Train, who retired as a rear admiral, is in the Columbia University collection. His son, Admiral Harry D. Train II, USN (Ret.) did an oral history with the Naval Institute in which he discussed visiting the Arizona as a youngster.

words, the stationing there was primarily political. As you probably appreciate, after a certain amount of time the fleet commander at Pearl Harbor decided that we had a little bit too heavy a force consistently too far advanced in his professional opinion. He therefore felt that it would be desirable to filter the battleships one at a time probably back to California and simply keep the smaller and faster and lighter forces out front at Pearl Harbor.

Now, of course, that meant that the admiral then put himself in a position where he was in some opposition with what the President's policy on the matter was.

John T. Mason, Jr.: The political policy versus the—

Admiral Struble: Well, the diplomatic policy let's call it, if you want to. You can call it political, but I think the President would have been inclined to call it the diplomatic policy. There's no argument in our government, the President must make the decision between what the diplomatic policy appears to dictate and what the military policy appears to dictate. And President Roosevelt decided that he felt that the presence of the fleet there in Honolulu was accomplishing his purpose vis-à-vis a warning to Japan. He considered it was better for it to be out in Honolulu than it would if it were returned to California, even though Admiral Richardson had proposed that the return be done kind of one ship at a time and slowly and not become a marked maneuver.

John T. Mason, Jr.: Consequently, the diplomatic decision being what it was, did the fleet take any precautionary measures that were extraordinary being based there in Honolulu? You say you were very busy in the fleet at that time and your state of readiness was extremely high.

Admiral Struble: At that time in the fleet we had splendid maneuvers regularly. The state of readiness of the fleet for action was splendid and continued so as far as I was concerned in the <u>Trenton</u> until in September a division of cruisers of which my ship was the flagship left and was sent down to Panama for the purpose of seeing if they could locate why a large number of our merchant ships leaving Panama were not arriving in Australia.

John T. Mason, Jr.: You say, of course, you were with the Trenton from January 1941 as skipper, and you say eventually the group of cruisers went down to Panama in the middle of the year.*

Admiral Struble: That's right.

John T. Mason, Jr.: Will you restate the purpose of that?

Admiral Struble: Of course, the Australians needed assistance and everything. We were trying to send supplies and so forth to them, and we did it through Panama. Now, the trip from Panama to Australia is a very long voyage. It's over twice as long as the average Atlantic passage.

John T. Mason, Jr.: Especially when you have to go eight or ten knots.

Admiral Struble: No, it isn't the speed that's involved; it's the oil supply. There was no oil supply available at that time between Panama and Australia. Therefore, the bigger, better, newer American merchant ships and so forth had to be used on that run. They were leaving Panama and sailing and then not arriving in Australia.

John T. Mason, Jr.: What happened to them?

Admiral Struble: Obviously they were sunk. So this division of cruisers that I was in was sent down to Panama with the idea of investigating this matter and seeing if there was anything that could be done to improve that situation.

---

* USS Trenton (CL-11), an Omaha-class light cruiser, was commissioned 19 April 1924. She had a standard displacement of 7,050 tons, was 555 feet long, 55 feet in the beam, and had a draft of 14 feet. Her top speed was 34 knots. She was armed with twelve 6-inch guns, four 3-inch guns, and ten 21-inch torpedo tubes. She was eventually decommissioned in 1945 after service in World War II.

John T. Mason, Jr.: But we weren't actually in the war at that point with the Japanese.

Admiral Struble: We were not at war with the Japanese, but the ships were being sunk. It wasn't Japanese that were sinking them.

John T. Mason, Jr.: They were German?

Admiral Struble: Yes, it was German. Certainly. Probably my best guess is that they were German submarines that had a small civilian ship from which they could refuel. They would rendezvous with each other and, say, a 6,000- or 7,000-ton merchant ship could refuel the submarine a long time. Therefore, that submarine could do an awful lot of damage. That undoubtedly was where a number of our merchant ships went.

John T. Mason, Jr.: And there was no communication? I mean, they just disappeared?

Admiral Struble: They just disappeared, which meant that the ship had been struck and sunk in such a hurry and so well that no news came, no word got out.

John T. Mason, Jr.: Well, what did your division of cruisers do?

Admiral Struble: Well, we immediately started to go into all the local ports to see what information we could reach and get at and also started to convoy the ships out a certain distance. It was not direct convoy, but we would go out a certain distance directly toward Australia with the idea of making the German submarines there apprehensive. There has always been a large amount of German sympathy in South America. Therefore, in most of the West Coast ports of South America there could very well have been good German intelligence that could be transmitted by radio to ships at sea.

It's my opinion that the effect of our presence finally affected the German intelligence so that the German operations went farther south. Do you understand me?

John T. Mason, Jr.: Yes.

Admiral Struble: The moment they did, the big ships we were sending through commenced to get through better. Therefore, it appears that we to some extent accomplished our purpose. Now, I believe that there is a record now existent that would indicate that at least one of those German submarines then went south around the Cape, the southern point of South America, and did some operating in the southern Atlantic before it was sunk. It wasn't caught until after we had entered the war. It was caught by cruiser—

John T. Mason, Jr.: The *Omaha*.

Admiral Struble: Yes, the same class as the *Trenton* was. It was in the Atlantic rather than in the Pacific.

John T. Mason, Jr.: Tell me more about that operation, because that hasn't been terribly much publicized.

Admiral Struble: Well, we didn't really concretely do anything. We never sighted anything; we never shot at anything. Therefore, we didn't feel that we had done anything. But the fact that the sub later left the Pacific and went over into the Atlantic accomplished our purpose. In other words, there is nothing for us to make a big shout about.

John T. Mason, Jr.: Did you have any kind of a liaison with some of our people in, say, Venezuela, who were doing some undercover work?

Admiral Struble: No, we were not in that intelligence game at all. Although every time we went into port, we would keep the American representative there acquainted, and the captain would have a thoughtful talk with the representative.

Immediately after Pearl Harbor, a force was organized of Army to go out to occupy one of the islands in the Central Pacific, approximately halfway between Panama and Australia.

John T. Mason, Jr.: Was this Palmyra?

Admiral Struble: No, this was Bora Bora. I believe that's the western island of the Tahitian group.

John T. Mason, Jr.: And that's what the division occupied.

Admiral Struble: The cruiser division took on all these merchant ships in convoy, and we put about 4,000 Army troops ashore with guns and so forth. I imagine that the shore guns that we took with us had been mounted, say, in about two weeks. Then the admiral who had been in my ship decided that he would leave me out in Bora Bora in command and that he would take the rest of the division back to Panama. So he transferred to one of the other cruisers and went back to Panama.

John T. Mason, Jr.: And left you with the Trenton there.

Admiral Struble: And I remained in the Trenton at Bora Bora until things seemed to be completely settled and then brought the Trenton back.

John T. Mason, Jr.: What sort of reception did you have from the French?

Admiral Struble: Well, the reception was very polite.

John T. Mason, Jr.: Which persuasion were they?

Admiral Struble: Free French. They were certainly polite and cooperative except that the young Frenchman who was representing Free France just didn't personally able to make any decision. It wasn't that he told us we couldn't do something, but he wouldn't agree that we should or could.

John T. Mason, Jr.: Was he a military man?

Admiral Struble: No, he was not a military man. He was quite young. Now, we had a very good relationship with him, despite this one little disadvantage that I have suggested to you. We got our troops in there and we landed them. We set up a very good station.

John T. Mason, Jr.: Did you have the assistance of a contingent of Seabees to do this?*

Admiral Struble: There may have been a small outfit of Seabees. Of course, there was an Army outfit who were capable of installing guns and doing that kind of work, similar to Seabees but that, of course, isn't what the Army calls them.

John T. Mason, Jr.: They were included in their own contingent there.

Admiral Struble: They were included in their own contingent. The contingent as I remember was the New Jersey National Guard. The <u>Trenton</u> stayed out there for another three or four weeks to be sure that the Army was all properly installed and that we had done everything we could before I went back to Panama.

John T. Mason, Jr.: Being in occupation in that island, what assistance would this render actually in affecting the merchant marine transports?

Admiral Struble: We set up a fueling station.

John T. Mason, Jr.: Did you build an airfield there too?

---

* Seabees is the nickname applied to members of the Navy's mobile construction battalions (CBs).

Arthur D. Struble, Interview #4 (6/18/76) – Page 136

Admiral Struble: There was then an airfield built, one of those temporary ones, so that a plane from Australia could come in.

John T. Mason, Jr.: That was very interesting. Where were you in the *Trenton* at the time of Pearl Harbor itself—the attack?

Admiral Struble: That was Sunday morning, wasn't it? The admiral and I had been ashore in Panama that morning playing golf. About ten minutes after we got back to the ship they brought this rush radio in, "Pearl Harbor has been attacked."

John T. Mason, Jr.: It was fortunate you were down there then.

Admiral Struble: The *Trenton* continued this type of duty around Panama, making one specific trip south along the whole western coast of South America, contacting consuls, etc., and then returned to Panama. It was about that time I got orders to go to Washington, back to the Central Division.

John T. Mason, Jr.: While you were still in that part of the world, part of the ocean, did the Galapagos Islands figure at all in the discussions?

Admiral Struble: It did, and I went out in the *Trenton* to Galapagos Island on a tour of inspection, preliminary to the Navy's intention with the Army to install a station of our own at Galapagos. But I never saw the station. Although I got out earlier for the preliminary survey, I left the ship before we finally established it.

John T. Mason, Jr.: I might ask you what were the special precautions to protect the Panama Canal at this time? Did we have radar installations?

Admiral Struble: We had radar and constant air surveillance on both sides all the time. We were pretty well protected. I think that's the way to put it. Now, of course, we had very strict entrance orders about ships entering from the Pacific so that nobody could come in and blast the canal. One of the worries of the Panama Canal people—not me, but naturally we were concerned with it—was whether the Germans would try some monkey business about mooring a ship up in the locks.

John T. Mason, Jr.: Some sabotage, which was rather feasible.

Admiral Struble: There's no argument; it's a very feasible thing. Of course, the dangerous thing would have been a Jap ship. You appreciate the reason, don't you?

John T. Mason, Jr.: Yes.

Admiral Struble: I mean, you appreciate why a Jap ship would be worse than a German ship.

John T. Mason, Jr.: In May of 1942 you left the Trenton, your relief standing on the dock waiting for you, and you came back to the Central Division. You must have liked that place.

Admiral Struble: Well, it was definitely an interesting office to be in the Navy Department because you really were at the center of things going on. Of course, when I went back at this time I became the head of the office. Previously I had been an assistant in the Central Division. Under war conditions, you had quite a large job.

John T. Mason, Jr.: When you got back Admiral Stark had already departed and Admiral King was CominCh.*

Admiral Struble: That's right. Admiral King was the boss, and Admiral Stark had gone to London.† Due to the war, I found myself talking to the Secretary of State much more

---

* In March 1942 Admiral Harold R. Stark, USN, was relieved as CNO by Admiral Ernest J. King, USN. King also served as Commander in Chief U.S. Fleet (CominCh).
† Admiral Harold R. Stark, USN, served as Commander U.S. Naval Forces Europe from 30 April 1942 to 15 August 1945.

than I ever had before.

John T. Mason, Jr.: This was Hull.

Admiral Struble: This was Hull. Cordell Hull was a very fine gentleman in my opinion. A very capable man. Unfortunately, maybe his health wasn't quite as strong as would have been desirable that he be.

John T. Mason, Jr.: He was quite elderly too.

Admiral Struble: He was elderly, yes.[*] That's right, he was elderly. But he was a very, very fine man. I found that I could often go to the State Department, see a very important man, and be back in 15 or 20 minutes with a solution that we needed on something that it was important that State agreed to before we issued the order.

John T. Mason, Jr.: The decisions were rapid and decisive.

Admiral Struble: That's right. That's what they needed to be in wartime, and I must say that I think that's what they were.

John T. Mason, Jr.: Was there a contrast in the Central Division from what you had known before the war? Was it streamlined?

Admiral Struble: I don't know what you mean. The Central Division had always been rather streamlined. For instance, one of the desks in the Central Division was in charge of Guam. It was the Navy man who was personally the center point at which the Navy in Guam would send its problems, etc. So it got right into the diplomatic channel quickly that way.

John T. Mason, Jr.: That was a dead end in 1942 when you came back.

---

[*] Hull was born in 1871.

Admiral Struble: I know, but I mean I was just illustrating the way the organization worked. I was a very busy man until November of 1943.

John T. Mason, Jr.: So you were there for a year and a half roughly speaking.

Admiral Struble: Yes.

John T. Mason, Jr.: Well, let's concentrate on that period. Tell me about some of the things you accomplished.

Admiral Struble: Well, one of the things, for instance, was this New York incident with the Free French off the <u>Richelieu</u>. Another—there were a very large number of French problems all over the world during that period that we were able to clean up so that we could go ahead with what we were trying to do in the war and still not be at odds with either the Vichy French or the Free French. Of course, we did business with that part of the French who were in local control of the spot where we wanted something.

John T. Mason, Jr.: Dakar was one of those places.

Admiral Struble: Yes. All those problems we managed to handle I would feel very smartly.

John T. Mason, Jr.: The Dakar situation concerned a lot of tonnage of merchant vessels that you wanted to get ahold of.

Admiral Struble: Well, all of those things as you appreciate were very valuable. I felt that that had been a very interesting and valuable assignment. But, of course, I also realized that I was ashore. So personally I wanted to get to sea when I could. Every now and then when I was in the course of business I would go up and talk to Admiral King personally. I'd ask him "When are you going to send me to sea?"

Arthur D. Struble, Interview #4 (6/18/76) – Page 140

John T. Mason, Jr.: He had a rule, did he not?

Admiral Struble: He was tough. He said, "You've got a job here. You go get it done. Some day you'll go to sea." I remember the day—I think it was in November—when I was sent for by the admiral who was the Chief of Naval Personnel, which meant the officer who assigned officers, who actually did it.

John T. Mason, Jr.: That was Admiral Jacobs.[*]

Admiral Struble: Was it Admiral Randall Jacobs then? Maybe it was the deputy then. It was the man who had had the Central Division that I told you about once before.

I think the important thing from my point of view was that I was asked if I would like to go over to England and be the chief of staff on the Navy side for the Normandy invasion.

John T. Mason, Jr.: Alan G. Kirk had been named, had he not?[†]

Admiral Struble: Admiral Kirk had been named as the man who was going to be there, and I was asked if I would go as chief of staff. I couldn't say yes quick enough!

John T. Mason, Jr.: We'll come back to the Central Division again the next time we meet. In the meantime, let's begin a discussion of the preliminaries to the Normandy landings.

Admiral Struble: Admiral Kirk was to be in command of the forces that actually conducted the landing. Admiral Stark, as you know, was the 12th Fleet in London. He was the senior American naval officer in the Eastern Atlantic. Kirk was designated as the officer who would be in command of the naval forces that made the landing and therefore

---

[*] Rear/Vice Admiral Randall Jacobs, USN, served as Chief of the Bureau of Navigation/Personnel from 19 December 1941 to 15 September 1945.
[†] Rear Admiral Alan G. Kirk, USN. His oral history is in the Columbia University collection.

in our amphibious system, which we had adopted by that time. He would be in command of the expedition until the Army was landed and the general had established himself ashore.

John T. Mason, Jr.: Kirk's title was in command of the Western Naval Task Force.

Admiral Struble: That was the title that we chose for the thing.

John T. Mason, Jr.: Admiral Stark actually had no operational units to be under his command?

Admiral Struble: A small amount, although some of the ships that were under his operational command at that moment might have been later at Normandy. But mainly the Normandy forces were going to be formed up and sent over just before we were going to make the landing so that the preliminary period from November on was to plan the invasion jointly with the British. There was, of course, a British naval officer, and there was, of course, the British Army. We had a number of our people. I suppose we may have numbered maybe 30 American staff officers who were Americans and working on the problem. The British had at least as many. Actually they provided more of the stenographic help, etc., probably a slightly larger number of personnel.

John T. Mason, Jr.: And Admiral Bertram Ramsay was the British senior officer.

Admiral Struble: That's right. He was the British admiral.

John T. Mason, Jr.: And he was over Admiral Kirk.

Admiral Struble: He was really senior to Admiral Kirk.

Arthur D. Struble, Interview #4 (6/18/76) – Page 142

John T. Mason, Jr.: In this early period of your planning, were you handicapped by the fact that President Roosevelt had not named the commander in chief for this whole operation?

Admiral Struble: Not originally. Actually since at least September or maybe August of 1943, there had been a number of Americans and a number of British who were jointly studying this problem and who were doing another very important thing. They were collecting a tremendous amount of information and knowledge about where we might land in France and about what we would be up against if we landed here or there or there.

John T. Mason, Jr.: That was the group known as COSSAC.*

Admiral Struble: I think it was. Of course, I never saw that or was never connected with that. But that had been there before I got there. They had done a splendid job, and they had prepared what I would call a preliminary approach to a landing plan. In other words, maybe a selection of whether we could go here or there and so forth and so forth.

As soon as Kirk and I got there, we got down to what I would call the employment of the information that had been collected and a much more detailed and closer approach to a landing plan. We had gotten it developed quite a bit by January or February, at which time Montgomery and some of the other people involved commenced to come into the picture in London.† As I remember, Eisenhower was appointed about February.‡

John T. Mason, Jr.: I think he was named by President Roosevelt in December actually, but he appeared in January.

Admiral Struble: All right, then that's when it was. Then with the arrival of the prospective commander in chief, which was Eisenhower, we then got to the point where

---
* British General Sir Frederick Morgan was Chief of Staff to the Supreme Allied Commander (COSSAC). General Dwight D. Eisenhower, USA, was the Supreme Allied Commander.
† Field Marshal Bernard Law Montgomery, British Army.
‡ Lieutenant General Dwight D. Eisenhower, USA, later promoted to four-star general by the time the operation took place in June 1944.

the planning became firm, much firmer. That didn't mean that some of the ideas we had in February weren't changed by June because they were. But the plan then commenced to get much firmer.

John T. Mason, Jr.: And you began to focus on a certain segment of the coast at that point, did you not?

Admiral Struble: We commenced to focus then on two points. The point that seemed to offer the most was right across from Calais. This narrow trip across the channel had two advantages. First, it was the closest spot from Britain over to the continent and second, you landed north of Paris. Now, that was advantageous because it meant we didn't have to take a large army and a large number of people around or through or adjacent to a tremendous big city. The third item, really, which is part of the second item, having landed at that spot you had a direct path to Berlin. So from the standpoint of which was best, I think you would have had to say that was the number one choice.

John T. Mason, Jr.: And may I ask was this a factor in the consideration? The city of Paris itself. You did not want to make it a battleground.

Admiral Struble: No, I would have said it was a more professional decision. I don't think we got to the point where we discussed consideration for Paris, because we hadn't chosen the path yet. If we had chosen that path, then we would commence to think in terms of would we go straight through the center, around the side, and all that.

    The other route was very good for—I said two, but there were really three reasons that I have given you—a short distance, the fact that you are already north of Paris, and the third fact that you had an almost direct route to Berlin, which is where we were going.

John T. Mason, Jr.: At the same time you needed a port somewhere near with facilities for landing, did you not?

Admiral Struble: Well, that spot on the French coast could have been developed into a pretty darned good harbor, and being such a short distance you could use a lot of small ships for some of your work. I think I would have considered that the number-one spot.

However, after you had selected one or two spots, of course, the other spot that we had selected as a very considerable possibility was Normandy, where we landed. Normandy offered the probability of a much easier initial attack. It didn't look as if we would run into quite as heavy and stout a resistance.

John T. Mason, Jr.: The Germans were pretty well entrenched along Calais, were they not?

Admiral Struble: Yes, and they had four Panzer divisions under the command of a general who was in Paris.[*]

John T. Mason, Jr.: How influential was the disastrous experience of the British at Dieppe in August of '42?[†] How influential was that in your thinking?

Admiral Struble: Well, I don't think that that affected our thinking much, because we realized that the British did not have anywhere near as much development of the landing business as we had attained already in the United States. Basically, we had given more peacetime thought to the amphibious landing than the British, and we had already made the North African landing with large forces. Therefore, I would say our experience and our ideas had attained a little more proof, if you choose to put it that way, than the British ideas.

Now, don't make any mistake, we did not try to argue the British system versus the American system. We never approached the subject from the point of view. I won't say that it was never discussed, but we didn't approach it from that point of view. We

---

[*] Panzer divisions operated tanks.
[†] On 19 August 1942, in order to test their own tactics and the German defenses, the Allies staged an amphibious assault on Dieppe, a small French port on the English Channel. Within a few hours, three-quarters of the invaders were killed, wounded, or captured. For an excellent overall account of the operation, see Terence Robertson, Dieppe: The Shame and the Glory (Boston: Little, Brown and Company, 1962).

approached it from the fact that we would make a plan and that at the place where the British landed they would run it. At the point where the Americans landed, the Americans would run it. In other words, the coordination of the naval ships and the troops would be kept American here and British there. I think all of us felt that it was very desirable to have an American responsible for the American landing and anything that went bad was under the American command and the same thing under the British.

John T. Mason, Jr.: That's understandable, certainly.

Admiral Struble: This was very clear. In other words, if somebody was going to be blamed for the Normandy landing as it happened, it was going to be Kirk and not the British admiral. Now, whether he had put another man under him who would make the landing for the British, it was up to him; it would still be British.

John T. Mason, Jr.: Did you have in the early stages of your planning any residue of resistance on the part of the British to a landing on the coast of France?

Admiral Struble: I would say there was no British resistance to the idea of making the landing. This problem as you appreciate received a tremendous amount of thought and discussion before. A lot of it had had discussion before the appointment of Eisenhower. But then with his appointment we went right into the—

John T. Mason, Jr.: That was the green light.

Admiral Struble: That was the green light. I think that Eisenhower made it clear that he accepted this idea, you might say, completely and that was the way it started to go. Now, I think the British admiral would like to have directly commanded the Normandy landing.

John T. Mason, Jr.: You mean Admiral Ramsay.

Admiral Struble: Admiral Ramsay, yes, he would have. He would have preferred, I think, if Kirk and I had more or less joined his staff and there had been only one admiral. But our conception, which we held to and argued for, was that there was an American admiral with an American staff and they ought to have charge and command the actual American landing. Anything that went wrong at that landing was an American responsibility.

John T. Mason, Jr.: Now, then you came to a discussion of landing supplies, the logistics of the whole thing. Did you think at all of Cherbourg and its availability or the problems of getting it to the point where it was?

Admiral Struble: Well, Cherbourg very obviously wasn't in competition with the place we landed. The place we landed was by far the best place for a big landing of that character, if you realize that our goal at this time was to put a new division across the beach every day at the Normandy landing. That meant that the supply problem the first day was for one division. That meant that the supply problem on the second day was theoretically for two divisions.

Now, actually the original landing was more than one division, and we did not get up to the division a day across the beach until maybe the end of the first week. But that was our goal—to try to put that much across all the time. Except for the period of the tremendous storm which I remember was on about D plus 13, we were able to operate that beach almost at full level all the time. But on D plus 13 there was a terrible storm that came directly around the channel from the north. It is not quite north-south; it is actually a little bit northeast and a little bit southwest. But it came right down with its full brunt on the Normandy landing area. We had in our area on the American side about 3,000 small boats; they were thrown up on the beach. Paddles maybe here and there. Those that were motorboats, maybe the engine had been conked and maybe it hadn't. The whole beach was just strewn with small boats. It was a tremendous blow to us.

Of course, I had gone ashore just as soon as I could get a boat in the water from the flagship and took a survey. My preliminary survey, of course, was very sickening. I wondered if we could recover in a week. But, by God, by a little less than a week later we were back up to full power again about getting people across the beach and getting supplies across.

Over at Utah Beach, which has a few little islands in front of it, the islands, had, of course, broken up the effect of the storm quite a bit.* While we had just as big a percentage of the small boats on the beach at Utah, the damages there were much less. Utah, I would have said, was back in commission about two days later.

But at the main landing, why, we just had some 2,200 to 2,400 small boats up on the beach, piled on top of each other. Oh, it looked like a wreck that it was going to take a hell of a lot of time to recover from.

John T. Mason, Jr.: What was the state of the British beach, which was north?

Admiral Struble: The British beach didn't suffer at all because of where the point comes out. Now, as I said, Utah had some islands in front of it. Omaha was a much wider, bigger open stretch of beach—a long stretch of beach. This is where we had some 2,200 to 2,400 small boats on the beach, and it was a wreck.

John T. Mason, Jr.: And the British were over here?

Admiral Struble: No, the British were way over here. Now, this is the English Channel coming down like this. This is England, this is France, and, of course, north of France. It comes down like that—not quite north and south, but northeast a little and southwesterly. Right about here there is a hook that comes out, and the British beach is over in here. So this hook of land prevented the British beach from being disrupted anywhere near as much as we were. Now, they were still disrupted because the heavy waves that came in did raise the water level at the British beach, but they didn't have the wave pounding of it. So I believe the British got their beach in operation in the late afternoon of that day or, if not, on the next morning.

John T. Mason, Jr.: As soon as the waters had subsided somewhat?

---

* The American landing beaches at Normandy were designated Omaha and Utah.

Admiral Struble: Well, the water subsiding wasn't the highly important problem, because the boat just wouldn't go in quite this far. The British didn't have a good beach like we had, though. They had a lousy beach in a way. You've got to hand it to them. They had much more of a beach problem. They would never have been able to handle supplies across their beach except just what was needed for the local contingent. The beach wasn't that good, you see.

John T. Mason, Jr.: Let's go back, sir, to that initial period after Eisenhower had been named and some of the conferences you had.

Admiral Struble: Naturally, the first job, in a way, that Eisenhower had was to collect the top important people for a consideration of the basic plan. Would they accept the Normandy coast landing, or would they take the shorter landing? Therefore, all of the talking that had gone on previously now went on again up on the higher Eisenhower level. That would have not gone into all the details that we went into on the lower level. But it became the question of well, will we take the Normandy landing or will we take the other landing?

John T. Mason, Jr.: I suppose on that level the political pressures were applied also, were they?

Admiral Struble: I don't think so.

John T. Mason, Jr.: Wasn't Churchill operating on that level?[*]

Admiral Struble: Oh, Churchill was always operating on every level all the time. Churchill was always in the thick of everything. You've got to appreciate that. He was liable to send for Eisenhower any time of day or night he wanted to talk to him. And he'd go through all this talk like you and I have been talking with him. There was no doubt in

---

[*] British Prime Minister Winston S. Churchill.

my mind that he was trying to persuade Eisenhower to do it this way. Eisenhower, of course, was very calm with Mr. Churchill. He was very deferential to his position, but he also stood up very much, I think, to his best military thought.

I think the top British people, as well as the top—now, I'm talking military—as well as the top American people all pretty much agreed that the plan we finally adopted was the better military plan. It was not going to be as quick and spectacular, but in our opinion, we thought it was surer.

John T. Mason, Jr.: You might tell me, sir, about the arrangements back in the British Isles, I mean how you accommodated this vast army of men and equipment necessary.

Admiral Struble: As the spring went on, all over southern England there were piles of this and that in all these little villages at the head of little small inlets that might exist. Supplies were getting piled up everywhere ready for the invasion. The location of the various ships—the American, British, and so forth—was all planned and arranged so that all could concentrate at the landing spot at the appointed time. Most of the American ships, for instance, were on the western side of England and Scotland and on the southwestern coastline.

John T. Mason, Jr.: Some of them were up in Belfast too, weren't they?

Admiral Struble: That is true. But most of the supplies were on England and to some extent in Scotland. The plan as we devised it on the American side started at minus 60 hours. In other words, two and a half days before the landing was made, some of the small ships started moving toward that area. Of course, they were very slow, and that's why they would have to be started early. I had small ships in the plan that left the vicinity of Plymouth as early as minus 60 and minus 55 hours and started heading up the channel all along the British coast. They would not turn south for the landing until after nightfall or until about nightfall on the day before the landing.

John T. Mason, Jr.: How was it possible, sir, to keep this somewhat of a secret, not to alert the Germans to the exact general time of the landing? How was this done?

Admiral Struble: The Germans were able to figure just as well as we, recognizing the tidal situation, the probable four- or five-day period once a month in which we would land. So the idea of our fooling them on that part of the problem we gave right up. You had to concede that they could figure it out.

John T. Mason, Jr.: I suppose that they had constant observation of the collection of materials from the air, did they?

Admiral Struble: Oh, yes, there was no doubt in their minds that we were stacking up and getting ready for the invasion. I'm sure they knew that and I think Rommel, as an example, knew or thought it was coming when it did.*

There is an interesting story there I might give you. Rommel was present on the Normandy coastline behind where we landed. I guess he had a castle maybe 12 miles inland from the shoreline. That's just a rough estimate, 12 miles inland. He had arrived there in about March, maybe April, and he had taken a look at the Normandy beach line and said, "Oh, my God, this sure as hell is a spot where they might come."

He had previously undoubtedly examined the landing place across from Calais and had estimated it as being a very probable landing area and had undoubtedly marked it as number-one guess at that time. He went into Paris to talk to the German generals there, and then he started down on the Normandy coastline. What he had done is he had started up in Scandinavia and had come down the coastline, working south.

John T. Mason, Jr.: Looking at all the possibilities.

Admiral Struble: Looking at all the possibilities. It was a good thing for us that he started up in the far north because he might have gotten to the Normandy area quicker.

---

* Field Marshal Erwin Rommel, commander of German Army Group B for defense against the Allied invasion of France.

Had Rommel gotten to the Normandy area much quicker, I feel sure that we would have had a much tougher time because I think he understood the problem and I think he was capable.

Now we go on with the story. He had gotten to the Normandy coastline, and he took one look and said, "This is certainly a very definite possibility for the American landing." He therefore went back to Paris apparently and tried to persuade the German general who was in charge of the four Panzer Divisions to order them to his command in Normandy. This, you understand, is a collection on my part of a lot of things I have heard. This is not intended to be a clear statement of fact. You understand?

John T. Mason, Jr.: Oh, yes.

Admiral Struble: I'm giving you kind of an appraisal of my own. I think it's interesting and you may choose to have it. He asked the German government in Paris for the Panzer divisions to be ordered to his command in Normandy. The German general wouldn't do it. He said, "I'll send you one for training purposes."

Rommel was given one Panzer division down in the Normandy area for training purposes. I don't know when he got those, possibly as early as April. That is not important to the story, though. So he brought that Panzer division up to the coastline right where the landing was going to occur, the bluff and all that, and he had exercises with this Panzer division for about a month in repelling an attack before we landed. So it does go to show that Rommel was a pretty smart, thoughtful person and that he was on the job.

After this period of training, the general commanding the Panzer divisions apparently had Rommel put that division back farther from the beach. He didn't like to keep them out there in an exposed position too long. Well, of course, that made them susceptible to American air and so forth. So the Panzer division proper, most of it, was withdrawn from the beach—a large part of it was withdrawn from the beach and taken inland farther and put into a more protective area for its location.

However, during that period he also must have dug all these little ground holes at the edge of the cliff where we finally landed. He had a string of these things dug along the edge of a bluff. The men had sights down on the beach and they were located in a tremendously powerful, strong position to repel a beach landing.

John T. Mason, Jr.: Well, this was more than just training.

Admiral Struble: The training had gone on then and had developed into specific fortification controlling the beach to prevent an attack. Now, at the same time, Rommel had studied the tides, and he had decided that our probable landing period would be these four days in the month. He was entirely accurate in that, as far as I know. He had his troops stationed at the beach as they were stationed at the landing and so forth. I don't think he covered the Utah area. I don't think he had considered that necessarily the probable landing point. He had some forces down in Cherbourg, but I don't think he thought of that as a probable landing point. He had a German admiral down there who would keep him informed of the tides.

At the time of Normandy, during the four-day period when we might have and should have landed, we had rough seas coming in from the west, very, very high, rough seas between Cherbourg and Plymouth, rolling in. They were big enough to have prevented us from landing with all the multitude of little small boats we had to have. We could have put our big ships out into that, but we couldn't put the small ships out in it. So we were delaying the possible landing a day at a time, hoping that it would subside.

On the day before the landing, and if I give you a good picture of it—well, I'll describe it to you. At Plymouth, where we were located, we were located farther out to the westward. On the other side, Cherbourg was farther to the eastward than Plymouth, and I would suppose weather-wise maybe as much as six or eight hours later on the weather than we are to the westward. So that at dusk, 6:00 or 8:00 o'clock on the night before the decision was made, we were farther out to the westward and we had a little better appraisal of the weather and we felt sure the waves were going down. In Cherbourg at the same time, the German army being farther to the eastward would still have had eight-foot waves maybe.

John T. Mason, Jr.: He didn't have the advantage of the Plymouth view.

Admiral Struble: Being to the westward. He was farther into the eastward, so that evening at 6:00 o'clock when he made his report to Rommel, he apparently told Rommel that the waves were eight feet high and he didn't think there could be an American landing. Of course, by this time a lot of our ships were already at sea going to where they belonged. But none of them had anywhere near approached the coastline so they wouldn't have been visible.

That evening at 8:00 o'clock in Plymouth we recommended to Ike that we go along with the landing. The German at the same time was probably recommending to Rommel that he didn't think the Americans would be landing.

I want to tell you one other thing in here quickly. Rommel, some time after that decision, said, "Well, this is the last day on which they would land, so I'm going off to Berlin." He got in his own car and started toward Berlin. Now, I can't tell you why he started to Berlin. There was a story that existed at one time that his wife's birthday was going to be in a couple of days so he was trying to get there and see her. But I think that a much stronger estimate on my part would be that he went to Berlin to get command of all the four Panzer divisions direct from Hitler.* And he would have gotten them from Hitler. When he got back we would have had a hell of a lot tougher problem a month later. Fortunately for us, the decision was made to go ahead. We had pretty rough water, but Rommel, who was on his way to Berlin, was no factor then in the landing.

Now, this is all speculation, but it's not bad speculation.

John T. Mason, Jr.: But intelligent speculation. Rommel had a great pull with Hitler.

Admiral Struble: Oh, there's no argument about that. Listen, I'm of the opinion that Rommel was a smart cookie and Hitler knew it. Hitler trusted Rommel. He had given him this special job—I'll bet you if Rommel had gotten to Berlin, he would have gotten the command turned over to him.

---

* German Chancellor Adolf Hitler, who was his nation's military commander in chief.

John T. Mason, Jr.: Let me ask, sir, in the months of planning when you went into the details of it all, did you appreciate fully the advantage you were going to have in terms of being in Plymouth and observing the water conditions on that side and knowing that there was a time lag on the other side?

Admiral Struble: That had not entered our planning or thought, but it did enter the situation about one week before the landing when we started to take a look at the weather all the time from the ships. Our flagship was anchored in Plymouth harbor.

John T. Mason, Jr.: Tell me about the anticipated use of the British idea of the Mulberry and how they entered into your planning.[*] Did the Americans appreciate this novel idea?

Admiral Struble: We did very much. We went for it. We thought it was a remarkable way the British organized and got the things built, and we felt that they did a superb job of taking them across the channel and installing them.

There was one thing that, of course, happened later, that we had not anticipated. It looked as if these tall concrete four-story buildings were very strong and everything. But it did prove in the worst storm that had ever come down the English Channel for the last 60 years—the one that came down that year. So that did break that up, as you know.

John T. Mason, Jr.: That really tested your mettle, didn't it?

Admiral Struble: Well, that broke up that harbor. We had had the advantage of the harbor, though, for a week almost. We had gotten a lot of things pretty well fixed up. It put us temporarily in a hell of a mess with the small boats, but all of that would have happened anyway whether we had the harbor or not.

John T. Mason, Jr.: Did the storm affect the British Mulberry?

---

[*] Mulberry was the name assigned to a large sort of caisson structure that could be flooded down in large numbers off the French beaches to form artificial harbors for the protection of Allied ships during the unloading process.

Admiral Struble: The British didn't have one. They didn't need one, and they were protected by the land that came out over their area.

John T. Mason, Jr.: I was thinking there were two, one in the American sector and one in the British sector.

Admiral Struble: Well, if there was one in the British sector I can give you no knowledge of it. I was never over there until ten years later.

John T. Mason, Jr.: In the planning stage was much consideration given to the other idea of a landing in southern France to divert German attention?

Admiral Struble: Well, there was talk of it, but none of us were interested in having it done. We thought we had all we needed planned up there, and we didn't figure that somewhat of a fake landing in southern France would be very effective unless it was done a fair amount earlier. If you did it very much earlier, you might give away the fact that it was nothing but a fake. You always have that possibility.

John T. Mason, Jr.: Because it was perfectly obvious that you were planning one on the channel.

Admiral Struble: Oh, they knew we were. Their air going over to England saw enough to know we were planning an invasion from England. I just don't think that we ever gave the idea to sally down there and so forth. My own thought was that it could only do harm.

John T. Mason, Jr.: You made an intriguing statement before when we were talking about Churchill. You said he was planning on every level. So obviously he was planning on your level. Can you recall any of the encounters with him?

Admiral Struble: No, I really had no encounters of that character with him. I met him, of course, a couple of times. He was a very brilliant person. There is no doubt that he had Eisenhower over to see him almost every other day there for the planning period and maybe sometimes oftener. He had ideas, he expressed them, he discussed them. That was common knowledge, I will say, in London. He had a very clever mind and he did think of things. So you might learn something from him.

But, of course, he probably made it pretty tough for Eisenhower who already had plenty to do without being called on all the time, as it were, for consultation.

There is a good story that I have heard of. I don't know whether to tell it to you or not.

John T. Mason, Jr.: Why, of course.

Admiral Struble: The story is that Eisenhower told Churchill one day at one of their meetings about two or three weeks before the landing. I think it was in that period—that the staff had strongly recommended that he establish a post in southern England where he would have good communications and everything else and that he be located there rather than on one of the ships going over. It seemed ridiculous to put the Supreme Commander on a ship which might just receive a bomb from a plane and be the place where the incident occurred. Anyway, from England he would have better internal communications available to him, and that's where he ought to be located. So he said after much argument, "I gave in to the staff, and I'm going to put my command post in southern England." That was settled.

Then a couple or three weeks later, the Prime Minister is supposed to have sent for him again and said, "Say, I've been thinking over this command post of yours down there. That's fine for you and that's where you belong. But in my case, it's a little bit different. "Now," he said, "which ship do you think I should embark in for the invasion?"

Ike said, "I strongly object to your embarking in a ship. I don't think you ought to go."

"No," he said, "what ship do you think I ought to embark in?"

Ike said, "I don't recommend it, and I don't want anything to do with it. Of course, there is no doubt if you decide to go down to the south coast and get on any number of different British ships that are there and tell them you are the Prime Minister, they'll take you over if you insist on it."

That was one of the stories floating around London.

John T. Mason, Jr.: It may be apocryphal, but it's nearer to the truth all the time.

Admiral Struble: But it's kind of interesting. I don't think there is any doubt that Ike's determined stand against his going and saying that he disagreed strongly with his going, probably prevented him from doing it. He wanted to go pull out his sword as he crossed the channel. Ike had decided finally that he wouldn't be going, so he didn't see any reason why Churchill should. And there were more reasons why he shouldn't have really. Because Ike was really a military man in command.

John T. Mason, Jr.: And Churchill was a naval person.

Admiral Struble: Well, yes, but he wasn't really in direct military command of the operation. That's always been an interesting story, in my opinion.

John T. Mason, Jr.: Tell me, in the planning stage what kind of a liaison did you maintain with the Joint Chiefs in Washington?

Admiral Struble: An occasional letter, but primarily Ernie King's office would send a man over to London every so often at what he considered a strategic moment. He sent over one of his top men during this period of about three weeks beforehand. The final clinching period of the final decision. We had a long talk with him.

Then he started over the succession of moguls, senior people of one sort or another, about a week beforehand. Some of them were going to be able to witness the invasion and others of which weren't.

John T. Mason, Jr.: But they were eyes and ears for him too.

Admiral Struble: Yes, and one or two of them had interest in specific things that they wanted to see how they functioned and worked and we were going to try them out. So they would be permitted to come over on that basis. We had quite a few people on our flagship when we went over—a pretty husky load of people.* A lot of them, though, were experts who were over there to try to decide whether what they were interested in would function as well as we had hoped and all that sort of thing.

---

* Admiral Kirk's flagship for the invasion was the heavy cruiser Augusta (CA-31).

Interview Number 5 with Admiral Arthur D. Struble, U.S. Navy (Retired)
Place: Admiral Struble's Home, Chevy Chase, Maryland
Date: Wednesday, 23 June 1976
Interviewer: John T. Mason, Jr.

John T. Mason, Jr.: Well, sir, this morning we are going to resume your story of the Normandy operation. Perhaps you want to begin your remarks by saying something more about the command setup and the relationship with Admiral Ramsay, the British overall naval commander.

Admiral Struble: Admiral Ramsay was the overall commander for Normandy under General Eisenhower, who in his status was the overall military commander for the invasion of Europe and subsequent operations. Admiral Ramsay had ordered Admiral Kirk to join his staff at some location in southern England where Ramsay's staff and Kirk and his staff would be jointly together operating under Admiral Ramsay.

Admiral Kirk was expected to recognize that he would operate under Admiral Ramsay's orders. His conception had been that he would go to sea actually for the invasion and be in direct command at the spot of the American naval forces there and therefore responsible for them to that extent. As soon as the landing was completed, the flow of troops and supplies across the beach was satisfactory, then Kirk would be disappear from the scene and some other representative of Commander 12th Fleet in London would be under Admiral Ramsay for that purpose unless in the meantime, the landing being successful, Admiral Ramsay also closed up shop.

So with that in view, Kirk expected to be in a ship and be over at the landing and be in direct control of both Admiral Hall and Admiral Moon.*

John T. Mason, Jr.: Was there any arguing about the two positions?

---

* Rear Admiral John L. Hall, USN, was Commander Task Force 124, the assault force for Omaha Beach; Rear Admiral Don P. Moon, USN, was Commander Task Force 125 for the landing at Utah Beach.

Admiral Struble: Yes. The British position was different. The British did not have this joint relationship of Navy and Army, where the Navy was in command up to a certain point and then the Army took over the command ashore when they were ready and prepared and so stated. In other words, Bradley went to sea with Kirk for the landing.[*] He went ashore from the ship and went around, and he and his staff did what they wanted to do in connection with the early day or two of the landing. As soon as they moved themselves and their command post over on the beach, then General Bradley became in charge ashore, and Admiral Kirk's responsibility was null in that respect. He was still in charge of the ships offshore to assist General Bradley's operation from then on.

John T. Mason, Jr.: How was it resolved from the British point of view?

Admiral Struble: From the British point of view, the Navy was more of an assisting force from the start to the Army and did not have as much control of the landing from the start as the American side did. Therefore, the moment the troops landed, the Army general was in command immediately. Do you understand me?

John T. Mason, Jr.: Yes, but the point I would hope you would make was how it was resolved—Kirk's point of view, the American point of view, versus Ramsay's and the British point of view.

Admiral Struble: Well, Admiral Ramsay finally accepted our idea for us. We went to Plymouth, and we handled it in the American custom. He handled the British landing in the British custom, but during that period when the landing was being made, we would have carried it out any order that Admiral Ramsay sent to us. Kirk would have carried out on his side with the American forces. But we would have been in command of doing it, and it would have been in our phraseology, let's say, and the details would be as we directed. And, of course, there were some differences. There were definitely differences in the way we thought these landings ought to be handled.

---

[*] Lieutenant General Omar N. Bradley, USA.

John T. Mason, Jr.: Yes. One point that was made by one man who wrote on the subject was that there was a difference in this sense: that the British in their op orders, so to speak, were much more specific. The total planning was at the top, whereas in the American way of doing things lesser commanders were given more authority to implement. And the illustration given was Ramsay's orders for Operation Neptune, which it was called, consisted of 1,000 typewritten pages, a very detailed thing, which was a little bit different from what the Americans would have.

Admiral Struble: Oh, yes, very different. Our plan as issued by Kirk was much, much smaller. Both Hall and Moon on our side had much more local initiative themselves in handling them. I guess that's pretty clear.

John T. Mason, Jr.: Yes. Tell me about the conferences that were held at the Eisenhower headquarters. This was outside of Portsmouth, at a country place that was taken over.

Admiral Struble: Yes. Well, of course, Eisenhower did not go down there until about the last seven to ten days, I guess, before the invasion. From that spot he expected to issue the decision that we would land at a certain time, on a certain day. Kirk was at Plymouth on the ship that was going to take us to the invasion.

John T. Mason, Jr.: The Augusta.

Admiral Struble: The Augusta.* The day before the landing—with the weather rolling in from the Atlantic quite heavily, but apparently from our point of view subsiding a little— the decision had to be made that night for the following day, you might say. Because that was the last minute, which would give the big ships and all that sort of stuff enough time to get over to the landing. That was the last day that we had figured would be a favorable day for the tidal currents situation for the landing.

---

* USS Augusta (CA-31) was commissioned 30 January 1931. She had a standard displacement of 9,050 tons, was 600 feet long, 66 feet in the beam, and had a draft of 16 feet. Her top speed was 33 knots. She was armed with nine 8-inch guns and eight 5-inch guns. Because she was configured as a flagship, she frequently performed that function, both before and during World War II. She was eventually decommissioned on 16 July 1946.

John T. Mason, Jr.: Well, there was a postponement of the day, was there not?

Admiral Struble: Oh, yes.

John T. Mason, Jr.: And this caused some problems.

Admiral Struble: Well, it meant that some of the ships at sea we had to turn around and not have them land a day ahead of time—small units. Actually, we didn't have any trouble that way, although we never really were sure that we had gotten all the little fellows turned around because communications with some of these log rafts that were floating over to the landing were—it wasn't like talking to a naval ship with good radio communication. As we previously discussed, at about 8:00 P.M. Bradley and Kirk and I went ashore in Plymouth to talk direct to General Eisenhower. He had made the appointment. We were to be there at about 8:00 o'clock, if I remember.

John T. Mason, Jr.: That was on the night of the fifth.

Admiral Struble: That's right. His British adviser—and he had some excellent men—had decided that the waves were definitely going down. There would be pretty good-sized waves, a good bit higher than we wanted, but that they thought it would subside enough that it would be continually getting better so that we could afford to try it out.

From Plymouth Kirk, speaking for both himself and Bradley—I think that Bradley did talk for a minute or two with Ike on the phone at that time—confirmed that we were favorable to going ahead with the operation. That was at the time that the Germans on the other side were getting their information from Cherbourg, which was 60 miles or so towards the eastward. The waves hadn't subsided quite as much there, and Rommel had apparently decided from his reports in Cherbourg that there was no chance of our landing that month, so that we'd undoubtedly put it off for a month. And he started for Berlin by automobile. So he was on the other side of Paris in an automobile when we landed, which did us no harm.

John T. Mason, Jr.: No, I guess not.

Admiral Struble: I think he would have put up a better fight against us on the Omaha beaches than the other people did that were left in charge.

John T. Mason, Jr.: There was another conference which I presume you attended—I know Admiral Kirk did—and that was the meeting at General Montgomery's headquarters at St. Paul's School in London on the 15th of May. Will you tell me about that meeting? It was very colorful, and it was a very important one.

Admiral Struble: This was what you could call the final briefing for the American and British sides with a large number of senior political people present. Actually the King was there that day.[*] What happened is that the Americans in order, Moon speaking first and so forth, would stand up and sketch what they were going to do. Kirk also spoke, and the British officers who were going to be in direct command over at the beach or maybe in direct command of aviation for this particular landing. Each officer would speak in turn.

They got about a little over halfway through the meeting, stopped, and had luncheon. It's my impression that the King left shortly after lunch. I don't think he stayed for the afternoon.

John T. Mason, Jr.: Schoeffel says he spoke at the end of the meeting.[†]

Admiral Struble: Well, then he did stay. The King spoke very well and very interestingly. He made a very fine talk. I guess he did stay there for the afternoon.

---

[*] King George VI.
[†] Rear Admiral Malcolm F. Schoeffel, USN (Ret.), is the subject of a Naval Institute oral history.

Actually on that occasion, I had taken over the general who was going to follow Bradley on the Omaha beach. He was from another army, and they would be coming in, as I remember, on about somewhere around the 13th to 18th day after the initial landing. He was the man who had the very famous movie.

John T. Mason, Jr.: You mean George Patton.*

Admiral Struble: Yes, George Patton. George Patton had been kept under wraps in northern England because of an incident that had occurred in the hospital that he was connected with. I don't know whether you remember that.

John T. Mason, Jr.: So you accompanied Patton to that meeting.

Admiral Struble: Patton and I sat together for both the morning and afternoon sessions. As he had not been in London previously, I was able to fill him in on quite a bit of the planning for the landing and so forth.

John T. Mason, Jr.: Admiral King was not there, was he?

Admiral Struble: No.

John T. Mason, Jr.: Was Stark there?

Admiral Struble: I think Stark was there. I don't personally remember.

John T. Mason, Jr.: This was kind of a verbal rehearsal of what was going to happen.

Admiral Struble: It was a kind of verbal rehearsal. For instance, when Moon got up and started talking about landing at Utah, the Army colonel or brigadier general who maybe was going to be landed at that spot could stand up and say, "Admiral Moon, can you tell

---
* Lieutenant General George S. Patton, USA.

me this—or tell me that?" Now, of course, once they went to sea on the operation, the American Army general who was going to make the landing would have been on Moon's ship with him, and those two people would be right together. While Moon would be giving the orders, the Army man could get into the picture and say, "Let's not do that. That's going to be terrible for us," or something like that.

John T. Mason, Jr.: I must ask you, because he was a very colorful character, was General Teddy Roosevelt there too?*

Admiral Struble: I don't remember. Of course, it was a pretty good-sized meeting. I suppose we had maybe a 100 senior people—Army and Navy and British and American.

John T. Mason, Jr.: The security precautions must have been very great.

Admiral Struble: Well, it was a boys' school, and all they had to do was send out a certain number of people early, probably the day before. The British Army people would clear out the building and be sure everything was secure. It was a boys' school that was at the moment empty.

John T. Mason, Jr.: Obviously reporters were not present.

Admiral Struble: No, reporters were not present.

John T. Mason, Jr.: Well, let's talk a bit about various aspects of the operation. For instance, communications.

Admiral Struble: On the American Navy side we had rather good communications. They had been established at least over a period of two weeks in advance to most places that were going to need communications. So we really had, I would say, excellent communications most of the time, very good communications to all the ships and so

---

* Brigadier General Theodore Roosevelt, Jr., USA.

forth. The only problem was that a lot of the log rafts and things of that sort didn't have any communications at all. Although a lot of them did have some listening and could hear orders issued.

John T. Mason, Jr.: Tell me about these log rafts. I don't know about them.

Admiral Struble: The log rafts were designed to be floated into the beach to be used in connection with building the harbor and that sort of thing, that was going to be put up with Omaha. They were going to be needed for early in the operation, so they had to be gotten over earlier.

John T. Mason, Jr.: How many personnel would be carried on a raft?

Admiral Struble: Leaving Plymouth, we steamed east for about three or four hours, five hours at least, until we got to the point where we turned south to go to the French coast. We must have passed at least half dozen of these great big log rafts. In the center of the log rafts there would be some sort of little metal stove arrangement where the boys would have a little fire and they would be cooking their lunch or dinner, as the case might be, as we went past them.

There would be on that log raft anywhere from six to ten men. They would be chugging along with a fairly good-sized outboard motor at the rear end; it was probably pushing them through the water about three or four miles an hour.

John T. Mason, Jr.: Kind of a precarious vehicle.

Admiral Struble: Well, they had to be put over there fairly early in order to get there anywhere near on time. Their timing wasn't to get there for the landing. Their timing was probably to get there by about two or three days after the landing, but they were already at sea. Our first units on the American side had gotten under way at minus 60 hours. That's two and a half days before the time of the landing. And that was the people that were up on the west coast of England and Scotland. They had gotten under way at minus two and a half days. Once they got to sea, some of these smaller little things like I just talked about—it was almost impossible to communicate with them. Even if they did get your message, you wouldn't necessarily know because very few of them could talk back to you. They might get a message and not necessarily be able to answer back.

John T. Mason, Jr.: There were what, 1,000 ships of various kinds involved?

Admiral Struble: Including these log rafts and everything, I would say yes.

John T. Mason, Jr.: Tell me about the shore bombardment. Was this under Admiral Kirk?

Admiral Struble: Well, in a way, but not actually. We had already in our operation plan stipulated that Moon would take charge of what happened over at his beach, and Hall would take charge of what happened at his beach. There were two separate beaches. So the man who was going to make the landing at that beach had the local command authority at that spot.

Now, Kirk, from where he was, could countermand or alter orders to either Moon or Hall, which by the way he didn't do. We never had any propositions of that sort. But sometimes we would alter our own previous instructions when we saw that something could be done that would make it better. We would send out an order to both Moon and Hall that our plans had changed to so and so and altered the plan if we wanted.

Now, of course, actually at the landing our ship was right off Hall's ship. We were right there where the landing at Omaha was being directed and in fact, we had a number of conferences the day of the landing. Kirk went over and called on Hall and came back very unhappy about 2:00 o'clock in the afternoon, I guess it was—or 1:00 o'clock maybe. I went over a little later, and we were still unhappy. We still hadn't decided yet that we were going to make it, although we all felt we would.

John T. Mason, Jr.: You mean you were unhappy because it was an uncertain proposition?

Admiral Struble: Oh, yes, when the troops landed, instead of being able to start the march against the enemy, they ran into this high bluff. They couldn't march up the bluff because up above the Germans had installed all these beautiful gun emplacements. They had a number of their good troops there and, boy, their rifle fire down on the beach was deadly. So when we landed on the beach which at low water was over a mile from the cliff—as the water came in it came up within about 200 yards of the foot of this cliff.

John T. Mason, Jr.: It was a rise of what, 20 feet or something like that?

Admiral Struble: Well, I don't remember that figure. It was quite a good rise and fall. So the early troops that landed really landed almost outside the rifle fire of the beach. But then they had to go all the way across the wet sand and attack this thing that was just looking down their throat. Of course, they edged off to one side, mostly to the eastward. When there appeared a good chance, they'd grab their rifle or what they had and make a run for it and get right up close to the bottom of the cliff.

Now, the German gunners with their rifles were up over them, and they couldn't shoot down at them. So they were perfectly safe there, but they couldn't go anywhere either.

John T. Mason, Jr.: And great numbers couldn't assemble up at the cliff either.

Admiral Struble: Well, actually great numbers did start to assemble. What they did was ease off down the beach to the left, staying up close to the cliff, until they would get down far enough away where the rifle fire from the top of the cliff wouldn't hurt them too much. A lot of them did collect to the eastward. Over to the eastward of what was the original spot for landing at Omaha there was an arroyo that kind of ran up. One of the conferences that I attended in the afternoon, at maybe 2:30, was with Hall and with the major general who was in command of the Army troops that were landing at Omaha.[*] He had gone in originally in one of the early landings, and he had been up in there, up

---

[*] Major General Clarence R. Huebner, USA.

against the cliff and all that and he knew the whole picture. Any idea of doing anything promptly appeared to be completely out of the question. But he hoped and expected that as soon as it got nightfall that these troops were free to maneuver more. They would go up the arroyo, get up behind the Germans, and maybe be able to knock out this favorable strong point before the next morning at daylight. That would then permit us free and easy landing. And that's what happened.

John T. Mason, Jr.: Why wasn't this problem anticipated in the planning?

Admiral Struble: Because we had no knowledge that this particular type of thing existed on the edge of that cliff. We did have some knowledge of the presence of Rommel and the presence of one Panzer division over in that area of Normandy. It was obvious to us that Rommel was engaged in preliminary anti-invasion tactics and so forth at this spot, but we did not know that they had developed anywhere near as strong a strong point as they had.

John T. Mason, Jr.: This implies that our intelligence of that beach situation wasn't as—

Admiral Struble: Oh, boy. The closer you got to that area, the less intelligence you got. The local people there don't come down very much anyway. They are very scattered. I believe Rommel had been there about six weeks or two weeks. He had recognized this as being a very dangerous spot. He had wanted to put all four Panzer divisions down there and get ready a big fight, but the German generals in Paris who were in control of the Panzer divisions would not give Rommel control of them. They did permit him to have one of the divisions and exercise as it were at resisting enemy invasion.

Now, some of the preliminary work that Rommel did made the Omaha landing much more difficult originally because the boys got very murderous fire on them as they landed and tried to cross the beach. Fortunately, I suppose if you got under way and went as fast as you could, you could maybe cover that beach the distance of rifle fire maybe in a fairly short length of time. You would be generally traveling over fairly firm sand until just the tail end of the beach in front of the cliff, where there might have been some of the really dry sand that was mushy and slow to travel in. But by the time they got to the soft sand, you might say, they probably had gotten out of the sphere of firing from above. I suppose the rifles couldn't shoot down like that because they weren't quite out to the edge of the cliff anyway. So they would have to shoot out. But the moment you got in like this you were perfectly safe.

John T. Mason, Jr.: Going back to communications, and this is kind of a footnote, the correspondence from the Augusta did complain about the antiquated methods of sending their messages back to the United Kingdom for transmittal to the States. They said they had to rely on the British system of sending a little dory type ship that went around from ship to ship collecting the messages. It was not very expeditious.

Admiral Struble: Well, the question of handling press had only received attention to the point of doing what we could with what we had and as we were equipped. Certainly our invasion forces were not as equipped as the press would have liked. They would have liked to have had much better service, which they would be able to get probably about two weeks or so after the landing. From that time on, they would again get back to better press service. But, of course, during the landing itself, that isn't really the most important fact.

John T. Mason, Jr.: Well, they think so.

Admiral Struble: Sure.

John T. Mason, Jr.: Tell me specifically about your own duties on the Augusta. How were you occupied?

Admiral Struble: Actually, as chief of staff, all of the messages that came into the flagship would come to me, and I would handle the messages, one way or another, no matter where they came from—ships or what. There were occasionally very important ones that I would prepare a reply to and would go off and find Kirk and talk it over with him and send it off. But I suppose I handled 90% to 95% of the messages myself. I handled a very large percentage of all the messages that came in myself.

The very important ones that I thought had maybe a little bit of a sticky part to them, I would try to find Kirk if I could and let him see the replies before we sent them out. Now, he and I kind of alternated with each other for the first week of the landing. I would get up earlier in the morning, maybe around 6:00 or so, and would take over the duty, as it were. Kirk would go to bed. From about 6:00 o'clock in the morning until about 6:00 or 8:00 o'clock at night, I would handle all the messages as they came in, taking those that I felt were something unusual or some major thing or something to Kirk. He then would get some rest and then he would take over along about 8:00 o'clock at night, and go up on the bridge. He and one of the staff, who was actually the gunnery officer, would take what Kirk and I called the night duty, watching from the start any movement that might come from Cherbourg around toward us over water at night. Of course, we had night raids, small stuff.

John T. Mason, Jr.: E-boats?*

Admiral Struble: Yes, that kind of thing. The gunnery officer had been with Kirk a long time. The two of them would be up on the bridge from 8:00 P.M. until, I would say, about 6:00 A.M. Now, I didn't always get to bed at 8:00 o'clock. I was often up later than that, but in effect Kirk took over the duty at that moment, and I was free to go to bed if I could. On the contrary, when I got up about 6:00 in the morning, by that time the danger of this night stuff was over, then he would go to bed and I would take over. I, of course, wouldn't have hesitated to awaken him during the day if there was something of very great importance. If I felt that I shouldn't make the decision myself without his knowledge, well, of course, I'd wake him up. That's more or less standard naval practice in things of that sort.

For instance, a certain amount of stuff went on for about 13 days at least off Omaha including the storms.

---

* "E-boats" was an Allied nickname for German motor torpedo boats.

John T. Mason, Jr.: The strain must have been pretty great then.

Admiral Struble: Well, it was pretty busy. Certainly for the first six or eight days it was pretty heavy. Initially we weren't too sure that we were well off and that we didn't still have serious trouble spots. Along about D plus two or three, Bradley finally decided to go ashore and set up his command post.

The moment that he went ashore, of course, he had to have radio and all that, whatever he needed. But the moment that he went ashore and told Kirk he was taking over, that was automatic. Bradley made that decision, not Kirk. Until that time, Kirk theoretically had been in charge of the joint operation, but the moment that Bradley established his command post ashore and said, "I'm taking over ashore," then that was his job.

John T. Mason, Jr.: Did you make an excursion ashore?

Admiral Struble: Oh yes, sure. I went ashore a number of times.

John T. Mason, Jr.: How soon did you go ashore?

Admiral Struble: I guess it must have been about one day before Bradley took over. Now, he was already over there. He was setting up his command post, but he hadn't yet informed Kirk that he was taking over complete command.

John T. Mason, Jr.: Had the gunners been silenced on the cliff by that time?

Admiral Struble: Oh yes, they were gone the next day. After the night of the landing day, these people that I told you got up the arroyo and came in from behind. Then the Germans that were there were all trapped. They couldn't go anywhere. They were in these beautiful places in the front of the cliff where they had these nice little spots dug out, but they could shoot down and give us hell. But they didn't have anywhere to go when we got behind them. So that ended that with a bang.

John T. Mason, Jr.: Did you make a trip to the Utah beach also?

Admiral Struble: Oh, yes. I went over there a couple of times by boat. Kirk went over a couple of times by boat.

John T. Mason, Jr.: You didn't go together?

Admiral Struble: Oh, no. We never both left the ship. One of us remained in the flagship. In other words, anything that came in, either he or I was there and could take prompt action on it. Of course, that was the main purpose of the chief of staff for Kirk.

John T. Mason, Jr.: An alter ego.

Admiral Struble: That's right. Somebody that was senior enough and had enough experience so that he could make the decision, bang, in the admiral's absence. I was also a rear admiral by then. I had been made a rear admiral before I left Washington.

John T. Mason, Jr.: Was there any danger from German submarines? Were they operating?

Admiral Struble: Well, the chance of German submarines coming in to try to operate against us was very remote because we were out in the open seas, and that's where they were doing their real work in getting things. Had they attempted to come in, say, from west of Ireland up in the channel, they would have faced so many problems of detection and the chances of their doing it were very remote. I think you've got to put it that way—very remote.

John T. Mason, Jr.: So there were actually not any there.

Admiral Struble: As far as I know, there was none. Now, one might have come in and snooped up on us and would not let himself get known. Of course, if he starts to try to shoot a torpedo at anything, he gives himself away too. In confined waters that isn't good for a submarine.

John T. Mason, Jr.: Your chief menace then, I take it, was in the form of the E-boats which operated in the channel.

Admiral Struble: Well, the E-boats were the things as I described to you that Kirk and the gunnery officer stayed up every night about. That was their specific agreed responsibility every night.

John T. Mason, Jr.: The E-boats didn't operate in the daytime?

Admiral Struble: Oh, no, they couldn't have. They had to have cover of darkness to have any chance at all.

John T. Mason, Jr.: They were very speedy, were they not?

Admiral Struble: They were speedy, but they would be a hell of a target for aviation in the daytime, and we had a lot of aviation. I don't know whether I told you, but I do think that the American aviation, which was located in England, discovered the Normandy landing on the American side.

American aviation did an excellent job of two things. I think they covered the air over the area quite well. Secondly, they certainly cleaned out the roads from south of us in France toward the beach. They covered those roads beautifully during daylight hours, and none of the three Panzer divisions that weren't already at the beach were able to get to the beach. But as soon as it started to get light in the morning, they had to scatter in the forest or something and sit there all day long until it got dark again before they could get out on the road and start moving down towards Omaha. So that was one thing that prevented those other three Panzer divisions that I mentioned before from getting into action quickly against us.

I'd say the daylight conditions probably existed for 14 or 15 hours a day. During that time, the American aviation from England would keep the Germans off the main roads. These troops just couldn't march. Of course, they all had equipment. They had to bring their ammunition. So they were just stymied for a large part of every day. They had to get off the road and park and wait until they could start again.

You know, if you take a division of troops and push them off in a big forest and then you come back to not too wide a road and start moving some place, your mobility is cut down very much. I would say that those fellows didn't get into good position to hurt Bradley too much until probably it may have been as late as plus eight or plus ten days. Bradley was able to get a pretty good start.

Now, the aviation did an awful good job of that. This was land-based aviation out of England. But it was American.

John T. Mason, Jr.: There was a preliminary bombardment, too, of roads and railroad connections and all the rest.

Admiral Struble: It was going on all the time. But the main effort of that character was not to the south toward France but was to the east toward northern France and toward, let's say, Berlin. The normal British operations. Now, both the British and Americans were jointly, in other words, attacking to the eastward before the landing. The American aviation shifted over and covered the area to the south, which, of course, was where we wanted to move and expand in there.

John T. Mason, Jr.: Now, there was the one incident that has been publicized. The American bombers dropped bombs that fell on their own troops.

Admiral Struble: That could have happened. That can happen in any war. That is sometimes an impossible problem. There is no easy way for a plane up at a fair distance overhead, going along spotting troops and deciding that yes, those are Germans or no, maybe they are Americans. There is no way that every little group of troops can be positively and quickly identified from high altitudes by an airplane. So I would charge no mistake to the airplanes involved. The Americans knew they were getting bombed; they got the hell out of there in a hurry. That's one of the problems in war. I don't think there's any way that you can solve that. Of course, as the two forces approach each other, you realize that there may be Germans just a block or two south of you.

John T. Mason, Jr.: There is almost a melding of the lines.

Admiral Struble: Yes, of course. Our troops were constantly advancing against the Germans. The Germans were not able to bring their mobile guns and stuff down the road toward us anywhere near as fast as I think they had thought they would be able to. Either that or the three German generals were a little stupid, whoever was in command, in not helping Rommel along and getting them down there a lot closer and a lot quicker. It looks like the Germans dropped the ball there.

John T. Mason, Jr.: There is one place in the operation I wish you would talk about a little more, and that is the mining and minesweeping.

Admiral Struble: The English Channel itself, except in certain spots which the British were familiar with, was fairly free of mines; they knew where they were and where they weren't. Of course, on the Normandy coastline, it was apparent to us up through I guess you'd say February or March maybe, that there had been no mining or attempt at mining in the area that we were interested in. Of course, we knew that Cherbourg Harbor would undoubtedly be mined. There undoubtedly would have been some mines, not directly in the channel, but maybe off the north coast at Cherbourg itself.

We didn't expect to go into Cherbourg, so that was no menace to us. So as far as we were concerned, the chances of mines at Omaha beach were nil. That condition existed until, let's say, shortly before the invasion when the British did get some intelligence that indicated that maybe in the Omaha-Utah beach area that some operational stuff was going on that might be mines. In other words, we did have some intelligence on that stuff about, I'll just guess, two weeks before. Now, where the British procured the intelligence I don't know.

John T. Mason, Jr.: Schoeffel says that there were nightly forays to the beaches on the part of a few men. Some of them actually landed on the beaches at Normandy to ascertain some of these things. Perhaps that's where it came from.

Admiral Struble: You don't know how long Schoeffel estimated that had been going on, do you?

John T. Mason, Jr.: No.

Admiral Struble: If that was done, it was certainly done without my knowledge. I would say that it was undoubtedly without Kirk's knowledge, because I feel sure that if Kirk had authorized anything of that character that he would have told me. I knew nothing of it. Now, if what Schoeffel said means the day before or something like that, that's an entirely different subject. If the day before the landing, he had run a small boat in there somewhere—I can't imagine his doing that.

John T. Mason, Jr.: I wonder, in connection with the forays we mentioned somewhere off the Calais coast, would you talk about the use of deception prior to the actual landings—the use of deception as a tool in the whole operation.

Admiral Struble: Well, a group of young men from the United States—fine, outstanding young men—had come to England, I would say, approximately two or three months before the invasion was due to take place. They were over there for the purpose of engaging and doing what they could in that type of counterintelligence and employing modern radio and sound type of weapons. A number of them were from the movie business. So they understood how lots of sound effects could be made and produced.

It was obvious to me upon talking to them that their ideas were a fine thing to try to do this, but they had no practical knowledge of the matter at all. So with Kirk's approval I had this group go down to one of the British training stations in southern England for about a month's training, during which period the British would tell them all the things that had happened in the English Channel previously, how it had been done, and so forth.

They wanted a ship about 60 feet or so on which they would mount their instruments. Their idea had been that the night before the invasion they would go in off, let's say, the coast off Calais if that was going to be the place where we weren't going to land and would start up this sound apparatus of theirs which noise would go in toward the beach. They would be far enough off the beach that they wouldn't be at all easily visible at night, but the sound would travel across the water. Sentries on the beach, hearing it, would think that it was a small ship anchoring and all that kind of stuff and putting out boats and create maybe a good counterintelligence action.

Well, that was done. Of course, the boys were hot to do it, and it was a dangerous type of operation for them to engage in because the Germans had a few fast boats around, and they would probably come out and shoot the hell out of them. But the boys did it, and as far as I know it was fairly successful.

We will never know on our side or probably never know how much intelligence information from those sentries got into the German system and how much it affected it. But any information that did get in from that operation would not only have gone to Berlin, but it would have gone to Paris where there were about three big German generals. People sitting in Paris hearing this stuff come in from Calais would say, "Oh, boy, this looks like the invasion. That's where it is." So that, of course, would have been good counterintelligence from our point of view. And the boys did accomplish the operation.

They were very hard at first because they were going to save the war and everything, and it was difficult to try to persuade them at first that there was a lot they still had to learn before they were going to be competent to do it. But we finally did get a ship, and they had it down on the east coast of England. It was all set in readiness to start out as soon as they got the word. Of course, we weren't going to give them the word until just before we were going to move. They all wanted to know what date it was. Of course, I wasn't going to tell all those boys what the real date was.

John T. Mason, Jr.: They were all in uniform?

Admiral Struble: Yes. Well, they weren't going to be necessarily. I don't know what they were going to wear on the ship. I know it started down there. When they came back to England, they all came down to see me and they said that thing had been very valuable. They were very glad they had gotten it. They were a good group. Daredevils, willing to do anything

Of course, if we could get a counterintelligence in that area about 24 hours in advance, that would be a good thing probably.

John T. Mason, Jr.: Yes, but coming dawn the effort would be canceled out, would it not, by visibility itself?

Admiral Struble: You never know how soon it will cancel out. But if you ever get the first message off and it looks like a landing is taking place, that is very disruptive to the other side because that message goes through with a bang. The later message that it looks like this may have been a fake is always way behind. So a lot of your purpose has been accomplished.

John T. Mason, Jr.: I see. It's simply like a report published in newspaper with a correction the next day.

Admiral Struble: Yes. So it isn't until the next day that the correction means anything.

John T. Mason, Jr.: And it isn't as widely read.

Admiral Struble: Before they get this correction, let's say the top man in Paris immediately fires back to his people and says, "Well, prove this has been canceled." He says, "Be sure now and know it's been canceled." Then the other end gets on the job and starts investigating, "Maybe we popped this thing off too quickly and we aren't sure." So that's the way this sort of thing works.

John T. Mason, Jr.: Would you tell me a little more about the floating harbors and about the construction and transporting the concrete pillars and that kind of thing? Did you get involved in that?

Admiral Struble: We were involved only in that we knew about it. We knew that the important one was going to be set up on Omaha beach because both the British beach and the Utah beach had protection from the north storm.

Now, there is often fairly heavy weather that comes down the English Channel. The English Channel is just like this toward your typewriter there—if that's Omaha beach, the English Channel just comes right down like this toward that beach. When you get over there closer, it turns to the westward and goes out to the Atlantic.

But the force of the storm, if it does originate and come down the English Channel, it usually increases its intensity, hits right at Omaha beach and there's a hell of a big storm. That is the one that put about 2,300 or 2,400 boats on the beach one night. Every small boat we had was way up high on the beach in the sand and a lot of the engines and propellers and everything else knocked up and so forth. That was quite a blow to us.

John T. Mason, Jr.: Is that the one that destroyed the Mulberry?

Admiral Struble: Oh, yes. Up until that time the Mulberry had been perfect. Oh, boy, it was sitting there, calm water inside, small boats and everything could enter; it had been swell. That was the day it went to hell. That was pretty heavy weather.

I had insisted myself on staying over there that long. Kirk thought that maybe we might go back to Plymouth quicker. But while we were going ashore at this moment, I had kind of felt it would be very desirable if we were sure that Bradley and his Army division and his supplies were all very safe before we left. Kirk had agreed. He said,

"Well, I don't know but what I'd do it the other way, but if you feel that this is desirable, we'll do it." That's the way you make decisions, and that's the way it happened.

So we were there when this big storm occurred.

John T. Mason, Jr.: How did it affect the Augusta?

Admiral Struble: Oh, we rode it out. She's a good, big seagoing ship. We rode it out without any trouble, but we couldn't put a boat in the water during that period. I guess there was a period of at least 12 hours when I wouldn't have thought of trying to put a boat down in the water off the ship. Maybe it was a little longer. There were such heavy seas. And, of course, all the stuff was up on the beach, away from the shore, and I suppose it took us in the neighborhood of three or four days to eliminate a lot of the trouble and at least a week to entirely recover from it.

John T. Mason, Jr.: Well, that justified your insistence on staying over there at that point, did it not?

Admiral Struble: It did indicate that in the case of this landing that maybe it was desirable for us to stay over there. Of course, the other point of view could just as easily have been expressed, which was that Admiral Hall maybe could have made all that decision and everything. But my thought had been that Hall's job was to do that kind of pushing, and our job was overhaul.

Normally out in the Philippines the thing was different, the major combat forces usually would have a tendency to get out at about the second or third day at least, if not earlier. But that was just the conditions as they were. Sometimes you can leave too quickly. I would say that my approach was a little bit on the safer side.

John T. Mason, Jr.: You mean it's more cautious.

Admiral Struble: More cautious, yes.

John T. Mason, Jr.: Tell me about the traffic to and fro across the channel—bringing supplies, unloading them, and going back. There must have been some tight control over the schedule, was there not?

Admiral Struble: Yes. That was all handled, though, from the English side. That was all under Ramsay, and he was handling all that from there. That was very well done on the whole.

John T. Mason, Jr.: There were a few collisions.

Admiral Struble: Well, yes, there was much small stuff that wasn't surprising. The size of this thing, of course, was really the big thing about it. It was a tremendously large operation and the largest one, I guess, that we'll ever hold. I don't know.

John T. Mason, Jr.: It certainly was the largest one up to that day.

Admiral Struble: There's no argument about that. That's right.

If you were going to install those harbors again on an open beach like at Omaha, it would definitely be desirable to make them stronger so they could withstand more pounding waves. Now, if you were going to make a quick landing that would be over in a certain number of days, well, then that wouldn't be so important. The thing about the Normandy landing was that once we established it and got the thing working we were expecting to try to put over maybe as much as a division in one day and all the supplies it would need, plus all the supplies that the previous troops already put ashore would need. So if you're going to do it like that, you don't know whether it's going to be as much as two months before you have another harbor through which you can operate which will be closer to your front lines and which will be capable of handling the stuff. But, of course, we did have such harbors farther up the channel so that if our troops had moved beyond that point we could then shift over our supply thing to the regular harbor. That, of course, must enter into the planning and thought.

John T. Mason, Jr.: Of course, the temporary harbor was destroyed by a storm which was the greatest in generations, wasn't it?

Admiral Struble: I think it was supposed to be the worst one they had had in 70 years. That's true. So it wasn't a good wind maybe in that way. You would expect to take a chance on it. The caving in of the harbors wasn't so good, but it wasn't so serious either. It didn't nullify the strength of the matter. It is one thought, though, that in the future if you were conducting an operation and there is a choice of a harbor that you might capture or an open beach that you might take instead, careful thought should certainly go into the matter that that harbor is very valuable to us and maybe we had better get it captured very quickly and have it open and ready as an alternate spot.

John T. Mason, Jr.: And not rely on the temporary.

Admiral Struble: And not rely on the temporary one forever.

John T. Mason, Jr.: Well, for the Normandy Landings, we did eventually attempt to clear Cherbourg, did we not?

Admiral Struble: Yes, I think we cleared Cherbourg and we also got charge of the coastline, too, as our troops got far enough along. Of course, the French people were with us, once we got there and were in control. So we had the French harbors that were normally up the channel a ways. Well, you didn't have them entirely, because once you did take over the land surrounding them, then you had to go through the necessary labor fixing them up to the extent that the Germans might have destroyed them.

But that was obviously the way to do it. I would suppose by September or October we had gotten well beyond Paris to the point where we could use anything along in there we wanted.

John T. Mason, Jr.: Including Belgium.

Admiral Struble: Yes. Belgium would have been reliable too.

John T. Mason, Jr.: How would you propose going about strengthening the Mulberry to withstand a storm such as did come along?

Admiral Struble: I suppose the only way to do it would be to have steel framing there.

John T. Mason, Jr.: These did not have?

Admiral Struble: No. They may have had one or two but not the number that was needed. A steel-framed structure might well have stood up because during the first part of the storm it stood up against some pretty good stuff. But eventually it went over. I don't think I could estimate. But I would think that some strengthening certainly would improve it the next time. And I'm sure that the people that built them recognized that and have already devised a method of doing some strengthening if they need to do it again. I'm sure of that.

Any construction man would have been working on that problem very shortly afterwards probably.

John T. Mason, Jr.: This is an illustration of man's weakness in the face of the forces of nature. It can be overwhelming.

Admiral Struble: You know, you have always got to take a chance in military operations. Usually there are a couple of choices like the choice of Cherbourg or the open beach. But the thing about the open beach which was it was so useful to us was that the plan called for both Bradley and followed by Patton could get moving in great quantity and strength toward Berlin as quick as they could. Therefore, there were a tremendous number of regiments and divisions that were to be landed and pushed into action. So I don't know, but if Cherbourg had been captured and the Germans had done some demolition themselves, I question that we could have gotten as good service as quickly out of Cherbourg as we did off the open beach.

John T. Mason, Jr.: The proof is in the fact that it did take quite a while to clear Cherbourg harbor once we were there.

Admiral Struble: That's right. Sometimes those harbor clearance jobs are very troublesome.

John T. Mason, Jr.: And that one was.

Admiral Struble: Yes.

John T. Mason, Jr.: Well, sir, when did the Augusta return to Plymouth?

Admiral Struble: As I remember, we left maybe about six to seven days after the wreckage of the Mulberry had been cleared away and things were commencing to work smoothly.

John T. Mason, Jr.: Did you have any VIPs visit you on board the Augusta while you were out there on the French side?

Admiral Struble: Eisenhower was out there. I don't remember any that were except military.

John T. Mason, Jr.: So you went back to Plymouth and then what?

Admiral Struble: We went back to Plymouth then, and I had said that I felt that we should make a fairly long, careful report. I don't think that Kirk entirely agreed with me that we needed quite as big a report as I contemplated, but I felt that this had been a very unusual experience and that if we got on the job and made the report right then and there, we'd have it.

John T. Mason, Jr.: You had an eye to the historical record.

Admiral Struble: Well, yes. This was going to be valuable in my opinion, and if we made a very good report of everything that had happened this would be valuable, library-effect for our future amphibious landing knowledge and everything. Of course, this was one specialized case. It would never be duplicated again probably, but all the things that you learn—any one of them might happen again, and the people who had read the record then would be able to evaluate their choice 20 years from now of doing something at a different place under different circumstances.

John T. Mason, Jr.: I would say you had an eye for the appreciation of the historical record.

Admiral Struble: Well, we spent in Plymouth then, I would think, and the whole staff was involved for about 20 days in making a very complete report. Then we went up to London. The staff filtered here and there. Kirk and I returned by air to the United States.

John T. Mason, Jr.: This was when?

Admiral Struble: Well, I guess it was in July. Kirk went back to be Eisenhower's principal naval assistant in Europe when he set up SHAEF headquarters in Paris.* Ernie King asked me why I hadn't stayed over there. I had been offered a job as chief of staff.

John T. Mason, Jr.: To Kirk?

Admiral Struble: No, to Admiral Stark, Com12thFlt in London. He wanted to know why I hadn't stayed over there and I said, "Well, I've been chief of staff now for a while. I want a command."

So he said, "All right. I'll give you a command."

---

* SHAEF—Supreme Headquarters Allied Expeditionary Force.

I would have thought I'd get a couple of weeks' leave, but 24 hours later I was on the way out to the Pacific.

John T. Mason, Jr.: Well, a war was going on, you know!

Admiral Struble: Yes, I asked for it and I got it.

John T. Mason, Jr.: Did you and Kirk have to make verbal reports on the operations when you got back to Washington?

Admiral Struble: I don't know how long Ernie King talked to Kirk, but I would say that Ernie talked to me for a couple of hours in his office when we got there, when I had told him what I wanted to do. He was very interested in certain of the subjects. He knew just what he wanted to know, and he wasn't interested in a lot of the other.

John T. Mason, Jr.: Do you remember what his particular interests were in the operation?

Admiral Struble: I think he was primarily interested, from what I recall, in whether we had a sound system of planning and conducting this type of operation. I think that was the basis of his thought. As he questioned me, I explained to him how we had tried to handle it and how we had insisted that we plan the American side of the invasion in detail ourselves. Not that we put all the details into the order that we issued on Kirk's level, but we kept those details either in Kirk's order or in the order that Hall and Moon put out as soon as they got our order. In other words, the landing of the American troops was entirely an American operation. But there was no argument in our minds, and we never tried to indicate to the contrary but what we would carry out any order that Admiral Ramsay sent to us.

Now, Admiral Ramsay wanted us to join up with him and so forth. Then there wouldn't have been an American record, and there wouldn't have been American responsibility if that thing had gone sour. One of the things that I felt very strongly was that we had to be in a position where we had had the power to control the American landing and therefore, subject to broad command from above. Then if anything happened, we had to face it; it was our responsibility.

John T. Mason, Jr.: This must have met with King's approval.

Admiral Struble: I'm sure it did. I'm sure that Ernie thought that was the way it should be done. Now, he had never told me that before. That's the way I had felt, and I had felt it very strongly. Now, the English approach would have been different. Of course, Admiral Ramsay was a very fine man. It was very difficult for Kirk to try to promote this idea to Ramsay, because he had known him well and they were very good friends and it was very difficult for him to promote it. As a matter of fact, I found it difficult to promote myself, but it was finally Admiral Ramsay's chief of staff and I that had the final meeting when the decision was reached. I'm sure that Admiral Ramsay was a little unhappy about it.

John T. Mason, Jr.: Tell me—you say there was some thought as to the need for this additional American naval command in the English Channel.

Admiral Struble: Well, very obviously Admiral King had felt the need of an additional naval command and had designated Kirk to be the man who would have the command. When I was asked if I would go over to London as chief of staff for this job, I was willing to go because I thought that we were now establishing new command principles and everything of that sort in connection with amphibious landing. We had had a certain amount of amphibious experience and the more we knew about it and the better we could develop it the better. So I accepted the job to go to London for this purpose and felt very happy about it.

Now, if Admiral Kirk and I had joined Admiral Ramsay's staff, we would not have produced anything but some personal knowledge of our own about the handling of the invasion. However, if we put our American principles and ideas into the American part of the landing, still carrying out any instructions that Ramsay might issue to us of a naval character and carrying them out, we would have an American record of what we did at the Normandy landing and the decisions and methods of accomplishment would have been completely American. Our approach and that of the British were not always in complete agreement.

John T. Mason, Jr.: Given the reports on King's attitude, do you feel that perhaps he felt more confident if there were an American naval commander over there in this particular operation?

Admiral Struble: I don't think it was a question of Admiral King's lacking any confidence in Admiral Ramsay. I think he felt that Admiral Ramsay was a fine man and everything, but I do think that he recognized that the British development of this particular type of business and our American development of it were different and, therefore, why not let each side accomplish their part of the picture in their own way? But there would be one naval commander who was in a position to issue the same order to Kirk that he issued to his own English admiral that was over at the post. And Ramsay had that authority. We would have carried out an order if we got it from Ramsay. Or, of course, as in any case, if a subordinate gets an order from a senior and there's something he thinks the senior ought to know, he can always send him a message and tell him so. It's not necessarily an objection to carrying out the order, but, "I'd like to be sure you know this and know that before we carry this order out." That's understood business everywhere.

You don't question the order of a senior, but if time is there and there is something that you think he ought to know, you could always send him a message.

John T. Mason, Jr.: I have another question, sir. Inasmuch as you and Kirk gained a great deal of experience in this operation, why did Admiral King not send Kirk to a billet in the Pacific? I know Kirk wanted one. Why did he not send him?

Admiral Struble: I have no reason to believe that Kirk was dissatisfied with the job that he got in Europe myself.

John T. Mason, Jr.: This is going to be out of sequence because this is an incident that occurred when you were the head of the Central Division.

Admiral Struble: You know, in this business of the Central Division, I often would be designated by Admiral King or maybe somebody else in the Navy Department to go over and testify before a committee of Congress on some specific question that had come up. Those testimonies, of course, were very important, because generally they involved highly secret matters at the moment, operational Navy matters. It was very important that detailed information concerning the subject not leak in any way. The subject on this matter was the submarine sinkings off Florida and in the Atlantic and what could be done about improving the matter and therefore the expenditure of funds by Congress.

I went over to this committee. The chairman was, I believe, Senator David I. Walsh, a very fine gentleman.* We had had sinkings off the Florida coast. We had submarine sinkings in the Atlantic, and we were engaged in a very tough operational problem to handle this. So I testified, gave a broad situation, indicated that we needed more money very much. However, due to the fact that the submarine menace was so touchy, I did not want to go into a lot of figures on how many ships had been sunk and of this sort of data.

The committee was quite quiet, and the chairman quite thoughtful for a few minutes. Then he said, "Now, Captain, of course we have to make a vote on this matter, and this is important from our point of view. Can't you give us some intimation of how serious this problem is in practical terms so that we can have a good reason for voting?"

I realized that that was certainly reasonable and proper, so I said, "Well, let me give you one statement which I will give you a fact and let that fact exercise your judgment in the matter and I'll guarantee that it is a fact. My statement is that we have lost off the Florida coast over 500,000 tons of shipping in one month."

The chairman thought it over carefully and accepted that for the committee and no further large amount of figures or discussion of the submarine problem had to go on.

John T. Mason, Jr.: You didn't say what month this had happened.

---

* David I. Walsh (Democrat-Massachusetts) was chairman of the Senate Naval Affairs Committee.

Admiral Struble: I didn't say what month it had happened, but I said, "has happened in one month recently." I may have put "recently" in.

John T. Mason, Jr.: I wonder if you'd give me the preliminaries to that story, because they have a bearing on the way Admiral King approached things.

Admiral Struble: He was doing one whale of a job with the submarines, and he was entirely right in trying to keep it secret. But somebody had to face the fact, who was going to testify on how much latitude are they going to be given? It was only by getting the facts that I could reach a conclusion that maybe one juicy fact, and this was the fact that was the better one for us to talk about—we didn't want to talk about what was happening in the Atlantic at that particular moment. We were having problems. So my statement, which was accurate, indicated to them that it was serious, and the members of the committee decided they could accept my statement that it was serious. That is the important fact.

John T. Mason, Jr.: The fact that you had to go and testify and testify in terms of a problem which was highly classified at the time says something about Admiral King's attitude toward publicity of naval operations. Do you want to say something about that?

Admiral Struble: Well, of course, Ernie was always very tough on unnecessary publicity about our operations, which any military man should be, particularly under war conditions. Some little tiny statement that doesn't appear to mean much, if overheard by somebody who shouldn't know about it, boy, it might give them inkling and a valuable bit of information goes to the other side that they shouldn't get. It's very obvious that under war conditions we had not only a problem off the Florida coast, but we had it also out in the center of the Atlantic temporarily. We were commencing to lick it, but the figures were large, and a long listing of them would have been terrible.

The more I talked, the more danger there was of more leaking. I said one thing. I think the committee appreciated it; the chairman certainly did. He said, "We'll do it, and we won't ask any more questions."

John T. Mason, Jr.: The Navy eventually had to loosen up a bit on its policies of revealing facts, did it not, because the Air Force in particular was so vocal about its accomplishments and the Navy was being obscured?

Admiral Struble: There was no doubt at times that what one service does can embarrass the other services. And I'm sure that that happened. However, I do think that in the case of the submarine sinkings at that particular moment it was desirable that it not become public knowledge that we were having one hell of a hard time, because it would just confirm to the Germans how successful they were being. They didn't necessarily know that they were as successful as we knew. No, they didn't necessarily know that. Why tell them?

Interview Number 6 with Admiral Arthur D. Struble, U.S. Navy (Retired)
Place: Admiral Struble's Home, Chevy Chase, Maryland
Date: Friday, 10 December 1976
Interviewer: John T. Mason, Jr.

John T. Mason, Jr.: Well, sir, we've had quite a hiatus in this series. I'm delighted that we are back again now and am looking forward to this most exciting story of the liberation of the Philippines. You had been with Admiral Kirk at the Normandy landing, and you returned to the States, I believe, in July of that year, '44. Do you want to take up the story from that point?

Admiral Struble: All right. I returned to Washington after the Normandy landing with Admiral Kirk. We flew back. We reported to Admiral King, and I thought I was going to get a couple of weeks' leave. But King had asked me why I hadn't stayed on over in Europe. I had been offered the post of chief of staff over there after the landing, but I had said no, I wanted to get command of something. I thought I would like to go out to the Pacific if I could.

John T. Mason, Jr.: And you were in a position to ask.

Admiral Struble: So I was told, "Well, you'll probably get a couple of weeks off then." I came back to the Navy Department the next morning and was met in the hallway. They said, "Admiral King wants to see you." Of course, I went up there right away, and I found out that rather than having two weeks' leave I was to leave Washington by air that afternoon to go out to the Pacific.

So I left Washington in a hurry, much to my wife's disgust.

John T. Mason, Jr.: I would think so.

Admiral Struble: I went out through Honolulu and flew down to Hollandia, which had been taken.* General MacArthur was moving in with his headquarters there temporarily, and Admiral Barbey was located there.†

John T. Mason, Jr.: Before you left Washington did you have some concept of what you were going to be asked to do?

Admiral Struble: I was told that I would get an amphibious command when I got out there. So I reported in to Admiral Barbey, who was the amphibious commander under General MacArthur.

John T. Mason, Jr.: Was the trip out very strenuous?

Admiral Struble: No, it was very pleasant and comfortable. The only problem we had was that as we got down in the Hollandia area, we had quite a bad storm and we had a bad half hour or 20 minutes maybe approaching that area because of the bad weather. The airplane had a pretty tough landing.

So then I reported to Barbey. At that time I became the third, I believe, of the rear admirals that Barbey had under his command who weren't in command of any particular ships or anything but whom he would appoint to take command of a specific landing.

John T. Mason, Jr.: Bill Fechteler was one of them, was he not?‡

Admiral Struble: Bill Fechteler was on one them. He had been out there; he was an experienced one. I then became one of those people who were available.

My first real command was the Leyte operation. When I first arrived out there, Barbey had told me that I would make the first landing in the Philippines. We thought at that time we would land on the island just south of Leyte, at the southern end, and work

---

* Allied forces had invaded Hollandia, New Guinea, in April 1944.
† General Douglas MacArthur, USA, Commander Southwest Pacific Force; Rear Admiral Daniel E. Barbey, USN. Barbey later wrote the book MacArthur's Amphibious Navy: Seventh Amphibious Force Operations, 1943-45 (Annapolis: U.S. Naval Institute, 1969).
‡ Rear Admiral William M. Fechteler, USN, later Chief of Naval Operations, 1951-53.

our way up through it slowly and then on through Leyte. But as time went on, MacArthur and Barbey decided that we could skip this southern landing and go right directly into Leyte.

John T. Mason, Jr.: What was their decision based on?

Admiral Struble: It was based on MacArthur's information out of the Philippines. You realize that a lot of the Filipinos were still very loyal to us, and we were getting some information out of the Philippines. So MacArthur was getting some information that he considered pretty sound and solid that, yes, there was something on Leyte, some troops, but it wasn't much and it would probably be knocked over. Going directly into Leyte advanced us maybe six weeks at least.

John T. Mason, Jr.: Yes. There were a number of Americans involved with guerrilla forces on the various islands, were there not?

Admiral Struble: That's true.

John T. Mason, Jr.: And MacArthur was in communication with them?

Admiral Struble: Yes. I'm not sure myself that his communication channel was with them or whether he also had maybe faster and better communication with some of the Filipinos. Maybe he had both. I think he had both.

John T. Mason, Jr.: And the various landings down south had been pretty successful, hadn't they, without too much opposition?

Admiral Struble: You mean the island hopping.

John T. Mason, Jr.: Yes.

Admiral Struble: There were one or two of those that were pretty bad. There was some pretty tough stuff there, as I remember, say, about three months earlier. While we were definitely making our way up all the time, we really had one or two heavy stops on the way north that were not at all easy.

The Japs were really fighting very tough. They had commenced to be very tough.

John T. Mason, Jr.: It was a last-stand sort of thing.

Admiral Struble: Yes. And each one became the last stand as we went north. Now, Leyte was a big island. The southern half had practically nothing on it, but in the middle part, which would have been the place, of course, where you would land, there was a fair amount of Japanese opposition. They did not think that we would come in there, although they knew we might. They weren't sure we would. But they didn't have too large a force. MacArthur was putting everything he had in that one landing. He thought he had enough, and he did definitely have enough.

Of course, Commander in Chief Pacific, Nimitz, sent down quite a bit of extra help for the landing on Leyte, and we had a pretty good force there to make a landing.

John T. Mason, Jr.: When did you begin your planning for the Leyte operations?

Admiral Struble: I would say about six weeks earlier, when we were still at that time planning on going in the islands to the south of Leyte. Then about two weeks after I had been planning that way, Fechteler was already working towards that island and had made a few small landings to the westward of Hollandia, just working their way up toward Leyte. So I was then planning on taking a small force up to Leyte a day or two before the landing and being sure that the entrance to Leyte Gulf was clear and to see if the Japs were in control of any of the islands at the entrance to Leyte Gulf. If they were, we needed to find out so that we could be sure to knock them out as we tried to take this large force of ships, which would just be merchant ships full of Army men, up and land them on Leyte.

John T. Mason, Jr.: Where were you doing your planning? Where was your base?

Admiral Struble: We had one ship that Fechteler and I and at times other admirals used as a hotel, you might say, a base of operations.

John T. Mason, Jr.: What was the ship?

Admiral Struble: The Blue Ridge.*

John T. Mason, Jr.: And this was an amphibious command ship.

Admiral Struble: Yes, she was a merchant ship fitted out to take a number of people and had good communications. She was not in any way what you would call a combatant ship.

John T. Mason, Jr.: What kind of staff did you have for planning?

Admiral Struble: I had a chief of staff and I would say about six to eight officers.

John T. Mason, Jr.: Skilled planners they were?

Admiral Struble: Well, the chief of staff was excellent; the number-one planner was very good, and a couple of the other lieutenants were quite capable.

John T. Mason, Jr.: When I said that, I was thinking perhaps they had had experience in the island hopping prior to that.

Admiral Struble: That's right. The chief of staff and I had not had any experience in the island hopping. I selected my own chief of staff and had him ordered to my staff, so he

---

* USS Blue Ridge (AGC-2) was commissioned 27 September 1943. She had a standard displacement of 7,431 tons, was 459 feet long, and 63 feet in the beam. She had a top speed of 16.4 knots and was armed with two 5-inch guns.

and I were not experienced. But the planners had been through a certain amount of the island hopping, so they were pretty familiar with the way they would advance north. They were familiar with working with the army and so forth.

John T. Mason, Jr.: And all the details that were required for a particular plan.

Admiral Struble: Well, yes, they were what I would call fairly experienced, pretty good youngsters. Some of them were regular Navy and some weren't.

John T. Mason, Jr.: This is when you began to set up the task force for Dinagat?

Admiral Struble: That's right. The original conception came after we had word that there were Japanese on the south side of the entrance. Dinagat is a little tiny spot on the south side of the entrance to Leyte Gulf.

John T. Mason, Jr.: A little island?

Admiral Struble: No. You see, Leyte is a great, big long island. On the eastern flank is the entrance. This is Leyte Island, and here's the big part of Leyte Island and here's one thing coming out this way and here's another thing coming out that way next to the entrance of this very large and imposing gulf. Now, on the southern part of that was Dinagat. The northern part was over like this, and the lighthouse was over here. There were no signs of troops or anything on the north side of the entrance, but there were signs of Japs on the south side of the entrance.

So I went up two days in advance of everybody else. I landed troops at Dinagat and took over that southern part of the entrance to Leyte Gulf. We had control of it, in other words. The Japs that were there were maybe as many as 50. The moment our force landed there and came after them, the Japs beat it and got out of the way. So there was no doubt about the fact that the entrance was going to be all right for the big outfit that was to arrive. I went in early one morning, and they were due about midday two days later.

John T. Mason, Jr.: Was there any minesweeping operations? Was that required?

Admiral Struble: There was with me, but not really under my command, a fairly good-sized minesweeping force. Temporarily, as we went up the Leyte Gulf, I was the officer in tactical command of my force and the mine force. But as soon as we got to the entrance to the gulf, I became more of an independent commander. I took over the south side of the entrance and started to investigate and be sure that the Japs couldn't interrupt the landing.

In the meantime, the minesweeping force had sailed from Hollandia two days ahead of me. I overtook them about a day out of Leyte and went in ahead of them. But as soon as we got to the entrance of the gulf, the minesweeper man came in and turned north as we were landing about five or ten miles at least, maybe 15 miles north of the entrance was where we were going to land.

So the minesweeper man turned north and started doing his minesweeping.

John T. Mason, Jr.: Were there any mines of any consequences?

Admiral Struble: They did get rid of a certain small number of mines, some that they swept and one or two that they didn't sweep. We had no mining problem; they handled the problem very satisfactorily.

Then the second morning was when the whole outfit came in about 4:00 or 5:00 o'clock in the morning, before daylight, and started up for the beach. By this time the minesweepers had gotten up that far, and they had eliminated most of the mines that were in the main track of the thing. I think one mine was discovered by one of the ships coming in and shot up itself. We had no mining problem.

John T. Mason, Jr.: Was the weather a factor at all in landing?

Admiral Struble: No, the weather was almost perfect. It really was fine. In the meantime, after I had landed my small force of Army men on this little point to the south,

I started cruising around the gulf a little. I had, as I remember, one or two single airplane attacks on me. Now those single airplane attacks must have come from Cebu, which is the next island over to the westward where the Japs had quite a bit of aviation. Those two individual attacks dropped bombs which didn't hit me.

John T. Mason, Jr.: They weren't kamikazes?

Admiral Struble: They were not kamikazes. They were just airplanes with the bombs.

John T. Mason, Jr.: What kind of coverage did General Kenney supply for your operation?[*]

Admiral Struble: We had no aviation from Kenney at that time. We were far too far away. We had to establish our airfield at Leyte, and then we commenced to have aviation. But the distance was much too far from him because we had avoided going to this southern island which would have been a jump before going to Leyte had we not eliminated it. I think MacArthur and Kinkaid were both very smart in agreeing to avoid the pass by the southern island and go right into Leyte.[†] That was really a very excellent decision.

John T. Mason, Jr.: So you were cruising around in Leyte Gulf.

Admiral Struble: Cruising around in Leyte Gulf. I had about 40 to 60 troops at the south side of the entrance.

John T. Mason, Jr.: How many ships did you have?

Admiral Struble: One.

---

[*] Lieutenant General George C. Kenney, USA, Commander Far East Air Forces.
[†] Vice Admiral Thomas C. Kinkaid, USN, Commander Seventh Fleet. Kinkaid was commander of the naval component of General MacArthur's forces.

John T. Mason, Jr.: Oh, you were without escort.

Admiral Struble: I was just a single ship.

John T. Mason, Jr.: What was your flagship?

Admiral Struble: I ought to remember that.*

John T. Mason, Jr.: You were cruising around in your flagship of the moment, and what was your purpose? Were you trying to entice Japanese to come out, or were you spotting or what?

Admiral Struble: I was trying to keep an eye, if I could, on the Dinagat force so that if by any chance any problems developed I could go down there and render help. Also seeing if I could get any information that would be useful to the incoming ships to let them know that things looked helpful.

When this one individual airplane came over and tried to drop a bomb on me, of course, that made me think. Instead of going farther up into Leyte Gulf at that time, I turned and came back toward where the Dinagat force was to be sure that a big air attack didn't start to develop on them or whatever it might turn out to be. And by the way, I did not have any more air attacks on me like that first one. I did see one other airplane.

John T. Mason, Jr.: Why was this? Were they unprepared for these landing forces at this particular time?

Admiral Struble: I don't think they expected the landing at Leyte. I don't think they had anticipated it at all. I think they felt sure we would land on the southern island as we had originally planned. I think they were getting ready to receive us down south and by bypassing it—

---

* Struble's flagship was the destroyer Hughes (DD-410).

John T. Mason, Jr.: They just couldn't adjust.

Admiral Struble: Well, my God, it would take a long time to bring their troops and forces from the southern islands up to Leyte. That was really a very fine decision that MacArthur and Kinkaid made.

Now, speaking in those terms, as I cruised around I ran into a small boat, a little sailboard effect, with about two or three Filipinos in it. So we went alongside of it and wanted to know what the hell they were doing and what was going on. I asked them first about the southern part of Leyte, in other words, south of where we intended to land. In the southern part there was a narrow neck, and we were wondering whether or not there were Japs there. There had been Japs there. In other words, would we have to block off this force that was south of where we were landing while we made our landing on Leyte.

These people told me no, that the Japs had generally left the island of Leyte. But, of course, when the big force came in behind me, I was then to take over command of a small segment of the main force that went up to the north into Leyte Gulf, let's say 20 miles, and landed. I was to take this small force south to this narrow spot that I talked about and to take care of the Japs that were there.

So I sent word back that it appeared that there was going to be little opposition at the southern landing. On the other hand, I didn't recommend that we shouldn't make it because of course this kind of information isn't always complete. But actually the Japs had withdrawn from the southern part so there was no need for me to take troops down and land them.

It was still dark when they came in the gulf. The big force went north. A couple of transports full of troops turned south with me, and I went down and landed them the next morning at this narrow spot.

John T. Mason, Jr.: Now this is what Morison refers to as your Palawan attack group?[*]

---

[*] Samuel Eliot Morison, whose Leyte is the 12th volume of his History of United States Naval Operations in World War II.

Admiral Struble: Yes, that's right. That was that attack group. Now, that was what I would call an abortive effort. We got down there and landed the troops promptly under gunfire. They marched ashore and didn't find anything. So the enemy had been removed from that area. Of course, that happens.

John T. Mason, Jr.: How did your troops react under circumstances like that, when they found no enemy?

Admiral Struble: Well, they all laughed. They all were amused. I think the men kind of said like something like this, "Say, the big boys made a mistake on that." I think the men were not critical, you know, but just were laughing, appreciating. So I landed them, and then I reported they didn't have anything there. Then we embarked them and took them back and put them on the tail end of the main landing.

John T. Mason, Jr.: Well, now the next thing you did, you were present at Tacloban, were you not, on October 20? That was when MacArthur arrived.

Admiral Struble: Oh, yes, sure.

John T. Mason, Jr.: That's an historic moment. Where were you at that point? Were you coming in with MacArthur's party?

Admiral Struble: No. That was that same morning that this happened up north of me. It was the morning that I had taken this force and landed it down south and we had run into no opposition. Of course, once you had made the landing and landed a lot of troops, two or three or four hours or so they had scouted around and hadn't found anything. Then the Army commander sent me word and said, "Hell, there doesn't seem to be anybody around here anyplace, any opposition or anything."

So then I communicated with Barbey and told him I didn't think we had anything down there at all and recommended that I re-embark the troops and bring them north, which I did. About the time I had gotten those troops back up to where the main landing had occurred, I imagine that the MacArthur incident, if you call it that, was probably over. I wasn't there and didn't see it.

John T. Mason, Jr.: I see. Then having brought your troops back up north again, were you free to go on planning for Mindoro or what?

Admiral Struble: Oh, no. I suppose an amphibious operation of the magnitude of this initial landing would be such that it would take at least two or three days for you to get everything organized. You would not send back any of your combatant ships during that period or send them elsewhere. But as the merchant ship types, for instance those that had brought troops and emptied them all, and those that had brought up supplies and they had been emptied—those type of ships would be sent back out of Leyte Gulf, back to Hollandia to be back at the source of supply where they could get reloaded and come back again.

So I would say the day after the initial landing, all of the troopships had been unloaded. I had gone through this thing to the south and had brought the troopships back up to the main landing because we weren't going to leave them down there. That next day then I was told to proceed back to Hollandia. Now, this is the day after. I was in command and convoyed a few little ships like my own, taking that big force of 50 transports and a certain amount of the empty cargo ships back to Hollandia.

John T. Mason, Jr.: Was there danger in a convoy operation of that sort? Were units of the Japanese troops stationed in the southern Philippines?

Admiral Struble: There is always a little danger. That was the reason we had a flag officer like myself take that outfit back. Barbey and Fechteler and Berkey were all remaining in Leyte, and I was to take this first big group of troopships and everything back to Hollandia to get ready for the next operation.[*]

John T. Mason, Jr.: Which was at that point intended to be Mindoro.

---

[*] Rear Admiral Russell S. Berkey, USN.

Admiral Struble: That was the idea. I had been told that I would make the Mindoro landing as Barbey and Fechteler had been the two primarily that had made the Leyte landing. So as soon as I got back to Hollandia, I started planning the idea of the trip out to the west to Mindoro.

John T. Mason, Jr.: Did you anticipate that Mindoro would be a very hazardous operation?

Admiral Struble: At first it looked very, very hazardous because we were going such a long distance ahead of ourselves.

John T. Mason, Jr.: That was 250 miles beyond Leyte.

Admiral Struble: Oh, it was more than that. It took me two and a half days to get over there. That's 60 hours. It must have been darned near 600 miles. Of course, when I made the attack, I had a very slow outfit because we had all these ships with it, an awful lot of merchant supply ships with us because the biggest thing we wanted to do was get ashore in Mindoro and install a new, big airfield. You had to have an awful lot of ships to take the airfield equipment and everything.

So I suppose we only made about ten knots speed on the Mindoro trip.

John T. Mason, Jr.: Somewhere very shortly the plans were interrupted, because you had to be taken off the Mindoro planning and focus on the Ormoc.*

Admiral Struble: I think I'll try to express it to you this way. I got the outfit back down, and I started the Mindoro planning. We realized that we were making a very large advance into what might be called enemy country. It was only partially enemy country,

---

* On 7 December 1944, the 77th Infantry Division, commanded by Major General A. D. Bruce, USA, landed unopposed about three miles south of the port of Ormoc on the island of Leyte in the Philippines. Ormoc was secured by U.S. forces on 10 December. The amphibious commander was Rear Admiral Struble, Commander Task Group 78.3, embarked in the destroyer <u>Hughes</u>.

though, because locally the natives weren't unfriendly. It was only the Japs that were unfriendly to us in this large area. On the whole, the Filipinos were all on our side. So it wasn't as if we were going into an area that was completely antagonistic to us. The local people weren't going to be antagonistic to us, but the Japs that were there were.

John T. Mason, Jr.: And the local people could be very helpful if they were on your side, could they not?

Admiral Struble: Not initially. Not until they realized that you had gotten in there and were established. They couldn't afford to show their colors too quick. I mean they couldn't. Hell, the local Japs would have watched them.

John T. Mason, Jr.: Self-preservation.

Admiral Struble: Self-preservation. They were very sympathetic and they were for us, but we had to get there in force and get established a little bit before you could expect them to unbend and entirely support us. But in my experience, the Filipinos—boy, as soon as we landed, they were hollering and yelling and were right with you. As soon as they realized you were there in force with armed troops and meant business, then they were immediately on your side. They couldn't afford to uncover their feelings too quickly.

Well, then about three weeks later, I guess, Barbey had already returned to Hollandia. Fechteler had been left in Leyte as Barbey's representative and in command, let's say, of the naval force that were operating in Leyte Gulf. Ashore there was a lieutenant general commanding a big army. He was, of course, really the senior officer present on Leyte, and he was fighting the Japanese. He had taken over the central part of Leyte, but this northwestern part was uphill, fairly rough, tremendously full of trees, a perfect defense spot for an outfit that was willing to fight to the bitter end.

If those people ashore were determined to fight hard, they had a very strong defensive position. It was uphill to go after them; it was heavily wooded. Ten men could hold back almost 100. It was a strong defensive position. The Japanese recognized it, that they could bring in ammunition and supplies to it from the other side.

John T. Mason, Jr.: From their own bases.

Admiral Struble: From their own bases to the westward, and they had them over in Cebu and everything so they were able to keep their defense force in northwestern Leyte supplied. Our Army, which was much stronger, just was held back. It was too strong a defensive position. You couldn't just rush in and try to capture it. Boy, you'd lose 10 or 20 men to one in the fight. The fighting was too expensive.

The Army general, I think, was excellent. I was very fond of him. He was a fine man. Then at the end of about three weeks, Fechteler, who had been handling matters, was called back to Hollandia to get ready for what was going to be his next job. And Barbey sent me up to Leyte to take over the job of being his representative there and the senior Navy man in Leyte.

In the meantime I would continue my plans for Mindoro. I could plan for Mindoro just as well up there as I could down at Hollandia. So that became my job, I would say, about three or four weeks after the initial Leyte landing and Fechteler went back then to Hollandia. Of course, as soon as Fechteler left, then I became the naval officer that would go ashore every couple of days and talk to the general's headquarters people and quite probably also talk to the general, keeping up a constant liaison between the forces on the water and the ones ashore. I know I was very impressed with the general's argument on why we ought to get out to Mindoro. I thought it was very sound and excellent. It might be a little risky, but it was a very sound, excellent approach, and bypass all these islands and places in between. If we let ourselves get bogged down trying to attack and take each little island individually between Leyte and Manila, hell, we'd find ourselves with months and months of fighting and work.

John T. Mason, Jr.: That was the same thesis that prevailed down below, wasn't it, when you were coming up from Hollandia?

Admiral Struble: That's right.

John T. Mason, Jr.: You skipped some of those.

Admiral Struble: That's right. We had made a skip coming up. Now the question came up, were we going to be willing to risk and take a bigger skip.

John T. Mason, Jr.: And who blocked it?

Admiral Struble: I won't say that anybody blocked it, but I would say people like myself—and I don't know quite how Kinkaid would express it and I don't know that Bill Fechteler ever commented on it, except I know when Bill asked me what I thought about it I told him. He said, "I agree." He said, "You ought to get all the help you can in that operation." He said, "I tell you one thing, if you want to help, you've got to fight for it." But we didn't have a lot of stuff, I mean, by the time—

John T. Mason, Jr.: You have to be pretty aggressive and go out and get it.

Admiral Struble: By the time we went into Mindoro, we had a much changed position. A large number of ships and forces had been sent down from the Central Pacific that had not been there before. So at this time when we were initially planning Mindoro and going over, we were trying to do it with what we had and it was a rather small force. So I think there was some justification for those of us who were planning on going to Mindoro and who said, yes, let's go, for us trying to put up a fight for more stuff with which to do it.

In any event, I took over then for Bill Fechteler, and it was kind of interesting because the senior officer up at Leyte Gulf had small problems all the time connected with the ships. There would be some sort of trouble over in the northeast of another island. We were on a kind of broad part of the island that kind of swung around like this—there would be problems over there. He'd have to send small ships and maybe a small force of Army to handle it. That kind of stuff was going on at the same time that we were planning Mindoro. I always said that Mindoro was sound and we ought to try to do it. But I also thought about it, to get a little more aviation help. This was the hardest help to get. I don't mean that the Army Air Force wasn't willing to do all it could. But they would say, "Oh, sure, we'll support you all we can." But they would never list exactly what it was going to be. So we were always pounding—are we going to have a big force out there or aren't we?

John T. Mason, Jr.: They were stretched pretty thin, weren't they?

Admiral Struble: They were stretched pretty thin, and in lots of ways, as I review it now myself, I realize that, by God, they couldn't guarantee much more than they did in the earlier days. Now, of course, once we got established on Mindoro and had an airfield there, then we could afford to leave all these little islands behind us where the Japs temporarily had forces. We could just afford to leave them and let them die on the vine. We didn't have to really go in and fight them to clear them out. Then we could fight in our own way at our own leisure.

Well, to go on, about two weeks before Mindoro Kinkaid and MacArthur both came back up to Leyte. I think MacArthur had been there. I don't know but what he had gone back to Leyte. I guess I had better express it the other way. I think maybe MacArthur had gone back for a trip to Hollandia but had come right back. But Kinkaid had remained down in Hollandia and had come up to Leyte about ten days, maybe a week before the Mindoro operation. We had a chance to have a good get-together in talk and discussion. At the final meeting, I had made my plea for a little more Army aviation out at Mindoro.

At the time, we didn't know—at least I didn't know—whether Kinkaid had some knowledge that it might happen. I hadn't had a chance to talk to Kinkaid before we had this joint meeting, and I don't think he knew at that time necessarily that we were going to get these forces from the Central Pacific. If so and he wasn't sure of it, why, I don't blame him for not discussing it. I mean, there was no good talking about the idea that maybe we'd get more.

But we all agreed that we ought to go ahead with the Mindoro operation. The new thing that came up was the general who was on Leyte Island—it was his desire to have a force move around to the western side of Leyte, which would mean that Cebu and the Jap air base and so forth was that much closer to you. That would give the Jap air base at Cebu an excellent chance to bombard the hell out of this little force that went around there.

Now, I say the little force that went around because it wasn't useful from the standpoint of what we were going to do, land troops. It was impractical to send any big ships around there due to the waters and everything concerned it had to be small ships. Therefore, you were limited almost to destroyers going around with you. As a matter of fact, that was the force that I had—a force of destroyers and small landing craft. We couldn't afford to take any of the big landing craft around there because they couldn't get in close. It wasn't a place where you could land troops from them.

John T. Mason, Jr.: Yes, and you're focusing now at Ormoc.

Admiral Struble: I'm focusing now in terms of Ormoc while we are still at Leyte. Now, I supported the general in his desire. I supported him very strongly because I could see it could be a very good land operation for them, to land troops behind the center of the Japanese strong point. I could see from the Army point of view it was going to be excellent for them. This strong point, if they continued to put men up the hills they were just going to lose them and it was going to be a terrible, dismal, long drawn-out and expensive thing for us. If we could land a force in the center of that Japanese group behind them, we could advance on them with more open ground and we could at least stop reinforcements coming into the Japanese. Then, being behind them, we could give them hell. We could give them hell instead. We wouldn't advance up the other side; we would advance from the westward. So I was in favor of doing it. Kinkaid said, "Well, all right. If you want to do it and you can do it, go ahead and do it. But we want you to go to Mindoro four days later."

That was all right. I didn't mind that. Mindoro was all planned, and the cruiser that was going to be my flagship to go to Mindoro had arrived. I had just moved on board it when they decided to make Ormoc landing. So I took a few of my staff and I went to a destroyer and we sneaked out of Leyte Gulf one evening and went way up south. We had to sneak out of Leyte Gulf and go way south to the tip of Leyte Island, turn to the west, and then almost immediately turn back and come way north. Leyte is a kind of long, very narrow island. So then we'd have to come back north. I had already planned the operation, and I arranged to go around down here about 7:00 o'clock at night, dark, so that when I turned north we would go up north to where we were going to land, Cebu being over here now—the Jap airfield. I wanted to turn into the gulf after dark so that if possible they would not have seen us turn north. As long as I was going south, they might well think we were going down to capture the south island. Even if they did happen to see us go south, which we had to do in daylight because we had to go slow. We were only making about eight or ten knots, a very slow convoy. But we turned after dark and headed north.

John T. Mason, Jr.: Were there any navigation problems?

Admiral Struble: There was a pretty fair navigation problem because, of course, there were no lights or anything. We found out we could see fairly well. Actually I had decided myself that with very careful safe navigation I would be willing to take a chance and do it at night, which, of course, added some problems.

John T. Mason, Jr.: How many troops were you shepherding?

Admiral Struble: I suppose 2,000, maybe a little more.

John T. Mason, Jr.: With supplies and everything.

Admiral Struble: Oh, yes, we had to give them supplies. Of course, it was inherent in this problem that we were going to have to keep this little supply line open to keep them going with ammunition and food and so forth. But we were headed north, a dark night, and I was in the flagship leading because I knew that I wanted to have the navigation right in the ship with me that was leading the column. It was a dark night, but we could see just a little every now and then. We generally would see ashore one of the prominent elevated spots. We would usually get a chance to locate it roughly enough so that we could tell our navigation was working fairly good.

Along about 9:30 or 10:00 ten o'clock, I think I had gone down off the bridge below to my cabin for a moment and I got a report that they thought they had heard an airplane. So I went back up on the bridge and I said, "Where was it?" Well, it was over towards Cebu and it seemed to be going south. They could tell that it was going south. We were here going north, fairly close to the beach. I decided that was going to be the best way not to attract attention from Cebu.

John T. Mason, Jr.: And with darkened ships, I suppose.

Admiral Struble: Oh, with darkened ships, of course. So I was still up on the bridge about 20 minutes later when one of the boys aft reported, "We think we can hear the plane behind us." Sure enough, he had turned around. He came over and he located us. He was flying directly over this column of ships.

The captain of the ship said, "Well, shall we get ready to shoot him down?" Well, I thought it over. That was a kind of funny but interesting one. Yes, we might open fire and shoot him down at night. But, I tell you, it was a pretty questionable proposition—very iffy. If we tried to shoot him down and failed, it would be very evident that he would report to the Japs that there were armed forces moving north.

John T. Mason, Jr.: It certainly would reveal you, wouldn't it?

Admiral Struble: Well, it would reveal a certain amount of more information to them.

John T. Mason, Jr.: The capabilities.

Admiral Struble: I don't know how much of this thing the Jap had already seen in the dark and could report. I decided to take the view that maybe he didn't know how big we were, so I would just sit tight and do nothing. If they didn't think we were as big as we were, all the better for us.

John T. Mason, Jr.: You didn't know whether you had been really detected or not as a task force.

Admiral Struble: I felt pretty sure that they had detected us, but the question was whether they would realize how big the force was that was there. In other words, how much attention they should pay to it. If there were just a couple of ships sneaking up there, why, it didn't mean too much. In any event, the whole evening passed off very uneventfully, and we got up off Ormoc in the early morning.

Now, the problem of landing at Ormoc was based on the situation that there was apparently no good place to land troops in quantity ashore. Of course, we had to put a fairly good-sized lot of troops in there.

John T. Mason, Jr.: Does this imply the jungle came right down to the shore?

Admiral Struble: Very irregular. Here was a nice dry spot where you could land and go in at 20 feet. Then you ran into a lake and a lot of trees and all that kind of stuff—kind of a bad landing area. There were two spots where we thought we might make it, and with a little help and a few logs ready and on hand we could maybe fashion a little walkway or something to take the stuff over. It was not a beach, in other words.

John T. Mason, Jr.: Yes. How good was your intelligence of the area before you came there?

Admiral Struble: We had practically negative information. I kept asking for it from the Army Air Force and didn't get it. Of course, I had been hammering the hell out of them. But it wasn't their fault, I guess. They just weren't able to get the plane over there low enough down to take the pictures that would mean anything. However, the night before we sailed, we got a few pictures that were taken from quite low down. My staff by that time, by the way, had gotten bigger and I had some pretty good boys. They went over these pictures and everything very carefully. They decided there were two possibilities where we could maybe run troops. It would be single column for a certain amount of distance, but it would only be about maybe two or three blocks of bad going. Then they would get on a road in an open area that would be pretty good for fighting offensively like we wanted to fight. The boys that were doing that work finally said, "We think you have a pretty good chance at either one or the other." So that was the basis that I accepted and went in.

We got up there and landed early the next morning, 7:00 o'clock, and we put up the gunfire. We didn't know whether there were any troops anywhere around there, but we knew where they might be if there were. So we put up a pretty good amount of gunfire as we went in. It didn't hurt us; it might help us. We had no signs of any opposition.

John T. Mason, Jr.: But you obviously had been sighted.

Admiral Struble: We had been sighted the night before, yes. So that went off very well. We came to these two broken spots that we realized were going to be difficult They had found with American ingenuity that with a little [unclear] there and a little there and some poles—of course, we had that stuff kind of ready and available—we were able to make a pretty good approach situation and get quite a few troops assembled out on this road in a fairly short length of time. Once that happened, then I knew we had it. Once we could defend the road both north and south, we could bring more troops in.

However, there was not a good beach or anything like that, so the landing had to move slowly. It just inherently had to move slowly. Now, the destroyers that were protecting me were out to the westward, kind of in a big circle—steaming around slowly.

John T. Mason, Jr.: They were in a sense pickets, I suppose.

Admiral Struble: That's what they were, yes. Of course, all the ships we took on this operation were fairly small ships, because I had wanted to make the approach the way I did, close up to the beach, and it was desirable to have only small ships involved. Well, we didn't have any big ones, anyway.

So I guess it was about 9:30 in the morning, we had the landing well under way, and we were certainly in control locally. We had accomplished everything we wanted up until then, and there was no doubt that we would complete getting the troops and the supplies in. The destroyers were just kind of cruising out between us and Cebu.

All of a sudden we heard enemy airplanes coming. Now, of course, the destroyers undoubtedly sighted them already and they told us. I was more inshore to be sure the landing was going. I turned around, and I could see, as I remember, there were either three or four planes in column coming over toward this area where we were. We were landing here, and they were coming over like this. They turned around quickly and started down, still in column. I've forgotten whether there were three or four of them.

John T. Mason, Jr.: That was a strange technique, wasn't it?

Admiral Struble: Very strange to me. It showed that it wasn't too well planned and too well coordinated on their part. Before it came down, there was one of our big new destroyers, broadside to them, headed over towards Cebu like this, and they crashed into that ship—just deliberately came down and went right into the side of it, just above the waterline, one after the other.

John T. Mason, Jr.: Amazing.

Admiral Struble: In other words, three of these powerful planes with all the stuff in them were wasted on sinking one destroyer. They didn't actually sink it, but they raised sure hell with it.

John T. Mason, Jr.: Now, up to that point, you hadn't been introduced to kamikaze techniques, had you?*

Admiral Struble: No. No, this was my first experience. I had heard about it, but this was my first experience. This was the kamikaze business. It was, "We expect to die; this is the way we are going to do it."

Well, if there were four planes, the fourth plane kind of detached itself and went over here and got shot down or something; I don't remember. But there were three or four. The first three all went and made a hole in the side of this destroyer in the boiler room area, and then the other two followed directly behind them.

John T. Mason, Jr.: This was the Mahan, was it?

Admiral Struble: Yes, this was the Mahan. The Mahan—isn't that the ship that was named after the famous writer?†

John T. Mason, Jr.: Yes, after Admiral Mahan.

Admiral Struble: Well, that happened and that was the first attack force, and then it was all over. I thought, "Boy, is this all it's going to be? Or is this just the first one and are we going to get more?"

In the meantime, a couple of other destroyers had come over and gone alongside the Mahan and had taken off the captain and the crew. Of course, the question was very obvious—was the ship going to blow up any minute? You could never tell under those circumstances what damage has been done. If they had only spread out a little bit they would have blown it up. But as it was, they put her in very bad shape. The three planes were gone and the fourth one was also gone by this time. The crew had been saved to the man. There was maybe a minor casualty or two. The next day you find out the

---

* Kamikazes were Japanese suicide aircraft that began showing up in the Philippines campaign in the autumn of 1944. The pilots attempted to crash their bomb-armed aircraft directly into American warships. Hundreds of them successfully hit their targets and inflicted great damage.
† The destroyer Mahan (DD-364), named for author Alfred Thayer Mahan, was so badly damaged by the aircraft attacks on 7 December 1944 that she was soon sunk by U.S. gunfire and torpedoes.

preliminary report was a little too optimistic. But on the whole, all the crew were off the ship, and she was a hulk with great big holes on either side of her and everything. That was when I made the decision that we were going to have a slow, hard trip home. We were going to have air out of Cebu all day long because when the word got back there to Cebu—Cebu was only over about 60 miles. It was a short trip for an airplane. That was their air base around that area, and they would probably be able to get air from somewhere else too and it was going to get very interesting before it was over.

So I decided that I was not going to attempt to save this hulk and take it back to Leyte Gulf. We already had more hulks on our hands than we needed, and it was safer and better to sink her. I told the division commander to sink her. He came back at me with "What with?" I said, "One torpedo." So she was torpedoed and sunk. It was a glorious end in a way. She would have been just housekeeping, and we would have had all that hull problem with us. Somebody would have had to tow her back, and whoever had to tow her back was going to have a towline to her. If we had air attacks on the way back, it was going to get tied to a bum thing and there was my idea. So I sank her.

In the meantime, we got the troops all landed and everything was going fine. We started to try to reorganize and start back. As always happens in cases like that, certain things hadn't gotten off certain ships for one reason or another. I wanted to be sure that everything that we brought with us that was to go ashore, got ashore, because there was no telling how soon the boys that were there were going to get resupplied. So I suppose it was maybe as late as 10:30 when we slowly hauled out and started south and straggled out. And, boy, it was a straggle. All these little small ships and everything we had that had brought supplies and everything.

Now, the destroyers were in pretty good shape. They were still cruising around in column, smartly. Of course, they weren't going anywhere because this big column of small ships wasn't organized yet. It took us quite a while to get them organized and going south properly. I remember some of the incidents that even before we started south, one or two planes came over from Cebu, individually or maybe a pair.

John T. Mason, Jr.: More kamikazes?

Admiral Struble: No, they didn't kamikaze. No, after the original kamikaze stuff, we only had about two or three bursts of kamikazes thereafter that were small—if I can put it that way. A lot of the attacks were absolutely not kamikazes. Anyway, they were more or less like fairly good-sized planes that were bombers and would drop bombs. They weren't kamikazes.

John T. Mason, Jr.: They intended to get back home.

Admiral Struble: Yes. They were sent out with the idea that they would return. I knew that those kinds of planes could easily make three or four trips between now and the time that the thing would be over—the coming of the next darkness. In the first start off, we were a very disorderly mass. The ships, of course, had been all scattered accomplishing the operation, and we had a hell of a hard time. I didn't want to hold any of them back that were up ahead, and I didn't see any necessity or desirability of trying to put them into good military columns or anything. The thing to do was to get them all there and get them started home. We were trying to keep the front ships from not running out too fast and trying to get the other ships organized.

    I suppose it was 1:00 or 2:00 o'clock in the afternoon before we got into any reasonable type of organization, with the exception of the destroyers. The destroyers were the biggest things we had and the most military and their commander was able to put them in shape. They were on the flank toward Cebu. I was in a destroyer myself. I stayed with the small ships. I didn't take my destroyer to join up with the destroyer force because I didn't think it proved anything. As a matter of fact, I thought it was better for me to be over in the center of this big mess and see how it was getting along. I could see things and do things to get them going.

    So we cruised onward, southward, and I kept asking, "Where the hell is the air support?" Just kind of spiking the Army Air Force a bit.

John T. Mason, Jr.: What kind of replies did they send up?

Admiral Struble: They never sent me any messages. They said, "Oh, things are going not too good, but it will be better." Something like that. I guess it was about 3:30 that I'll pick up the story.

We hadn't had an attack for a certain amount of time. We had gotten the ships pretty well organized. They were going along pretty well together, and the destroyers were over on the flank towards Cebu. All of a sudden, a pretty damned big attack was on, a pretty well organized attack.

Now, there were a couple of kamikazes in that. I was in my flagship, in a destroyer in the mess of small ships. The destroyer division was over as a pretty good unit about, I suppose, a half a mile away from me. A kamikaze came in and very definitely had decided that I was the flagship, I guess, because she was very definitely headed for me. I went down to the captain from the flag bridge and I said, "Well, keep moving and keep turning.* It looks like he's after you. He's coming down." The captain handled her very skillfully. I have forgotten whether she touched us just slightly—I think she did. I think she tried to graze the after part of the ship as she came down. But she didn't get us. Of course, then she hit the water and she was gone. She was gone and sunk, and I thought the captain handled her very well. He put a turn on her and then the kamikaze kept turning on us. As he got down right close, the captain gave her a harder turn and I guess put on more speed—probably put on full speed and had the engine room all set. We made a turn and pushed away this way. She hit the water close to us, hit us, but we got out of that one. And he was, of course, gone then. He had hit the water by that time, and he couldn't get back up.

Now, in the meantime, there had been maybe as many as two or three or maybe a few more kamikazes in that particular afternoon attack. At the same time, there were also a number of bombers of a different type of craft that were dropping bombs at us. I suppose that it was about the time that some of the bombing had developed that the Air Force showed up in force. I must say their fighters when they did come in went right after them.

Down where I was, I never got a report on it. I never knew what the hell happened, but I believe that the Army Air Force probably got a number of the Jap planes.

---

* The commanding officer of the <u>Hughes</u> was Commander Ellis B. Rittenhouse, USN.

They certainly did go after them. That was clear. You'd stand there and you'd see one dogfight going on. Well, that's all you saw, you were watching that, you see. I thought the Army Air Force when they did come in did beautifully, fine. They broke it up, and we had no more attacks that day.

Pretty soon, about the time we were at the southern tip of the island, it got dark, and then we were on our way home. We got in early the next morning.

John T. Mason, Jr.: You must have breathed a deep sigh of relief.

Admiral Struble: Well, it was. We had had quite a few kamikazes—the afternoon attack, I don't know, I can't tell you. Here's what happened. You realize I had planned and was going to go to Mindoro. I had a cruiser waiting for me in Leyte that my clothes were on and everything else and I was going on to Mindoro. Of course, after this day was over and we were on our way home, I went down to take a sleep. I got up the next morning and we were in Leyte. I got packed to go over to the other flagship to start talking Mindoro, and I don't know whether if any or very much of a report of that action ever went in.* I doubt very much that my report on the thing amounted to anything.

Well, boy, when this was over, I immediately was interested in getting over on a cruiser and getting ready for Mindoro. I think I sailed for Mindoro two or three days later.

John T. Mason, Jr.: As a matter of fact, there were some losses. I mean the <u>Ward</u> was lost also.

Admiral Struble: Was it?

John T. Mason, Jr.: Yes, the <u>Mahan</u> and the <u>Ward</u> were sunk, and the <u>Little</u> and the <u>Lamson</u> were severely damaged.

---

* Admiral Struble's flagship for that operation was the light cruiser <u>Nashville</u> (CL-43).

Admiral Struble: Well, we had had kamikaze attacks; there was no doubt about that. But as I tell you, I have nothing in my mind—I have no remembrance of signing a report of the action.

John T. Mason, Jr.: You were immediately occupied with much bigger things at that point.

Admiral Struble: That's true really. I think you can understand that.

John T. Mason, Jr.: Tell me, what was your personal reaction to kamikazes, this being your first introduction?

Admiral Struble: Oh, boy. There's no argument in my mind that they were a Goddamned powerful weapon. The Japs had something that if they were going to develop further and harder was going to be something that we had to develop a counter to more than we had. The kamikaze business was quite serious at that time in my mind. I didn't talk to Kinkaid because Kinkaid was down in—

John T. Mason, Jr.: Down in Hollandia again?

Admiral Struble: I guess so.

John T. Mason, Jr.: MacArthur had established his base by that time in Tacloban, had he not?

Admiral Struble: MacArthur was there. No, I think I'll change that a little bit. I think that was when Kinkaid came up. He came up about the day afterwards, not the day of—you see, this thing had been planned in a hurry and gone ahead with. I got back to Leyte Gulf and got over on my cruiser flagship and started to go ahead with the Mindoro plans. I would say it was either the next day or the day after that that Kinkaid arrived from

Hollandia maybe. So I think I did have a chance to report to him verbally on the subject, but I don't remember ever having made a written report at all.

John T. Mason, Jr.: How did you react to this statement which I read somewhere? I think it was General Krueger who said later on that this action of yours at Ormoc was really the decisive action in the Leyte battle.*

Admiral Struble: I think that it was very fine. I agree that it had some very considerable effect.

John T. Mason, Jr.: It split the enemy forces.

Admiral Struble: If we had been bogged down and we had problems, we would have eventually taken over Leyte island. But if we had sat down there and doggedly fought it out on the island, would we have had the foresight to go right on up to Mindoro then? I don't know of anybody else that had backed him, but that was the reason I had disagreed so strongly with Kinkaid on the thing that said I thought we ought to try to help the Army out if we could, and I felt that we could. So then he had in effect said, "Well, all right. You go ahead and see what you can do about it."

But then I believe he did come up the next day and maybe was there. I'm not sure whether I reported to him personally about it or not. I'm really not. I have some recollection that, yes, he did come up and knew about it, and we sailed off on the other expedition.

John T. Mason, Jr.: Morison also reports that General Kenney was of the same mind. He backed the Ormoc expedition.

Admiral Struble: Well, from my point of view, the Ormoc thing was a natural and a very fine operation. I can see why Kenney certainly should have backed it, because from the air point of view, if we could accomplish that operation, he wouldn't be kept so damned

---

* Lieutenant General Walter Krueger, USA, Commanding General Sixth Army.

busy and held down on Leyte anywhere near as much as he was either. It would have freed him, which would have been good.

Our problem, frankly, was taking that northwestern part of the island and I think it was a very important one.

John T. Mason, Jr.: Well, they certainly didn't give you a breather.

Admiral Struble: Well, they couldn't have. In the meantime, Mindoro had all been planned. The ships had been assembled, the whole machinery was going.

John T. Mason, Jr.: So the landing there was contemplated then for the 15th of December.

Admiral Struble: The landing had been scheduled. The agreements with the Pacific Fleet and everything on the forces that would be assembled where—it wasn't just only the forces that I would command and take out with me. It was a bunch of cruisers and a bunch of other ships that by that time would be located to help me out if they were needed. All those things had already been put in the mill and agreed to. It would have been a big mistake to have held it up. I agree with that.

John T. Mason, Jr.: Maybe at this point I should ask you to comment on a problem—I hope that it doesn't divert you from the story itself—about the assembling of ship units from Nimitz's forces in the mid-Pacific to MacArthur.* It created a problem from time to time between MacArthur and Nimitz in that it seemed that MacArthur was never willing to release these ships once he got them under his control.

Admiral Struble: Well, now you see, the last statement you made—that's just human and natural. When you are doing this kind of business—and I think I have talked to you enough and described some of the problems about why we didn't have enough stuff—you hardly ever have enough of what it would be desirable for you to have had. That was

---

* Admiral Chester W. Nimitz, USN, Commander in Chief Pacific Fleet and Pacific Ocean Areas.

consistently the way down the Southwest Pacific. We were running it on a shoestring down there.

In the meantime, the Central Pacific—and I would say wisely—had the biggest assemblage of naval power and had to keep it in order to have it available if and when they had a good crack at the Japanese naval power. Until they had destroyed a good amount of the Jap naval power, if in the central Pacific they still didn't maintain a strong position and a readiness to take it as quick as they could, they might lose their opportunity.

Therefore, Nimitz's view of keeping everything he possibly could up in the north and have it ready to go after the Japs was, in my opinion, a sound decision. I think he sent enough down for us to accomplish Leyte. Now, those of us who were making the landing didn't think he had sent too much, but as it turned out, he had.

Now, when it came to Mindoro, it certainly would have been desirable if we could have had a little more available earlier. But as I review what happened, he sent us enough quick enough. A couple of times we were pretty close with some of that help coming.

By that time, the planning was also going ahead, not only for Mindoro, but for our landing up on the main island of Luzon. So we hadn't overlooked the big primary mission. We were planning for it, and I think on the whole Nimitz got the stuff down south at the time when it was needed and we had it available later at Leyte when the Japanese battleships showed up. Remember? They put on a relatively poor performance. I mean, we did very well. The ones that came around Leyte certainly were handled in beautiful style. The ones that came the other way, well, it wasn't all quite so proud on our part. Possibly, I would say, a discussion might go on whether at the later battle when the Jap big battleship outfit came across from Manila over toward Leyte.

[Tape turnover]

John T. Mason, Jr.: Off tape, you have been discussing in very broad terms the strategy in the Western Pacific. Suppose, sir, you repeat some of this and begin by talking about the two approaches to the Japanese mainland, the naval approach through the Central Pacific and the MacArthur approach through the Philippines.

Admiral Struble: Well, in view of what you said, I'll try to give you thoughts, not that I necessarily had all of them at that time, but that have developed in my mind and which I think got pretty well settled after the war was over. And that is that in connection with the broad Pacific problem, I think that it was splendid that MacArthur was given control of the Southwest Pacific, was given reasonable naval assistance, was given pretty good Army assistance, and started the development of freeing some of the islands and areas that the Japs had taken over. This was a concrete sign to all the world that we weren't just trying to get rid of Japan, but we were also interested in freeing these other peoples of the world that had been subjected to Japanese power.

John T. Mason, Jr.: These were the political overtones.

Admiral Struble: These were the political overtones coming into the problem. As soon as it had been determined that that broadly would be our approach, I think that the Central Pacific within reason did its best to provide good naval assistance to MacArthur and his forces, certainly not all that would have been desirable, but probably a fair adjustment of the forces for and at the time.

Now, considering what was happening as MacArthur went north, which he did very well and very fine, the Central Pacific was constantly going after and combating the Japanese naval problem as it existed in the rest of the Pacific, and that problem was primarily and purely naval. A few landings maybe on one or two islands might have been appropriate in the northern part of the problem, but they weren't really the big amphibious operations. They were only something connected with smaller islands.

John T. Mason, Jr.: And they didn't involve freeing captured people.

Admiral Struble: That's right. They weren't really involved in freeing the captured peoples and that sort of thing. I think that the Navy during that period with its submarines and its constant menace with its fleet for the Japanese fleet did remarkably well. I don't think they would have done anywhere near as well on what I will call the naval problem as they would have done if Nimitz had been put under MacArthur and MacArthur had authority to order all the naval help that he would think he might want.

So in my opinion, that solution from the broad strategy point of view was sound and excellent.

John T. Mason, Jr.: There had to be the two separate areas.

Admiral Struble: There had to be the two separate areas to have the dominance of naval problems in the northern part of it but the dominance of the shore problems in the southern part.

John T. Mason, Jr.: What determined this type of strategy? Was it just happenstance? Was it the set of circumstances that determined it? Or was it some wisdom on the part of Washington commanders?

Admiral Struble: I think it was wisdom on the part of not only the top people in Washington but also the top people in Honolulu as well as the top people in MacArthur's command. MacArthur actually, I think, recognized a number of these things as time went on. I think he felt maybe that he might have accomplished some of the things he did quicker if he had had more and all the naval help, but a lot of the things that did happen up north never would have happened if MacArthur had had complete control in the early part. So I think from the standpoint of the United States and the bigger problem that the broad adjustment of command strength and power was very well done in World War II and I think its readiness to transfer all of it to MacArthur if and when we landed on Kyushu was clear and that MacArthur at that time would have had it.

John T. Mason, Jr.: There were two dual commands in operation without any overall attention. How did this affect Navy men like you who were serving in one camp being actually by affinity part of another camp?

Admiral Struble: Those of us who were down in the Southwest Pacific with MacArthur realized that he didn't have all the naval power that he could use. We were constantly trying to help him get more. On the other hand, we couldn't help but recognize the sensible approach of the use of naval power if it was accomplishing something up north. On the whole, I think we did very well. I think MacArthur really felt so. But he was a fighter for his part of what he thought ought to get done. I don't believe that the Army ever realized the tremendous value of the naval submarine effort and the presence of the fleet up north which did restrict Japanese naval operations quite a bit and did clip their wings quite a bit and eventually, of course, it resulted in our closing in on them.

I do believe myself that we did a good thing freeing the Philippines, having MacArthur in Manila, and accomplishing it not by something that the Japs had decided to let us have but by kicking them out, by getting them out ourselves. I think that was very important. Politically it was very important.

John T. Mason, Jr.: From a world point of view, it showed our strength.

Admiral Struble: The world could not help but admire that we had done all this work in the Southwest Pacific that we did. We had freed peoples that had been taken over by the Japs on their initial overrun.

John T. Mason, Jr.: Did I infer from one of your remarks off tape that there were actually two different independent plans for our eventual occupation of the Japanese mainland? Was there one developed by the Central Pacific? Was there one developed by MacArthur? And did they differ one from the other?

Admiral Struble: I don't think you can put it in the phraseology the way you have. I think you must look at it this way: long before the accomplishment was to be done, people had a number of different ideas. There had been, for instance, an idea that we might land troops on China territory, more or less closer to Japan, which could have been very easily accomplished. And then we would have had a specific force that could be launched from there against Japan, as well as the use of all the naval power and everything else against Japan to the landing.

There could be the direct approach of landing at Kyushu, which had been considered. And there could also be a more direct landing on Japan contemplated so that basically I think that there were three things that might be considered. It's my opinion that in the final evolution of the matter that the approach of landing on Kyushu was the best of the three, and it was the one that had been finally jointly agreed to by the Navy and Army departments and by the two big principal commanders out in the Pacific and it was on the books.

So in my opinion, the eventual solution was a fine solution, just like I feel that the solution that was devolved between the Americans and the British and to some extent a little French knowledge possibly, but the French weren't really involved, of the Normandy business. Two people got together, and they eventually reached a fine conclusion. I do believe that the preliminary Normandy stuff reached a far better solution than a lot of those that were discussed.

I think that actually the Pacific ended up that way. I think if we were going to have to settle the war by landing on Kyushu and we would have had to do it, unless the decision had been made about the atomic bomb, I think it was the best solution for Japan. We didn't land at Kyushu. We would have had heavy losses in Kyushu. We would have been successful and having been successful, I think after the Kyushu landing, Japan would have folded up just like it did later. We didn't know it, but the surrender of the Japanese would have been so remarkable that we never could have contemplated it beforehand.

John T. Mason, Jr.: Because in a sense the American didn't understand the—

Admiral Struble: Japanese psychology. We did not understand all of that perfectly. I think one of the most remarkable things is the complete changeover that the Japs made after the bomb was dropped. Listen, Kyushu would have been like dropping the bomb but not as effective really. Dropping the bomb was much more dramatic, much more worldly, a much more unusual thing. And the Japs immediately said, "Why, this is terrible." But then they did what they would have done when they decided to quit. So, in my opinion, we would have made the Kyushu landing, but I believe that possibly before we left Kyushu the Japanese people would have said, as they did after the bomb dropped, "We're wrong. We accept it. We'll go ahead for the better." And that's the way they did it. And that's what I think would have happened, even had we made the Kyushu landing.

John T. Mason, Jr.: Shall we go back to Mindoro? Ormoc had been accomplished, and you had gone back to Leyte and had no time whatsoever plunging from one operation into the other. You boarded the flagship at this point, which was the Nashville.

Admiral Struble: That's right. The cruiser Nashville.

John T. Mason, Jr.: She had been, as somebody said, MacArthur's favorite ferryboat.

Admiral Struble: Well, she was often used as the flagship for somebody. We had prepared a plan that involved, as I remember, 60 hours from Leyte to the landing at Mindoro. Of course, we would go south out of Leyte. We had to go west, and end up eventually going north for a little while to land on the west side of Mindoro.

Mindoro wasn't too far away from Manila, but our information was that there were not any Japs on Mindoro Island. There appeared to be no reason for having any there. Mindoro was not a large island and of no particular strategic value apparently, at least for the other side. But for us going in and trying to get Manila, Mindoro would amount to an island fairly close to Manila, south of it, and a good position from which we could direct an aviation field and communications facilities fairly close to Manila. From there we could be in a position to assist an awful lot for an eventual landing on the island of Luzon to end the matter. All the way along, the American opinion had not been that we should try to capture each little spot and get it done and then go on to another little spot. But after we got landed in the Philippines, we'd get down to the heart of the business as quick as we could.

John T. Mason, Jr.: Mindoro was not contemplated as an easy operation, however, was it, because of the closeness to Japanese airfields?

Admiral Struble: That is correct. We did not expect much. We thought in planning the operation that they might have a hundred people there or something, but we didn't think it would be a big force. So we planned on landing in the early morning. I planned a full heavy bombardment of the beach and everything so that if there were any dugouts or strong points, we would attempt to destroy them before we landed. We did not have solid information to indicate that they had any such things, but neither did we have solid information that they didn't have them.

John T. Mason, Jr.: By that, I take it that we didn't have any American friends that had remained on Mindoro.

Admiral Struble: No, I don't think there were any Americans. I question whether there were any foreigners on Mindoro, and there were very few Filipinos. It was not a populated island at all.

John T. Mason, Jr.: Is it unfertile or what?

Admiral Struble: No, I guess it's just never been used much for anything. I think that's the place for it, but it would make an excellent stopping-off spot, and it would be a splendid place for our small boats to have a little bit of a harbor, a place to supply. There's no doubt about it, we could direct excellent radio activities. It would be very useful, not only for communications but also for the Air Force in operating on Manila, which of course was our final objective.

I planned it was going to take 60 hours at the speed that I could travel with this great big kind of a cluttered-up force, which did involve my cruiser flagship and then involved one cruiser division that was under Berkey.* It would be the principal supporting force that we would have as regards powerful strength. Then we had a fairly

---

* Rear Admiral Russell S. Berkey, USN, Commander Cruiser Division 15/Commander Task Force 75.

good destroyer force with us. And then, of course, we had a large amount of ships that involved all the supplies and all the stuff that we expected to put ashore there to build the station for ourselves.

John T. Mason, Jr.: In addition to the building of the station and the airport, how many men were you contemplating landing there?

Admiral Struble: I have forgotten the exact amount, but I would imagine it might have been 500 to 1,000.

John T. Mason, Jr.: Not really a large number.

Admiral Struble: Not really a large force but enough to defend the local situation. We didn't anticipate much of a reaction from the Japs to our landing there in an attempt to take it back from us, if we once got it, because we would get enough aviation out there quickly to make it a very hot spot for somebody to come attack. In other words, they'd have had to have ships at sea and everything to bring down their forces. Now, we had already planned a landing on Luzon that was going to take place, as I remember, on about the 15th of January. But, of course, that landing would obviously be contingent on success at Mindoro and the fact that we could be ready to meet that success with observation from Mindoro on Manila and the Luzon area by virtue of being closer at hand. We could not expect to have any kind of observation like that unless we had something like Mindoro.

John T. Mason, Jr.: Now, even before you landed on Mindoro, you almost came to grief. Do you want to tell me about that?

Admiral Struble: Well, we knew that our action at Ormoc would fully alert the Japanese to the fact that we were moving west a little bit. It was reasonable to suppose that when they would find out that we had started some other forces west and they might even be headed at Cebu, we had to expect possible kamikaze and possible other air attacks from the moment we left Leyte.

In this large, slow force, I had four cruisers and maybe as many as 18 destroyers. We left in the late afternoon or evening from Leyte, and we were cruising along the next morning south of the big Jap air base. If they did have observation planes out, we did not know it. We didn't sight any. But, of course, this was a tremendous force of ships that we had scattered, a big outfit. I would say that some Japanese observation plane from Cebu had undoubtedly sighted us from high up in the air and had decided that there was no use telling us that he had seen it. He had disappeared back into the clouds and had gone back to Cebu and told them that he thought there was an outfit there.

It's possible that the next plane that came out, which was a kamikaze, had been sent out deliberately to see what was out there, make a report, and if there was a ship there, go in and sink it. It doesn't add up that the first man, therefore, could have known we were quite as big a force as we were, but he might know that there was a ship there. Otherwise, it wouldn't have seemed to be sensible to have sent out a kamikaze unless there was something there. So I believe that they had some idea that one or more ships were out there, and the kamikaze was sent out on the basis that it was just a little outfit rather than a big one.

Now, why my force did not sight that kamikaze earlier, I do not know. However, the man that was the kamikaze was apparently pretty damned bright because he had his plane very low, just over the water.

John T. Mason, Jr.: Just so he could escape the AA.

Admiral Struble: So he escaped all of our observational methods at that time and got in quite close to us before we recognized he was there. I had my flagship on the forward starboard post for big ships. The basis of that was the area from which attack might come, and I'm a little chagrined that we didn't spot it sooner. We should have, in my opinion.

John T. Mason, Jr.: There were many other instances, however, in the Western Pacific.

Admiral Struble: However, we did not spot him. Outside of me was a ring of destroyers, of which I would say there were about three destroyers that were on a circle maybe two miles out; they might have spotted him. But, by golly, none of them spotted that fellow until he was practically passing over that destroyer screen. He was very low down over the water.

Of course, the moment that happened and we saw the kamikaze coming, the ship immediately jumped around and got guns trained and ready. Some of the destroyers did some shooting at this kamikaze, but, you know, if the fellow's at a distance and coming at you you've got a steady target. But if he gets close to you, he's changing position all the time and he's a much more difficult target. So he just went through that destroyer screen like nothing. While there was some gun shooting out there, none of them got him.

John T. Mason, Jr.: He was a horizontal target.

Admiral Struble: That's right and it's very difficult to get if he's close.

John T. Mason, Jr.: He's moving so rapidly.

Admiral Struble: He's moving so rapidly by comparison it is very difficult to stop him. So he went right through that destroyer screen and nobody got him.

Now, about the time that he got, I would say, a mile from us, the ship began shooting. She may have opened up a little earlier. But, again, he apparently was headed to pass us. He apparently hadn't spotted us, or maybe he knew we were but he was going to go in the center more. So he kept coming on the course he had that was going to take him reasonably well astern of us.

Of course, the men on the ship were apparently doing all they could to try to bring him down, but it was a very difficult target and they weren't at all successful. The kamikaze came in, of course, at high speed. He came in astern of us, but in the meantime at the latter part of this thing, had decided. "Oh, there's a great big good ship; I'll take it. So as he got practically astern of us he turned directly toward us.

Well, again, we had a shot at him but we didn't hit him. He came in and deliberately kamikazed right at the base of the foremast of the ship, which as you know is always the place where the bridge is and where the admiral is and where the captain is.[*]

John T. Mason, Jr.: The heart of the ship.

Admiral Struble: The heart of the ship. Now, he did a lot of damage, but he hit the flag bridge, which is the bridge that I would normally be on. Of course, we had certain casualties in my staff that were the result of that.

On the Nashville the captain was using a higher post than my spot.[†] There was a higher post above them, a little smaller bridge, a little tiny thing. But he was using that as his observation post and it was where he was running the ship from. It was not bothered by the kamikaze attack, and he was able to handle the ship and so forth after we were kamikazed.

Now, as the kamikaze exploded, the impact of this explosion was pretty much in a large number of directions. It was primarily down and to the rear of the mast structure that he came into. Of course, my staff were on the bridge and were all right in the line of fire at that time, right where he came in.

John T. Mason, Jr.: Including your chief of staff.

Admiral Struble: Including my chief of staff, yes. He was right there. I had been up on that bridge talking to the chief of staff, I suppose, a couple of minutes before this thing occurred. The chief of staff had been saying, "Admiral, I think we have gotten the outfit in the best kind of shape we can get it." He said, "You know these fellows, they don't have much power. When they get behind they straggle a little. You're pushing them in some ways about as fast as they can go, so if one of them straggles out a little bit, we've got to leave him there or we've got to slow down the whole shebang."

---

[*] This incident occurred on 13 December 1944.
[†] The commanding officer of the Nashville was Captain Charles E. Coney, USN.

I said, "Well, I'm not going to slow down, so we'll continue at ten. I think you've got things in pretty good shape, but any time you get a straggler, have one of the destroyers go over with him and see if he can help him or if necessary, give him a tow for a little or something because I don't want to let this thing start straggling. We've got to get to Mindoro on time and we've got to keep our speed."

So the chief of staff said, "Well, I think we're all right. That's what we're watching." And everything was calm.

I said, "Well, I think I'll go out and look up ahead." I left the port after corner of the bridge, walked across to the starboard side, and walked forward on the starboard side of the forward end of the bridge. That therefore put me diagonally opposite with the bridge structure and everything in between the spot where the kamikaze landed. That's how I got out of it. I was standing right where the kamikaze landed and would have been right in the middle of it, if I hadn't said, "Well, it looks like the whole force and everything is in good shape. I'll go out and take a look out ahead." And I had gone just diagonally away from it. I put the big structure between us and where the kamikaze landed.

By that time, we didn't know it was coming in. And it wasn't until after I got out on the starboard side. I immediately went back and hollered at everybody, "Hell, there's a plane coming. Let's get everybody alerted." And I went back out and went to this forward part to watch the kamikaze.

John T. Mason, Jr.: Where was General Dunckel?

Admiral Struble: General Dunckel was down in his cabin, which was directly below us, below the superstructure.* He was on the starboard side of the ship, and the damage occurred on the port side. Of course, general quarters had been sounded. Everybody on the ship had been alerted before the hit occurred, but just before. I mean, seconds before was all the alerting that had happened. So Dunckel, I believe, had come out of his cabin and was out on the starboard side of the main deck, out in the open, but on the starboard

---

* Brigadier General William C. Dunckel, USA.

side, and the kamikaze came over here on the port side. In this ensuing debris and everything that flew, I think that was when he was hit. Wasn't he hit in his hand?

John T. Mason, Jr.: I don't know, but his chief of staff was killed also.

Admiral Struble: Oh, yes. Well now, I can't tell you how he was killed, but Dunckel was hit by something in the right hand and knocked down and stunned a little bit. I didn't see Dunckel for about 30 minutes, because I started to tour the ship right away to see what had happened down below.

John T. Mason, Jr.: You weren't stunned then in any sense.

Admiral Struble: Oh, no, I wasn't stunned. The moment this thing happened and I realized it, I started crawling up the mast on the forward part of it. I went up and up until I got up to where the captain was. The captain, as I told you, had gone up to this upper, small station. I went up to that upper small station. I said to the captain, "Well, we've got to be worried about other attacks. How are we coming along? How are we doing?"

He said, "We can steam all right. There's no problem. But I'm afraid we've got quite a bit of damage in people hurt. But we're all right. We'll still go on." So I stayed up there with him, I guess, for three or four or five minutes trying to assure myself that the flagship was able to go on and it didn't have any problem in that respect.

I said, "Well, I guess you'd better stay up here because you've got control from here. You better not start moving control away from here until we're sure where we stand." He said he thought that was what he ought to do and he was going to stay there.

So then I said, "Well, I send a message." He had signalman there on his bridge so that while our main flag signaling had been cracked up by this kamikaze attack, he had a signalman up there with him. So I said, "You signal over to Berkey and tell Berkey assume OTC until further orders."* I got an answer back, "Affirmative." So that put Berkey in command. He realized, of course, that we had been hit. So then, of course, I didn't have to worry about the whole force. Berkey, you see, would be that.

---

* OTC—officer in tactical command.

I stayed up there a few more minutes, and then I decided I'd go down below and find out what the damage was. Of course, the wreckage and the damage on the levels was terrible. People were here, people were there. My chief of staff was quite badly hurt. Actually, as you know, he died.*

I got down to the level below that and there were a lot of people running around and everything. Things seemed to be in fair organization. I went down a deck below that to the wardroom. All the doctors were there, and things were apparently going ahead in good style. That is the time I remember that I found Dunckel. Dunckel was the head Army man. He was a brigadier general. He was lying there and seemed to be passed out. So I went over to the doctor and said, "Doctor, I want to..."

He said, "I'm too busy. I can't talk to you."

I said, "Now look, I'm Admiral Struble, and this is kind of a command problem and this is a little important. I don't want to keep you from some medical work, but I want to ask you one question about a man over here in the corner. It's fairly important because I decided that I will probably leave this ship and will maybe send it back because of the terrible amount of damage."

And the doctor says, "Oh, yes, sir."

He came with me and we went over in the corner of the room and I said, "This is General Dunckel. If I go on I'll have to take him with me. He's got to be able to transfer to a destroyer and go along with me." I had already realized by one look at that ship that I wasn't going to take her along. I realized I wasn't going to take her on. There were just altogether too many people wounded.

John T. Mason, Jr.: Most of the personnel.

Admiral Struble: So many people were wounded that it was obvious to me that the only thing I could do was send her back to Leyte Gulf, where they would get some hospitalization. And for the ship, there was no use trying to take her on. So the guy came over and examined Dunckel's hand. He said, "Well, it isn't too bad. We've got it

---

* The chief of staff was Captain Everett W. Abdill, USN.

fixed up. You must tell him he can't use that hand and to be very careful of it. When will he be moved?"

I said, "I probably won't move before early afternoon."

He said, "All right. I'll keep an eye on him during the morning. He'll be able to do. But you'll have to have somebody pack for him."

I said, "How will he be when he gets on the destroyer? They can probably give him some sort of a private room or semi-private at least and there will be a pharmacist's mate there that can take care of his hand all right."

"Oh, yes," he said, "this isn't serious enough. The pharmacist's mate will know how to handle it." But he said, "Tell him one thing. Don't put anybody in the room with him. Keep him quiet and don't give him any problem until you get out to Mindoro."

John T. Mason, Jr.: Two days hence.

Admiral Struble: Two days hence. So that was all right. Then I was commencing to feel that I had a little grip on the thing and went up on deck and went all around the main deck. The main deck, the forward main deck in that cruiser—you know what a turret is, how there's an overhang on a turret? Underneath the overhangs of the turrets and that sort of thing were all these groups of people, most of them wounded.

I was looking for the aviation man. I hadn't found him. Nobody had seen him, and I finally found him up underneath the forward turret, a very fine person.

John T. Mason, Jr.: And he wounded too?

Admiral Struble: Oh, boy, he was badly wounded. He had gotten a very bad wound. Well, I really was very worried about him. So I left him and went around begging a doctor. In the midst of one of these things you think it's a funny thing that the boss can't wham, wham, wham. But he can't. You're your own messenger boy and everything. I could have had a messenger boy. There were plenty of them. But I went around and looked for the doctor, because I didn't want somebody else to do this for me; I wanted to do it myself. I finally found a doctor and I explained to him who I was. I don't think he knew me. I had only been on that ship a couple of days. I said, "Well, I've got the head aviation man over here underneath turret one's overhang and it looks to me like he's pretty severely wounded." I said, "I'm going to send this ship back to Leyte Gulf tonight as soon as it gets dark. I'm not going to send her in the daytime, because it might be recognized that she is weakened or something and it might encourage a big air attack on her."

John T. Mason, Jr.: That would finish her off.

Admiral Struble: "So she will proceed with us until darkness and then I'll turn her loose and she'll go back to Leyte Gulf tonight at high speed, which she can do very safely. It's very good travel here and she'll be there late tonight or early in the morning." I said, "I think I probably ought to send this head airman, but if I'm going to send him I want to know because I want to try to locate the fellow that's going to take his place and be sure I've got him ready to work."

So the doctor went with me then. He stopped what he was doing and said, "All right. This is pretty important. I'll go with you." He went over and looked him over and he said, "When we get over there now, you just don't talk too much because maybe I don't want to talk in front of the man, and therefore you better wait until I see him and then talk to the man for another couple of minutes and then leave. "Then you come talk to me, and I'll tell you what it is. So that's what we did. And he said, "No, no. He can't go on. I'm afraid he's very, very bad."

So I said, "All right."

By this time, two or three or four of my people had collected and were following me around, my own personal people. So when I got through with that job, I said, "Well, boys, it's perfectly clear. I'm going to call a destroyer alongside, and we will take Jones and Smith and so-and-so and so-and-so and so-and-so." I outlined the members of my staff I was going to take along with me. I said, "You tell all the other staff people that you see that they are to go back with the ship."

So then I got them started working on the problem, and I took my aide because I had located him in the meantime. Then he and I went up to my cabin. I had—I've got to show it to you, it's up in the attic—kind of a big box about this long and this wide and this high with one of these hooks on it. That was the place that I kept my papers in.

John T. Mason, Jr.: Oh, sort of a chest.

Admiral Struble: Kind of a chest for my papers. It was where I kept all my secret information and all that kind of stuff. So I told the aide, "Now, I'll close this up here, and you're to get this in the destroyer this afternoon when I leave the ship." So then I decided I had handled that part of it.

So then I went back up on the bridge, and I went up through the stages of the bridge. By that time people were scattered out everywhere. I didn't see anybody I recognized and went on up to the captain's bridge. I found out he had come down to his main bridge then and that with the number of wounded, everything was a tremendous mess.

He said, "Well, Admiral, I was going to ask you if we couldn't go on. But I decided that you know best. When are you going to leave the ship?"

I said, "About 2:30 I'll call a destroyer alongside, and I'll try to have my staff assembled by that time. We will leave the ship, and then you and the staff remaining will drop back to position. Then tonight, as soon as it is dark enough, you can return and head back to Leyte Gulf at a pretty good clip and get in as early as you can in the morning. They'll know you are coming, and they'll do the best they can for you hospital-wise."

I believe that I was told that he had some 350 people on the casualty list. That doesn't mean they were all dead, you know.

John T. Mason, Jr.: About 50% of them were, though.

Admiral Struble: Yes, a large number.

John T. Mason, Jr.: You did want to say something about your chief of staff.

Admiral Struble: Yes, my chief of staff, who I think I mentioned earlier in this slightly, was a very, very fine man and, of course, I lost him on this occasion and it was a very, very big blow.

John T. Mason, Jr.: He wasn't killed outright.

Admiral Struble: No, when I saw him, he had a very heavy wound that had broken up one arm and wrist and so forth had gashed into him. The ship sailed that night and I never had any further word from the doctor. I suppose by the time I got back from Mindoro, we were doing something new and we were going on.

John T. Mason, Jr.: Yes, the next step for you.

Admiral Struble: Yes, the next step.

John T. Mason, Jr.: It really was.

Admiral Struble: But he was a very fine man and we certainly lost a very valuable person from the Navy at that time.

John T. Mason, Jr.: How did you then manage without a chief of staff? Or you got another one immediately?

Admiral Struble: Oh, no. The Mindoro planning had all been done. We made the landing.* We had no problem with the landing, so it was just a question of when I got back to our base, I got a new man. As a matter of fact, I got a new flagship too. I went from a big cruiser down to a little Coast Guard cutter. But the Coast Guard cutter really proved to be very good because it was small. It could get into little harbors, and it was all I needed to take my staff with me.

---

* On 15 December 1944 U.S. forces mounted an amphibious invasion of Mindoro, an island just south of Luzon in the Philippines

John T. Mason, Jr.: Yes, in the places you were scheduled to go.

Admiral Struble: After Mindoro, of course, we had to plan and make the landing, not the major landings in Luzon which had been previously made about a couple of weeks after Mindoro, but we made a landing close to Manila on the seaside shore and went into—

John T. Mason, Jr.: Zambales.

Admiral Struble: What's the name of the Navy spot there?

John T. Mason, Jr.: You had to plan the landing for Subic, coming after Mindoro. But tell me about Mindoro itself now. You said there was no opposition.

Admiral Struble: There was no opposition to the landing. We made our big gunfire assault on the beach. It actually proved to be unnecessary. But we didn't know that it wasn't necessary. The troops unloading and the supply unloading at Mindoro were simply remarkable. How we unloaded as much equipment and troops and everything as we did in one day, I'll never know. But people realized we were quite a ways out front, and they certainly did work to get the stuff over on the beach so that I was able to sail about 7:00 o'clock that night from Mindoro to go back to Leyte. I had thought I would have to run over one day, but I didn't.

John T. Mason, Jr.: The mission was accomplished.

Admiral Struble: We got out about 7:00 P.M., and as we stood out, I saw a minesweeper that was commanded by a man that I was very fond of, an old friend of mine. His minesweeper had run aground on a slightly elevated spot off of the beach where we had landed. Actually as we pulled away from Mindoro the tide was going down, and it was getting to be low tide. He was caught fast on this little bump of ground. He says, "Admiral, you aren't going to go off and leave me."

I said, "Oh, yes. This big slow convoy is on its way. Now, when high tide comes I hope you can make good arrangements now and get off the beach all right. Then you put on the best speed you can and you ought to overtake me tomorrow sometime."

John T. Mason, Jr.: And did he?

Admiral Struble: He did. By that time, I realized that the chances of him getting into trouble was very little, and I had a hell of a lot of small ships to try to herd back so I didn't want to waste the time. We were very slow and were going to have to take a slow trip home.

John T. Mason, Jr.: I don't know who made this statement, whether you are credited with it or somebody else. But on the operation at Mindoro they said that this was an amphibious group commander's dream. Was that your remark?

Admiral Struble: No, I didn't make it, but I might have made such a statement. Of course, it was very simple and very easy and turned out very fine. I had too many little small ships that I had to get home to stop and help him off when all he had to do was wait for the coming high tide which would take him off and he would overtake me.

It took us about the usual 60 hours to return to Leyte Gulf at comfortable, slow speed.

John T. Mason, Jr.: And you weren't harassed on the way?

Admiral Struble: Without any harassment or any problem. So the actual trip was in itself a very simple, easy one to handle except for the initial kamikaze.

John T. Mason, Jr.: What about the men who were on Mindoro, who were setting up the base and so forth? Were they bothered by the Japanese air?

Admiral Struble: They had been attacked a couple of days before I landed. But actually the Japs paid hardly any attention at all to Mindoro in the future. They didn't pay any attention to it and they didn't go after it.

John T. Mason, Jr.: Does this mean that they didn't really suspect that it would be very harmful to them?

Admiral Struble: I think they realized that the main attack would come against the island at Luzon, and they didn't think that Mindoro would help us very much in doing it. Actually the fact that we could put up a little airfield there that could get a little bigger, the fact we could have good communications from there, probably helped us more in our attack on Corregidor than they realized would happen.

John T. Mason, Jr.: This is what you had planned anyway, wasn't it?

Admiral Struble: Yes.

John T. Mason, Jr.: You had anticipated that it would be helpful.

Admiral Struble: We just figured it would be and it was. I think in closing I would like to make one statement about what a fine man my chief of staff was who had been with me previously in my amphibious landing and who lost his life in the attack we had soon after we left Leyte Gulf. He was a very fine capable officer.

John T. Mason, Jr.: Thank you, sir.

Admiral Struble: Now, do you want me to go on.

John T. Mason, Jr.: You said that you were put in command of the forces on Leyte when you returned there after Mindoro.

Admiral Struble: When I returned there after Mindoro. I made a few minor landings around in that area and then about late January took the force up and landed them on the west coast just north of and near Subic Bay. The troops then marched over and took over Subic Bay.

John T. Mason, Jr.: Was this the force that was intended to cut off the Japs on Bataan or kept them from getting on to Bataan and holing up there?

Admiral Struble: No, that was different. All of those things were going on after I got back to Leyte Gulf and during the period when I acted as the man in command in Leyte Gulf still. Those attacks would come out of Leyte Gulf, but they wouldn't be under my command.

John T. Mason, Jr.: I have a note here to the effect that on the 29th of January you landed 30,000 troops near a place called Zambales.

Admiral Struble: That is just north and on the west coastline of Luzon. Those troops when landed, of course, became a part of MacArthur's movement on Manila.

John T. Mason, Jr.: I also note that for the landing of those troops you really met no opposition.

Admiral Struble: That's right. We had no opposition at that landing. The following day we moved in from the sea and into Subic Bay. The Japs were then leaving Subic Bay to retreat toward Manila. Fortunately for us, we had no Japanese opposition then or in Subic Bay. That could have been nasty because it has a rather high nice rounded little island, and it would make it very difficult to pass too easily. But they had decided apparently to get out so we had no trouble on the Subic Bay trip.

John T. Mason, Jr.: Even though you didn't have any opposition in landing 30,000 troops, it seems to me that is a considerable operation.

Admiral Struble: Oh, it was a good-sized operation. And I then stayed in Subic Bay in command until about ten days or so later when we went down and made the attack on Corregidor. I was in charge of the attack on Corregidor.[*]

John T. Mason, Jr.: That brings back lots of memories. Tell me about that.

Admiral Struble: That was interesting in that it was decided that we would have an air drop on Corregidor and the air would come from Mindoro, which had been established. Up on top of Corregidor was a great big field that was used as an Army training field. It was a quite big fine space, and it was up on top of the island so you land on top and you could come down on people. Whereas we coming in on the water level were pushing in from the bottom trying to go up. So far it looked as if our attempt to land troops the next day across a very narrow slit of land was going to be pretty bad because they would be just sitting on the shore peppering us.

So it was thought that the airdrop was a good thing. In the airdrop the first day I had noticed that as the men cascaded out of the planes and dropped down that a number of them fell short, and it was very nasty for them. Any of them that went down and were over were very difficult to pick up. Very late that afternoon I had a report that a large number of our aviators dropping down on the top of the rock had had broken shoulders and so forth.

So I decided that the necessity for any further airdrop was over. We did have men on top that had been dropped there by air the day before, the first day, and I was going to be able to land troops from the beach now that could get up on top; that part was accomplished. So I sent word to Mindoro not to send up any more air troops. I said to send them up by destroyer to Subic Bay and that I would land them over the beach.

The Air Force took offense to this. They wanted to have another airdrop, but I bucked them strong and said that I thought it was a very unnecessary risk of very fine aviators and I couldn't see it. So they gave in, and we did put the second contingent of air

---

[*] Corregidor was a heavily fortified island at the entrance to Manila Bay. Its American defenders surrendered to the Japanese on 6 May 1942. The U.S. invasion to recapture the island began on 16 February 1945.

in over the landing. There was no doubt about it, the airdrop was a success. It was a method of getting your people up on top, but after you've done it once, it is not the sensible way to run in more troops. So the Air Force finally gave in and we ran the troops in the next day across the beach.

MacArthur came down about two days later.

John T. Mason, Jr.: And returned to the place where he had left.

Admiral Struble: That's right.

John T. Mason, Jr.: Were there Japs in the tunnels?

Admiral Struble: There were still Japs in the tunnels. But once we had a few men located outside the tunnel with control of that entrance, they couldn't get out of either. So we had the top hand.

John T. Mason, Jr.: What did you do with them, just leave them there?

Admiral Struble: We just left them there until they decided to surrender. We usually had two little spots located outside each entrance place like this, a crossfire controlling it, and all we did was sit around and wait until they gave up.

John T. Mason, Jr.: You mean a sentry booth?

Admiral Struble: That's about the idea. But that was the only thing to do. There was no use trying to go in and bring them out. Two men inside would have killed 12 or something like that.

John T. Mason, Jr.: It would be a bloody duel.

Admiral Struble: Well, it was just useless.

John T. Mason, Jr.: How long did it take to subdue them?

Admiral Struble: Well, when MacArthur was there I don't think we had cleaned out all the spots yet.

At that landing we had moved in and had pretty good gunfire from Berkey's outfit and from a couple of British ships. Our landing was touchy on the beach, which was sort of narrow, and bad for about four or five hours. As soon as we got enough troops and we could move on the surface reasonably, we eliminated that problem from then on. Of course, the next day I specifically put up quite a fight to avoid another airdrop because I had seen when the people reported to me from the beach the number of broken shoulder blades and things they had among the aviators and I didn't think it was a necessary thing to do.

John T. Mason, Jr.: No.

Well, our taking of Corregidor must have had a certain amount of an emotional impact, did it not?

Admiral Struble: Oh, yes. Once you took the entrance to Manila, why, Manila wasn't feeling so good.

John T. Mason, Jr.: Were you involved in the recovery of Fort Drum?

Admiral Struble: No. It was then that I went back to Leyte and became the man in charge of the house there with instructions to make landing in a number of the southern islands and assist with air support and so forth to the Army in landing here and there and so forth.

John T. Mason, Jr.: Well, that we'll reserve for the next time.

Interview Number 7 with Admiral Arthur D. Struble, U.S. Navy (Retired)

Place: Admiral Struble's Home, Chevy Chase, Maryland

Date: Wednesday, 15 December 1976

Interviewer: John T. Mason, Jr.

John T. Mason, Jr.: Admiral, it's good to see you this morning. Off tape you've just told me a rather humorous incident in connection with Corregidor. I wonder if you would put that on tape for me?

Admiral Struble: All right. After the airdrop on Corregidor early in the morning, we commenced a landing from small boats on the island. By about 10:00 or 11:00 o'clock in the morning we had established a very nice direct landing from small ships on Corregidor and had started troops going up to the top of the island where the Air Force had dropped troops to effect a juncture with them and then eventually, of course, continued the elimination of all the Japanese on the island.

As this pursued, the Japs had steadily withdrawn into the tunnels at the base of the island. A tunnel would start in and run straight for maybe six or eight feet and then curve around so the people on the inside were protected up to the last minute and people trying to come into the tunnel were in a pretty bad way because right around the corner they had people waiting for them who could pop them off as soon as they showed up.

The Americans found out that some of the Japs on the inside could talk English, so they would holler at them and say, "Why the hell don't you come on out and fight?"

The answer from the inside by some Japanese that could talk English was, "Why the hell don't you come in and get us?"

John T. Mason, Jr.: It was a stalemate wasn't it?

Admiral Struble: Of course, it was becoming a stalemate. We just had to take our time or suffer heavy losses, which, of course, were not at all necessary. We bided our time, and eventually the Japanese started to come out and surrender. Then we cleaned the island up on the lower levels, where the tunnels were, as well as the island top.

John T. Mason, Jr.: Did they surrender in any great numbers? One is always led to believe that they sacrificed themselves rather than surrender.

Admiral Struble: That is true, and there were not a large number of Japs on that island. But they put up a terribly tough fight when we first landed, during the airdrop and during the first half hour of the landing from small boats. But thereafter they realized that they were done for and that they would either have to surrender or we were going to just sit it out until they did. So eventually—I would say about two to three weeks after we first landed—most of them had realized that the only thing they could do was to surrender or—and this is what a large number of them did—they would sneak out at night and get in the water. Maybe they would be able to pick up a log or some sort of a piece of wood to ride, and they would try to get off Corregidor and get back over on the mainland, under which situation they could rejoin their own Japanese outfit that was already around Manila getting ready for wherever the Americans might land.

John T. Mason, Jr.: Did many of them succeed in that fashion?

Admiral Struble: I suppose maybe as many as two-thirds of them that left the island made it to the mainland all right and got away. The average might have been a little bit higher. But a fairly good number of them did. The amount that eventually surrendered because they were holed up in tunnels and they couldn't get out because we were controlling the entrance to the tunnel—I suppose we controlled most of entrances to tunnels on the island after about the first week or ten days so that this process of leaving the island individually took place in that first week or ten days. After that they had to either surrender or come out fighting.

John T. Mason, Jr.: So you did take some prisoners.

Admiral Struble: We took a certain number of prisoners on the island after things settled down and they realized the hopelessness of their situation.

John T. Mason, Jr.: Now, were they interrogated? Was there any information you could obtain from them of value?

Admiral Struble: No, by that time the people that knew much were all gone. I think we got very little information.

John T. Mason, Jr.: So they were simply put in some sort of stockade.

Admiral Struble: Oh, yes, surely. If they surrendered, we gave them a fair break, of course.

John T. Mason, Jr.: Yes. Well, now, the campaign went on. You weren't immediately involved in Lingayen, but tell me about it.*

Admiral Struble: I think that's an interesting thing that maybe we might mention a little bit. When we got back to Leyte, of course, the big thing was going to be this big advance on Lingayen. It was the biggest assemblage that we had had as far as I know in the Pacific in the line of combatant ships and all that sort of thing and certainly very definitely in the amount of troops that we had afloat who were going to be landed. The Lingayen outfit was due, as I remember, to pass probably some two weeks to 20 days after I had gone out to Mindoro.

They would pass Mindoro. They would go past Manila, they would get out on the west coast of Luzon in a big open gulf called Lingayen, from which they could march south and a little to the east directly on Manila in very good fighting conditions. I mean reasonably clear ground so that the strength of our military and the strength of our

---

* On 9 January 1945 Navy amphibious forces put Army troops ashore to begin the invasion at Lingayen Gulf, which is north of Manila on the island of Luzon in the Philippines.

support of the military would be useful to us and would give us a better break in fighting the Japanese.

So the big push on Lingayen had been really started and most of the ships collected, not at Leyte Gulf, although a lot had come into Leyte Gulf. The big gathering for Lingayen—principal officers and everything—had occurred at Hollandia. They came then from Hollandia, picked up a certain amount of forces at Leyte, and went on to land at Lingayen. From there it was a very direct, standard type of military operation towards Manila.

It had also been previously planned that about the time the forces that landed at Lingayen were approaching Manila from the northwest and had Manila surrounded and so forth. An additional small landing would be made at a little spot on the open beach just northwest of Subic Bay. Subic Bay was a spot that would make an excellent naval harbor for our ships if we did not decide to stay in Manila. Actually, Subic Bay had always been an important spot for naval ships. So after Lingayen and after the forces were well established in their attack on Manila, I landed a division of Army troops on the oceanfront just northwest of Subic Bay. Those troops were going to land and start toward Manila, which they would do by going through Subic Bay.

John T. Mason, Jr.: Kind of a pincers movement.

Admiral Struble: Yes. Of course, a relatively small force, but it would also be able to capture the land adjacent to Corregidor from which the Japs might be able to launch continual little harassments. But this new Army division that landed there would not only be coming at Manila from the southwest but would also be able to affect the flank of Corregidor.

John T. Mason, Jr.: Did you anticipate a great deal of opposition there at the landing on the beach?

Admiral Struble: No. All of our information indicated that we weren't going to have it, and we didn't. We didn't have any opposition on the beach. We had very minor opposition that really meant nothing in Subic Bay. So both of those landings and operations were accomplished with hardly any casualties.

John T. Mason, Jr.: Did you take the necessary precautions in terms of minesweeping and so forth, and bombarding the beach?

Admiral Struble: Well, the ocean beach very obviously had no mines, so there was no problem there. We did make a slight effort to ensure that there were no mines at the entrance to Subic, and there were not. So we went right in to Subic. We were supported there by a cruiser division that had probably been in the Lingayen operation and had been held over to handle this second operation.

John T. Mason, Jr.: Was great opposition anticipated in the Manila area?

Admiral Struble: There was a considerable number of Japs, who, up until the time we had landed and gone through Subic, were roaming that country west of Corregidor and who were putting up opposition. However, the moment that this division landed on the coast, we started across where Subic Bay city is, you might say, and heading up towards Manila, the opposition disappeared quite rapidly. They all retreated on their own main body. So we took over Subic Bay. Of course, it was very valuable to the Navy because we could anchor ships in there and anchor supply ships and all that sort of thing.

Now, we did not make too heavy an effort to try to clean out Corregidor with a bang because it was going to be tough fighting there, and we were just going to sacrifice unnecessarily if we tried to march in with a bang. However, as soon as the Japs realized that they were getting undercut behind themselves in Manila Bay, then they finally gave up on the island.

John T. Mason, Jr.: Were you the one who developed the strategy of a gradual taking of Corregidor, I mean without the frontal assault idea?

Admiral Struble: Well, of course, we did have a frontal assault, you might say.

John T. Mason, Jr.: But I mean in the easing up.

Admiral Struble: The further development of it naturally developed on the spot. I encouraged the Army people and tried to provide everything we could from the naval angle, to take it slow and easy and not unnecessarily try to barge in because we had no great purpose in capturing it except for the fact that it was fine for us to be able to announce that Corregidor has been recaptured. Of course, that was done when General MacArthur and Admiral Barbey and others all came down for that ceremony, you might say, when the flag was rehoisted.

John T. Mason, Jr.: That was a highly emotional moment too.

Admiral Struble: Right. To MacArthur as well as everybody else.

John T. Mason, Jr.: Well, you accomplished this landing on the beach above Subic Bay; what was your next move?

Admiral Struble: Well, I remained until after the surrender of Corregidor and then I went back to Leyte. In the meantime, all of the senior people—both the Army and the Navy—were commencing to center in Manila after we had taken over Corregidor and hoisted the flag. Manila, in general terms, had come under our control. Then Kinkaid and MacArthur and all of them moved up.

John T. Mason, Jr.: Manila itself, Manila Bay, was not a very [unclear] place for ships at that point, however, was it? It was in pretty horrible condition.

Admiral Struble: Yes, but not that bad. No, it was all right. That became the center of things. When I got back to Leyte after the landing at Lingayen and the one at Subic Bay, then I became the senior man in the whole southern area from the Navy point of view because Barbey and everybody else was up in Manila, which was where they belonged and which was where the future planning was going to take place. I guess I was the SOP at Leyte for a month or two months down there, kind of mopping up and going to some other islands.[*]

We did make a few more landings. One of them in particular was at—what was the place where the Air Force was?

John T. Mason, Jr.: Well, you landed at Panay and at Negros, the northern part of the island.

The reason I brought up Manila Bay is because Admiral Sullivan told me some years ago about the condition of it.[†] He was the salvage man, and he was called to Manila as soon as the troops took it. He told me about the horrible conditions of the bay, the sunken ships and all the rest of it.

Admiral Struble: I'm sure there were a tremendous number of sunken ships and everything. That was a big job for the people who had the job of cleaning it out, but it isn't very dramatic. It was just a hell of a tough job for the fellow who had to do the cleanup.

John T. Mason, Jr.: Yes.

Admiral Struble: I don't see anything else about it that needs—from our point of view.

John T. Mason, Jr.: No. Shall we turn our attention to that southern area that you were engaged in mopping up? Morison says that General MacArthur wanted to capture Iloilo and Cebu City and use them as staging points for troops that were to be redeployed from Europe, with the idea of the forthcoming direct assault on Japan. That was back of the plan for taking these areas.

---

[*] SOP—senior officer present.
[†] Rear Admiral William A. Sullivan, USN (Ret.), was the subject of an oral history that Dr. Mason conducted under the auspices of Columbia University.

Admiral Struble: That is true. We went to a number of specific spots in the southern islands where we practically had little or no opposition so that in those southern areas there could have been a considerable amount of ships and troops assembled and formed up. Of course, the final attack going north to land on the Japanese island of Kyushu would have been a tremendous force, and you couldn't assemble it all in any one bay or spot. Therefore, it would have been assembled, I suppose, in as many as a half a dozen different spots, one of which, of course, would have been Leyte.

But when you put in a good size force like that, it's well to scatter them around because a large force needs the space. Now, the units that would assemble the ships would all be able to assemble at sea north of the Philippines as they headed north and get in the formation and order that they would be needed to attack Japan. So that was really advanced planning for the actual landing on Japan, what you are talking about.

Now, of course, from MacArthur's point of view, I think he felt it was valuable to pay some attention to most all of these Philippine Islands and in effect have them removed from Japanese supervision by the presence of some Americans in ships and ashore to show the Philippines that we had lived up and come back to rescue them, not just talked about it but had come to these islands.

John T. Mason, Jr.: And that we were actually doing so.

Admiral Struble: That we were actually doing it. Now, of course, in all of those later operations every now and then we got a little bit of a fight. As we moved in to land, there might be a few Japs there, but relatively small numbers. There would be maybe some little fight put up and it would dissipate. They would retreat and run off and try to get away, and we'd move in and take over the place with very little opposition.

John T. Mason, Jr.: Now, Morison does make the statement that there were maybe 30,000 Japanese in the Cebu-Panay area.

Admiral Struble: Well now, Fechteler made the landing in Cebu. I guess he had been in the Manila area and was coming down to the south and eastward going to Leyte.

Fechteler had come over from Leyte with a force that made a frontal attack on Cebu. It was a toughie, and they had pretty heavy opposition from the Japs on Cebu. But after about two or three days of a little bit of touch and go fighting, you might say (I had been over to the westward), I came over and joined up with Fechteler for this landing that he had made on Cebu.

John T. Mason, Jr.: Did you bring amphibious forces with you?

Admiral Struble: Oh, yes, I had amphibious forces that I had used in Panay so that when I got over to Cebu, Fechteler's landing was under pretty good control. I mean, there was still a group of Japs and a certain amount of gun power and everything at an elevation of 200 or 300 feet up—kind of on the hilly country above the city. They were still a little bit pestiferous. But Fechteler had completed the landing very successfully and it was done when I got there.

However, as soon as I arrived he went back to Leyte, and I took over the further cleanup and completion of the Cebu landing. Then from Cebu I went over to Leyte and by that time everybody had left Leyte and I became the SOP to further handle this southern area for additional small landings that the Army would make here and there. As I told you previously, this really showed our good intentions and the fact that we had personally come to the islands to clean them up.

John T. Mason, Jr.: Now, if there were 30,000 Japanese on Cebu, what happened to them?

Admiral Struble: Oh, there weren't that many. There may have been 3,000, not 30,000.

John T. Mason, Jr.: Were they wiped out or . . . ?

Admiral Struble: Well, they disappeared. A lot of them retreated by ship. Actually, they didn't entirely retreat. A number of those who put up quite a fight at Cebu actually went north on the island, and there was no advantage in trying to charge into areas where the other fellow had all the advantage on you. So we just sealed off areas in the north part of Cebu until they surrendered rather then try to go in and dig them out. A few people at the end of a tunnel or a few people in an important spot can cause one hell of a lot of trouble for a pretty good-sized force and cause an awful lot of casualties. So there was no use in our pursuing the actual elimination of these last outfits. It was smarter for us to just get them surrounded, get control of the main body of the country, and then just sit it out on them.

John T. Mason, Jr.: And then time would take care of it.

Admiral Struble: And then time would take care of it; that was the proper way to do the fighting. Now, we were doing that all over the southern part in a number of places. Generally the Japs would concentrate and go to one spot, so we would automatically get maybe three-fourths of them out without any effort by going in and saying hello.

John T. Mason, Jr.: The indication is that the Japs were largely in the cities and towns, because the rest of the islands were controlled largely by guerrillas.

Admiral Struble: Of course, the principal towns or places are where the supervision had always occurred from that island so that was the place you had to take over. If you had a military force located in one spot that was still able to roam much and do much, then you did have to go in and try to get rid of them. That's the cleanup. It isn't of tremendous importance, but there is no particular advantage of putting your own armed forces in to dig them out when the advantage is three or four or five to one from the other fellow and the number of people that are going to get killed.

It was just like the reason for going to Ormoc. If we conducted our frontal attack on the Japs instead of sneaking around the back and catching them from behind at Ormoc, we would have lost three or four times as many troops as we did lose by doing it the way we did.

The cleanup job is never attractive. This is what happened to me after I took over Cebu; I had to stay there for a couple of weeks. Then by the time I got ready to get up, I had the cleanup problem. However, I suppose I stayed there in the cleanup spot for about six weeks maybe and then I got word that I could go back to the United States for a month's leave. So then I departed. It was obvious that this landing in Japan would probably not take place before September.

John T. Mason, Jr.: Now, before you resume the story at that point, tell me about the landing and the need for the landing at Macajalar Bay. This was in Mindanao and this was in May.* I understand that we were meeting opposition from the Japanese on Mindanao.

Admiral Struble: We did not have an easy or a good approach to that landing area. It was tough, a little tough. We had to go through with it because it was big enough to eliminate.

John T. Mason, Jr.: That again was something reminiscent of Ormoc. You went around to the top and came in.

Admiral Struble: That's right. That's what happened. When I got to the landing that you're talking about, they had conducted the maneuver where they had gotten around behind the Japs. The Japs had departed but they had also had to scatter. So by the time I got to that island—which was broadly this kind of run-around job that I had gotten, that had been accomplished and the Army general who was there in command—I left first to go on back and take a look at Cebu and he left I suppose about a week later after he reported that he was through down there. It was all done. Maybe it was a couple of weeks later before he left.

MacArthur had a couple of lieutenant generals under him and one of them who had been up in the campaign for Manila was sent back to Leyte for the Army just like I was sent back there for the Navy to be in broad command of this cleanup of the southern island group.

---

* Mindanao is the farther south of the Philippine Islands. The Japanese invaded it on 20 December 1941, and the Americans surrendered it on 6 May 1942. The U.S. Eighth Army began a series of invasions of the island on 17 April 1945, and fighting went on intermittently until the war ended in August of that year.

John T. Mason, Jr.: Were there any particularly interesting events in connection with the mopping-up exercises that you might put on tape?

Admiral Struble: Well, until we cleaned out the ability of Japanese air to operate against us, for example, at Ormoc, the job of the Ormoc resupply—you realize I had made a landing and put an outfit there and had had a fairly good amount of supplies with them, but a week later they needed gasoline and more supplies. So the Ormoc resupply which for a while we had to make the same route that I had made, and until we got the Japanese air out—I guess they were about 50 or 60 miles away from us. Until we got that cleaned out, we did have quite a problem there. While those Japs—as long as they had airplanes, as long as they had gas, which they had apparently a very good supply of and so forth—they were able to raise hell around Ormoc for us even after we had cleaned out Ormoc. But we didn't clean Ormoc up in five minutes. It took quite a while before we had gotten the surrender of Ormoc.

John T. Mason, Jr.: What about—in any one of these islands, did you run into any mining that was troublesome?

Admiral Struble: No, we thought that we were probably going to either Cebu or the island just to the westward. I had taken mine forces in those areas, but I had come from the west—that's where I had been—so that I was in the island to the westward of Cebu. There is one spot there that would be excellent for them to have mined which we approached very gingerly and so forth. We did not approach Cebu as gingerly, although we did have a little mine group going in there ahead of us, but we didn't need to. There was no Jap mining at Cebu.

John T. Mason, Jr.: How do you account for their failure to have planted mines?

Admiral Struble: Well, I imagine it would have been because it's quite a way from Japan down there. The mines would not have been in the Philippines; the mines would have had to have been in Japan. For quite a while of the period that we have talked about, their ability to bring mines down from Japan to use in the Philippines had been tremendously curtailed by our own naval operations—the submarines and surface that had been going on, but north of the Philippines against the Japanese Islands.

Halsey and Nimitz's operations there were shutting the Japanese off from sending stuff south, getting anywhere.* It's true they could run a military force out of Japan. Unless you intercepted that specific military force, you couldn't stop them; they could run a military force out of Japan all the way down to the west of the Philippine Islands without any trouble. But that military force would have taken with it a certain number of tankers for gas and everything, but they couldn't carry down tremendous large amounts of military supplies and mines and things. That had been sealed off already by the central Pacific operations.

John T. Mason, Jr.: Supplies of that sort had to come by convoy under special guidance.

Admiral Struble: Yes, and boy, they would run into Halsey and his outfit and would be demolished.

John T. Mason, Jr.: That's a logical explanation for their failure to have done that.

Admiral Struble: Yes. They hadn't gotten to that point before our opposition, and particularly this naval opposition which was directed from Honolulu because that thing started up as early as we could develop it. We realized—the Navy realized very much the importance of trying to seal off Japan as quickly as we could. We were going to do that from the sea, we weren't going to do it form the land.

We were eventually, apparently, going to have to recapture Japan from the land, by landing troops, but we didn't need to do that to stop anything except fairly good-sized, fast naval forces from operating. As you know, until we had gotten into the Philippines in pretty good force, the Japanese were able to operate their number-one seagoing outfit,

---

* Admiral William F. Halsey, Jr., USN, served as Commander Third Fleet from 15 March 1943 to 22 November 1945.

both to the west and to the south of the Philippines, and there wasn't a hell of a lot we could do about it because we couldn't go off chasing. But we could keep Japan itself sealed off which was the important touch.

Now, I think that General MacArthur at times felt that he didn't get as much Navy as he should have down there under him. But he didn't need the Navy under him and it should never have been put under him. The constant naval work against Japan was going on before MacArthur ever got out in the western Pacific and it was most important. We were commencing to give the Japanese an awful lot of problems at home. We couldn't keep their submarines from leaving Japan and coming out and attacking here and there. We couldn't necessarily get a surface force of their battleships and carriers if they left Japan and decided to go let's say down to Taiwan and bombard it and so forth. We couldn't stop that.

But if they did come down to Taiwan to do that, then our central Pacific naval force being ready could maybe give that force that they send down there hell before they got back to Japan again. You see the idea involved?

John T. Mason, Jr.: Yes.

Admiral Struble: Now, this was the strategy that was sound, and it was right. Nimitz was entirely on the right track in every way when he insisted that the naval forces ought to stay under the command of the central Pacific and that it was their job to sequester, etc., Japan.

John T. Mason, Jr.: Now, when you say that, that the naval forces should not have been put under MacArthur, you don't mean that the Kinkaid command was unnecessary?

Admiral Struble: Oh, no, I didn't say that. The point was—yes, when MacArthur got to the place where he needed naval support, a very good admiral went down there to be under him and assist his military operation to the greatest extreme that they could. But they could only do it to the extent of the forces that were given them by the Central

Pacific. That was the major spot for naval operations to be controlled from and it was the right spot.

Now, for instance, when we went into Europe we eventually agreed—we did happen to have an American become the new Supreme Allied Commander for the ground forces in Europe. Well, that was fine. Whether it was an Englishman or a Frenchman or an American has some political and other angles but also the man that was chosen proved to be a very capable supreme commander. There was no doubt about it, he did a very fine job.

Now, there was no necessity for tying up a large number of naval forces to Eisenhower. Those naval forces could be better employed doing a large number of other jobs until the day arrived when they made the landing on Europe. Then on that day, a hell of a lot of naval forces would be pushed in and used, temporarily, under the naval officer who was Eisenhower's principal naval officer. But there was no use giving those ships to that fellow in the six or eight months that we took to plan the final details of and accomplished the landing at Normandy.

I went over in November. I suppose I was over there six months. We didn't need these large naval forces until they were brought together and organized and used for the landing.

John T. Mason, Jr.: And the same thing pertains to the Philippines.

Admiral Struble: Why, of course, in the reverse direction, you might say.

John T. Mason, Jr.: Yes.

Admiral Struble: Now Eisenhower, when he came to London, Kirk and I talking to Eisenhower's people—why, of course, we'd agree, yes, we can do that. Yes, we will have that, we will handle that. But we didn't have to have the ships right there under our immediate command. And the fact is that except for the naval forces that were under Jimmy Hall who was going to be one of the principal men to land the troops at Europe, we didn't need the naval forces there.

In all fairness to the British and the French and others, when it came to the landing at Normandy, the Supreme Commander was an American—Eisenhower. He was also an Army man so that the two Army men, one British and one American, that were going to land at Normandy were going to be under Eisenhower. Montgomery was going to land the British Army troops and he was under Eisenhower, just like Bradley was under Eisenhower.

Now then, the British—this was right in their home territory, and they had a pretty good navy—they were able to know and operate and handle all the local naval problems better than we as Americans were. So it was perfectly proper to make a British vice admiral the principal naval officer under Eisenhower for the Normandy landing. The <u>principal</u> naval officer.

John T. Mason, Jr.: That was Ramsay.

Admiral Struble: Yes. It's also just as true as it was previously when I talked to you that Ramsay did not have to start taking control in November of the naval forces that he was going to use for the Normandy landing in June or May. He didn't need to run them in the meantime.

John T. Mason, Jr.: It's a good thing he didn't because they were in the Mediterranean and all over.

Admiral Struble: They were doing all sorts of useful things. But Kirk and I would say to Admiral Ramsay, "Why, yes, we'll have these naval forces available, and we'll agree to put this into the plan for the landing. But in the meantime you're not going to be in command of them."

Of course, actually one of the commands got over there a little bit early, and Ramsey would have liked to have taken control of them. He was going to be the big naval commander for the landing. But we maintained our position that no, Admiral Ramsay was going to be the principal naval officer at the landing; as I explained things to Admiral Ramsay and his chief of staff, neither one of them liked that part of it. But I said, "The moment we start the actual movement of troops and all that, you will be in position to give us a naval order and it will be accepted and we will carry it out."

There was never any idea on my part but what we had an outfit under Mort Deyo—some cruisers—and we also had a battleship division for a while that we had used at the landing on Normandy.* Once the Normandy landing started, had Admiral Ramsay sent us, "Send battleship division so-and-so," it would have been done. We would carry out naval orders that we got from him without any hesitation. We would have then told Bradley, "I'm sorry. We told you we could do so-and-so, but we're not going to be able to."

But somebody has to make those decisions as you're fighting. Now, of course, that would have meant if Bradley didn't like something that we were going to do, he was in a position to talk to Ike and say, "We wish you wouldn't have those Navy ships do so-and-so." Ike was then in a position to talk to his naval officer, Ramsay, and say, "Ramsay, I don't think we ought to do that." And they would talk about it and figure it out. That's the only way to run these shows: have clear lines of command and authority.

So if you've heard a lot of talking about all of this, you've got a pretty good discussion of it. I can tell you that Admiral Ramsay would much have preferred that Kirk and I, as naval officers, come over and operate under him.

John T. Mason, Jr.: Well in advance.

Admiral Struble: Yes. In advance we were agreed that we were going to plan and discuss and do anything. When it came the time for doing it, it was important that the naval planning that we had made for the landing with Bradley be thoroughly understood by Bradley. We and Bradley were in thorough cahoots, and if some higher authority had to change something, we were Bradley's men to holler for help. We would have objected to a naval order that we felt was going to hurt Bradley very much in any way. If something that we were going to change would have been better for Bradley, maybe the

---

* Rear Admiral Morton L. Deyo, USN, served as commander of the bombardment group for the landings at Utah Beach on 6 June 1944.

other way, but it was also a useful thing, then we would agree to it. That's the only way you can work it.

John T. Mason, Jr.: To go back to the Philippines and the mopping-up exercise, is there anything of interest to relate about the guerrillas on these various islands? I saw a note to the effect that Colonel Peralta, who was quite a character on Panay, had his guerrilla forces operating in a very effective way.*

Admiral Struble: I just can't answer that question and help you out. I really can't. I know that just what you discussed happened, but I didn't have—you see, I went back to Leyte, was the SOP, and theoretically would have been connected with a lot of these things. But then after I had been at Leyte as the SOP for a certain length of time, we were getting ready for the attack up north, but it was a long time off. So I was sent home on a month's leave.

When I came back after a month's leave in the United States, I was, naturally, flying west. When I got to Honolulu, I reported in, expecting that I would be probably ordered down to the Philippines as I had been previously. Nimitz in the meantime was no longer at Honolulu. He had moved out to Guam. So then I was ordered from Honolulu to Guam. When I actually got to Guam I was told, "Well, we're not going to send you down to the Philippines, we don't believe. So you just kind of wait around here to see what's going to happen."

John T. Mason, Jr.: Did you confer with Nimitz?

Admiral Struble: Oh, yes, sure. Actually, I didn't talk to Nimitz when I first got there for about two or three days because he wasn't there. He was off traveling. But I did, of course, see him when he got back.

Then I was held at Guam. This was about—I guess I was back in the United States until May. My wife and I went down to the Florida coast and just lolled in the sun and so forth. I didn't try to do any business at all with the Navy. We went off and we

---

* Colonel Marcario L. Peralta of the Philippine Army organized an effective guerrilla force on Panay.

came back and just at the end of leave time—I believe that I started out after I had been here a month.

[Note: At this point there is a gap of a few months that was intended to be discussed during the next interview but was not.]

John T. Mason, Jr.: But now we are going to September of 1945 after the Japanese surrender when Admiral Struble takes command of the minecraft in the Pacific Fleet, and his task was to clear mines in the Western Pacific.*

Were you elated at this new assignment?

Admiral Struble: Well, of course, it was a very good job. It was not the most important or one of the really exceptionally important parts of the Pacific Fleet, but it was a major command in the Pacific.

John T. Mason, Jr.: Well, in retrospect, it was of paramount importance, wasn't it?

Admiral Struble: Well, then, of course, the question came up, what would you be doing? And, of course, to have the assignment of cleaning up all the mines in the Western Pacific and so forth in the postwar occupation of Japan and everything was bound to be important and possibly difficult, because there would be a tendency for the personnel to want to get home and they should get home after the war. But it was also important to get rid of the mines for the safety of everybody who was going to be running around in the next six months out there.

John T. Mason, Jr.: I would think that your command at that point had high priority.

Admiral Struble: So I was on the small flagship that we had in Okinawa, and it became apparent that in connection with the post-surrender activities that we would operate for

---

* V-J Day—Victory-over-Japan Day, 15 August 1945, marking the end of hostilities in the war in the Pacific. The formal Japanese surrender was on 2 September on board the battleship Missouri (BB-63) in Tokyo Bay.

some fair amount of time out of Okinawa until we had cleared the entrances to Japan and were sure that we had a certain large number of ports where we could properly and safely land.

John T. Mason, Jr.: This all had to be planned in conjunction with General MacArthur in this new command, did it not?

Admiral Struble: This very definitely would be under General MacArthur. There would be no argument now. With the war over, the part about Japan would be under General MacArthur, and he was the man who was designated also to accept the surrender as the principal officer. Of course, Admiral Nimitz was recognized and everything, but he was recognized after MacArthur, as it were, because he was not going to be the principal man in Japan in the future, the surrender having occurred.

We had a fair amount of minesweepers. We had a large number of spots that required minesweeping, and it was certainly important that we open up a certain number of harbors in Japan with careful minesweeping as soon as possible.

John T. Mason, Jr.: Where did you assemble these minesweepers from?

Admiral Struble: The minesweepers actually were mostly already assembled in Okinawa getting ready for the attack on Japan, so your force was there and that was where you would operate from.

In addition, all of the postwar paperwork would have to be accomplished in Japan while you were doing minesweeping. This involved handling all the papers and a large number of recommendations that had been made for awards to officers and men in the minesweeping business as they had approached and gone up that far north. It meant a lot of paperwork to change over from the warlike status to the peacetime solution and to all of these recommendations for awards for minesweeping people for the last three or four months. Of course, unfortunately, as the new commander of that force, I had no connection with it during the war while this was going on.

Naturally, the man who had been fighting the job for a long time wanted to go home, and I can certainly understand that.

John T. Mason, Jr.: Let me ask you a question now. This is the nature of digression, I suppose. What was your basic attitude toward awards and decorations?

Admiral Struble: My basic attitude was that a large number of people deserved proper awards, and it was bad that two or three people maybe would be remembered for the first attack on, let's say, Okinawa. It was important in my opinion that because the war was over that we shouldn't just quit and say, "Yes, there are three or four or five people that ought to get an award." And then wash out everything else that had gone on. There were many people that had done well and many people that should be remembered. Now that the war was over, it ought to be done very carefully and methodically and properly. In a way, I felt that taking over this job, I had not been in a position to know about them personally, but there were others aboard that I would have on my staff and we could and should do our best to clean up the awards that were right, proper, and necessary. At the same time, we would go ahead with our minesweeping orders and business.

So I guess that we had assembled by that time a great big box that was four by four by about six feet tall full of papers for awards to various people that had been in this business.

John T. Mason, Jr.: And you as the new commander had to give approval to each and every one.

Admiral Struble: Oh, yes. You had to go over every one carefully. I had to get a new chief of staff, so the two top people in the Mine Force were not the real Mine Force people that had done the job. However, we did our best. We worked long and hard hours on that part of it. In addition, of course, most of the staff of the Mine Force were still there. They all wanted to go home. My attitude toward the Mine Force Pacific Fleet was that I could not afford to send too many people home in a wholesale fashion just because the war was over. We still had a very important job that was dangerous and had to be done.

The minesweeper was a small ship. It had a lieutenant or maybe a lieutenant commander in it, but it also had on board it at least one, sometimes two, very experienced older chief petty officers who knew the job and who were going to be important in doing the minesweeping that we had to do in the next three to six months before we would have the minesweeping accomplished. In all of these harbors of Japan where we had put in mines, it was important to have experienced people on these ships that knew what they were doing so we wouldn't risk the lives of people on the minesweepers by not having experienced men doing the work.

John T. Mason, Jr.: Well, how did you succeed in dealing with this business?

Admiral Struble: It was very difficult because the Congress and everybody in the United States wanted to send all of the people home who had done the fighting as quick as possible.

John T. Mason, Jr.: And those who had the necessary number of points were automatically, I thought—[*]

Admiral Struble: That is true, and I just simply refused to send these top chief petty officer people on minesweepers. If there were two and they were both good, you could send one of them home. But if there was only one on the minesweeping who was the only experienced minesweeper man on that ship, I said, "I'm sorry, but you've got to stay until we've done our job."

John T. Mason, Jr.: You must have been unpopular with some of these people.

---

[*] For the demobilization of the U.S. armed forces after World War II, the services had a point system to determine individual priorities for leaving the service. Points were awarded for length of service, overseas service, battle stars, decorations, and dependent children. Those with the highest number of points were the earliest discharged.

Admiral Struble: Very unpopular and a hell of a lot of objections were coming all the time from Congress in Washington, why didn't I send people home? But I just said I didn't think it was honest and safe for the individual ships. We had to have one excellent top man who knew his business on that ship, or it couldn't be done. So I kept them on, and I was very unpopular for the next four or five months.

John T. Mason, Jr.: How long did it take to shake down the thing?

Admiral Struble: I would have said by the following March we were getting in good shape. It seems to me it was about March that I permitted the first squadron to go home with all the people on board. However, I must say that although the Navy Department sent me all the messages and all the thoughts that came up on the subject, they never canceled my order.

John T. Mason, Jr.: You must have had tacit approval on the part of Admiral King and others that this was the right policy.

Admiral Struble: Well, very obviously the people in the Navy Department recognized I was right. While they sent me messages that included what some of the prominent Congressmen felt and thought, I just didn't do it.

John T. Mason, Jr.: In general, can you say something about this Magic Carpet procedure?* I mean about the release of military people immediately following the war? The advisability about this? The wisdom of it?

Admiral Struble: I would say that on the whole there was no reason why a large amount of the combatant ships and the combatant people shouldn't go back home. They could always come back again if they had to. Therefore, the ships could go home and all the people who were in those ships could go home with them and should go home with them.

---

* Magic Carpet was the nickname for the use of Navy ships, including combatants, to bring servicemen home to the United States from overseas once World War II ended.

But in the case of minesweeping, I felt it was very desirable to keep the structures that were there. I think I authorized the second squadron to depart in a fair amount of time thereafter.

John T. Mason, Jr.: I was thinking of the whole policy in terms of the problems that continued on into the peaceful period following World War II. There was a potential enemy still fairly well armed. What about the wisdom on our part of disarming so rapidly in face of that?

Admiral Struble: I think you've got to recognize a fleet is capable of doing one thing and then doing another very rapidly. So the ships could be brought together and brought back again in a hurry if they had to. I think we had every reason to feel that the Japanese surrender was honest and straightforward. So while we had to keep a few of the combatant ships out there, I don't think we did need such a large number. You could afford to send most of the combatant ships back.

But in my opinion, the minesweeping business was sufficiently dangerous for the next three to four months that we shouldn't send the minesweepers back. It was only the minesweepers I felt that way about. Had I been the chief of staff to the rest of the combatant fleet, I would have been content to send a lot of them back and would have done so.

John T. Mason, Jr.: Would there not be some wisdom in a policy of gradualism rather than the precipitous way in which . . .?

Admiral Struble: There undoubtedly might be some ideas of the fact that it would be better that way. But on the whole, the war was over. I think we were all convinced of it. It had been a long, drawn-out war, and I think the idea of getting as many of the combatant ship people back in the States was a good idea.

Now, we didn't keep very many of the Navy ships around the Japanese islands, and I don't think we needed them. But I did think we needed to keep all the minesweepers and not simply because it was my command but simply so that we could get this minesweeping work done properly and safely. Although the Japanese helped us, they became one of my problems because they wanted to have their ships do it too. They said, "We should do part of it."

John T. Mason, Jr.: Do penance.

Admiral Struble: Do penance, that's right. But they wanted to and they were very strong for it. I recognized I had to agree to that and let them do some of the minesweeping. But then I found out my own minesweeping people were raising hell because the Japs didn't understand minesweeping the way we did. It was very difficult to try to combine the Japanese and an American minesweeping unit. The Japs were perfectly willing to work for us. There was no question of command or any of that kind of stuff. They were quite willing to work for us, but they wanted to do part of it.

Well, we had a couple of accidents that were caused because the Japanese didn't understand our methods. They were wanting to do too much too quickly, and we had some minesweeping accidents. They were our own fault in a way, but they were caused by the way the Japanese were wanting to be too active to help and our intercommunication was not always completely and thoroughly understood.

Therefore, when we were going to enter some of these principal harbors of Japan where I knew we had dropped by air a lot of very dangerous American weapons, I felt we had to have that operation controlled very much in the hands of the Americans who knew their business when we went in to do the minesweeping. As a matter of fact, although we got lots of civilian and other experts, we could not agree among ourselves on the plan for sweeping some of these bigger harbors. Therefore, as the boss man, although I was not really a minesweeping man, I had to make the final decision on how we would sweep out some of these areas. I never hesitated making them. I listened to what all the experts said, but I found out that they always had different ideas.

These mines that we dropped by air were dangerous, and we didn't want to kill any of our people while trying to get rid of them. We were on the whole very successful. We did have, of course, some accidents.

John T. Mason, Jr.: Did you encounter any feeling on the part of American personnel towards working with the Japanese? Was there any feeling, a carry-over from the war itself?

Admiral Struble: No, not because of the war but our experienced minesweeper captains preferred to do the job themselves if we were going to do it and not have the Japanese connected with it. They realized that when I, for instance, took a group of Japanese small ships and assigned them to one of these American commanders, he had a hard time commanding them because he and the Japanese outfit didn't do things the same way and they had an awful hard time communicating properly with each other.

Therefore, the American squadron and division commanders that I had under me really would have preferred to do the job entirely themselves because they would know what they were doing and they would know their people would know what they were doing.

John T. Mason, Jr.: Was General MacArthur aware of your problem? What was his attitude towards this cooperation on the part of the Japanese naval forces?

Admiral Struble: Well, he sent for me a number of times. I'm sure he was aware of it because I told him. However, he never tried to supervise in the slightest. He said, "Arthur, it's your job. You've got to go get it done."

John T. Mason, Jr.: Well, he was happy to give the Japs a job, was he?

Admiral Struble: He recognized the part of using the Japs as much as you could, and he told me clearly and frankly, "If and when you can use them, I think it's a healthy thing to do." But he said, "You have to make the decision—you and your own people. You've got to make yourself what's the safest way to do it and you go ahead and do it that way." And he said, "I will back you up on keeping your experienced men here until it's done."

John T. Mason, Jr.: Good. Did he give you a list of ports priorities—as to what ports he would prefer to do?

Admiral Struble: He told me what would be best from his point of view, but he never tried to dictate. I found him an excellent military man to work for.

John T. Mason, Jr.: What were some of the other problems you encountered in the sweeping process?

Admiral Struble: Well, of course, some mines had dragged and others had undoubtedly become obsolete. But we didn't know that. We did want to allow more time before you'd get into every area where there might have been mines. So we tried to select, first, the important places that were needed in the connection with our return of Japan to normality. And there were a number of big harbors, so we would select one harbor and would try to make a fairly wide path up through that harbor so it could be used for merchant ships and other ships and then try to mark off the parts that hadn't been swept and let time take its course in handling some of those. We went ahead on the problem of sweeping a specific path in each of the important harbors.

John T. Mason, Jr.: Do you imply that some of the mines you would drop would become obsolete?

Admiral Struble: Ah, yes. We knew whether those that we had dropped were still active and when they would become obsolete.

John T. Mason, Jr.: What sort of life span is there for some of these?

Admiral Struble: You can arrange that a mine deaden itself, if you want to, and when.

John T. Mason, Jr.: And we had done that?

Admiral Struble: Well, we had kept track of everything we had put down. So we had a certain amount of knowledge ourselves. But we, of course, were always careful. If we felt that a certain amount of mined area was dead, we would generally play on the safe side and count on more time.

John T. Mason, Jr.: Now, you are talking in terms of how many thousands of mines constituting this major problem?

Admiral Struble: Well, I must say I've never asked for that figure, and I don't think I can afford to give you one. But we did know where our most dangerous ones were. The American mines, by the way, were the most dangerous ones planted. They were the ones that we had to put our specific attention on. They had been dropped, as you know, by air.

One of the problems of air-dropped mines that you had to concern yourself with was that the airplanes could go up over a certain harbor in Japan at, say, 1:00 or 2:00 o'clock in the morning. They would drop a group of mines as the plane went on and they would attempt to drop them in a certain spot in the harbor from A to Z. Well, they would have been dropped from maybe 8,000 feet. Now, there is no doubt about the aircraft's ability to navigate, but it was a little difficult for them to be sure if they were exactly where they wanted to be at the time they started dropping mines.

John T. Mason, Jr.: The same problem as dropping bombs, was it not?

Admiral Struble: Yes, exactly. They'd run a stick of them, eight or ten in a line. Actually, that bunch could be right where they were supposed to have been dropped or under certain conditions in navigation and clouds and all other matters, they conceivably could have been a mile away. So then you had several of these long harbor entrances in Japan, and one of the first ones that we wanted to get cleaned out was one of the longer ones. Maybe it ran 20 or 30 miles, so you had quite a bit of area that you had to sweep.

Now, the sweepers that went in there were always susceptible to being blown up by our own mines. So it increased your necessity for determining how thoroughly you would sweep for the mines and where. Of course, it was impossible for us to sweep all of those large areas. The only thing we could do was try to sweep a path, make a channel that was safe and take our chances.

John T. Mason, Jr.: Now, your problem must have been complicated greatly by the Japanese mines as well. Did they not mine some of their areas for protection?

Admiral Struble: They were very, very cooperative. They really wanted to sweep all of their own mines themselves and accept the danger of it. So from that point of view, our immediate cooperation with the Japanese minesweeping people was very fine and good because they would say, "Oh, so-and-so harbor mine. Dangerous."

If I saw no reason to go in there for the next six or eight months, I'd say, "All right. We won't worry about that harbor. You keep shipping on. You go back and clean up sometime. But in the meantime, I want to get a number of specific harbors cleared up that were of importance right away to both you and to us." So we swept the principal harbors of Japan that needed it. As I remember, by March we still had a certain amount of harbors that I felt needed some American minesweeping, but I believe we sent the first big squadron of ships home then. So I guess they had been there by that time from. . .

John T. Mason, Jr.: From September to March.

Admiral Struble: Well, we didn't get started up probably much before October.

John T. Mason, Jr.: Did you get any help from the American Naval Mission, that survey under Admiral Ofstie that was in Japan?[*]

Admiral Struble: I don't believe that they affected us too much. We had an almost immediate cooperation directly from the Japanese minesweeping people. We really did. Of course, if we wanted some information, we would send word to Tokyo. Tokyo would get the information from the Japanese and send it back to us. So we didn't attempt to enter into the relations and arrangements that were going on in Tokyo at all.

---

[*] Rear Admiral Ralph A. Ofstie, USN, senior naval member of the U.S. Strategic Bombing Survey.

John T. Mason, Jr.: I seem to remember having read somewhere that a couple of our submarines were involved in the operation of locating mines and that sort of thing. Was that true?

Admiral Struble: I was there about six months, and midway in that we did have some operation with American submarines. They were also concerned with some mines that we had dropped in the Guam area. We were also, as I remember, going to have some tests of our own up in that mid-Pacific area near Guam. So up in those areas we did have some submarines and some of our minecraft operating in conjunction with each other for that purpose. I would call that a postwar activity and not a war effort. It was a further development of some of our equipment and ideas. But that was for the future and not for the immediate major problem that we had with the Japanese of restoring the harbors.

John T. Mason, Jr.: You mentioned the Guam area and the mines there. We did mine the harbor there, didn't we?

Admiral Struble: Oh, yes.

John T. Mason, Jr.: I was wondering if some of the ports up in the Hokkaido area had been mined. Did you attempt to do anything about them, or were you merely concerned about Kyushu and that area where most of the commercial shipping was done?

Admiral Struble: We were really concerned in addition to the eastern side and the south side and a certain amount of the western side of Japan. On the western side we left the Japanese more or less entirely in charge of everything north of Sasebo. And on the eastern side, more or less everything north of [tape turned over and material lost]

John T. Mason, Jr.: What determined the end of your operation?

Admiral Struble: Well, Tokyo and south was all cleared up, which was one of the principal areas. Then you had the big southern area of Japan, and you had north on the west side about a hundred miles, maybe a little more. In other words, the harbors on the southwest, south, and the southeast of Japan had been cleaned up and were opened. We felt that in most cases in some of the northern spots that letting time take its course was the best answer, but the Japs worked that out by themselves.

John T. Mason, Jr.: Did you do anything with Hiroshima and Nagasaki?

Admiral Struble: We swept at Nagasaki. We didn't do anything at Hiroshima. We only did a very minor amount of sweeping in spots in the Inland Sea. We were pretty sure we knew where the danger spots were, and we had gone after them.

John T. Mason, Jr.: I was wondering whether there was any particular danger of radioactive material still in the area at Nagasaki when you swept so soon thereafter.

Admiral Struble: Well, of course, there was possibly a certain amount of danger from the bomb drop, but that was over pretty much on the beach. The Japanese themselves kind of marked off certain areas, and then I didn't have anything to do with that.

John T. Mason, Jr.: I know. But I wondered if there wasn't some concern on your part since we didn't actually know too much about the duration of that danger, did we?

Admiral Struble: I think that's true, but I think we had warned the Japanese very much about getting into those areas where the bomb had dropped, the land areas, and they were just kind of marking it all off and waiting for further word from us and so forth. But I couldn't tell you about that part of it because I had nothing to do with that.

John T. Mason, Jr.: I see.

Admiral Struble: I would have been gone by about the time they had finished. The Air Force would have been the people that would have handled an inspection of the areas where the bomb dropped and have made the decision for the Japanese on what was safe and unsafe.

John T. Mason, Jr.: You said earlier that because of the willing cooperation of the Japanese in the sweeping operation that there were several accidents. Do you want to tell me about them? What were they?

Admiral Struble: Well, I'll give you one example. We had a squadron that was doing minesweeping. In a given location they might cut the wire or cable holding the mine about six feet above the bottom. All right, the sweeper would cut the cable to the mine. The mine would then bob up to the surface. Now, there were also some ships that were following the people doing the sweeping. The mine bobbed up, and a couple of good rifle men would shoot that mine up and try to explode it if they could.

Now, those sweepers that were coming along with the riflemen in them couldn't get too close to the mine squadron that was cutting the cables because one of those ships could explode itself on the mine that just popped up. That happened.

John T. Mason, Jr.: It's a question of timing.

Admiral Struble: That happened. It was unfortunate. It was American minesweepers that had cut the mines. It was the Jap minesweeper that was following too close that hit the mine and exploded. Now, the Japanese were not worried about it. They accepted that as one of the dangers of the thing. But, of course, as we tried to tell them, "You got too close." We didn't want to criticize them, but you can get too active and too energetic sometimes in an operation. It would have been better if they had been farther back.

Well, those are the difficulties that you enter into when you have two nationalities and different means of talking. I am sure the American minesweeper that was cutting the mine cables told them very carefully and surely what to do. The Japanese minesweeper man apparently didn't understand it accurately enough; one of his minesweepers got up too close and got sunk.

John T. Mason, Jr.: Maybe his reflex was too swift.

Admiral Struble: Well, these are things you run into, don't you see? You've got to be careful cooperating. People don't speak simply and easily to each other in a joint operation.

John T. Mason, Jr.: I understand that very well. Now, they weren't all the same type mines, were they?

Admiral Struble: Oh, no, they were entirely different types.

John T. Mason, Jr.: How do you detonate a contact mine from the other kind?

Admiral Struble: Well, with a contact mine you drop an anchor, and you have a cable on it. Preferably the contact mine floats underneath the surface so that it isn't visible.

John T. Mason, Jr.: But attached to a cable?

Admiral Struble: Attached to a cable so that it isn't on the bottom. If it's contact, it's got to be up to the point where the ship will smack it. So it must be, say, anywhere from about six feet under water to not much over about 20; otherwise a big ship coming in won't hit it.
    Now, if you're mining by air and you're dropping these mines down, you may be dropping them down with a cable that will take them under water or maybe even above water or maybe kind of just more or less barely afloat and hardly visible.

John T. Mason, Jr.: In other words, you have to be pretty knowledgeable of the water depth where you are dropping them.

Admiral Struble: Yes, you do, of course. So a lot of the airdrops that were made at night undoubtedly were not right on the beam always. Now, those mines should have made themselves safe a certain number of months later.

John T. Mason, Jr.: I take it that our mines were somewhat more sophisticated than the Japanese types.

Admiral Struble: Oh, yes.

John T. Mason, Jr.: I once asked somebody in connection with the Korean conflict about the mines used by the North Koreans, and I was told that they all dated from World War I.

Admiral Struble: Well, I think they did.

John T. Mason, Jr.: But our mines as we dropped them in Japanese harbors were more sophisticated and more developed.

Admiral Struble: They were. You see, you might decide to mine a certain area yourself with modern stuff because you don't have enough ships to keep on station to guard that spot. If the other fellow wants to try to come in there now that you are fighting the end with a ship, why, you'd just as soon mine it yourself and you know it's done so you don't go in there. When he comes in, he'll get popped.

    Now, I have this connected with the Koreans later too.

John T. Mason, Jr.: Yes, I know. We'll get you to talk about mines in Korean waters later on.

Admiral Struble: Well, I don't know too much more to say on this. If you're interested in MacArthur, I'll tell you a little more.

John T. Mason, Jr.: Oh, yes indeed, I am. Tell me something more about your relations with him at that point.

Admiral Struble: MacArthur sent for me to come to Tokyo occasionally, and I would tell him how we were coming along and what was going on. As I guess I've previously said, I found him an excellent military man to work with. He was decisive. When he sent for you, why, you would talk to MacArthur and nobody else. You knew what was what and it was settled very easily and quickly. So I found him a fine man to work with.

John T. Mason, Jr.: What was your estimate of his staff? I've heard so many conflicting opinions of the staff and how they prevented people from getting to the general.

Admiral Struble: Well, I never ran into that problem with him.

John T. Mason, Jr.: No, you were one of the privileged.

Admiral Struble: I was one of those who, when I came up, saw him and he never had his staff around to complicate the matter. Or if he did, it was a discussion that he wanted his staff to hear. So from my point of view, from another service, he was an excellent man, as far as I was concerned, to work with.

Now, I am sure that General MacArthur had about three or four times as many people wanting to talk to him as he was able to handle. Therefore, his staff had to protect him, as it were, from everybody that wanted to talk to him. I imagine that in the early days in Tokyo, there were an awful lot of Americans that came over that wanted to talk to him. It wasn't really necessarily on business. So I assume that his staff felt that it had to try to shield him. Under those conditions, the staff always get to feel too important maybe rather than less. I think that's the way it works out.

I've heard stories, of course, about MacArthur, and I'm sure that he couldn't talk to everybody so there had to be some system of eliminating those who could and those who couldn't. I can only speak really for myself on that.

John T. Mason, Jr.: Well, you were always in a position with the general of being an operational man who had important things to do, and he was interested in getting the things accomplished.

Admiral Struble: That is correct. So I was a privileged person in that respect. Of course, by the time we got into the Korean business, he had known me before, and so I always talked to him in private and we always had a good, simple, easy conversation. I found him quite reasonable to do joint business with.

He'd say, "I understand you are doing so-and-so. Why are you doing that? I think it would be better for the Army if you did it the other way."

Of course, the people kicked to him about the way I was doing something over in Korea. I'd say, "General, this is my approach on that. I think thus and so, and I just told the Army representative there that we weren't going to do that. It wasn't good business."

I'd explain it to MacArthur and he'd say, "You are right. Stick to it." Because he thought so. If he didn't, he talked with me some further. But I found him a very good military boss and a good man to do business with myself. He didn't always agree with you, but if I didn't agree with him, my experience was that I could always tell him. If I had a good reason, he always accepted it.

John T. Mason, Jr.: Did you find him to be the brilliant man that he was reported to have been?

Admiral Struble: Oh, he was definitely a very brilliant man; there's no doubt of that. I wouldn't always have done things maybe the way he did. I think politically he was probably a little bit tough with other people. I felt it was a very unfortunate incident the way he and Truman got into contact with each other, and I think under unfavorable conditions.* I think Mr. Truman, in a way, was too thoughtful about MacArthur. I don't think he ever should have gone halfway out or part of the way out to Japan the way

---

* Harry S. Truman was President of the United States from 1945 to 1953. In 1951, During the Korean War, he relieved General MacArthur of command in the Far East because of his perception that MacArthur was insubordinate.

he did.* I think that was a big mistake. I think if President Truman thought that he and MacArthur were not working well together, he should have sent him a message to come to Washington and talked to him across his desk in the White House and straightened it out.

John T. Mason, Jr.: You feel that going to Wake was in a sense acknowledging MacArthur's political clout?

Admiral Struble: No, I don't think it was acknowledging his political clout, but I don't think it was the way to solve the problem that existed. He was the President. If they were getting at outs with each other, order him back to Washington and talk it through and get rid of it. Regardless if MacArthur says, "It's too important out here from the military point of view for me to leave."

Truman should have said, "Tell your second in command to take command, and I'll be responsible for anything that happens while you're gone." That's what I would have liked to see him do. That's what I think is the proper thing for him to have done. The only other answer was for him to go out and talk to MacArthur in MacArthur's office, but not in the presence of a hell of a lot of staff on either side. You're never going to settle that kind of a problem unless you settle it on the top level between the top people involved.

John T. Mason, Jr.: I've heard some criticism leveled at MacArthur and others of the military nature because they, in a sense according to the critics, tended to mix a military thing with politics. The critics claim that this could never be.

Admiral Struble: Well, I think my solution is the right one.

John T. Mason, Jr.: You'll stand on that.

---

* Truman and MacArthur met at Wake Island in the Pacific in 1950, several months before Truman relieved MacArthur.

Admiral Struble: I'll stand on that. In doing business with MacArthur I found out if you were able to talk to him personally and you discussed the thing frankly, you usually reached an answer. There was no reason then why that thing shouldn't have worked out with MacArthur working with Truman. And if there was politics involved, all the more reason why he should have ordered him to Washington.

John T. Mason, Jr.: Well, one sees in retrospect that FDR also handled him rather gingerly on occasion, and the inference is because MacArthur had a political connection.

Admiral Struble: Well, he was an important and capable man, and there was no reason why he shouldn't have handled him with some reasonable situation. But I still get back to the idea that I'd have ordered MacArthur back to Washington if I had been Truman. Then I think the thing might have been handled and accomplished. But to go part of the way out and then have all these staff present and everything . . .[end of the tape]

Interview Number 8 with Admiral Arthur D. Struble, U.S. Navy (Retired)
Place: Admiral Struble's Home, Chevy Chase, Maryland
Date: Thursday, 6 January 1977
Interviewer: John T. Mason, Jr.

John T. Mason, Jr.: Well, sir, we begin a new chapter, chapter 8, and we begin a new year in this marvelous account of your career. After you had finished the sweeping operations in the Japanese coastal areas, you left that command and you assumed another command of amphibious operations in the Pacific Fleet. This was in June of 1946. Do you want to pick up the story at that point?

Admiral Struble: The headquarters of the Commander Amphibious Force Pacific Fleet was located in San Diego on what we might call Coronado Island. It's really a part of San Diego Bay, and it's really a part almost of San Diego city except it is a little independent town itself.

John T. Mason, Jr.: And now connected by a very fine bridge.

Admiral Struble: And now connected by a very fine bridge. The importance of amphibious operations had been extensively portrayed in World War II. It became apparent—at least to those of us who were Americans—that it required considerable thought and attention for the future to develop the technique of naval and land forces working together in a landing which could then become a very strategic point in further land operations.

John T. Mason, Jr.: Let me ask—were there not some at that point who thought in terms of discontinuing any amphibious forces?

Admiral Struble: There was a certain amount of thought that more or less, well, that's been done, we may have to go through this again in another war. But there was a tendency to play down the amphibious technique. Having been at the Normandy landing and then having been through the campaign in the Philippines, I realized that the technique should be developed for the future so that the weapons and the advancements in the future would be brought into and become a part of the new amphibious technique if we were going to have one.

John T. Mason, Jr.: You certainly were the ideal appointee for that job at that moment, weren't you?

Admiral Struble: Well, there were many who had had more experience, let's say, in the Pacific technique of amphibious operations, probably in the Pacific Fleet under Admiral Nimitz but purely limited to the problems that they handled in World War II. I think my experience was a little broader in that I had been in the Atlantic and had been part of the Normandy landing, which was a tremendous landing of Army troops. I concluded that careful thought had to be given on how to handle Army landings, particularly if they were going to be big and provide for the proper coordination of Navy and Army efforts smoothly and easily and to the best interest of the combined operation.

Now, the amphibious people operating out of Pearl under Admiral Nimitz were mainly island hopping and making landings on specific islands and were just getting ready for the big landing on Kyushu in Japan when peace was declared. The point there is that while the Marines were the obvious soldiers that we used in our amphibious training in the Navy because they were a part of the Navy, you might say, they were not going to be the larger operations of the future if they were held. Because if the operations became very large, they were sure to involve Army troops; therefore the Army point of view had to be very carefully handled. So if the development of further amphibious techniques for the future was going to be accomplished, it would be done by the Navy at the amphibious base in southern California.

The Marines, of course, cooperated easier, quicker, and better with the Navy because they were accustomed to and were a part of the Navy.

John T. Mason, Jr.: There was a compatibility there.

Admiral Struble: There was a compatibility that already existed.

John T. Mason, Jr.: Well, how did you go about your command then?

Admiral Struble: The main thing was to start, and we did start. There was, of course, a base of Marines in Southern California. They were as interested in the amphibious business as we in the Navy were because they realized how important it could be.

John T. Mason, Jr.: And they had such success.

Admiral Struble: And they, of course, had had very considerable success in their amphibious landings. So with a certain amount of amphibious forces available, we commenced a system of, I will say, joint Navy and Marine training in Southern California. We developed a certain number of techniques that brought in the Marine experience of all World War II, wherever it might have been, and brought in presumably all of our own amphibious experience, whether it might have been in the Atlantic or the Pacific or where.

John T. Mason, Jr.: Can you cite some of the most successful of those techniques that you coordinated at that time?

Admiral Struble: Well, the technique of having better small boats to put the troops ashore was given thought, and we did develop some in that respect. However, being peacetime you could not expend large amounts on new equipment at that moment. You could design your equipment. You could figure out if and when we build some more of these, this will be a desirable change. But you couldn't with all the expenses and everything that we had had, expect to go ahead and immediately build up new forces. So we were conducting our amphibious training exercises in general with the equipment that we had at the end of World War II.

Now, our first training exercises were entirely with Marines. Having gotten together quite well—the Marines were very interested in it. They felt in a way that they were the father of it, and they were very interested in it and went after it very strongly. The Marines, of course, were much better for an amphibious landing from the Navy point of view because they knew how to handle the shipboard end of it more easily and were accustomed to it. A new Army contingent from, let's say, the central part of America would not have had any previous experience maybe in that sort of thing. It would be difficult from both their officers and their men to accommodate easily to it.

So after a certain amount of development of our own basic Navy-Marine Corps techniques and training, we then branched out into a larger exercise in which we expected to have Army troops cooperate.

John T. Mason, Jr.: Was this your operational idea?

Admiral Struble: Well, I'm expressing it as my idea simply because this is the way it was developed. Some of the thoughts that I've expressed were ideas that I had myself, but much of the contribution also was made by people who had been through World War II in different places. Both Marines and Navy people would recommend changes, and we would sift it out at this amphibious base. Actually, of course, at the moment I would make the decision on how much we would try to include it in what appeared to be our new technique and how much we would hold onto what we had already employed in World War II.

We did have some training exercises with Army forces from the Presidio. It was always difficult to handle new Army troops who had never had any training in an amphibious landing because they just aren't accustomed to small boats landing on beaches and so forth. Even on the coast of southern California I remember one time in particular when we were having a big training exercise, and I realized that things weren't going well. I went ashore in one of the landing boats, and we had breakers that were a little higher on the beach than it would have been desirable to land in.

I had been in a lot of this stuff before, of course, and on the boat that I went in on, I said, "Well, coxswain, let's go in. This is it. It looks pretty heavy." We charged in, and the boat that I was in capsized. We were underneath with our feet on the sand, with the water around us, and with the boat overhead. Then we took another roll and we came out all right and got ashore. But it was perfectly obvious to me that we would stop any further landing boats going in at this time because the waves were too heavy for proper landing of our boats.

John T. Mason, Jr.: You would lose personnel.

Admiral Struble: Why, you would have had tremendous personnel losses. So this is one of the conditions in an amphibious operation that can defeat you very badly. So careful appraisal of the beach and of the weather conditions at the beach are essential to success and very particularly essential to a large operation of any size. Otherwise, you could have a terrible problem on the beach. If the other fellow was much on the job, he'd wipe you out very easily.

So I think the trend in our operations was to try to develop a little better boating if we could. Some of the ideas on the techniques required a definite training program for the future to accustom the Navy, the Marines, and to some extent the Army in our probable methods of employment in the future.

John T. Mason, Jr.: Now, as you worked with the Army from San Francisco, what problems did you deal with?

Admiral Struble: We faced the landing of mostly green Army troops. A large percentage of these Army troops would have been new boys who had been enlisted and brought into the Army after World War II. There were always a few experienced Army noncommissioned officers in any organization like that, but the bulk of these troops would be brand-new youngsters. So they needed training from the ground up and under very good conditions initially until they became familiar with what was involved.

Now, the Marines—by virtue of constant and regular training and working on this matter—were up-to-date more on the ability of the average Marine personnel to get into boats and be landed ashore and recognize what the conditions might be like. Now, of course, if you landed in a cove or if you landed in something approaching a harbor, why, you landed under flat conditions. But there were lots of times during World War II when you couldn't land under flat conditions. In particular, Normandy is an excellent example.

If we had tried to land a day earlier than we did at Normandy, we could have had one hell of a mess because a few determined Germans quite possibly could have kept us off the beach if we had tried to land under very bad conditions.

John T. Mason, Jr.: You had this big operation off San Diego in November and December with the Army. An Army infantry division? An Army engineer brigade?

Admiral Struble: Yes.

John T. Mason, Jr.: Plus planes and all the rest.

Admiral Struble: This would be a pretty good sample of what would be needed in another big amphibious operation if it were held. We held that on the beachfront off San Diego.

John T. Mason, Jr.: Now, as in retrospect, were you happy with the results of this operation?

Admiral Struble: Yes, I was. Of course, individual parts were bad, such as the incident I described in the boat that I went in myself that turned over and rolled around. Now, for those of us who were in that boat it was just an experience and we had no problem. But had that boat been full of Army troops it could have been calamitous.

John T. Mason, Jr.: However, I can see some advantage for you in terms of leadership. Here was the head man going in and hazarding his life.

Admiral Struble: Well, I was criticized for that.

John T. Mason, Jr.: People who were concerned about your welfare.

Admiral Struble: Well, people who thought I was taking it too far maybe. They didn't think it was quite necessary for the senior man to demonstrate quite so fully.

John T. Mason, Jr.: It also demonstrates your eagerness to make the thing work.

Admiral Struble: Well, I felt that I had better go in and see how it was going on the beach. I found out that we had to slow down a little and wait until there was a little more change in the tide which would effect the landing and make the possibility of boats capsizing much less. All of these matters are connected with the tidal situation—low tide, high tide, tide going in, and tide maybe going back out—in regards to the ability of the small boat to maneuver and land on an ocean beach.

John T. Mason, Jr.: In retrospect, how did the Army command react to this combined operation? Were they pleased?

Admiral Struble: They felt it had been useful. They were a little concerned about our landing Army troops if the boating conditions were going to be as bad as I had happened to have in the particular boat that I went in in. Now, that, of course, is sound. If that boat had been full of men, we would have lost a large number and have had a lot of casualties. It wouldn't have been very good for amphibious training. Fortunately, nobody was hurt and all we did was get wet.

John T. Mason, Jr.: The Army then continued to cooperate with you in these?

Admiral Struble: The Army felt very strongly that the amphibious operations could well be necessary and employed in the future. As far as I was concerned, they were willing to continue joint training and operations in a reasonable amount. The Army naturally is thinking in terms of handling large numbers of troops; therefore, the amphibious training which we were doing on beaches like that was going to be landings of supplies and of smaller amounts of men involved. There was going to be a sample of that type of work rather than, for instance, a larger landing such as Normandy where we were going to put a large number of troops and would necessarily have to have a much better factor and a much safer beach and/or harbor on which to land Army troops. Because not only would Army troops be necessary, but large amounts of equipment and supplies would be immediately necessary in large quantities to push those troops inland. Do you understand?

John T. Mason, Jr.: Yes, and I understand also that you were just dealing in sample landings, small landings.

Admiral Struble: That's right.

John T. Mason, Jr.: You must have had a great deal of interest evidenced in Washington at these operations that you were conducting. You must have had a number of observers from Washington.

Admiral Struble: I don't remember any observers that came out from Washington.

John T. Mason, Jr.: Nimitz had become CNO at that point.[*]

Admiral Struble: Yes, but this was just good standard amphibious training and other things going on. I think everybody realized that until you knew where you were going to land, you might have a different problem. So it was basic training that we were going in for, and I think we found out one thing—that we could conduct basic training on the Southern California beaches. But we did have to watch our weather conditions carefully for basic training for new people who had never been through the training before. You could get pretty heavy rollers and you could roll over a good size Navy boat and you could have a lot of casualties like the one that we went through.

---

[*] Fleet Admiral Chester W. Nimitz, USN, served as Chief of Naval Operations from December 1945 to December 1947.

John T. Mason, Jr.: Since weather was such an important factor, who produced your weather reports? Who gave you all the detailed data which you used?

Admiral Struble: Well, of course, our broad weather system in the United States today produces information like that regularly all day long almost in our weather reports, so that we had pretty good weather reports. We had good weather reports, of course, in California. The only thing we learned a little more than I had previously thought was that on that open beach off southern California under certain tidal conditions and wind conditions together, you could get a much heavier chance of upsetting and overturning a boatload of troops than we might have anticipated.

Of course, one thing that was important. Had that boat been heavily loaded, we would have charged in and gone up on the beach, I believe, safely. Probably if we had a heavy boat, we would not have turned over.

John T. Mason, Jr.: When you had this combined operation in '46 with the Army, there must have been quite a large flotilla involved. Can you give me any idea what the extent of the operation and the ships you had?

Admiral Struble: I just don't know. It was a fairly good-sized operation. We had, I suppose, maybe 300 or 400 Marines that we were landing on the beach. But that isn't a big landing when you think in terms of Normandy. But in terms of peacetime operation, it was a good-sized landing.

John T. Mason, Jr.: The Army division, an Army brigade.

Admiral Struble: Well, I suppose the Army that we landed on that occasion probably totaled 800 or 1,200 troops, maybe—somewhere in that area.

John T. Mason, Jr.: Admiral, this was back in the '40s when you still had certain command relationships which were somewhat difficult to achieve, I would imagine. Do you want to talk about that whole subject? The Army was a new element that you were incorporating into a joint amphibious operation. You had some working arrangements with the Marines, but with the Army it was somewhat different.

Admiral Struble: Well, of course, it was expected that the Marines as a part of their basic purpose would become experts in amphibious landings and that the command relations involved between the Navy and the Marine troops who were landed would be very clear and understood and could be handled very easily and well. They had been.

But now we were training for the future and, of course, in the future we had to consider the idea also of landings with Army people. In the case of Army landings, they might be small ones like some of the training operations we were having with the Marines or conceivably you could have a fairly large landing. Under those conditions, it is well to thrash out the command relations between the services involved and have them understood in advance.

Of course, my experience in World War II happened to be in a very large landing at Normandy where the importance of the Army command was much greater and bigger once the things was started and accomplished than it was before the landing was made and had been a success. So the Navy was highly important at Normandy until we had gotten the troops established ashore for a couple of days and had things started. Thereafter it was an Army show, not really a Navy show—if I may describe it that way. Of course, at Normandy our purpose had been to try to achieve the idea of putting a new division of Army troops across the beach at least about five days out of seven every week. Therefore, you had to have supplies going across that same beach for the troops that were already ashore and those that were coming and for all of the Jeeps and/or other equipment that they had with them.

Of course, normally you would try to work through a port such as Cherbourg that you would capture initially and then handle your supplies and the handling of further troops through a port. But in the case of Normandy, Cherbourg was not a good bet for us initially so we had chosen this coastline as the spot where we landed. We had thought that we could use it successfully at least for a couple or three months, by which time we undoubtedly would have Cherbourg in our pocket. Then we would be handling further merchant shipping, new troops, new supplies, and everything through a recognized and developed port.

So my idea when I was ComPhibPac would be to develop ideas that would be suitable, not only for a Normandy of the future, but also for a lot of small landings that we had made that were most successful at the moment in handling a smaller but an immediate local problem.*

John T. Mason, Jr.: That was no mean task.

Admiral Struble: Well, it was interesting. I think we did pretty well in the broad development, and we even went so far as to get into the oil business. I think this is rather interesting if I can put in a little time on it.

John T. Mason, Jr.: Surely.

Admiral Struble: The proposition of oil out of Alaska had been carefully considered and developed a certain amount. The question had come up whether we could take amphibious boats and so forth that we already possessed and get up on the northwest coast of Alaska, high up, and land equipment and supplies for three or four months in the summer. These things would not be used, of course, for an amphibious landing but would be used to possibly develop pipelines from oil that was known to exist in Alaska. It would then move by pipeline from Alaska to points in the United States, possibly as far east as Minnesota. Or it might be handled by pipeline to southern Alaska, possibly even down into British Columbia to some port so that oil could be regularly taken out of the ground and shipped, say, 10 or 12 months out of the year.

John T. Mason, Jr.: You were anticipating problems that developed 30 years hence.

---

* ComPhibPac—Commander Amphibious Force Pacific Fleet.

Admiral Struble: They were problems that were known to exist. At that time the oil people realized that if they could only figure out some very reasonable way of handling that oil, it was very valuable.

John T. Mason, Jr.: Of course, you were thinking in terms of the Navy landing up there.

Admiral Struble: No, I wasn't thinking of Navy landing up there. I was ordered as the Commander Amphibious Force to go up to Alaska the following summer in about June and investigate what we with our own current materials could do to assist in getting equipment into northern Alaska. The purpose would have been then for us, with some of our forces and things, to have assisted, let's say, the development of commercial oil in the future for the betterment of the United States. We would have nothing to do with where the pipelines went or who did the work or anything. But we might be able with our particular types of ships and small boats to assist in getting some equipment up there early. This the government could afford to do very well if it was going to be very valuable to the United States to get it done.

John T. Mason, Jr.: What was the result of your expedition up there?

Admiral Struble: I reported that we could use amphibious shipping between two and maybe three months in the summer. We concluded that we could take in fairly good-sized loads, we could land them on the beach in northwestern Alaska, and we would not need any harbors. But they would only be useful for a two-month period, possibly a little more, during the summer months. Later, as time went on, I believe it then developed that it was going to be better to throw this back possibly to the development of Alaska. It would probably be better to construct a pipeline down into southwestern Alaska rather than an overland pipeline into the central part or the northern part of America.

John T. Mason, Jr.: At that point you were not dealing so vociferously with conservationists either.

Admiral Struble: No, we hadn't gotten into that part of the problem yet. We were just giving a little naval assistance to what was a big government project on how to handle oil out of Alaska. I think it was a very legitimate thing because it was good for us to get a certain amount of experience and knowledge and so forth for ourselves up there.

John T. Mason, Jr.: Were you doing this not only as Navy, but were you doing it under the aegis of the Interior Department as well?

Admiral Struble: Oh, no, no. This was purely Navy at the time. We were using our forces for investigating purposes, which would be turned over broadly to the government as soon as they were produced. We would not really become the actors very long if we started that summer or the following summer to do this.

Now, actually, about two years later, after I went back to Washington, I went up to Alaska as the Navy member of the Joint Chiefs of Staff. The CNO was unable to go, and I as OP-03 went up.[*] I was the junior member on the JCS, and I was part of the Alaskan trip that Bradley and the Air Force Chief of Staff went on one summer.[†] Our purpose was to see what we were going to do about cleaning up our military forces that had been up in Alaska and what we were going to try to keep. We wanted to see what we thought was useful to maintain there and how much of our Army and Navy forces we could get out of Alaska if they were not necessarily going to be useful for the future. The Joint Chiefs had a quite successful trip, and we agreed on most of the problems better than we often did when we were back in Washington.

John T. Mason, Jr.: You got a different perspective off in the field.

To go back to the other subject we were discussing, the subject of command arrangements, when you were working on amphibious operations with the Army, what was the net result of your efforts down off San Diego?

---

[*] Admiral Struble served as Deputy Chief of Naval Operations (Operations) from 1948 to 1950.
[†] General of the Army Omar N. Bradley, USA, served as Chairman of the Joint Chiefs of Staff from 1949 to 1953.

Admiral Struble: We adopted a number of modified rules, you might say, and I think they were much better for the future for all kinds of operations. We were going to include an early arrangement with the Army. I was quite familiar with the Army, particularly after the Normandy landing where I talked with the top Army people. I realized that their command relations were much more important than possibly I myself had previously given thought to in connection with a big landing like Normandy. We had to be prepared to support their command relations very early and at the start of the big landing.

Now, I eventually got back into that business a little in the Korean War, when I happened to be out there.

John T. Mason, Jr.: But you did work out something in San Diego with the Army then that was satisfactory to both parties?

Admiral Struble: Yes. We realized that the Army had to be in command of any large amount of troops once they got ashore and that the Air Force and the Navy had to arrange things so that they very promptly took a secondary status as soon as the troops had gotten well landed and were, in a way, on their own.

John T. Mason, Jr.: What about the Marines?

Admiral Struble: This, of course, was difficult for the Marines because if the Marines were in a landing such as Normandy, where it was going to be practically completely an Army affair, the initial Marines that were landed had to have the freedom of movement as military people when they first landed. But it was probably going to be desirable to phase them back out of that landing rather than continue them in the landing very long. They were professionals who had assisted in making the landing. They probably ought to be brought back out, and the whole thing would become Army with naval assistance as early as possible.

John T. Mason, Jr.: The Marines then become almost a part of the Navy.

Admiral Struble: The Marines would come back out and go to some other job. Now, when we landed at Inchon, which we'll discuss later, I'll describe to you some of the practical applications that I tried to put into effect at some of those landings.* We were certainly at that time engaged very much in primarily a military operation in Korea and, of course, in which an Army general was very properly the senior military man involved.

John T. Mason, Jr.: Now, I understand, Admiral, that the Army no longer engages in amphibious exercises. Is that not true?

Admiral Struble: I can't say definitely, but very obviously the further development of amphibious warfare now has got to stay with the Navy and the Marines. They will try to develop the technique but certainly should at all times face the fact that sometime in the future maybe we'll have a big Army landing. At that time we mustn't be too hidebound by our own previous rules and be prepared to cooperate with the bigger issue, which is getting a large number of troops ashore in a hurry and making the Army as mobile and as much in charge as possible.

John T. Mason, Jr.: Well, that being so, sir, why wouldn't it be advisable to continue exercises with the Army in peacetime just so that it would work more efficiently when the emergency arose?

Admiral Struble: I would advise myself, certainly, that the amphibious training of the future, which will probably be more out of San Diego than any other one spot, should go on and that the Army should be included in alternate years or occasionally. A certain number of Army officers and men need to get a certain amount of training. They would then get a certain amount of status in their own service as being someone acquainted with amphibious operations. Under those conditions, a certain amount of Army officers and a certain amount of Army men of the future would be available presumably for the Army

---

* On 15 September 1950, U.S. troops under the command of General of the Army Douglas MacArthur made an amphibious landing at Inchon, the port for Seoul, South Korea. The surprise landing, 150 miles behind enemy lines, temporarily turned the tide of war in favor of United Nations forces.

to use for that purpose, ten years later as having had a little amphibious training and experience. But in peacetime we can't maintain the expenditures of large amounts of sums to try keep it all in training. It gets to be too much big money.

John T. Mason, Jr.: That's the major problem then.

Admiral Struble: That is going to be the major problem, and I think we ought to go back to what we were doing before World War II. But bear in mind the fact that a little Army training and a little Army knowledge among officers is very valuable to the amphibious business. If enough of those people were trained from year to year or in odd years and so forth, the Army could order people who had had some previous experience with the thing when they were younger but preferably would be ordered then 10 or 15 years later when they had gotten older but hadn't forgotten what they had learned.

John T. Mason, Jr.: Yes. There would be a certain reservoir of talent.

Admiral Struble: That's right. A reservoir of talent in the Army to try to work with the Navy in the problem which is sometimes essentially Navy and should be determined by a naval officer.

John T. Mason, Jr.: All of that makes very good sense, but the money is the factor.

Admiral Struble: Yes. Now, for instance, with MacArthur at Inchon, just to speak with a little bit of an example—MacArthur had been the boss down in the Philippines when I was there. MacArthur knew me a reasonable amount. Well, when it came to this landing at Inchon, he wasn't worried at all turning over complete responsibility for the landing to the Navy. Now, there was hesitancy on the part of some of his aides and other Army officers in this matter, but no hesitancy on MacArthur's part in my opinion.

John T. Mason, Jr.: And experience had been the reason.

Admiral Struble: Yes. Joint operations and the experience had been the reason for it. We had no trouble in the slightest operating with MacArthur and the Army troops as we were going into Inchon.

John T. Mason, Jr.: Well, then, sir, as you reflect on those two years in San Diego dealing with amphibious problems, you must have found it a very fruitful thing.

Admiral Struble: I found it interesting trying to indoctrinate a certain number of Navy people. We had to recognize that the amphibious operation was simply a means to an end for the Army, and it was not the means to an end for the Navy. It was eventually an Army proposition that was going to be important. Because once the Army troops landed, unless it was rather minor and it was the Marines that landed, it would not probably remain under Navy control and shouldn't be expected to.

John T. Mason, Jr.: Now, you were trying to amalgamate, as I see it, in this time within the Navy, two distinct experiences in amphibious operations: those which you had experienced with MacArthur and those in the Central Pacific under Kelly Turner, which were somewhat different.[*]

Admiral Struble: I had not been under Kelly Turner until just before the surrender, so that my amphibious experience in the Southwest Pacific had primarily been under the broad command of MacArthur.

John T. Mason, Jr.: But my point is that there was some difference in the two kinds of operations, was there not?

Admiral Struble: There was quite a bit of difference between the two operations. One of the reasons was the fact that MacArthur was interested in restoring the Philippines at the same time he was advancing a war against the Japs. And that's important. There will

---

[*] Vice Admiral Richmond Kelly Turner, USN, was probably the Navy's most experienced flag officer in terms of amphibious warfare during World War II. He was in command of various operations from Guadalcanal to Okinawa.

always be an argument, I suppose, whether MacArthur's idea of trying to free the Philippines was a political purpose that should have gotten quite as much prominence at the moment in our war plans as it did from MacArthur. I think actually we were probably fortunate that in conducting a military operation in the Philippine area we had an Army officer do it that had been there previously. In many ways he exercised very good broad control of military forces in those areas. He did participate in freeing the Philippines, and at not a very great additional expense to the basic military operations that were necessary anyway. We couldn't very well leave the Philippines behind our backs.

John T. Mason, Jr.: Something had to be done about them.

Admiral Struble: So MacArthur was probably an excellent man to have had command there. I think his relations with most of his Navy subordinates such as Kinkaid and Barbey and, for instance, in a very small one, myself, were excellent.

John T. Mason, Jr.: But the fact remains that there was some difference in the island hopping in that area from the island conquering in the Central Pacific, and now in your command at San Diego you were combining the experience of the various men who had been in these different fields. Did you have any problem with that?

Admiral Struble: In general, I think, some of the people who had been in the mid-Pacific felt that their method of conducting amphibious operations under the fleet commander was the way to do it. Well, it had been successful in the mid-Pacific, and the fleet commander who had commanded the fleet would be the principal naval officer going in to land and take a small island. Now, the Marines were probably going to be generally and basically the military element involved in capturing this island. So it was somewhat all in the naval structure.

Now, it did put Admiral Nimitz then in a position there as commander of the mid-Pacific to control the military operations that went on in the capture of these islands so that the main naval purpose of eventually shrinking down and closing in on Japan went on. That proposition of developing this enclosure of cutting in on Japan and eliminating these islands from any Japanese control was probably much better handled by a naval officer out of Honolulu, and I think Admiral Nimitz did a very splendid job handling that particular thing. His main purpose was isolating Japan; he wasn't interested in freeing the Philippines. That was not a part of his purpose, and it shouldn't have been a part of his purpose, and it wasn't mixed up in it. That's why initially, probably Nimitz was the man to have had control of all this Pacific area, including the ground operations that were going to go on.

Now, the minute that the Japanese surrendered, then Nimitz's purpose was done. Japan was no longer our enemy. I think it was reasonably logical and good that from then on MacArthur as a land man was much better to take over the further handling of matters in Japan, which he did, and which I think he did very successfully.

John T. Mason, Jr.: Am I correct in thinking then that in the background of your thought as you describe these various operations is the fact of geography? It was the determining factor, was it not—the nature of the Central Pacific in contrast to the nature of the South Pacific.

Admiral Struble: Our important thing in the Pacific operations had to be obviously the eventual surrender of Japan. That had to be the number-one item. And in handling that number-one item, it became desirable to be sure we had cleaned up the Southwest Pacific area, which included the Philippines, and that there were no longer Japanese bases down there—air, naval, or even military—that could be on our back side and interfere with us. It was desirable for us as one of the big free nations of the world to consider breaking the Japanese yoke on the Philippine area at the same time we were moving forward elsewhere, because you still faced a threat. You had to get in to eliminate the navy and eliminate their possibility of operating out of Philippine ports. You see, they could do a hell of a lot of harm to us with submarines and other naval ships if they were allowed to operate freely out of the Philippines.

MacArthur's ideas were incorporated into the idea to free the Philippines. I just feel that the so-called Nimitz-versus-MacArthur dispute should be completely dropped, and we should recognize the considerable value that we got out of both things. In particular, I think we should drop the idea of the younger people, the commanders and so forth, who said, "Well, gee, we got a destroyer back from the Southwest Pacific today and, God, wasn't it run down!" In effect, he's criticizing the people in this other theater. That's no good. That should be eliminated. I suppose you must give the President the credit for the way this thing worked out. His idea was to keep both MacArthur and Nimitz in the picture and each responsible for and given credit for what he did.

Now, actually, when you came to the surrender it was more appropriate under the circumstances for MacArthur to have accepted the surrender. Why? Because he was going to continue on as the head man in Japan. So that was very important. But I think the fact that he was allowed to accept the surrender does not mean that he, MacArthur, contributed a greater amount to the eventual surrender of Japan than Nimitz did. History should record the two gentlemen very favorably. In my opinion, if you feel you must give one a little more credit than the other, I would give Nimitz slightly more credit for the defeat of Japan than MacArthur. But then immediately follow up and give MacArthur the full due that he deserved in handling the surrender and further handling of Japan.

John T. Mason, Jr.: That's a very fair statement to make. It does delineate the two roles, the different roles.

Well, going back to the problem there and your staff, the people you were working with in San Diego—you had Navy men who had had experience in the Central Pacific. You had Navy men who had had experience as you had had with MacArthur. My question was then: did you have any difficulty in amalgamating the two points of view within the amphibious operations you were conducting there off San Diego?

Admiral Struble: Oh, no. Every now and then you'd get a youngster who was very sure of himself because he had had a very good experience but a very small experience of a bigger issue. He'd fight for a while on the subject and want to talk about it. But I think everybody realized that we had to get together and be able to handle an amphibious operation better in the future. The Army was not going to do it, and they shouldn't be expected to. Therefore, the Navy was going to have to use some of its money in the

Marine Corps to keep the thing alive for the future. I tried to [unclear] the money angle in Washington. The broad Navy money does include the Marines, as you realize.

John T. Mason, Jr.: In that particular time, which was in the late '40s, the personnel situation in the services was at times almost catastrophic. Did this affect your operations in any way?

Admiral Struble: No, we hadn't commenced to get that effect too badly. There was a very fine Marine group in San Diego that I saw quite often, and with a couple of the older Marine officers, I disagreed with them to some extent. But I think they all realized that we had to have a broad view of the result and that they couldn't make this too much of just Marine command problems. Of course, if they did, they would then eliminate the bigger landing if we ever had one.

John T. Mason, Jr.: But I was thinking in terms of immediacy, the lack of sufficient personnel to operate your ships and so forth.

Admiral Struble: Oh, that always happens. I felt that we were getting enough men and ships and things to go ahead and consolidate and attempt to be sure that we had the better ideas that we learned in the Pacific war amalgamated into the final results. Now, there was a little proposition there, of course, in Kelly Turner, the man who was the amphibious commander under Admiral Nimitz. He was a very excellent man. He was already a rear admiral by the start of the war and deserves probably more credit than anyone among the senior officers of the Navy in the development of the amphibious business for use in the war. So he and Nimitz and their people were developing the amphibious doctrine very well and very usefully.

Kelly Turner was a brilliant man, and he developed it. But I do not necessarily agree with all of the ideas that Kelly Turner had, because I don't think some of them would have been as applicable for use in the Southwest Pacific. In other words, a broader point of view on it was needed than what Kelly thought was the Amphibious Force Pacific Fleet answer. He had it for the Central Pacific and conducted the Japanese war. I don't think he would have been the man to have tried to continue it after the war because I think he was a little bit inclined to make it too specific, based on the Central Pacific island-hopping campaigns.

John T. Mason, Jr.: Could I suggest an illustration of the point you are making? The possibility in terms of planning for these operations, the great large-scale planning that Kelly Turner engaged in, the small-scale landing that was developed in the South Pacific.

Admiral Struble: I don't think you've got that right when you talk about the large-scale operation and the small-scale. The biggest operation that we were going to have was going to be the attack on Kyushu, wasn't it?

John T. Mason, Jr.: Oh, yes. But I mean—

Admiral Struble: The biggest amphibious operation we ever conducted in the Pacific would have been the landing at Kyushu. Now, I do not think that Kelly Turner was necessarily more competent to plan and carry out that operation than the people that handled Normandy, which was a bigger operation.

John T. Mason, Jr.: What I meant was, I was thinking in terms of the island hopping in the Southwest Pacific, say, from Hollandia on up until you got to Leyte Gulf, all the small islands. These were short-term planning operations for these various islands in contrast to planning for Saipan, which was a great gathering of planners.

Admiral Struble: In most theaters, you have a lot of smaller operations and every now and then a couple of big ones.

John T. Mason, Jr.: Yes.

Admiral Struble: Now, I think you've got to put it that way. There were a large number of smaller operations in the Pacific; each individual small island became a small thing.

But the way it was handled in the Pacific was splendid and best because the commander of the fleet who was out there looking for Japanese ships and everything, and who had an overall responsibility for this little island-hopping operation under Kelly Turner going along all right and being protected, made it better for the fleet commander to be the boss.

Now, I get back to the fact that it was probably better in the Southwest Pacific command area for an Army officer, namely MacArthur, to be boss. Do you see?

John T. Mason, Jr.: Oh, yes, you made your point and you made it very well. But let me shift a bit and let me say that when you were engaged in these joint operations off San Diego in the late '40s, what concept did you have of the possibility of future amphibious operations against a potential enemy? What were you thinking in terms of in the long future?

Admiral Struble: I had no specific area in mind, but I realized that I had combined personally the experience at Normandy, the experience in the Southwest Pacific, and eventually a certain amount of experience close to and connected with the command out of Honolulu. I thought that this was the time to convert that broad experience into something that would be useful, no matter what happened throughout the world in the future. You just couldn't try to make your stuff too specific.

Now, later in the Korean business, I had to sometimes disagree with a man who was a good amphibious man and who had done very well under Kelly Turner.* The fact is he had been one of Kelly Turner's bright young men and had done very well for him. But he was, in my opinion, too indoctrinated with the Kelly Turner method and thought it was the only answer. I recognized that sometimes in the Korean business a little Southwest Pacific experience wasn't at all harmful.

John T. Mason, Jr.: Now, just one more question, sir, in terms of amphibious operations. In the '40s when you were out in San Diego, the only potential enemy the United States

---

* This is probably a reference to Rear Admiral James H. Doyle, USN, who was Commander Amphibious Group One during the Inchon landing and Hungnam evacuation in 1950. As a captain he had been one of Turner's senior staff officers.

would dream of possibly was the Soviet Russia. So did you think at all in terms of any amphibious operations that might be directed toward Russia at some time in the future?

Admiral Struble: No. I was at that time trying to develop a philosophy and what I just quoted to you about my idea about Nimitz and MacArthur. I want you to realize I didn't have that idea at that time. I have evolved a lot of those things carefully and thought at the time and also since. I felt when I was in the Southwest Pacific that a pretty good job was being done, and while I was a little doubtful at times whether this freeing of the Philippines was a good thing or not while we were doing it, I eventually came to the opinion it was a good thing.

In the meantime, I realized that the Central Pacific had done a beautiful job on their island hopping and everything and that they were right. But in this final big landing that we were going to make it was going to be commanded by MacArthur. I believe that it was right that our forces and people should all be acquainted with and see generally and broadly the same idea rather than have two completely separate methods. Now, the Nimitz method which was illustrated by Kelly Turner's view was certainly a fine and splendid way of handling what they did in the Central Pacific, but it doesn't mean for one minute that it was the only answer to every amphibious problem that would come up in the future.

John T. Mason, Jr.: I'm delighted, sir, to have your considered reflections on this whole subject of amphibious operations.

Admiral Struble: I felt very definitely at that time that we should learn carefully and well from what we had rather than letting the idea develop you were a Kelly Turner man or a Dan Barbey man, for instance. Or were you a Nimitz man or were you a MacArthur man? Those are the ideas that I thought we ought to eliminate. Instead, we should have a broad view of how is the best way to solve these problems. Now, any idea of attempting to study any particular part of the world for the practical solution of the problem would probably be a waste of time.

John T. Mason, Jr.: So I get back to my original observation that you seemed to be the ideal man for that job at that time.

Well, sir, now we are going to another assignment in April of 1948. You returned to Washington from San Diego and became Deputy Chief of Naval Operations for Operations, which was known as OP-03. You were also naval deputy on the Joint Chiefs of Staff. Was this something that you looked forward to with great pleasure?

Admiral Struble: Oh, yes. This meant that I was going to be in the same type of planning and everything that we just mentioned except that instead of being the case of one type of military operation known as the amphibious landing it became operations of all types.

John T. Mason, Jr.: A much broader scope.

Admiral Struble: A much broader scope.

John T. Mason, Jr.: Now, Admiral Nimitz had left Washington. He had served as CNO for a couple of years, and Admiral Denfeld had become CNO and was in office when you arrived.*

Admiral Struble: That is right.

John T. Mason, Jr.: Had you worked with him before?

Admiral Struble: Yes. I had served with Denfeld in the Navy Department, not directly under him but close to him about twice previously. I had been with him in the Navy Department just before Normandy. He and I were not in the same job at all, but we knew each other quite well.

---

* Admiral Louis E. Denfeld, USN, served as Chief of Naval Operations from December 1947 to November 1949.

Arthur D. Struble, Interview #8 (1/6/77) – Page 312

John T. Mason, Jr.: So you had a good working relationship.

Admiral Struble: We had a very good working relationship, excellent. OP-03 can be a very important and very valuable man to the CNO if they know each other and so forth. It's a very important thing for the OP-03 to be regarded well by the CNO because the CNO is often called out of town and his OP-03 is often the man that ought to act for him when he is gone. If he isn't fully convinced of his OP-03, he's hesitant to let him handle problems when he isn't around.

John T. Mason, Jr.: Well, OP-03 in a sense runs the Navy Department, doesn't he?

Admiral Struble: I wouldn't say that, no. You see, this Joint Chiefs of Staff means that the services are going to try to get together beforehand and have the same point of view on a future war or a future problem. That means that the man that is the deputy that goes with CNO to those meetings is a man that has the most information on it in the Navy Department. He has even more than the CNO because he goes to more of the meetings. The fact is he ought to go to every meeting.

Now, of course, if he's on leave for a week or two or he is sick or something he doesn't go to the meetings. But he's the one man that often has more continuity on that subject than even the CNO himself. Why? Because the CNO has to go off somewhere to do this and to do that, so he doesn't get to go to quite as many of those meetings as the deputy does. Now, if the VCNO goes instead of the chief to the meeting when the chief is away, he again only goes to maybe six or ten a year.[*]

John T. Mason, Jr.: Just to lay the groundwork for that period when you served in that job, we might say something about the fact that it was the time that Louis Johnson was the Secretary of Defense and there was a great cutback in monies that were available for the military.[†]

---

[*] VCNO—Vice Chief of Naval Operations.
[†] Louis A. Johnson served as Secretary of Defense from April 1949 until September 1950. He cut back substantially on defense expenditures, a program that had to be reversed with the beginning of the Korean War in June 1950.

Admiral Struble: Well, that great cutback in money, of course, was one of the military's biggest problems, based on a certain sized establishment and a certain amount of money that was available. All of their plans were labeled in that direction. Now, although there was going to be less money, you couldn't necessarily give just a proportionate cut to everybody. Why? Because maybe just two months earlier a fine new program for submarines had gone in effect; it was needed very much, and it had gotten started. Well, were you going to start cutting that thing before it got off the ground? You had to try to support that contract, so you had to try to find out where in the hell you were going to take the cut. You're going to have to be hard on something. In general my experience was that just to try to take a graduated cut all through the department isn't the answer. It's to try to find the place that can accept the cut better and easier under all the circumstances involved.

John T. Mason, Jr.: I introduced that element of the reduced expenditures to indicate the fact that your task was much more difficult.

Admiral Struble: That was one of the big problems. For instance, if you wanted to try to take a cut out of aviation, by God, the aviation people could scream to heaven, and they could produce a hell of a lot of good reasons why you shouldn't cut it. Well, then you had to say, "Well, I'm not going to cut this aviation thing. Aviation is as important as hell and it shouldn't be cut right now." So you look around and make certain cuts. Then at the same time you are getting ready to submit the next year's thing, and, of course, aviation is going to ask for the same thing they had asked for the year before. That was when you had to tell aviation beforehand, "Oh, no, we didn't give you a cut on this last thing which you might well had to have your share of, but your new year's program has got to make some decisive cuts somewhere and you are the fellow that's got to do it yourself. You have three or four months now to get ready for how you are going to cut." That was my conception of how OP-03 ought to try to operate with the other people.

John T. Mason, Jr.: That was not easy to accomplish with Admiral Radford as OP-05, was it?

Admiral Struble: Radford was really VCNO.* He was a shade above. He was really between me and Denfeld except that—whereas most of the other OPs would always go to Radford before they went to Denfeld—as OP-03 I was often with Denfeld direct for two reasons. First, he'd send for me and second, we were the team that went together to the JCS. So he'd send for me and he'd say, "What are we going to do about that at the JCS meeting?"

Well, invariably, after leaving Denfeld's office, I would go right in to Radford's office and tell him what the hell was up and what we were going to do. Now, that gave Radford an opportunity to object if he thought he wanted to, but it also gave him an opportunity to be thinking about it and he knew what I had advised the Chief to do. He could then think it over, and he could come back down and argue with me and say, "Look, I'd like to recommend this." He and I could then discuss that matter. So OP-03 had a special meeting as one of the OPs and I would say a special responsibility to both the Chief and the VCNO. I am sure that I maintained my responsibility to the VCNO in good style because Radford always, I feel, had great confidence in me. He realized that if something was going on that looked like it would develop here or there, he could get word from me about it.

I might not agree with what he proposed, but if he did disagree with what I thought, he was always in a position—because I had let him know what was going on—so that he could go into CNO and say, "Look, I don't know. I think I would prefer this." And they could talk it over. This is cooperation. I think I cooperated very carefully on this subject, and I think it's very important.

John T. Mason, Jr.: When it came to matters that pertained to naval aviation, Radford could be a very tough adversary, couldn't he?

---

* Vice Admiral Arthur W. Radford, USN, served as Deputy Chief of Naval Operations (Air), OP-05, in 1946-47. As a four-star admiral he was Vice Chief of Naval Operations from January 1948 to April 1949.

Admiral Struble: Yes. Radford and I didn't always agree, but, of course, I was the fellow that was going to preside maybe two or three days later in next year's layout for the thing and aviation was going to come in. If I disagreed with him, I was going to say so. At that time, I would tell aviation I wouldn't agree to this or that. And I said, "You might as well let Radford know because I'm going to tell him myself that I disagreed and why. I think, broadly, disagreement is necessary. I don't think aviation should expect next year to get this."

In other words, I didn't try to slip it over. I talked frank facts. Now, Radford by that time had come to realize that I was the fellow that had to coordinate the damned big schedule. That was the way it was done. He, Radford, didn't ever have to do it. When I did it, he knew I was going to make what I thought was the best solution. He was going to be promptly told by me what had happened, and if he thought aviation needed some better thought, he could think it over, he could work out what he considered a better solution. Or he could go in to CNO and say, "I don't like what Rip proposes, and I'd like to have it changed to this." He could do it either way he wanted, but I never tried to eliminate him or slide anything by him. And that's the way those things have got to work, in my opinion, if they are really going to work right. I think that both the CNO and the VCNO had plenty of confidence in the way as OP-03 I did it because I never tried to put anything over on either one of them. But if they were both out of town, it was me that made the decision and I made it at that time the way I thought it ought to go.

John T. Mason, Jr.: In the light of the fact that money was very scarce, you had your problems in terms of doing something that the Navy had not done prior to World War II and that was to maintain a fleet in the Mediterranean and one in the Pacific simultaneously. This created a problem, didn't it?

Admiral Struble: This created a problem of the size of the fleets concerned. I think the basic idea of commencing to get some Mediterranean Sea experience and everything was very important, and I considered it more important than maintaining just the size of the Pacific Fleet. So I did go for an increase in size in the Mediterranean, which immediately meant that the Pacific was going to get cut.

John T. Mason, Jr.: The number of carriers had been reduced drastically, had it not?

Admiral Struble: Yes. Money, of course, is the source of all evil. If you are only going to get a certain amount of money, you've just got to figure out how you are going to use it yourself. I favored holding on to submarines. I favored holding on to carriers. I was sure we needed a certain number of destroyers. We certainly needed a certain number of light cruisers. If we had to cut something, I thought we would be the most capable in the future by taking out the battleships because they were, in my opinion, the least valuable of the types I just mentioned.

John T. Mason, Jr.: Of the capital ships.

Admiral Struble: For the initial start of a new war. Now, the battleships could always be called back if they had to be and recommissioned. But I questioned in my own mind if they would be the valuable pieces of machinery at the start of a new war. They didn't have the mobility of the other ships; therefore, much as I had been a battleship sailor myself, I preferred to take the cut there rather than elsewhere.

John T. Mason, Jr.: And the Navy at that point was ready to accept that thesis?

Admiral Struble: Some were and some weren't, but lots of them maybe hadn't thought it over as much and as carefully as I had and had had the same experience. The man that has had experience in one type ship is always bound to see the value and the use of that type ship more than somebody else. I had had fairly broad experience, and I think I tried to reach a broad conclusion.

John T. Mason, Jr.: All right, and in the light of that statement, what role did you assign to amphibious operations when you were in OP-03?

Admiral Struble: A slightly decreased status, because I felt that after we got into war, money would become available, and the amphibious angle could be more quickly brought up than some of the others.

John T. Mason, Jr.: Small boats could be built very rapidly.

Admiral Struble: Yes, and probably would be a different design anyway. It was much more liable to happen with small boats.

John T. Mason, Jr.: Now, you were talking in terms of maintaining the fleet in the Mediterranean. What responsibility was the U. S. Navy prepared to take over from the Royal Navy at this point?

Admiral Struble: Well, of course, in the past the Royal Navy had occupied certain areas around the world, and they had a very good reason for doing it because it was connected with their governmental control and/or interest in some of those areas. For instance, Singapore. For instance, the Mediterranean.

Now, obviously, we did expect England to be one of our best supporters and allies. We understood and talked easily and well with the English. We had just had a great war experience with them, to wit, the Normandy landing and so forth. So we were able to make a better gauge of what we might expect from the English, what they would do, and that they would do it well. Therefore, there was a natural tendency to, if you could have the English do something, to have them do it. They obviously weren't going to be able to do something then you had to figure maybe, well, maybe we ought to put some sort of an American increment into a certain area, not necessarily with the idea that we would be the only NATO—just to use an expression—the only NATO outfit in the area.[*] But there being no other NATO outfits in the area, then how much of an outfit could we put into an area that would be of some use and could we afford it?

We couldn't, of course, assume complete responsibility, as it were, for the whole Mediterranean Ocean, and we shouldn't have tried to. But we could put a nucleus outfit

---

[*] NATO—North Atlantic Treaty Organization, which was established in 1949.

into the Mediterranean. We could gain more experience in the Mediterranean, and we could be prepared then with thoughts and ideas and plans developed presumably by the senior officer that we put into that area of what might be modern thinking for that area. There was no reason why such ideas couldn't be secretly implemented with the British, at least, so that both countries would appreciate the situation and be prepared to put more stuff in if they had to and maybe with a minimum amount of current stuff there because all of us handled a few more commitments than we had the ability to provide for.

John T. Mason, Jr.: What role did you assign to Western Europe as such at that point? It was not in a very good state of affairs there.

Admiral Struble: The ground problem basically in Europe would be handled at least initially by Western Europe. We had to have plans to back up Western Europe based on our World War II experience that if something developed in Western Europe, it had to be Western Europe itself, basically, that provided pretty much for handling the first part of the problem. But we had to be prepared undoubtedly to avoid the disastrous thing we had gotten into in World War II with Western Europe almost taken over by Germany, with only England sitting on the outside by itself. So in my opinion, the British could support this and we could count on them to support it. The French were undoubtedly familiar with the problem. Boy, they had suffered it and realized it. But whether the French would necessarily be quite as heavily minded toward the defense of Europe was something that had to be determined by how willing they were to attempt to limit their problem out in the southwest. France had quite a large commitment . . .

John T. Mason, Jr.: In Indo-China.

Admiral Struble: Yes. Temporarily, I believe, it was tied into the French commercial situation in a way that made that part of the world very important to France.

John T. Mason, Jr.: Yes, her economic situation was pretty sad.

Admiral Struble: Well, there you are—and France can't afford to give up her economic problem. If the southwest area development was very important to them, then you couldn't count necessarily on France being able to support the Europeans' responsibility that we might wish them to undertake. You couldn't expect it.

John T. Mason, Jr.: Were we that realistic in Washington at that moment?

Admiral Struble: Well, I was possibly somewhat more realistic than some of the others. Of course, these were all ideas, you realize, at that time. Now, we are talking about it so many years later that anybody could say, "Gee, that's just hindsight he's talking." But it wasn't exactly that.

John T. Mason, Jr.: Well, because I realize that there were men who were pretty parochial in their point of view.

Admiral Struble: Well, for instance, it's my opinion that the immediate post-World War II problem, I believe that this government—now remember at that time, I wasn't OP-03.

John T. Mason, Jr.: Immediately postwar, no. You were out in San Diego.

Admiral Struble: Yes. But what I started to think of was that my next connection with this type of thinking at that time—I realized we had a problem in Southeast Asia and I felt that we ought to do something about it. I felt that we should try to strengthen the broad position in Southeast Asia. But at that time, none of us thought very heavily of doing other than just general support.

John T. Mason, Jr.: You mean by general support, we had an erstwhile ally there—France.

Admiral Struble: Yes, so we would support them a certain amount. Now, I guess there is an important thing that goes on there and I've forgotten exactly the date.

Interview Number 9 with Admiral Arthur D. Struble, U.S. Navy (Retired)
Place: Admiral Struble's Home, Chevy Chase, Maryland
Date: Thursday, 13 January 1977
Interviewer: John T. Mason, Jr.

John T. Mason, Jr.: It's great to see you on this chilly morning, sir.

Admiral Struble: Oh, this is sure good cold weather! I don't think we've had anything like this in Washington for a number of years.

John T. Mason, Jr.: No, indeed we haven't. You were about to resume your story by telling me about a very significant trip you made to Singapore sometime early in 1948. Do you want to take up the story at that point?

Admiral Struble: Yes. I went by air out to Singapore, where I talked to both the British and the French about Southeast Asia.

John T. Mason, Jr.: Let me ask you a question or two. What kind of preparation did you make for this trip and under whose orders did you go? The CNO?

Admiral Struble: Yes, I was ordered out by the CNO, and I'm sure that the State Department was conscious of what was going on. In other words, it was not a strictly naval matter.

John T. Mason, Jr.: And what kind of preparation did you make for your conversations out there?

Admiral Struble: Well, I studied the paper they had sent to me and a certain amount of information that they thought existed. I went out to make a survey to see if I agreed with their current position.

John T. Mason, Jr.: Give me the feel of the problem.

Admiral Struble: I think the interesting thing is that we had the case of the British in Singapore and the Malayan Peninsula. Although it was now '48, the British had not advanced very far above Singapore, and they were hardly one-tenth of the way, let's say, up the Malayan Peninsula. However, at the southern end of the Malayan Peninsula they did have a good, firm strong spot. The natives that were under their control were with them. They knew who the natives were. The natives knew who they were, so they had what I would call a pretty firm status.

They were slowly advancing up the Malayan Peninsula, probably not much more than a couple of miles at any one time. Then they would stop and, as it were, reestablish their front line a little, get all the villages in that area indoctrinated, get both the British and the village people all acquainted with each other, before they decided to try and take over another couple of miles.

John T. Mason, Jr.: What was the principal obstacle to their progress?

Admiral Struble: It would work out like this. Let's say that here's a village, say, a mile behind the front line. It's a good village, maybe 80 to 90 people in it. They are working hard, and they are trying to go ahead and keep their country, maintain it.

All right, some day, possibly in the late afternoon, there will be a raiding party from up north of, let's say, 20 to 30 men. They'll move in and take over the village. They would move in very carefully and try to circle the village and be sure that nobody got out of the village to let anybody know that they were in the village.

John T. Mason, Jr.: I see. And who were these?

Admiral Struble: The people from the north differ from the people in the south but all still related.

John T. Mason, Jr.: Were they of a Communist frame of mind or what?

Admiral Struble: I don't think I could answer that from memory, but they were from the other side. It's just like North and South Vietnam in a way. It was the difference between one outfit and another outfit.

They would circle the village. They would stay there and live high there for two or three days off the village food. Probably the women in town had a pretty hard time. They would keep their circle around the village to be sure that nobody left. The first thing and the most important thing they told people is that if anybody starts to leave and we catch them, you all will get it. In other words, they were very brutal in their appraisal.

So of course, with the number of people there accounted for, let's say 30 or 40 or 50, if anybody was missing at the roll calls it would be apparent that somebody had slipped out. Then they'd just raise hell locally. So by the time the man that had slipped out got down to where the British were and they organized something and came back out to the village, it was all over. The British point of view apparently was developed on that idea. They weren't going to get anywhere until they were sure that the outfit that was behind their front lines was entirely with them and therefore they could count on an advance of two miles. If they made it, it would be theirs.

This sounded very sensible to me, practical, hardheaded military thought. And they were making it, they were doing it. Of course, they were training these villagers the best they could, those up front, to have a couple of the young lads—preferably youngsters between 16 and 18 or 20, very young, capable, energetic, able to go through the hills. They were trained so that if a village were invaded, one of the youngsters would do his damnedest to drop down behind bushes or something or maybe even go in the opposite direction, maybe a little north or something, to get out of the way. The villagers would all have to be trained to say, "Oh, yes, everybody is here. Everybody is accounted for." Although, of course, all the villagers would know that one wasn't there. But that didn't make any difference. If these fellows came in and stayed there, that fellow had a specific spot where he was told to go to, usually something that he could reach in somewhere between about six and ten hours. Being a young, active man, he would be able to travel day and night.

So he'd get word quickly to the British, and then they would come out and quite possibly be able to surround the village and get the northern people eliminated and make the village safe. Well, the British felt very strongly that while their system was awfully slow, it was sound and produced the results.

Now, in my own mind, I felt this sounded very good and I so reported.

John T. Mason, Jr.: With whom did you talk?

Admiral Struble: Well, I made the regular report to Washington.

John T. Mason, Jr.: No, but when you went out to Singapore, with whom on the British side did you talk?

Admiral Struble: I talked to the head general that was there. There was a fairly senior Frenchman over from Vietnam who also was there at the time.

John T. Mason, Jr.: The Frenchman, I believe, was General de Lattre de Tassigney.

Admiral Struble: That's right. And General Harding was the British guy.

John T. Mason, Jr.: Well, did you visit any of these villages in Malaya?

Admiral Struble: I took a quick trip which somebody on the British side, I think, put up for me and it gave you just a little idea. But of course, the only place that I saw, they weren't far enough away from Singapore yet to be quite up more in the forest and upland stuff. But you got the idea. You could see the situation. I was very much impressed, though, with General Harding's determination to take his time and do it carefully and soundly and not try to establish a record for going too fast.

John T. Mason, Jr.: Was there any request of the U. S. Government through you for any assistance in this? Any supplies or anything of that sort?

Admiral Struble: The British made no request. The French, of course, needed help, and we were giving them some assistance. And, of course, the French would have liked to have gotten anything they could and a lot of it right away. But in my report I favored the British system and therefore did not believe that we should try to fight the Vietnam War on what we called recognized methods, methods that were used in Europe and everything. I felt that the care that the British were taking to be sure that they had a native area behind them that was solid was most important.

I've always felt that just in a big broad way that that was one of the lessons that we didn't learn until after Vietnam was over.

John T. Mason, Jr.: On this particular trip you also visited the French in Vietnam, did you? Where did you meet with de Lattre de Tassigney?

Admiral Struble: He was over in Singapore. He had come over to Singapore. I had to talk to him there. I don't remember going to any spot in Vietnam. In other words, I don't want to make myself a Vietnam expert. I didn't enter Vietnam. I got these impressions from just talking broadly on the subject. It is my opinion and it was my opinion then that the British method was a sound one, and I think frankly that had that method been adopted in Vietnam, it would have been better for all of us, whomever might adopt it and however they might try to do it.

John T. Mason, Jr.: How did it happen, sir, that you, a naval person, went to talk with two Army generals, one British and one French?

Admiral Struble: Well, it was military men talking to each other. I was probably sent out there because I had been connected with the State Department on this OP-03 type of duty before. Therefore, I imagine that the State Department felt some confidence in my ability to make an appraisal. Now, of course, you have got to understand that that was long before we went into Vietnam.

John T. Mason, Jr.: That's one of the very interesting points about it. This happened in the late 1940s before we actually got embroiled in any way, but it does indicate our interest as a government in that whole situation down there.

Admiral Struble: Well, this was a very serious matter. My trip was just a minor little thing in this matter, and I don't think it ever received too much attention at that time in the State Department. I am sure a couple of boys read it, and they might have said almost anything. This was long before the Vietnam thing developed, but I think it's interesting to realize that at that time our English friends were attempting a different method of handling the problem and it appeared to be going pretty good. It was smaller by comparison, a much simpler system to handle because they had one narrow peninsula. If you made an advance and tagged it down pretty well, you had it. So it's very easy after the fact to say we ought to learn more about Vietnam than we did. So I don't want that point of view to get in too heavy.

I do think it does show that as we developed that idea more at that time we might have done a lot better for ourselves.

John T. Mason, Jr.: What was your impression of the French general?

Admiral Struble: He had been a pretty successful man on the battlefields of North Africa and of Europe, and you couldn't discount him as being the top man and so forth and so on. The only thing that I would say as it appears is that we adopted the wrong method. Had we adopted what at that time was the British method in the Malayan Peninsula, then it might have been a lot better for us later in Vietnam.

John T. Mason, Jr.: Have you any idea why we didn't adopt the British method later on?

Admiral Struble: Not the slightest. I tell you, if you think it over carefully, you realize that was in 1948—we hadn't yet had Korea. We hadn't yet settled down the Philippines and Japan and everything else. That was still the big problem for us, by far the big problem for us.

John T. Mason, Jr.: That was a very interesting episode and you came back and prepared a report on your observations.

Admiral Struble: Yes, I prepared a report, I'm sure.

John T. Mason, Jr.: Did you keep a copy of that report?

Admiral Struble: Well, you see, it would have been a secret report so I wouldn't have kept a copy of it. That would probably be in the old files of ComPhibPac many years back. I don't know but what it's fairly secret still, although as you realize, you yourself have a knowledge of another report that was very similar. The situation would appear to indicate that the British themselves made that very clear to the proper people a couple of years later. But, again, it didn't take. That's the point, isn't it?

John T. Mason, Jr.: Yes, that's the point. Well, apropos this discussion of your trip to Singapore, you discussed that you talked with the British general and the French general of the situation in Indo-China. I have knowledge of the fact that later on, in the early '60s when we were becoming involved in Vietnam, that a representative from British Malaya was present on several occasions in Saigon and once in Pearl Harbor to tell our military people about the British effort in Malaya—how successful it had been over a period of 12 or 14 years that they had been engaged in this operation and they had finally succeeded. It was a very slow, difficult thing they had accomplished, but they had and they presented this information to our people. That's an interesting point of view.

Now, sir, going back to OP-03, would you talk a little about what was the thinking of the Navy about its future in this era of so-called peace that was opening up before us?

Admiral Struble: Well, the Navy was convinced at that time that they had been fairly successful in both the Atlantic and the Pacific in their operations that had gone on. Therefore, the necessity for a large number of radical changes did not appear to be immediately on the agenda. But it was apparent that some of our ship sizes and capability could be much better altered for the future to fight the same kind of a war we had just finished fighting.

In general, the improvements which we were asking for and were trying to get in the Navy were those that would do just that—improve the Navy that we had at that time but, in general, along similar lines.

John T. Mason, Jr.: No innovations.

Admiral Struble: I wouldn't say no innovations. At that time we were commencing to study very much the submarine problem and what advances we could make. We appreciated after World War II that the submarine was still a very important weapon and that we undoubtedly would offer some unusual advances if we kept after them. So the submarine was, I think I would say, the number-one improvement on the list. It would not necessarily have been the most expensive, but I would say that that was the thing we were thinking of very highly.

Now, improvement in aviation was very important because aviation was found to have a larger effect probably in any future war than submarines might have. But, of course, the expense of going into large aviation things was going to be much more probably than our expense in submarines.

John T. Mason, Jr.: Were we thinking in terms of a new type of carrier, or were we completely satisfied with the Essex class which had been so useful to use in World War II?

Admiral Struble: No, we felt that it could be improved. Now, we weren't sure exactly the way the improvements would go. The aviation people had a number of different ideas. Any changes of any marked character in connection with aircraft carriers would have been very expensive. Therefore, from the standpoint of people like myself, that was a subject we had to go into and study thoroughly, but we also had to be careful before we went into construction and decision on that because of the tremendous expense involved.

Arthur D. Struble, Interview #9 (1/13/77) – Page 328

John T. Mason, Jr.: You were under some difficulty, were you not, in that it was a time of economy. Louis Johnson was Secretary of Defense and was noted for his determination to cut down on expenses and forces and the like.

Admiral Struble: We were about to be cut below what we were getting unless we could get somewhere some help to hold pretty much to what we had and at least be able to convert by eliminating some of the things we had by putting it into these two areas which we definitely needed to keep investigating and improving.

John T. Mason, Jr.: You did actually reduce the number of active carriers, did you not?

Admiral Struble: Yes. We had already because after any great war things have to be put back in shape. The military has to reduce its spending markedly, and temporarily they are in a bad way for doing what they feel would be the better thing to do. So the amount of active forces had been cut. A lot of ships, all of which expenses had been eliminated, were put in mothballs. And our look at the future, both in the submarine and aviation, was indicating that it was going to cost money. It was going to be expensive.

John T. Mason, Jr.: Now, there was another area I think of that we were beginning to be interested in and that was in terms of missiles. We had been much impressed by the German efforts with the V-2.*

Admiral Struble: Well, I think I would class that as a part of our standard equipment almost by this time. New, yes, but almost obviously we had to go into the missile business and we had to study it carefully.

John T. Mason, Jr.: Did you get involved in that at all?

---

* The V-2 rocket bomb was first successfully fired on 3 October 1942 at Peenemünde, Germany. It was a liquid-fuel rocket, 46 feet long and weighing 13 tons. It carried a one-ton warhead. The German V-2 offensive against the Allies began in September 1944 and ended in March 1945; it involved some 5,000 rockets.

Admiral Struble: No, only in a broad way about how much of the money could we afford to put into the missile business, recognizing that it was something that would be worthwhile advancing. The missile business is much more of a joint business than either the airplane carrier or the submarine.

John T. Mason, Jr.: You mean joint with the other services.

Admiral Struble: Yes, joint with the other services.

John T. Mason, Jr.: What was the attitude of the Army at that time? Were they experimenting with the missiles?

Admiral Struble: As far as I know, they were. They had many ideas; they were up against the money problem just as much as the Navy was, and we were not getting ahead, I don't believe, with the amount of money that we were spending on that idea as fast as most military men would feel that we should. We needed more money in that area.

I think on the Navy's list we probably would have put new carriers and new submarines just ahead of the missiles. The other services, I think, would have been inclined to put the missiles first and the submarines and the carriers out. Actually, I think probably that the Army from their point of view would have felt that the missiles were number one and really we had enough submarines and carriers already. I'm just trying to give you an idea of the way the other fellow would look at it.

John T. Mason, Jr.: Was there any sense of compulsion in Navy circles in terms of missiles because of what we thought the Russians might develop?

Admiral Struble: Well, of course, one of the basic facts of the missiles was that it was just as well known to the Russians as it was to us.

John T. Mason, Jr.: Did we have any concern then that the Russians might go ahead and develop missiles?

Admiral Struble: I think we had every right to believe that the Russians would probably be doing just as well as we could. We didn't know if they had more money than we did. If they did, they would be doing better. I think it's just as simple as that.

John T. Mason, Jr.: So we did feel some compulsion about it?

Admiral Struble: Well, we were, yes. I don't see how you can expect that they wouldn't take advantage of that knowledge as much as we did. And it definitely was a source to be gone into. I think that it was a source of a new thing that should be developed slowly because it would be so easy to develop what appeared to be a pretty good thing. You've got a good design. It sounded pretty good, and at the moment it's better than anything we had for this sort of thing. It would be very easy to adopt that and go in and spend a hell of a lot of money for a hell of a lot of them in a hurry, and that would be a mistake.

I think the development should have been started properly, relatively at a somewhat minor rate of flow, until you had had more experience and were more nearly sure of what you were putting your money into. That has always been our experience, in my opinion, in the armed services. The new things should be examined carefully; they should be tested. We shouldn't get into production too quickly, particularly as production in the American method is a very expensive matter.

John T. Mason, Jr.: What you are saying is, it is a matter of proportion keeping these . . .

Admiral Struble: It's a matter of proportion. I am sure that we are going through that same thing right now in a way with some of the problems we have got.

John T. Mason, Jr.: Well, sir, there was a great fracas in Washington in Congress and Denfeld, the CNO, was dismissed from office and Admiral Forrest Sherman came in in his stead.* Was Forrest Sherman actually the choice of the Navy?

Admiral Struble: I don't think you could say who was the choice of the Navy because I don't believe actually that the Navy had quite expected that to happen.† Although before it finally happened there were many people who had an idea it was going to. But that didn't happen over a long period of time.

John T. Mason, Jr.: No, it was very precipitous.

Admiral Struble: Yes, it was very precipitous, so there had been no studied thought about who was going to be the next CNO. You don't usually have that studied thought on the matter until it becomes apparent it's only going to be a few months. Then you start to study the people at the top and so forth.

Forrest Sherman was relatively young. He was a very capable, bright, and brilliant man, there's no doubt of that. He had been my predecessor. He was OP-03 just ahead of me. Now, I think he was a very capable man; I think he was a good CNO. I think he was bright to jump on the problems of the mess we had in Korea, and I think he did jump on them very promptly and thoroughly.

Now then, if you want to discuss the problem of the CNO broadly, I must discuss it in slightly different terms, I think. I think I'm a little conservative. I think my idea would be that you shouldn't necessarily just select the young bright boy because he's so bright and everything. I think it is wise for the young, bright boys to all go through the training camp and not be jumped two or three steps simply because they are real bright.

Now, at the time you are about to select the CNO, there may be quite a few very fine older men at the top of the list. But if they aren't really of the extra high caliber that we need, then I think you have to go a little deeper. But I don't think you should go deep

---

* Admiral Forrest P. Sherman, USN, served as Chief of Naval Operations from 2 November 1949 until his death on 22 July 1951.
† Sherman's predecessor, Admiral Louis Denfeld, was essentially fired because of his support for naval aviators in their battle against the Air Force, which was trying to take control of all military aviation.

just to say I stuck my finger in the pie and pulled the plum out. I would prefer to see the CNO generally, broadly taken from the upper half of the list of people available. The fact is with the number we have today, I would say maybe the upper 25% to 30% on the list, rather than go deeper.

Now, if you are dissatisfied for one reason or another, if you didn't think the man's experience was broad enough, I wouldn't take one of the lower people simply because they were very bright and brilliant. And that's what Forrest Sherman was. He got it early.

John T. Mason, Jr.: And in a general sense you prefer that a man have thorough experience in the field.

Admiral Struble: More broad, thorough experience. I think he becomes the better man. I really do. And I see no reason to select the younger man unless you don't have a man of quite the caliber; then I'd go deeper. That's really your proper choice, go deeper a little more.

John T. Mason, Jr.: What contact did you have, if any, with President Truman when you were OP-03?

Admiral Struble: I guess I saw him two or three times when I would take over some sort of a special message that I knew about and it was better for me to take it over to the White House. The White House has many levels and grades. There are some messages that you want to be sure to get up to the top and not go through too many grades.

John T. Mason, Jr.: I was thinking at that time that the Navy was fortunate in having a very good man in the White House, Admiral Dennison, who was an awfully good contact for the Navy in there, wasn't he?*

---

* Rear Admiral Robert L. Dennison, USN, served as naval aide to President Harry S Truman from February 1948 to January 1953. He eventually became a four-star admiral. His oral history is in the Naval Institute collection.

Admiral Struble: That's true. The Navy has always taken the contact with the White House as being quite a serious matter.

John T. Mason, Jr.: Well, sir, did the Joint Chiefs have any idea that something might develop in Korea? There were certain rumblings, were there not, when you were still OP-03?

Admiral Struble: I think I would put it this way: if you specify Korea, I don't think we were quite as much aware of the possibilities of the North Korean attack as we were very considerably and broadly concerned with the Far East problem. I think that we all felt—at least certainly in the Navy and maybe a little less in the Army, but I think the Army was feeling pretty good, too—we thought that the Philippine problem was coming along fair. But the Philippine-Chinese and Japanese problem—if you mentioned all three of those names—wasn't too happy. Therefore, we still had a problem out there that we ought to keep our hands on. Does that explain it to you?

John T. Mason, Jr.: Yes.

Admiral Struble: That would have been, I think, our broad view.

John T. Mason, Jr.: You had that concern, but at the same time, with this whole emphasis on cutting down on forces and the drying up of funds, you weren't able to plan too heavily on adequate means of coping with the situation, were you?

Admiral Struble: Well, of course, in peacetime like we were just facing, it was apparent to all the Joint Chiefs of Staff that we just couldn't make tremendous expenditures at that time beyond some reasonable addition that we were going to try to get from the President on the current budget. Naturally at that time we tried to filter the budget. We had given quite a bit in some areas, but they had taken out a couple of big lumps at the last minute and it was very unhappy. This was just before I left Washington when that situation existed. I don't know but what the President at that time was doing his job in saying that he wasn't going to go any higher. But a couple of the boys that were out to raid for other things had stepped in and tried to convert some of the proper military money to ends that they considered more important.

John T. Mason, Jr.: What, for instance?

Admiral Struble: Well, I was trying to remember the thing that was about $800,000, if I remember. It was put through. You know the younger man who came into the government service temporarily, and then went up to New York and became the head of a big firm and was very successful for three years and then dropped out of the picture? I've forgotten his name now. But he was the man. I felt that he was diverting $800,000 in a way simply to assert his authority almost.

He had come up to Washington and gotten a good job. He was a very bright person, but he was pushing it awfully heavy. I didn't think that was a good thing, and actually his wishes were finally not allowed. The military people kept the money they needed. The Army had definitely taken a very big cut already. The Navy had definitely taken a big cut. I believe the Air Force had gotten fairer treatment from the Army and Navy in the division of the amounts of money. It was in a position where probably they needed if possible a little more money for advance things, and I felt they had a right to it. I didn't think they should take anything from the Army or the Navy, but I felt that if they could get $800,000 more I would have been glad to agree with it myself. Because aviation was getting important, and there was one thing that happened about that time that demonstrated it to me and in which I sided with the aviation against the Army on the decision.

When they vote—and there are three of you—it's kind of a two out of three thing. Broadly the Army and the Air Force have a tendency to agree with each other quicker because they are more similar services than the Navy. The Navy is a little different from them, although not so different from the Air Force, but in general our stuff is more expensive. A big ship is a very expensive thing to build.

Of course, the Air Force stuff was commencing to become very expensive too. But we found out one thing when we got stuck on the Berlin Airlift business.* Back in 1945, as you know, we had been prevented from marching a certain amount of troops into Berlin and conducting the finish of the war. Then a bridge had been carried away, and we thought it had probably been done deliberately. The question of marching troops into Berlin was not so good.

The Army wanted to go in for a land campaign and force the march in. On behalf of the Navy I agreed with the Air Force that we should just start an airlift. That way we didn't have to be fighting anybody on the ground, and we didn't have any rifle fire to get into the picture. Probably we could have a few planes flying around that would protect the airlift within reason, but if the airlift was brought down, we'd probably know who did it and it would be a clean-cut thing. So I voted for the airlift, representing the Navy, and, of course, the air people voted for it. The airlift proved to be a solution to the problem. It took a little time, but as we kept it going and improved a little bit, why, it was recognized by the Germans that they might as well give up the idea. We were going to have control of our own entry into Berlin.

John T. Mason, Jr.: You mean recognized by the Russians that we were going to have control of our entry.

Admiral Struble: Well, of course, the Russians also recognized it. But there had been some feeling on the German part about them controlling the roads as went into Berlin, so our basic problem in this was with the Germans. But in doing so, what we did was all right and the Russians could recognize it and they, of course, weren't going to stop it. It was none of their business. They had to have their travel in and out of Berlin on their side. We had to have ours on our side, and our solution was probably not going to cause another war. So the Russians really had no legitimate argument. But that was a hard-ought battle for a while.

---

* On 1 April 1948 the Soviet Union began a land blockade of the Allied sectors of Berlin, preventing overland transport from West Germany. U.S. and British airplanes then began and airlift that flew food and coal into the city until the blockade was lifted on 30 September 1949.

John T. Mason, Jr.: Yes indeed it was.

Admiral Struble: It was a good thing they did it.

John T. Mason, Jr.: What was the President's attitude towards the Joint Chiefs, and how much did he use them? What was his particular approach to the Joint Chiefs when you were there?

Admiral Struble: I think he was very sympathetic to the military. When some of these military things came out—let's say like this airlift—I feel sure that the appropriate military man explained the things to him carefully. Now, of course, at that time the head of the Joint Chiefs of Staff was a retired Navy admiral who was in the White House and who was still active in that capacity after World War II.

John T. Mason, Jr.: This is Fleet Admiral Leahy.

Admiral Struble: That's right. Now, we had a very fine man. Leahy was splendid. The Army and the Air Force recognized Leahy as a splendid representative for all of the military with the President. He had the President's confidence. He knew when to take something in to him, and he also knew when not to, which is always good. The fellow that gets to taking too much stuff in all the time is not what you want for that kind of a job.

John T. Mason, Jr.: What was your relationship with Leahy?

Admiral Struble: Excellent. Leahy, of course, attended the meetings of the Joint Chiefs of Staff. Leahy would drive over from the White House, pick me up at the Navy Department, and stop at the front door of the Pentagon. I'd be all ready and I'd jump in. He took me a ride over and he'd give me a ride back, which was very convenient. That also gave me a chance to talk to Leahy a little bit. He was a very fine, thoughtful, very thorough all-around military man.

John T. Mason, Jr.: He very often in the Joint Chiefs spoke for the President, did he not?

Admiral Struble: Oh, yes. He was in a position to say. "I don't believe the President this . . ." or "I don't believe the President that . . ." There's no doubt in my mind, I'm sure that both Bradley and Vandenberg felt very good toward Admiral Leahy.* He was a very splendid, all-around excellent chief of the Joint Chiefs.

John T. Mason, Jr.: Did you enjoy your assignment as OP-03?

Admiral Struble: Well, it's difficult to answer that question. I think I appreciated it very much, and it was a very important assignment. I realize that carrying out the job was very important, and I don't know that I have ever put in longer hours all the time on the job than I did when I was OP-03. I often came home with a large number of papers at night. Right after dinner I would sit up above where the fireplace is and read for two or three hours. Then I would get up early the next morning and go down to work and do it again the next day. As OP-03 I suppose that 80% of the time I was down there on Sunday. So it was a long, hard-working job really.

However, it was compensated because you felt you were really getting something done. It was a satisfactory job for your own self-esteem.

John T. Mason, Jr.: It was peacetime. Why was the job so demanding at that point?

Admiral Struble: Because we had so many world problems, in Germany and elsewhere. The problems of troops. The Joint Chiefs of Staff agenda was just full of problems all the time, and we were having a terrible time getting them settled. And we were having a terrible time keeping a reasonable amount of money in the defense establishment to meet the needs that we really had. We had not been able to keep together what had been a tremendous force during the war. At the same time we wanted to advance one or two of

---

* General Hoyt S. Vandenberg, USAF, Chief of Staff of the Air Force from April 1948 to June 1953.

the few new ideas, such as the idea of the missile. The missile was here, and we weren't getting the money needed to improve it and make it something.

John T. Mason, Jr.: Did you as OP-03 have any direct relationship with the Congress?

Admiral Struble: I had a relationship with the Congress only when I was sent over by the Secretary of the Navy to talk direct to them. I did that a number of times.

John T. Mason, Jr.: You only went then for specific problems.

Admiral Struble: That's right, sometimes very extra special and specific.

John T. Mason, Jr.: But no routine appearances.

Admiral Struble: No, no routine. It wouldn't have been a good thing for the man in OP-03 to be over there all the time. He's bound to talk too much.

John T. Mason, Jr.: Well, sir, we come to your next assignment as Commander of the Seventh Fleet. How did your assignment there come about?

Admiral Struble: I think that a new Seventh Fleet Commander was due to go out, and I think that they decided that my knowledge from OP-03 was a good thing for a man that was going out to the Asiatic at that time.* It did look as if the Asiatic area generally was a concern. I don't want to say the Korean problem, although we all know that a problem did exist in Korea, one existed in Taiwan, and a certain amount of the problem had drifted down into the Philippines. So I think they thought my previous experience in the Navy Department would be suitable for the man going out on the job.

---

* Admiral Struble took command of the Seventh fleet on 19 May 1950, just over a month before the start of the Korean War. He held the billet until 28 March 1951.

John T. Mason, Jr.: Yes, as a matter of fact, to underscore that point you just made, you went out in May to assume command of the fleet, and in June we find you in Manila conferring with Louis Johnson and with General Bradley on the Philippine situation.

Admiral Struble: That is correct.

John T. Mason, Jr.: Can you recall any details of that?

Admiral Struble: No, I can't recall the details except I think I can say this. I felt that my meetings with Bradley and Johnson were fine. I had only been out there, I believe, about a month or a month and a half at the time. But I think most of the things I said were corroborative of what my own views had previously been when I was the deputy on the Joint Chiefs of Staff. Of course, talking to Bradley was very simple and easy because we had been together when he was still on the Joint Chiefs.

John T. Mason, Jr.: There was some continuing concern, I think, in the Philippines about the Huks and their rebellion against the central government.

Admiral Struble: Well, I think I would say that that situation seemed to be improving. Therefore, I think that both Bradley and Johnson were satisfied that probably the Philippines were settling down, although the progress was never hasty down in the Philippines. Things are accomplished over there very slowly. That's probably due to climate.

I would have said that they weren't happy too much, but they weren't dissatisfied. But they were, of course, being in the Far East like that—just like a number of us that were out there—wondering how it was going to get along.

John T. Mason, Jr.: What was the state of the Seventh Fleet when you took over?

Admiral Struble: A very big title of a very small force.

John T. Mason, Jr.: Would you elaborate on that?

Admiral Struble: Well, I think I had a couple of cruisers and some destroyers and—

John T. Mason, Jr.: An aircraft carrier?

Admiral Struble: No aircraft carrier at that time. And I think I had all the forces that were needed to get around in that Southwest Pacific area properly to find out what was going on and so forth. I was in a position to take my flagship over and visit Vietnam by going over to their major ports on a trip. That way I was in a position to keep the Navy Department somewhat up to date on how things broadly were going in the area. I think it's valuable for one Navy man that he make a report of that character. I think, of course, it's valuable for another Army man ashore somewhere to be making reports of that character. I think it's also desirable for maybe an Air Force man to be making reports like that.

I have no doubt that the Army and the Air Force were giving reports from the Asiatic area in general and from the Philippines. We should have been. I think it's desirable for each service to give a certain amount of its own reports from their own people because sometimes they will be different from what the Navy got, for instance, by virtue of the fact that the Air Force and Army men are bound to have more contact with the local Air Force and Army people. The Navy man is a little more liable to have contacts with the naval forces. But in general, all three of their reports were a little bit different, and it's probably a good thing because when they all get back to the Defense Department they'll get coordinated and they'll probably have a better all-around answer.

John T. Mason, Jr.: Your primary mission as Commander of the Seventh Fleet was to be eyes and ears and to watch the situation out there.

Admiral Struble: To a certain extent that is true. But there is also a job inherent in that situation for the Commander of the Seventh Fleet to circulate around. For instance, sometimes I was going to be visiting Vietnam. Well, if you go up there as Commander of the Seventh Fleet, you'll get a pretty good reception in Vietnam, you'll get around a little bit, and you will enhance maybe the local reports from a captain in the Navy who was stationed on Vietnam. You will get to talk to some of the higher people where the need probably was. And you may get some franker talk.

John T. Mason, Jr.: So there was a diplomatic aspect to the job too.

Admiral Struble: Oh, there has to be. The Seventh Fleet was bound to be that type, even more than the Army man ashore in the Philippines. The Army man's job in the Philippines is pretty much limited to the Philippines. But the Navy and the Air Force men in the Philippines were more liable to visit Vietnam and Taiwan and so forth than the Army man. You can understand that.

John T. Mason, Jr.: You must have been happy at the fact that General MacArthur was in Tokyo, and here you were to go out and command the fleet in that area.*

Admiral Struble: Well, of course, my experiences with General MacArthur have always been very good. When I went out to the Philippines earlier, General MacArthur was on his way back up from the Southwest Pacific and had gotten as far as Hollandia. I had gone through Pearl Harbor and had talked there with Nimitz and was going out to be a rear admiral amphibious landing man after the Normandy bit. When I went down and joined up at that time, Admiral Kinkaid was there and was a very fine Navy commander locally. I saw MacArthur, and I started to see the way he handled the amphibious business in the Philippines and, of course, also the political business, which you were bound to see at the same time.

John T. Mason, Jr.: You had that as background when you went out here to the Seventh Fleet.

---

* General of the Army Douglas MacArthur, USA, commanded Allied occupation forces in Japan from 1945 to 1951.

Arthur D. Struble, Interview #9 (1/13/77) – Page 342

Admiral Struble: That's right.

John T. Mason, Jr.: So you immediately made contact with him again. Did he have any—?

Admiral Struble: I didn't immediately make contact with him again because this time when I went out with the Seventh Fleet, MacArthur was up in Tokyo. He was no longer in the Philippines. He was in the Philippines during the Philippine campaign when we took it back.

John T. Mason, Jr.: Where was the Seventh Fleet based when you went out in 1950?

Admiral Struble: It was based in the Philippines. In fact, I was the man in the Philippines then.

John T. Mason, Jr.: How much use was made of Sasebo and any of the other Japanese ports by the Seventh Fleet in 1950?

Admiral Struble: By about the 20th of June the Seventh Fleet had left the Philippines and was on its way north through Taiwan en route to Japan where the Seventh Fleet would be temporarily under MacArthur for Japanese area, which MacArthur controlled. The fleet was basically under Radford at Honolulu as a part of the Pacific Fleet.[*]

So the relations of Commander Seventh Fleet with Chiang Kai-shek on Taiwan were conducted through Radford in Honolulu.[†] I left, got up to Japan, and then I was conducting any negotiations I did under MacArthur.

John T. Mason, Jr.: Where did Admiral Turner Joy fit into the picture?[‡]

---

[*] Admiral Arthur W. Radford, USN, was Commander in Chief Pacific Fleet from April 1949 to July 1953.
[†] Generalissimo Chiang Kai-shek served as President of Nationalist China on the mainland from 1943 to 1949 and as President of the Republic of China on Taiwan from 1950 until his death in 1975.
[‡] Vice Admiral C. Turner Joy, USN, was Commander U.S. Naval Forces Far East from August 1949 to June 1952.

Admiral Struble: Admiral Turner Joy was MacArthur's number-one naval officer. He was the commander of naval forces under MacArthur. MacArthur had a certain amount of small naval forces under him. When I left the Philippines and went up into Japan, I went under Joy as MacArthur's military officer and temporarily wasn't under Radford. Actually, I was under Radford still in my responsibilities to Taiwan. When I first went back to Taiwan and the first arrangements that I conducted with Chiang Kai-shek, I reported immediately to Radford because he was my boss for that purpose.

I then got up to Tokyo, and I immediately visited General MacArthur. I told him and Joy the same thing, because I obviously shouldn't be under both of them.

John T. Mason, Jr.: It was a very confusing command, wasn't it?

Admiral Struble: Well, not confusing. There was no reason why I couldn't do it and do it properly. But as I told General MacArthur the first time when I talked to him, I said, "General, this is a little embarrassing to tell you what's going into Pearl Harbor on this matter, but, of course, my instructions on that matter came from Pearl Harbor. I want to keep you up to date and Joy up to date."

He said, "You know, I think Taiwan ought to be under us up here now."

I said, "I, of course, have no objection. But as you know, I can't order that. What kind of order the man in Pearl Harbor will give me about this I can't say, but I must report what goes on to him until the situation is clear. I believe it's just a matter of time until it will be cleared."

John T. Mason, Jr.: And was that the case?

Admiral Struble: Well, of course, as soon as the Korean War started, then it was recognized that the Seventh Fleet ought to be under Japan. And it was recognized then that the defense of Taiwan, which had been given to Commander Seventh Fleet, had to be properly then under MacArthur.

John T. Mason, Jr.: Now, before that happened, when you went up to see Chiang Kai-shek under orders from Admiral Radford in Honolulu, what was your mission?

Admiral Struble: Well, Chiang Kai-shek, of course, was concerned about the safety of Taiwan from the mainland. A clean-cut case. He was concerned with this diversion going on up in Japan and with MacArthur being forced to concentrate his attention on operations in Korea. He was afraid that Taiwan was going to be left out on the end of the stick—that it would be an appropriate time, maybe, for the mainland to decide to invade Taiwan. The people on the mainland might feel it was the logical time for them because the Americans were all tied up, up to the north. These are the kinds of things that you have to think about beforehand.

John T. Mason, Jr.: Do you recall your first meeting with Chiang Kai-shek?

Admiral Struble: Very well.

John T. Mason, Jr.: Well, tell me about it.

Admiral Struble: Well, I went up in the morning. It was pretty much of a private call. Chiang Kai-shek was in a big chair, and his interpreter was sitting right at his left so that he could talk into his ear whenever he chose. I was talking English to Chiang Kai-shek. I am sure that he understood most of what I said in English to him. However, I believe it's only honest to say that it is questionable if he had 100% understanding. He might have had 80 or 85%.

John T. Mason, Jr.: Therefore, the interpreter.

Admiral Struble: So therefore, the interpreter was justified and proper.

John T. Mason, Jr.: Did Chiang speak English himself?

Admiral Struble: He very rarely spoke much English, but he understood considerably more than he spoke. He would occasionally speak an English word to you, as he has to me. Not at that time, though, when we were going through this other system. He said, "How do you do."

Now, after I had spoken in English, then the interpreter would repeat it to him very carefully and thoughtfully. He was not loud, but I could have heard him, of course, if I had chosen to. Then Chiang Kai-shek would think about it, and then he would be ready and let his interpreter know. Then he would talk to me in his own language when he said the thoughtful things he wanted to say. His interpreter would convert that very carefully to English, and I would listen to him. Then I would reply.

Now, I was seated on a divan about eight or ten feet in front of him. Seated alongside of me was Madame Chiang Kai-shek, who could speak, of course, English very thoroughly and perfectly and knew what was said also in the other language. So as soon as he was done, she would start talking to me. Then when he had gotten through, then I would speak again. That's the way the conference went. I don't know how long it lasted—for an hour and a half maybe. But I'd be talking to Madame most of the time when I wasn't talking to him in English.

John T. Mason, Jr.: You were speaking on the same subject to her?

Admiral Struble: Not necessarily. As a matter of fact, a number of them were quite different. One or two were about the United States. How does this go down there, and how does something else go down there? And then sometimes, she would kind of worm into these current problems: "Well, I don't know that I understood what you said exactly about this fleet business of why the mainland probably isn't going to attack." You see, she sometimes would get onto that part of the mess with some questions herself.

John T. Mason, Jr.: It must have been a very demanding kind of a conference.

Admiral Struble: It was. It was a very demanding type of conference for you. Boy, you felt you had to be alert as hell because of this constant interplay.

I explained to Chiang Kai-shek very carefully that I felt pretty sure that with the fleet up north with things the way they were, that I doubted if the mainland was going to invade at this time. However, I said I couldn't help but agree that it certainly was a possibility if they decided they wanted to do it. I would keep the best possible eye on the subject that I could, and I would let him know as soon as I could if I felt there was any information that made me worry about an attack on Taiwan.

John T. Mason, Jr.: Did you and the Chinese on Taiwan feel that the mainland Chinese had the capability of invading?

Admiral Struble: Oh, they had the capability of invading if they chose to do it because they could put small boats on the shore, more or less abreast Taiwan. It wouldn't be a long trip over, and while the Taiwanese had some defenses of their own, the mainland could mount without too much trouble a pretty strong force, with their small boats. If the small boats got through and made a very effective and strong landing on Taiwan, they could probably take it over. So it wasn't to be just laughed off.

John T. Mason, Jr.: Were your assurances reassuring to him at that point?

Admiral Struble: Well, I told him one thing, "I'll guarantee you that while I'll be working with the Seventh Fleet up there in Japan, if there is an invasion and a buildup, I will leave promptly and come south and at high speed. I think I'll get here in plenty of time to be able to break it up." In other words, the fleet would get out in the channel and break up the mainland boats and crews coming across. It would be easy for us to do it. I had the kind of stuff that could do it, and I felt I would get there in time to do it.

Well, of course, that was some comfort to Chiang Kai-shek, but not altogether. He said, "Well, why don't you leave ships here when you go north? You take some north, you leave some here." Well, I had so few ships that I wasn't going to break them up. If I was going to go up to Korea for any real problem, as it appeared that it was going to be a real problem, I wanted to take up practically everything I had. However, I estimated that in easily 18 hours I could be down south abreast Taiwan, and I felt that I was sure to have at least 18 hours of notice. So if I had that much, I could come down and raise hell with the probable attack on Taiwan before it happened.

In the meantime, I was going to sharpen my intelligence about a possible landing from the mainland. I wanted to try to inspect it all very carefully, every day if I could, to be sure that there was not a buildup abreast Taiwan on the mainland to do it. It could not come up from the southern cities because the mountains in between precluded them coming that way.

John T. Mason, Jr.: And come from Amoy and thereabouts.

Admiral Struble: Well, it had to more or less come from the capital down to the southeast toward Taiwan. If they wanted to use troops that were down south, they would have had to send them north on the train, and having gotten them up north, then bring them down to the beach with heavy mountains stuck in between.

John T. Mason, Jr.: No, they couldn't bring troops up from the Canton area.

Admiral Struble: That's the idea. They had troops down there, but they were stymied unless they got them up and brought them back down again.

John T. Mason, Jr.: How adequate was your intelligence setup about affairs on the mainland?

Admiral Struble: I can't tell you what the intelligence on the mainland was. That would have been run from the Navy Department as part of their intelligence business.

John T. Mason, Jr.: And the CIA also.[*]

Admiral Struble: And the CIA, etc. Those reports would, of course, come in to General MacArthur from Washington. I would not have those reports until, let's say, MacArthur

---

[*] CIA—Central Intelligence Agency.

or Joy told me. Or they were sent to me by dispatch, if it was considered necessary. But I had some aviation that was under my control to the extent that from the island of Taiwan certain aviation could go up and take a look at the coastline so that we could make an estimate of that character. Now, it was my opinion that any large amount of troops that came from Canton down through the coastline—it's a fairly reasonable trip and a lot of ground in between—that a good aviation coverage of that area ought to bring something to light and it was a pretty fair intelligence thing.

The other thing, of course, was that there was every reason to believe that our planes could pretty easily make a very good search of the coast abreast Taiwan and to the north, and it would be fairly solid. So with that amount of aviation information, it seemed to me that we were almost sure to get a pretty fair crack at information that would be as much as 24 hours in advance.

John T. Mason, Jr.: What was the situation on the offshore islands, Quemoy and Matsu, when you were there?

Admiral Struble: As far as we knew, they didn't really affect the problem in the slightest.

John T. Mason, Jr.: Did the Taiwanese have them manned?

Admiral Struble: They were, I would say, practically neutral territory on both sides at that time. Now, of course, I guess both sides had plans maybe for occupying them, but neither one had yet done so.

John T. Mason, Jr.: That's very interesting, because it wasn't too long afterwards that this was in view.

Admiral Struble: Well, of course. Now, very shortly after my first visit to Chiang Kai-shek, the subsequent visits that I made down there were under General MacArthur's broad cognizance. In the meantime, I feel pretty sure that Radford had arranged probably that the forces which were on Taiwan which were previously more or less under him were shifted to be under Joy. In other words, the thing was tightened up because obviously there was going to be only one set of forces when we got into this Korean business and we were getting into it deeper. We knew that by that time. We couldn't afford to have two sets of forces out there.

John T. Mason, Jr.: What use was the Seventh Fleet making of Okinawa?

Admiral Struble: No use at all.

John T. Mason, Jr.: None at all.

Admiral Struble: No.

John T. Mason, Jr.: One other question about General MacArthur's naval units in Japanese waters: did he have control over the Japanese home defense forces?

Admiral Struble: Well, he was responsible for the defense of Japan, so through the Japanese part of his job, they were all under his control, I guess you'd say. As long as he would be fighting for their defense, they would certainly be fighting for him.

John T. Mason, Jr.: Well, they had a certain number of small naval units, did they not?

Admiral Struble: Yes, but they did not have anything that we wanted in the Korean business. I would say that broadly, certainly it's true, advisedly we might have wanted to try to run some things across the channel between the two places and maybe use a few, but I don't remember.

John T. Mason, Jr.: They didn't have any minesweepers?

Admiral Struble: They did have some minesweepers.

John T. Mason, Jr.: Admiral, I'm gong to ask you this question again. You intimated several times today in your conversation that the high military echelon felt that something was going to develop in the Korean area. When it actually broke out on the 25th of June of 1950, did it happen as you had anticipated?

Admiral Struble: Well, of course, you see what you're asking me now is really what MacArthur himself thought in Japan, because he is the one who had that worry and responsibility from the military point of view rather than Radford. It was apparent to me by this time that I was going to be operating under MacArthur in the future rather than under Radford and that the possibility of Korean trouble was certainly imminent. Whether it would or would not break, we were all gambling in our own minds. I think that MacArthur by that time had commenced to feel pretty strongly on it. I think that he jumped on it because he felt it would happen, but I don't believe he had actually moved many troops from Japan. I doubt if he moved any of them. Does that answer your question?

John T. Mason, Jr.: Yes, it does.

Admiral Struble: From my own point of view then, I still expected to make another trip to Taiwan on this Taiwan business and, of course, would require MacArthur's instructions now rather than Radford's instructions. I probably took a destroyer from Okinawa up to Japan, paid a visit, talked to Joy and to General MacArthur, and at that time discussed the deployment of the fleet from Okinawa up to Japan. My memory is not clear whether Joy and MacArthur at that time told me to come up immediately or whether just to be on very short notice and come up in a hurry. I do remember that when we left Okinawa, we left in a hell of a hurry. So I have a feeling that probably not too long after I got back to Okinawa we were sailing north to Sasebo.

I remember one thing, that is that the Chief of Naval Operations himself was out in Japan very shortly after the thing started to develop. And I remember that after Sherman had arrived at Tokyo he came down to Sasebo to talk to me. Joy accompanied him. So I'm not sure how much time was involved, but I might have remained in Okinawa for another couple of weeks and then started north to Sasebo.

John T. Mason, Jr.: In this book, The Sea War in Korea, the intimation is that MacArthur and others thought there was a possibility of air attack on fleet units in Japanese waters. Was that a real fear?

Admiral Struble: Well, there was nothing to prevent an attack on fleet units.

John T. Mason, Jr.: It would have been Russian planes, would it not?

Admiral Struble: I don't know whether they would be Russian or Chinese. Those were the two people who might want to get their hands into it. I don't think there is any way to drive that point other than to leave it broad like that.

John T. Mason, Jr.: There wasn't any certainty as to who was actually involved in this.

Admiral Struble: I don't think at that time that you could say that it had been established that it was Russian help for this problem that we had to worry about or it was mainly China help with this problem that we had to worry about, or both. I don't see how you could figure that one out.

John T. Mason, Jr.: Well, sir, by the 28th of June, three days after they crossed the line, they had taken the capital, and the United Nations Security Council had called upon its members to take some action to bolster up the South Koreans.

Admiral Struble: I think the mainland attack at that time finalized the idea that the North Koreans were coming south and were going to try to take over the whole country. I think that is established. The North Koreans, I said, were going to come south and take over the whole continent.

John T. Mason, Jr.: Not only were going to, they practically did right then, didn't they?

Admiral Struble: Well, that's the point, yes.

John T. Mason, Jr.: They had 100,000 men.

Admiral Struble: That's established. But at that moment, I don't believe that we were sure that any of those 100,000 were yet established as being either Russian or mainland Chinese. I have to get back to that part of it. We have not yet established that fact. At the present time, they theoretically are all troops helping. I think possibly—I'm certain they were Russian troops.

John T. Mason, Jr.: No, they were oriental.

Admiral Struble: It's my opinion that very shortly after that attack on Seoul that MacArthur and company had decided that the mainland Chinese were going to be interested but were not going to be interested in Taiwan probably. Now, when they made that estimate, if they did, I can't tell you. They wouldn't have talked to me about that particularly, you see, anyway. They'd be talking to me about my problems rather than that.

So I think, from my knowledge, you've got to attack the problem that way, that there was probably some backup being provided, but I doubt if we were in a position to determine which it was. Later, when they were deployed and they started south on the eastern side of Korea, I think you had some intimation then that they were maybe Chinese help rather than Russian help. I think there was some period in there where the mainland Chinese had said to Russia, "Don't you send troops. We'll send them if they are needed; therefore, we will have troops down there and they will go and you will not." Now, this is speculation in my mind. I don't know why I phrase it that way, but I think that was the way the situation turned out. In other words, mainland China was commencing to worry about this border and was probably telling Russia, "Don't you get into it; we'll get into it."

John T. Mason, Jr.: Now, on the seventh of July the United Nations, through the Security Council, called upon the United States to name a commander in chief to coordinate the United Nations effort in Korea. Did this make any immediate change in your status?

Admiral Struble: Oh, no, no. Nothing at all. That was merely a legality.

John T. Mason, Jr.: It had already been determined that MacArthur was to be the commander in chief.

Admiral Struble: Well, of course, he was going to be the commander in chief of our forces. But there's a legality involved there in that we wanted to try and force an issue with China and/or Russia that they were attacking U.N. forces. That was the legality.

John T. Mason, Jr.: Oh, I see. It was a collective thing. Well, it did mean something in terms of your naval forces at that point. Some British units were able to join up with you, were they not?

Admiral Struble: Yes, they did join up with us. That, of course, again was almost a kind of demonstration. We employed a couple of small cruisers they had. They were valuable, because they would go to individual spots. They knew the area, they were dependable. They could go up off so-and-so and tell you what they thought.

John T. Mason, Jr.: Did you not also have the use of a British aircraft carrier for a time, the Triumph?

Admiral Struble: Yes, and that tended to make it a U.N. force. But practically, from the tactical value, it was a hindrance rather than a good thing. However, the moment it arrived and joined up with our carriers, it did make it a U.N. force, if we wanted to say so. Of course, we were trying to push the U.N. proposition.

Now, we are getting down to whether we're talking practical military facts or whether we're getting off into diplomacy.

John T. Mason, Jr.: Well, in practical facts, why was it a handicap to have a British carrier?

Admiral Struble: Because she was small and slow, and she was going to operate in the center of the other carriers. We had to protect her. I mean, if she was going to be with us she had to be in the center and we couldn't outrun her if we wanted to. All we had to do was take the faster ships off and leave a few destroyers with her and hope to God it would turn out all right if it happened.

Now, I don't believe, to my memory, that we separated them more than a couple of times. The operations on the west coast were such that we didn't need the speed of our own carriers. There was one time on the west coast we had to rush north in a hell of a hurry. We had to send our fast carriers on at their best speed.

John T. Mason, Jr.: How were you using the carriers?

Admiral Struble: Well, we were using them to bombard shore troops whenever we felt we didn't have enough ground strength to stop them. That was the basic fact.

John T. Mason, Jr.: The planes then were being used in terms of close support of the ground troops, were they?

Admiral Struble: Well, close support of the ground troops really in attacking the other fellow's troops; that is close support—if you want to call it that.

John T. Mason, Jr.: Give me a definition for close support in terms of using fleet air units.

Admiral Struble: Well, real close support would be where the units up in the air and the units on the ground could talk to each other and function together. When we sent these airplane task units in on the west coast from the carriers, send in maybe 20 planes in a group, we'd say, "A certain thing is going on here; clobber the boys on the other side." They weren't necessarily trying to coordinate with our ground troops and support them in their advance. They were clobbering the troops coming south. Do you understand the difference there?

John T. Mason, Jr.: Yes, I do.

Admiral Struble: That means that the man up in the air with these 20 planes goes up there. He makes the decision. He tells them when to let the bombs fly, and he hopes to hell he hits the right forces.

Now, down in the southern part of the peninsula, where we were having hand-to-hand fighting of ground forces, we would have to have good ground communications from our forces to the fellows overhead because these forces are so close to each other that they've got to be sure he hits the fellows on this side and not the other fellows on this side. Close support, you see, is much more difficult by air. There is nothing that can be much worse than if your own air force gets after your own troops. It's very demoralizing.

John T. Mason, Jr.: Did this happen at all in Korea?

Admiral Struble: Well, once or twice it looked like it almost might have happened. But on the whole, we avoided it. But it's a dangerous thing and you've got to be sure what your aviation is and what it's doing and what it's capable of doing. This stuff that we're talking about now, in which the British might have been involved, would have been the kind where they would have been attacking the enemy. They would not have been in close support with our own troops because I don't think they had yet developed the communications and the clarity of thought on it.

John T. Mason, Jr.: And it called for basic training, too, did it not?

Admiral Struble: Well, it called for basic training and preparation. Yes. I hope you see why I'm being a little careful on some of these things. You're trying to make the case sometimes so simple that if I simply say yes, I won't be stating the military problem.

John T. Mason, Jr.: I don't expect you to simply say yes. I think you're too smart for that.

Admiral Struble: This is sometimes more complicated than you can imagine. I would think that some of the British units may have gotten into action fairly early, but it would have been independent raiding that they would have been doing. They would have been told that north of a certain latitude on the west side or north of a certain latitude on the east side, just bomb everything in sight. It isn't going to be us. I imagine that's the type of order that would have been issued.

John T. Mason, Jr.: Well, some of the naval units were engaged in shore bombardments. Could you not use the British in that way?

Admiral Struble: We did use the two British cruisers. They were very experienced, and they could get into the job much better than our aviation could because it's a much simpler job. We had the two cruisers, and it's my impression that we at that time that you mentioned were operating them independently. They would go in on their own orders, and they were told to bomb a certain village or a certain area. If they got any signs of life or any back talk, you might say, they were supposed to let us know promptly. But they were sounding out areas that we wanted to find out whether there was Korean and/or anything else that was liable to be dangerous.

I don't believe we used them on the big middle trend down on the way to Seoul and south. As you know, the North Koreans got a long way south before we stopped them.

John T. Mason, Jr.: For the first 82 days of the conflict, it was just a kind of a holding operation on our part, wasn't it?

Admiral Struble: Oh, it had to be. Oh, yes, it's all it could be. We were being pretty careful about our operations at that time. I was handling the west coast at that time. I wasn't using anything except with all the care that I just told you about. Now, after we landed at Inchon, then we had the problem that it was almost impossible for us to use the foreigners or anybody else in air of that character in support of the attack on Seoul because it had to be very closely coordinated or they would be getting our own troops. In other words, they had to be working then through the Army units that were with our advance troops because they were so close it was a very touchy problem. We just couldn't let anybody in then with broad open gunfire.

That was one of the things that was so valuable in the roads from the Normandy landing south, where the Germans were trying to bring up troops to Normandy to reinforce them. During the day our troops weren't supposed to be in the picture, and that was so that our aviation could bomb any damned thing on the road that they could find; any troops marching just had to be enemy. So therefore our troops couldn't march on those roads.

Interview Number 10 with Admiral Arthur D. Struble, U.S. Navy (Retired)
Place: Admiral Struble's Home, Chevy Chase, Maryland
Date: Wednesday, 19 January 1977
Interviewer: John T. Mason, Jr.

John T. Mason, Jr.: Now today, sir, we are coming to one of the really classic examples of an amphibious landing, the one at Inchon, the one that is going down in history as an extremely successful and an extremely difficult operation. You were informed sometime in August, I believe, that you were to be in charge of this operation. Would you take the story from this point, sir?

Admiral Struble: Admiral Sherman had come out from Washington and had flown into Tokyo and talked to Admiral Joy and General MacArthur, I am sure. He had then decided to come over to Sasebo, which is on the west coast of Japan, and come down and see me, Joy, of course, being with him. On the occasion of that visit which, as I remember, lasted overnight, there were, of course, a number of talks with both Admiral Sherman and Admiral Joy. So I'll try to say who said what, but there may be a little bit of a possibility of memory on which one told me what.

However, there was no doubt as far as I was concerned that they were seriously considering the west coast landing at Inchon. I was informed that I was to command the operation, and we better get on the job and get it going quickly. It was suggested that the sooner I got up to Tokyo with four or five or half a dozen people that I needed, that the planning could get under way and be accomplished.

John T. Mason, Jr.: At that point had they determined on a date?

Admiral Struble: Well, I would have said they generally thought it was going to be about the middle of the month.* I don't believe that the exact date had been fixed, but it was approximately fixed.

There was no particular Seventh Fleet situation that I had that couldn't be handled entirely competently by my chief of staff. He had a very small force at that time, you understand. But what I had to do was, without robbing my own chief of staff when I left, I had to select a certain number of good people with experience, if I could, to plan a very large overall operation. We had to coordinate a lot of small forces here, there, and so forth.

John T. Mason, Jr.: At that point you were well aware of the difficulties of that proposed operation, weren't you?

Admiral Struble: I realized that there were going to be a large number of difficulties. One thing in particular was that it was not on the coastline, so you didn't come in from the sea and make an attack on it. It wasn't really a river; it was a little bit more like coming into the capes and up into Baltimore, we'll say, from the Atlantic Ocean.

On the other hand, the width of the water involved was not at all as wide as, for instance, Chesapeake Bay. The width of the water generally from the sea up to Inchon was much more the width of a river. At times it was spread out a bit and there'd be maybe some little islands, as it were, and so forth. But I think you could call it more a river than certainly a big bay like Chesapeake Bay.

John T. Mason, Jr.: Do I understand that when Admiral Sherman came there that he was less than enthusiastic about this spot for a landing?

Admiral Struble: I wouldn't say he was less than enthusiastic about the spot for the landing, but he recognized that if you could get a better place you'd be better off. I think I'd put it that way. In other words, he wasn't holding back on an operation or on getting

---

* On 15 September 1950, U.S. troops under the command of General of the Army Douglas MacArthur made an amphibious landing at Inchon, the port for Seoul, South Korea. The surprise landing, 150 miles behind enemy lines, temporarily turned the tide of war in favor of United Nations forces.

something done, but if there had been a better spot, that would have been more desirable. Because he recognized that this long trip up an inland river, as it were, before you got to where you were making your landing wasn't too good.

John T. Mason, Jr.: Is it not also true that General Collins, I guess it was, was not very happy about the prospect?[*]

Admiral Struble: I would say that General Collins was more conservative and less sure of making the decision of Inchon than the Navy. Joe definitely had a few more misgivings about parts of it. Of course, he did recognize that a decision was going to have to be reached, and we were going to have to go ahead with it.

John T. Mason, Jr.: Now, how did you personally feel about this landing at Inchon?

Admiral Struble: I felt that the landing at Inchon would be a very strategic matter, excellent. From looking it over carefully, nothing could be better from a strategic standpoint in going after. The question became then one not of listing and fighting all of the problems that were going to be ensued, but it was to go ahead and discuss it and handle them carefully and accomplish it.

John T. Mason, Jr.: Tell me about your trip to Tokyo then and how you went about planning for this.

Admiral Struble: The main point that was involved in this trip was that General Collins had practically made up his mind, I believe, to go for the Inchon landing, although he was still thinking over it. He realized that he had until the next day to make up his mind to the decision. He was still trying to get information and investigate this to see if it was the thing.

In the meantime, I think Admiral Sherman had decided, "Well, this looks like it is going to be it, and we might as well get on with the business." The only difference

---

[*] General J. Lawton Collins, USA, was Army Chief of Staff from August 1949 to August 1953.

between him and Joe Collins was that he had made up his mind by that time; Joe didn't make up his mind until the next day when the conference was held in Tokyo. He was certainly entitled to hold up his decision until he listened to all the talk.

John T. Mason, Jr.: You were present at that conference in Tokyo.

Admiral Struble: No.

John T. Mason, Jr.: You were not.

Admiral Struble: Oh, no.

John T. Mason, Jr.: That was the conference with General MacArthur.

Admiral Struble: That was the conference with General MacArthur and the chiefs from Washington and the Joint Chiefs people from Washington. I was not present there. However, Sherman told me, "I feel pretty sure it's going to go through. I'm convinced it will be a good one."
    I said, "Well, I thought it might myself."
    So he said, "Well, you collect a staff right away, and you come up tomorrow or the next day to Tokyo and be all ready to go ahead and make the plans for the operation."
    That's what Sherman told me. Joy had not been at all as specific as Sherman in his statement to me. I had just said, "All right, I'll come up and bring some people with me."

John T. Mason, Jr.: Was he enthusiastic about it?

Admiral Struble: Well, I think he could have been withholding what you might call the final decision on his part until the next day, waiting to see what was said at the conference before he gave it his all-out approval. I think that would have been quite a reasonable situation, don't you know. Why try to make the decision before the meeting is held? Why not listen to all of the talk and then express yourself? And that's sound, of course. So there shouldn't be any criticism of either Joe Collins or Joy in withholding their statements until they attended the final conference.

However, as far as I was concerned, I was told to get on up to Tokyo and go ahead with the idea because Sherman said he was sure it would go through. Now, I decided I'd need about four or five really good people. I looked around for a number-two man who had had amphibious experience in World War II and so forth, who knew what it was all about and who was a good, capable man. That turned out to be Captain Sharp, who was then commanding a destroyer squadron in Sasebo.[*] So I went over to him first thing the next morning and said, "Now, you've got to pack up and go up to Tokyo with me tomorrow."[†]

John T. Mason, Jr.: All right, sir, whom else did you select?

Admiral Struble: These were people that weren't usually with me that I had selected specifically for this job. So about a day and a half later we flew up to Tokyo and checked into Joy's office. We were given a room in which we could operate. We spent about a day or a day and a half getting organized in that room and starting to make a general idea of what the plan should encompass, what should be involved, and how much, and so forth.

I would say about two days later, having gotten things pretty well lined up, I went up to have a conference with Joy on the subject. Unfortunately, he was just leaving his office at that moment and he referred me to his plans officer at that time. Joy was going somewhere. So I went around to talk to his plans officer, who proved to be a very nice young man that I remember, maybe a lieutenant commander. What he had prepared was a little statement that said, in effect, we would land on Inchon on the west coast and so forth. But, of course, it was not at all a plan, just a kind of a statement of intention.

---

[*] Captain U.S. Grant Sharp, USN, Commander Destroyer Squadron Five. Sharp eventually became a four-star admiral and Commander in Chief Pacific. His Naval Institute oral history discusses his role with Admiral Struble in planning for the invasion at Inchon.
[†] For the purpose of this operation Admiral Struble became Commander Joint Task Force Seven, giving him joint-service authority in addition to his Navy-only role as Commander Seventh Fleet.

I talked to him for 20 or 30 minutes on the subject of information and recognized that he was very young. I don't know how long he had been in the job, and I realized that he was not the man to help me prepare the plan. So I thanked him and went back and figured out who was around or available and so forth that we ought to talk to. Of course, obviously we wanted people like Doyle. Doyle was the admiral who was doing the amphibious training at that time in the Far East. The purpose of that had been to send out maybe a certain number of Marines from the West Coast and have them given a good training exercise in amphibious business out in Japan. It was an area in which there might or might not later be trouble. This, of course, hangs onto the work I previously told you about in San Diego.

The Marines were going to be assembled in a fair amount of strength in California and be taken out and shipped to Japan and have amphibious training and come home. Those of us who were interested in the amphibious business realized that it was good stuff and ought to be gone ahead with. Actually, on the Army side—and I guess to some extent more than most—Omar Bradley was not so sure that the amphibious training needed to be pursued too heavily. Of course, Bradley himself had been at Normandy, and he recognized that while we had a lot of problems, it did get him started on the continent in good style for the later operations against Germany.

However, I think he may have thought that the chances of another Normandy were very remote and probably are. But that doesn't mean that the amphibious technique shouldn't be developed. Of course, the Marines are very interested in the amphibious technique because it does give them a specialty above and beyond just being straight foot soldiers. The Marines wanted to continue the training because they felt it could be worthwhile. I think they were entirely right.

John T. Mason, Jr.: They certainly proved it in Korea.

Admiral Struble: It proved its value right there at Inchon—that the ability to do that was worthwhile. So we started ahead with the plan, and I suppose in about a week, maybe five or six days, we had prepared what was the final Inchon plan. During that period, I had, of course, consulted with Doyle who was the local amphibious man under Joy. I had consulted with the Marines who were there locally and would obviously be involved in the landing, and had had long talks with all of them and long discussions.

John T. Mason, Jr.: What about General MacArthur? Did you talk with him?

Admiral Struble: Yes. I suppose MacArthur sent for me maybe a half a dozen times during this period in the preliminaries up to the landing.

John T. Mason, Jr.: Did he have any input into the planning himself?

Admiral Struble: Oh, no. Of course, I think it's fair to state that MacArthur knew me much better than he knew Joy. I had worked for MacArthur in the Southwest Pacific, in the landings throughout the Philippines and everything. So he knew me personally, and we had often discussed this kind of business before. Now, I'm not sure whether Joy had previously been with MacArthur or not, and it might be that MacArthur may have had a tendency to send for me more often when he possibly should have sent for Joy because Joy was really the Commander Naval Forces Far East, which was under MacArthur.

Of course, in discussing with the Marines and with, for instance, Doyle and so forth, all of these amphibious experiences were different. The Central Pacific had a little different approach to the amphibious landing than did the Southwest Pacific. I was a Southwest Pacific man. The way it had been developed down there had been very effective and operated very well. I feel sure that the way it had been developed in the Central Pacific had been excellent. However, the two methods of development were to some extent different and the two cases were different. In a way I feel that the Korean business was more nearly like the Philippine business than it was like the Central Pacific business.

Now, Kelly Turner, the man that had been Doyle's boss in the Pacific amphibious business, was one of our top early amphibians. So naturally Doyle was, let me say, a student of Turner's system, whereas I had been a student of the other system.

John T. Mason, Jr.: Yes. A practitioner.

Admiral Struble: Well, all right, I had been a practitioner both at Normandy and out in the Philippines. So there were differences when I got together for the first talks with the head Marine and the Marine planners. Of course, Doyle was the same way. There were differences of opinion.

In the Central Pacific they had a much more rigid command of it developed. Down in the Philippines, we had developed things under Dan Barbey, the Navy man who had immediate command of amphibious operations under MacArthur. Dan Barbey was a very practical man and he had in general handled the amphibious matters—considering the particular operation involved and what it needed—with a more practical approach.

I was inclined to be one that felt the rules for each operation should be somewhat conformed to but figured out for the specific operations rather than just sticking to rules. In any event, we got along fairly well, as far as I can see. Doyle, I think, would have done some of the things differently than I would have done if he had been in command. I don't see how in general terms he could have reached anything much different. But he might well have.

The Marines, I would say, were a little different from the Army in that they felt that they were already expert in the business, and therefore their method of doing it had to be thus and so also. However, we really had no problems on the landing in preparing the plan. It was quite detailed, as I felt it should be, and it was an endeavor to land—if and when we could—with as little opposition as possible at that point of landing. We wanted to do that in order to get established as early as possible and then be able to put up a better fight and stay there.

John T. Mason, Jr.: Did you have knowledge that the enemy had troops in that area?

Admiral Struble: There were bound to be a few troops there. We had estimates, but I think in your approach to how many troops they had there, you had to be careful. It would be smart to overestimate rather than to underestimate. They very definitely had forces on Wolmi Do; they very definitely could shoot at planes that came in there and that sort of thing.* So there were definitely planes there.

It is also true that Inchon is the western end of the railroad that comes down the east side of the Korean peninsula. Then after you get to Wonsan, the railroad breaks and comes across over to where Seoul and Inchon are. Do you see the picture?

John T. Mason, Jr.: Yes, I've got a map right before me.

Admiral Struble: Which meant that North Korean troops could be put into Inchon very quickly or reasonably quickly. It also meant—and I realized this due to my previous experience in World War II—that that railroad could bring in mines. Mines are fairly good sized. You don't just put some of them on a wagon and go somewhere with them. They are rather heavy. So the railroad being in Inchon meant that mines definitely had to be considered a possibility.

John T. Mason, Jr.: But you had no intelligence of the fact that they were?

Admiral Struble: We had no intelligence that there were or there weren't. Of course, a minefield could be built up over a period of two or three days maybe, if the mines are there and they made up their minds where they wanted them.

Now, one of the bad parts about the Inchon operation was that you started down, as I remember, around 100 or maybe a little over 100 miles of what you might call a curving river. But I want to stress that it was really called a sound rather than a river. In effect, it would have been like coming up a very narrow Chesapeake Bay with twists and turns.

John T. Mason, Jr.: Now, that was a part of the hydrographic picture. How did you deal with this whole thing?

---

* Wolmi Do was an island connected to the mainland by a causeway. It controlled the approaches to the landing beaches at Inchon.

Admiral Struble: This hydrographic picture indicated that, if they chose, they could give you trouble on the way up that long channel. After you got to it, they could definitely give you quite a bit of trouble if you brought up fairly good-sized ships such as cruisers for bombardment purposes. They also might have to go through minefields on the way up. We were pretty sure there weren't any minefields there at the time. Whether there might be in the future or not, we didn't know.

John T. Mason, Jr.: Now, there was the element of surprise. This was to be entirely an unsuspected sort of an operation, was it not?

Admiral Struble: Very much. I think the success of the operation was based on the fact that we do it as quick as we could and that we have the best chances of surprise.

John T. Mason, Jr.: You've been talking about the element of surprise. I'm conscious of the fact that the base of operations at this point was in Japan. It has been said that this operation in the final stage was called Operation Common Knowledge because Japan was not the most secure place in terms of intelligence. There were too many agents snooping around and that sort of thing. Can you comment on that?

Admiral Struble: Well, I don't know how many agents there were around and how much information was leaking out of Tokyo, but I question that this specific thing got out. I am sure that the enemy probably had agents around Tokyo who knew that General MacArthur and his elements were all studying and working on this problem of Korea. But that, of course, they would have known any way.

John T. Mason, Jr.: As it turned out, was there any evidence of the fact that they knew anything about this specific operation?

Admiral Struble: I don't believe that I would classify the knowledge that I will give to you later as being something that indicated that they knew that the operation was going on. However, I'll make the statement that the Russians had long been mine-minded. The

Russians have always thought that mines were an excellent weapon, so that the moment you get anybody who is going to be supported by Russia maybe a little in the matter, you should be very suspicious of mines because your enemy would be getting mines then from Russia. If the Russians wanted to support the North Koreans, I am sure that their advice would be, "We'll send a lot of mines to you. We'll send experts who know how to put them down." Of course, the record of the war clearly indicated that they did recognize that, and they did send lots of mines down.

John T. Mason, Jr.: But they hadn't really gotten them down yet?

Admiral Struble: So where the mines were that they had given to the Koreans we didn't know. We had no intelligence, as far as I know, that indicated that they had any mines at Inchon or that they had any mines at Wonsan.* But certainly we could suspect it, and I was one that suspected it very much.

There had been some bombarding here and there going on and some air bombardment. I decided that, rather than attempting to keep everything away from Inchon, the approach was to try to gradually increase that type of business but not make it too marked so that you were apparently selecting Inchon or anything. So therefore we continued planes going over a little bit occasionally, but we also did bomb both north and south on the coast.

John T. Mason, Jr.: So they couldn't pinpoint any—

Admiral Struble: So apparently Inchon wasn't pinpointed too much. As a preliminary operation, I decided that we would want to run up a certain number of ships that were going to be up there during the operation itself. We would want to run up the river and show ourselves off Inchon and make a little bit of a fuss—not too much to make it prominent but to get some idea of what was involved.

---

* Inchon is a port on the west coast of South Korea; Wonsan was a port and stronghold on North Korea's east coast.

So as concerns our big menace—mines—they couldn't take any action that would hurt too much in less than three days. On the troop subject, yes, we were concerned if they had a lot of troops up at Seoul that they could push down through Inchon in a day. So I proposed in my own mind to run ships up, have our Air Force ready and have a good one-day attack on Inchon. Then we would withdraw all the forces and take them back out so that it might appear to the other fellow that we had decided to make an attack on this side and had come up the river for a day and made the attack and then had turned around and left.

John T. Mason, Jr.: You felt this wouldn't tip your hand at all.

Admiral Struble: Well, I felt, yes, you might say it would tip it a little, but the withdrawal of the forces and so forth—that idea was employed simply to make it appear that it had been a one-day effort, you might say.

John T. Mason, Jr.: And meanwhile, you would gather some knowledge.

Admiral Struble: That's right. And in the meantime, we had been employing some air operations along the west coast for three or four days to a week maybe. Those I endeavored to scatter very much, making it appear more that we were hitting important spots in the peninsula rather than that we were attempting to pinpoint where we came in from, which wasn't necessarily the Inchon area. In other words, the carriers might be 50 or 60 miles north of there and be launching their planes. They could also come down past Inchon on the way back to the ship and drop a few bombs in there and so forth.

John T. Mason, Jr.: You were employing a certain amount of deception.

Admiral Struble: Well, attempting to, of course. I think that that was desirable in that case, although as I say, we had no evidence of any mines. But that long, narrow almost river all the way up to Inchon was bad and offered a mine man a great opportunity to give you trouble.

John T. Mason, Jr.: Were you worried about the kind of tides in that area?

Admiral Struble: We weren't worried about them. We knew about them and what they were. They were very bad for us.

John T. Mason, Jr.: The rise and fall of the tide determined the actual date, didn't they?

Admiral Struble: At least initially they affected it in that you could only land troops in the Inchon area for about, I would say, one hour twice a day at a period of the year when you had the high tides. It was preferable for you if you had high tides at the time that you were there. I would estimate at Inchon your tidal height at high water might vary as much as 12 to 20 feet, depending on the period in the month. We would naturally want to land at Inchon at those higher of the high tides because it would give us a better opportunity to get any small boats ashore and get the men and materials over. If you went in and had a six-foot bluff in front of you, it was going to be tough handling supplies. So naturally, that determined to some extent the date, and then that affected the rest of the planning.

Now, I deliberately went up the river the day before, and we had some bombardment that was intended to get everybody accustomed to what was going on and how it worked out. As I remember, we had been up once before, and that was about a week earlier.

John T. Mason, Jr.: On this particular occasion, you went yourself, did you?

Admiral Struble: Oh, yes. I went up with the ships. I wanted to see what it looked like. Now, the first time we went up, we anchored south of Inchon by about four to six miles and bombarded the city from a distance with gunfire.

John T. Mason, Jr.: Did you discover anything on Wolmi Do?

Admiral Struble: Oh, yes, sure. There was stuff at Wolmi Do. Our air cover in that area had also found that they got fired at from Wolmi Do earlier. So we knew that Wolmi Do was capable of putting up a certain amount of antiaircraft for us.

The gunfire that would come out of Wolmi Do would be only medium- to short-range stuff as regards where the ships could anchor. When we went up the first time, the ships were probably firing at about 12,000 yards, so that would be about six miles. We were firing in at the city from outside. Of course, when we went in for landings, we went in much closer, but we were restricted from employing our boats and landing them ashore for one hour, maybe, more or less, every 12 hours as the tide went up and down.

John T. Mason, Jr.: Well now, the fact that you had met some opposition from Wolmi Do meant that you had to put Wolmi Do out of commission before you could attempt your landings?

Admiral Struble: No, it meant that we had to put Wolmi Do out of commission in order to get the best landing places for handling goods which was the front of the city down facing to the west.

John T. Mason, Jr.: Is that what you called the "Green Beach"?

Admiral Struble: Yes. Now Green Beach was the best beach—no, Red Beach was the best beach for our purposes, which was on the face in front of the city. Green Beach was the next best, which was off Wolmi Do. Blue Beach, which was way around to the right, was very good—it wasn't a good beach from the standpoint of going in for an attack and getting men ashore and starting your operations there, but it was the beach from which you could land troops closest to where the road went to Seoul and you could, if you got troops ashore at the beach, then be in control of the crossroads of the roads going to the eastward and you could separate and segregate the city itself by having control of that spot in the road.

John T. Mason, Jr.: Also control of the railroad?

Admiral Struble: Well, yes, also control of the railroad then. You'd be out where the railroad and the road—there was a big fine road there, a road and a railroad—where they went to the eastward. If we got ashore in some strength landing around to the right, then you would have control of egress and ingress into and out of the city itself.

John T. Mason, Jr.: Now all of this you were able to determine long before, while you were drawing up your initial plans.

Admiral Struble: Oh, yes. All of this was understood and the plan basically was that we would go in and along about, I suppose I would say 6:00 or 7:00 o'clock in the morning, maybe somewhere along in that period of time, but in the first landing knowing that we were going to Wolmi Do in particular, we could fudge I suppose an hour or so on high tide on the frontal landing. So we would make our first landing in the morning, right at Wolmi Do, and we would try to get in to red beach if we could which was the entrance into the city. Here's the city and here's this little island right out in front of it and you could go in and if you could handle the gunfire on Wolmi Do, you could land some troops and start to get ready to take over the Wolmi Do island.

If you got in here a little bit further this way but on the beach proper going to the city, which is where Red Beach was, you could start landing troops and equipment quicker and better than you could anywhere else. So the idea was that our landing in the morning with preliminary gun bombardment and, of course, with air applied, then we would put the troops in.

Now that landing was completed, I suppose, by around 9:00 o'clock.

John T. Mason, Jr.: And from then on until evening, you weren't able to add to the—

Admiral Struble: No, you weren't able to send in boats and get anywhere because all they would be up against was just a frontal cliff.

John T. Mason, Jr.: A palisade, sort of thing.

Admiral Struble: A palisade effect. So the people that were landed in the first landing were not going to see any help until the afternoon landing, which as I remember, was about 6:00 P.M.

John T. Mason, Jr.: They had to be self-sufficient then.

Admiral Struble: They had to be self-sufficient until we got in again in the late afternoon.

John T. Mason, Jr.: How many did you land originally in that first landing?

Admiral Struble: I suppose we got about 300 or 400 men on Wolmi Do and possibly a little more on Red Beach.

John T. Mason, Jr.: Were they Marines?

Admiral Struble: I would like to say they were all Marines, but I'm not positive. I think we had intended to try to for handling goods, which was the front of the city down facing to the west.

John T. Mason, Jr.: Is that what you called the "Green Beach"?*

Admiral Struble: Yes. Now, Red Beach was the best beach for our purposes; it was on the face in front of the city. Green Beach, which was off Wolmi Do, was the next best. Blue Beach, which was way around to the right, was very good. It wasn't a good beach from the standpoint of going in for an attack and getting men ashore and starting your operations there, but it was the beach from which you could land troops closest to where

---

* For diagrams showing the various landing beaches at Inchon, see Robert D. Heinl, <u>Victory at High Tide</u> (Philadelphia: Lippincott, 1968).

the road went to Seoul. You could, if you got troops ashore at the beach, then be in control of the crossroads of the roads going to the eastward. You could separate and segregate the city itself by having control of that spot in the road.

John T. Mason, Jr.: Also control of the railroad?

Admiral Struble: Well, yes, also control of the railroad then. You'd be out where the railroad and the road went to the eastward. If we got ashore in some strength, landing around to the right, then we would have control of egress and ingress into and out of the city itself.

John T. Mason, Jr.: Now, all of this you were able to determine long before, while you were drawing up your initial plans.

Admiral Struble: Oh, yes. All of this was understood, and the plan basically was that we would go in and along about, I suppose, 6:00 or 7:00 o'clock in the morning, maybe somewhere along in that period of time. In the first landing, knowing that we were going to Wolmi Do in particular, we could fudge I suppose an hour or so on high tide on the frontal landing. So we would make our first landing in the morning, right at Wolmi Do, and we would try to get in to Red Beach, which was the entrance into the city. If you could handle the gunfire on Wolmi Do, you could land some troops and start to get ready to take over the Wolmi Do Island.

If you got in here a little bit farther but on the beach proper going to the city, which is where Red Beach was, you could start landing troops and equipment quicker and better than you could anywhere else. So the idea was that our landing in the morning with preliminary gun bombardment and, of course, with air applied, then we would put the troops in.

Now, that landing was completed, I suppose, by around 9:00 o'clock.

John T. Mason, Jr.: And from then on until evening, you weren't able to add to the—

Admiral Struble: No, you weren't able to send in boats and get anywhere because all they would be up against was just a frontal cliff.

John T. Mason, Jr.: A palisade, sort of thing.

Admiral Struble: A palisade effect. So the people that were landed in the first landing were not going to see any help until the afternoon landing, which as I remember, was about 6:00 P.M.

John T. Mason, Jr.: They had to be self-sufficient then.

Admiral Struble: They had to be self-sufficient until we got in again in the late afternoon.

John T. Mason, Jr.: How many did you land originally in that first landing?

Admiral Struble: I suppose we got about 300 or 400 hundred men on Wolmi Do and possibly a little more on Red Beach.

John T. Mason, Jr.: Were they Marines?

Admiral Struble: I would like to say they were all Marines, but I'm not positive. I think we had intended to try to put Marines ashore entirely on the early morning landing. But very obviously, in order to put ashore the number of troops that we needed, we were going to have to start putting ashore Army also. My remembrance would be that in the morning landing we only had Marines in the landing force, because of their greater knowledge and previous experience in the amphibious business.

John T. Mason, Jr.: What was the total overall contingent that you planned to land?

Admiral Struble: It must have been a total of some 10,000 maybe, something of that sort.

John T. Mason, Jr.: Army and Marines.

Admiral Struble: Army and Marines. Of course, the Marine contingent would have been relatively a little bit smaller. The final Army count that were to be landed there probably would have been about somewhere around three-fourths of the contingent, and maybe one-fourth of the contingent would have been Marines. Now, of course, in the landing of the Marines you were going to have much more experienced people in this type of business.

John T. Mason, Jr.: Now, what about the air support? This was the Marines and the Navy?

Admiral Struble: I believe our big carriers were the ones that provided air support at Inchon. I'm not sure whether or not the small carriers with the Marine fliers were actually employed at the landing.

Air support came from the large carriers Philippine Sea (CV-47) and Boxer (CV-21) and the escort carriers Sicily (CVE-118) and Badoeng Strait (CVE-116). Now, the sum and substance of the first day was tied up with three things. The first was, did we get ashore on Red Beach, and were we going to be able to push troops and equipment across Red Beach and through the city and on their way to Seoul? If we accomplished that, we were in fine shape. That was our best bet for handling what we wanted to have happen.

The second bet in this matter would become—if Red Beach was not successful—would be able to land on Wolmi Do, take over the island, and then land from Wolmi Do across the natural approach to the city. You realize that Wolmi Do was connected with the city by a fairly good road. That would have been our second best bet on that matter.

Now, the third thing, which was the landing swinging way around to the right, was very definitely the poorest of the three possible landing areas . . .

John T. Mason, Jr.: The Blue Beach.

Admiral Struble: The Blue Beach, which was more affected by the tidal situation and the mud situation. In other words, the boats couldn't be too heavily loaded or you couldn't get to the beach. Of course, you would have only had it for 40 or 50 minutes or so every 12 hours on the high tide.

And that is the summation of the three beaches that we had open to us.

John T. Mason, Jr.: The three options.

Admiral Struble: Three options. We were going to use all three if we could.

John T. Mason, Jr.: Before you actually tell me about the first day's operation, I wonder if you would tell me about your conference with General MacArthur the night before?

Admiral Struble: The conference with MacArthur the night before would have been very brief and just said hello and we're glad you're here and all that sort of thing. I don't think it could have amounted to any more than that. There was no special news. Everything seemed to be going fine.

John T. Mason, Jr.: And he was filled with confidence.

Admiral Struble: Oh, yes. He was filled with confidence, and he was very happy about it. I told him that I would stay on my flagship for the first bombardment in the morning.[*] When that was over and I had evaluated a little bit what I thought our performance had been, I would come over and call on him. Of course, we would not be able to handle troops again before about, say, 5:00 or 6:00 in the afternoon. So I went over the next morning, as I remember, around 9:00 or 10:00 o'clock. We had the first landings, we knew what had been proved and where we were. Of course, all of MacArthur's people wanted to go with him, and all of the press wanted to go with him. So I had my barge pretty well loaded down with people; I suppose there must have been about 20.

---

[*] Admiral Struble's flagship during the operation was the heavy cruiser Rochester (CA-124).

John T. Mason, Jr.: And you took them back to your ship?

Admiral Struble: Oh, no. Going in to take a look at what it looked like close aboard.

John T. Mason, Jr.: Oh, I see. How far had he been standing out in the command ship?

Admiral Struble: Well, the command ship probably was anchored out about three to five miles from Wolmi Do.

John T. Mason, Jr.: So you had that trip into the Green Beach?

Admiral Struble: Well, no, we didn't go into the beach. We went in to a spot about two or three miles to the westward of Wolmi Do. Now, the Marine went in with us. He persuaded me that a hell of a good rifle shot could take a good potshot at us. That looks like a pretty long range for rifle fire, but I guess he could have been right. So I was careful about taking the general in too close to Wolmi Do Island.

John T. Mason, Jr.: Your barge could be easily identified as the commander's barge.

Admiral Struble: Well, I don't know that they were so thoroughly acquainted with naval ships and barges and everything that they could have recognized that it was my barge. But they could have seen it easily as a reconnoiter party coming in to take a fairly long-range look at things. So we went in and we spotted the island. We could see that things looked very calm and reasonably peaceful from our point of view. There was fighting going on in Wolmi Do. We didn't have physical control of Wolmi Do, although we apparently had gotten troops off Wolmi Do. We had definitely gotten some into Red Beach, but it had been a pretty tough proposition; it wasn't good.

John T. Mason, Jr.: There was real opposition there?

Admiral Struble: Oh, it was real opposition, enough to make the city still a little questionable in my mind.

John T. Mason, Jr.: As to whether it would hold or not.

Admiral Struble: As to whether it would hold or not. So I had a little reservation about the complete success of Red Beach at that time and I think properly so. So from the standpoint of what we were up against, I'm sure I didn't communicate it to MacArthur at that time other than that the morning's operations had been okay and we'd have to see how the evening's operations went before we were too happy.

I had made up my mind to come in in the early evening and watch the landing at Blue Beach myself. However, I was willing to take MacArthur and his aides and a certain number of press in about 10:00 o'clock in the morning to see what had apparently happened around Wolmi Do and we could take a look at it. That didn't really give the enemy any information. They knew we could run the boat in and back out by that time—a small boat and so forth. It didn't necessarily mean it was the landing, but then they should have known by that time that it was the landing. So I wasn't attempting to conceal too much.

Now, I came in myself in the late afternoon for the second landing of the day. I went to Blue Beach, the one around to the right that would land troops outside the city. Blue Beach was going to be a mess to get into, but if we could get a reasonable number of troops over on the beach and then they could get up to the crossroad spot, they would have control of the egress and the ingress from the city towards Seoul.

Well, it was a mess, as we thought it would be. However, the Marines, with their usual adaptability to problems of that character, went ahead, tore down a couple of spots here and there, and got the boats in. We got a reasonable number of troops landed at that beach just as it was getting dusk and dark.

John T. Mason, Jr.: A reasonable number—what would that be?

Admiral Struble: Probably 200 or 300. They were in a position definitely to get up to the crossroads so that by the morning daylight they would have control of the crossroads if Seoul started sending down reinforcements.

From my own point of view, I went back to my flagship that night but did not stop at MacArthur's ship and tell him I had been in there. I possibly sent him a message to tell him that things looked like they had gone well at the afternoon landing.

John T. Mason, Jr.: And this pertained to all three beaches in Wolmi Do and the Red Beach also? Did they land in the afternoon there?

Admiral Struble: We made landings at all three beaches to the extent that we could. I think we got a reasonable amount of troops landed at Wolmi Do, and I think we made a couple of blocks' progress up in Red Beach from where we had landed originally. Originally, I think the boys that made the first landing got tied down pretty quick. It was daylight, and they weren't able to do much advancing. But we did get another outfit in the afternoon, when it was getting dark. Their predecessors had arranged for them, you might say, and they would be in good position then to start out and do something as soon as it got light.

John T. Mason, Jr.: And again, it was all Marines for this landing in the afternoon.

Admiral Struble: I'm not positive. We might have started by that time to infiltrate in Army, too, because, of course, we were landing much more Army. The chances are that the whole landing was Marines, although there could have been some Army on Red Beach and Wolmi Do.

Now, to get back to this other landing: I want to give you my impression. I got back to the ship. I had seen a lot of troops get in on Blue Beach, and I realized they would have control of that crossroads the next morning, so I went and had a good night's sleep.

John T. Mason, Jr.: I was about to ask you if you could sleep that night.

Admiral Struble: I slept that night for the first one in a few days.

John T. Mason, Jr.: It had been accomplished and what you had anticipated.

Admiral Struble: I felt very confident after I saw that beach landing. Now, it was a messy spot and I realized that there was no use counting on that beach to put much stuff ashore. I realized we had to control the key spot, and in a day or two we'd be putting them ashore pretty fast over the other beaches that we had gone through in the morning.

John T. Mason, Jr.: But the whole operation was governed by the tides in that you could only do it twice a day.

Admiral Struble: You could still only land twice a day at high tide with troops.

John T. Mason, Jr.: Was that different from any other amphibious operation you had participated in?

Admiral Struble: Very different. Probably very different from any other amphibious operation that we will contemplate. There was the big gamble that you were making. Your inability to get troops ashore quickly, except for one hour out of 12, meant that the stuff you landed originally had to be able to take care of itself for 12 hours.

John T. Mason, Jr.: And be self-contained, and they were at the mercy of the enemy.

Admiral Struble: Well, if the enemy had had a well-organized ground force, they could have wiped out that beach probably by the end of the daylight, and then we would have had a mess.

John T. Mason, Jr.: Now, about mines. You discovered no mines?

Arthur D. Struble, Interview #10 (1/19/77) – Page 382

Admiral Struble: We had been in and out of that previously making bombardments, you understand. Big ships of cruiser category. So as far as I was concerned, I had decided we didn't have any mines to face going back and forth, up and down the river. I'll call it a river because it's much more of a river than it was anything else. So I had my big ships in the afternoon before the landing and bombarded. We had come out the river successfully and no mines. At 10:00 o'clock the next morning we started up the river again, so I felt that we were going to be okay.

John T. Mason, Jr.: As you discovered later, they had anticipated laying mines, did they not?

Admiral Struble: Well, this I would tell you—that about D plus three, one of my officers came ashore and he had been out that day.* He had been out to the railroad yard, and he had discovered on a number of flatcars a large number of Russian mines. So the Russian mines had arrived at Inchon probably just around about the time of the landing. Maybe they had been there for two or three days beforehand, but they hadn't had time to make their plans and get ready. So it is just as well that we landed at Inchon when we did.

John T. Mason, Jr.: If the mines had been laid, how much more complicated would your operation have been?

Admiral Struble: Well, an attempt to sweep ahead of you going into Inchon would have been a mess.

John T. Mason, Jr.: It would have taken up too much of your time, wouldn't it?

Admiral Struble: Minesweeping is slow stuff, and it would have been a mess, so it is well that we didn't put it off any longer than we did.

---

* D plus three means three days after the first day of landings.

John T. Mason, Jr.: And a question about these Russian mines: Were they old-fashioned types, or did they constitute a new kind?

Admiral Struble: Well, the Russians are very mine-minded people. They always have been; they've always liked them; they've always been ready to use them. They built good mines. I would say that the mines that they had shipped to the Koreans quite possibly were not their latest, most up-to-date type. But they would have been capable if they had been used. If that river had been pretty thoroughly mined, I don't believe we would ever have gotten up to Inchon. It would have been that big a menace; there's no argument about that.

That thing had enough narrow spots and everything in it, so it was almost a river. It was a very considerable hazard for us because of its length—it wasn't just a few miles, it was a long, long trip.

John T. Mason, Jr.: If I may digress for just a moment on the subject of mines—it is my understanding that the U.S. Navy had never been terribly concerned about mine warfare except when we approach a war or get into a war. But in times of peace, we are not very much concerned about it.

Admiral Struble: I don't think I'm enough of a mine expert on what we do in peacetime with them to try to evaluate. I think that mining is not considered one of our major efforts. As a matter of fact, I had had some mine experience at the end of World War II, but my interest after getting back from the war was in the development of the amphibious business and not in the development of the mine business. I had seen some of the effects of mining and what it could do, but I wasn't the mine man. So my knowledge of our peacetime effort and how it was getting along was nil. I don't remember much mining attention that went on on the Pacific Coast, California and so forth. As a matter of fact, I'm pretty sure that the head of mining was probably in South Carolina. How much our mining was developed between World War II and Korea, I just couldn't tell you.

John T. Mason, Jr.: Tell me about your reconnaissance of the beach and the kind of greeting you got.

Admiral Struble: As we got in close to Blue Beach, it occurred to me that it was a good thing we had Marines on the beach because there was going to be a lot of make-do necessary. An old Marine in there saw this small boat coming in and asked, "What the hell are you doing out there?" He gave me hell.

I said, "Well, it's all right. We'll take care of ourselves out here. If you're coming down this way, we'll back out of the way a little more." I felt very good about it because it was obvious to me that there were some damned good people on the beach. They were coming back towards the area where I was and seeing if they couldn't develop a better landing place. You might say, "The Marines have landed now. The situation is well in hand." That was the way I felt when I left and went back to the ship.

I only took one or two of the people on my ship with me because I had no desire to overload my boat, nor did I want to get off the track too much by going into a spot that might develop into a lot of problems. But I still wanted to see for myself if it looked like it was going all right, because it was an important key at that moment to the solution of the problem. Those boys on that beach got in there in the strength that they were going in that evening. They were going to be up at the crossroads the next day, controlling the roads to and from Seoul. We would make heavier landings in the face of the city, but we would have more time if we had some of our troops outside of the city protecting anything from coming in from the outside against us.

John T. Mason, Jr.: Well, you had a good night's sleep and I trust a good breakfast the next morning. Then what about the operations on D plus one?

Admiral Struble: Well, that just developed into dealing with the top of Wolmi Do Island. Of course, the people that were up there couldn't get ashore, and they didn't have any place to go, but they could still fight like hell. The question was whether it was going to be the best thing to just bomb the hell out of them or whether we could force them to surrender or not.

In the meantime, we very definitely had to get Red Beach opened up in strength and capable of sending troops down outside the city and then on their way towards Seoul. The second day was pretty successful, but I would say that from the standpoint of our knowledge of it back where we were, we didn't get quite as much information back as to how well we were doing as we actually were doing it. I would have said that the Army commanders who landed and pushed forth recognized that they had a hell of a tough fight at the start the following day. They didn't want to make any overconfident statements, and I guess they didn't.

John T. Mason, Jr.: What was the solution to the contingent of Koreans on Wolmi Do?

Admiral Struble: That was just a case of segregating them and letting them die if we wanted to.

John T. Mason, Jr.: Well, what did you actually do?

Admiral Struble: We just adopted a semi-passive thing because I always favored avoiding losing troops simply to capture something if it could be solved by taking time and letting it die on the vine. I mean, I've always favored the troops at that time. It's no use forcing to fight something unless it was really important.

John T. Mason, Jr.: Then the enemy of Wolmi Do didn't constitute that great a problem?

Admiral Struble: Not after we had gotten as far as we had and not after we were able to bomb the hell out of them with airplanes. And the airplanes were very safe; that was the way to bombard them.

John T. Mason, Jr.: Incidentally, did the enemy have any planes at all?

Admiral Struble: Oh, no, no. I don't remember any enemy aviation being involved.

John T. Mason, Jr.: That was a great aspect.

Admiral Struble: My attitude has always been, working with Army, I want to give them every break I could and not give them any impossible problem or ones that would lose lots of troops just to save the day unless that day was of great importance. That's always been my attitude from my side of the amphibious operation.

John T. Mason, Jr.: Now, I do have another question that does come to mind and this pertains again to the tide. It had been written in various places that the 15th of September was the last date upon which you could really undertake an operation of this sort in that particular place. This operation began on the 15th of September but continued on for days thereafter. Was it affected in any way by the tide?

Admiral Struble: No, because our ships were able to go up the river and anchor off Wolmi Do. And if we had control of the area and everything where we landed, all we had to do was have a few lights and you could bring in boats and land stuff at night. We had no enemy that could prevent it, don't you see? So by about the third day—this is when I guess MacArthur and I went in and went outside the city to see the troops advancing toward Seoul.

John T. Mason, Jr.: Tell me about that incident. That's a famous incident.

Admiral Struble: Well, that was famous because MacArthur was there.

John T. Mason, Jr.: How did it happen that he did this?

Admiral Struble: Well, MacArthur was always the type of man that liked to see for himself. It's fine to get a report from a subordinate; it's possibly finer to get a report from a subordinate that he knew and was very confident of; but the best of all is to go yourself and look.

John T. Mason, Jr.: Did you have any qualms about having him go in with you?

Admiral Struble: No, I didn't. If we had gone a day earlier, I would have had qualms about doing it. I didn't think the commander in chief should be subjected to a spot where we would give the enemy too good a crack to let one fellow with a gun take a potshot at him. So it was important to me from my point of view that we had gotten troops outside of the city. In other words, they had gotten to the crossroads that I had mentioned, and they were now outside of the city headed toward Seoul. The man in there felt fairly confident of the situation, and he felt that he had a good control of things and he took MacArthur in.

John T. Mason, Jr.: Who was this, the Marine general?

Admiral Struble: I'm inclined to believe that the Marine was still in command of the landing force at the time that we took MacArthur ashore. But the Army was commencing to holler for control ashore and it was about to transfer to them proper. Does that explain it?

John T. Mason, Jr.: Yes. So you went in and you got in a Jeep.

Admiral Struble: We got in a Jeep and we drove out, I suppose, as far as a mile or two beyond the city. We got out of the jeep and walked out on sort of a promontory where you look down and ahead on the road going to Seoul, which we were commencing to clear to the eastward.

John T. Mason, Jr.: But you were almost in the enemy line, were you not?

Admiral Struble: Well, the enemy had been pushed back on a fairly broad front for about a mile and half or two miles outside of the city.

John T. Mason, Jr.: And you had gone a mile yourself.

Arthur D. Struble, Interview #10 (1/19/77) – Page 388

Admiral Struble: Well, we went about a mile. That's just a rough guess. We didn't try to go all the way out to the farthest advance post, but we went well out to where we could look well ahead and see things and see that everything looked very clear ahead. That doesn't mean that the Army had yet gotten that far and were in complete control of it. But it was apparent that we were on our way to Seoul and it was only a matter of time.

John T. Mason, Jr.: How did MacArthur react to what he saw?

Admiral Struble: Oh, he was very pleased, of course. He couldn't help but be very pleased. He was ready to go back. Just like I was, although I wasn't able to get away as quick. But it looked like it was in the bag and done.

John T. Mason, Jr.: Well, the actual landing operation comprised how long a period of time?

Admiral Struble: I'm not positive whether Doyle went back in the command ship that he had come in or not. But I believe that he stayed on there a little longer.

John T. Mason, Jr.: And took over from you?

Admiral Struble: Oh, yes, I would have turned over to Doyle, as regards my contact with it. Now, any control of Army troops that I might have been considered to have up until that time, I had turned over to the Army commander the day before.

John T. Mason, Jr.: That was General Almond.[*]

Admiral Struble: Yes, and the Marines were annoyed that I had turned over to him rather than to the Marines—General Smith.[†] Now, therein and thereby you get into local stuff. As far as I was concerned, initially I had done my planning with and everything with the

---

[*] Major General Edward M. Almond, USA, had been MacArthur's chief of staff. He then became commanding general of X Corps and assumed command of operations ashore on 21 September.
[†] Major General Oliver P. Smith, USMC, commanding general of the First Marine Division.

Marines. But when the Army landed and were going to be in command of the troops going to Seoul, I felt that Almond was the man I had to turn over to rather than the Marines. Now, the question of the Marine getting the command from me rather than the Army had never come up that I know of, nor had the Marine ever consulted me and made any fuss about it. It was my opinion that at that time the Army man who had landed was in command of the troops, and I turned over the problem to him.

John T. Mason, Jr.: And that's the way it was.

Admiral Struble: That's the way it was. Now, the Marines were unhappy about that. They would have preferred, I think, if I had turned the command over to them and let maybe the Army take over command from them, which they undoubtedly would have been in a position to do immediately as soon as I left. I do think myself that that was carrying the command business a little bit far on who was to be in command.

John T. Mason, Jr.: Would you say maybe that that was a fine point of service etiquette?

Admiral Struble: Well, it could be considered a point of service etiquette, but I think the main thing that was involved was the fellow that was going to be in command from then on was the one that ought to get the command and not maybe somebody who might be in there just temporarily. It's a fine point, which, of course, was a very strong point from the Marine point of view because they feel that they would like to stretch their control of amphibious operations. Now, my experience had been in a much bigger operation, where, of course, the Marines have no control of troops in the landing.

John T. Mason, Jr.: You wanted to comment on the fact that it has been written that this was the turning of the tide—this landing. This made all the difference in the whole picture in Korea.

Admiral Struble: There's no doubt in my mind that Inchon very definitely turned the tide from what had been a fairly bleak look at things to a much better picture. It was not the end of the war in our favor, but it was very definitely a tremendous big blow in our disgraceful defeat.

John T. Mason, Jr.: Before that time it had been a holding business, even a retreat.

Admiral Struble: Before the time, it was getting to be a retreat almost back into the ocean—almost.

Interview Number 11 with Admiral Arthur D. Struble, U.S. Navy (Retired)
Place: Admiral Struble's Home, Chevy Chase, Maryland
Date: Thursday, 27 January 1977
Interviewer: John T. Mason, Jr.

John T. Mason, Jr.: Well, sir, as usual, it is very good and very stimulating to see you.

Admiral Struble: I got your message, and you've got my considered opinions on amphibious operations and command, anything further on Inchon, and then you've got minesweeping operations at Wonsan. The only fourth item that I might suggest adding a little, or maybe you may not want it, is the air operations around Christmas up north.

John T. Mason, Jr.: I indeed do. Yes, indeed. I was just giving you these points as a starter. The one in particular that I want to stress with you is the amphibious operations and command, because you said you had some very decided opinions on that. At this point, have you a few more observations to make about Inchon and the landing there.

Admiral Struble: As you realize, the plan for the second landing was successful. Within a short time we had troops outside of the city on the side towards Seoul and who were very rapidly in control of that area. Had enemy troop action developed against us at Inchon from Seoul coming down the main road, which is frankly the only way it could come, we had quite a good-size force on the outside of Inchon on the road toward Seoul. So we were both in excellent position to protect the further development of Inchon as a place to land troops, supplies, etc. We were also, of course, in position to start marching toward Seoul. As this was the only way by which the people in central Korea could come against us, we were in a much better position to defend ourselves if they did try to put large forces against us.

    Now, this, I think, is one case where I'll make a point on amphibious command. This illustrates, in my opinion, why the amphibious commander who is going to land the troops and so forth and who is an expert at it should not be in chief or high command of the whole thing at that time. If you want to make the man who is the overall commander in command of everything, it's fine. He will normally issue instructions to the amphibious commander if you want to separate him from them with the situation. He will issue instructions to him on what to do, but he is always in a position to make the higher, overall decision if it appears necessary. Generally, the amphibious commander is the one who should have actual operations of the landing, but he is not necessarily and often wouldn't have been the one to make the final, overall decision where something was going to be altered for an obvious reason that had come up.

John T. Mason, Jr.: He's there on the beach so he knows what's going on at that level.

Admiral Struble: Yes, he's handling all the troops. But if North Korean action had developed heavily in the direction of Seoul down toward us, the man to command was not the amphibious commander at Inchon. The man to command then was the man who had control of fleet aviation, etc., and who would have then been the one responsible for our defense of our position in Inchon against somebody trying to come in. Do I make the point for you?

John T. Mason, Jr.: Yes, you make the point.

Admiral Struble: I don't think there is any other point on Inchon of importance at this moment. The landing was successful. The troops and supplies went ashore. We were on the road toward Seoul and quite quickly. As a matter of fact, our advance on Seoul became very successful.
    We were also protecting our west coast position by advancing on Seoul.

John T. Mason, Jr.: Yes, indeed. So you had turned your attention elsewhere at that point, did you?

Admiral Struble: No, I stayed at Inchon long enough so that if a situation had developed where we had to go on the defensive, I was in command of the naval air that was present.

It was probably the only air that we had that would have been present or could be. Under such conditions, I would have taken over direct operational control of the matter. As long as it was purely an operation of landing and so forth, I was perfectly content, of course, to let Doyle go ahead and do it. Do you understand the distinction there?

John T. Mason, Jr.: Yes.

Struble: Now, actually there was another similar case. You remember that we had advanced up north, and then we got pushed back and we had to get out in a hurry from the northern part of the east coast. Do you remember that?

John T. Mason, Jr.: Yes.

Admiral Struble: That's right. Now, the amphibious commander, who was Doyle, was sent up there to evacuate it.* He did a splendid job. He did a very fine job in the evacuation. But he should not have been the overall commander there. Why? I wasn't there when Doyle started it, but I went up there very promptly and I was in command of the carriers and so forth. I should have been in chief command again for that evacuation, in my opinion.

Now, actually, I would not have stepped in on Doyle probably and issued even the slightest order, but I should have been in a position where I could. It should not have been handled from Tokyo to Doyle, in my opinion. It's much sounder command relations to have the other fellow in command.

Now, during World War II we had a few cases, particularly in some of the islands, where a fleet commander—or probably someone comparable—and the amphibious people would be haggling with each other as to who was in command. In my opinion, I think I've made it pretty clear and why, I believe that the fleet commander, if there is one, for instance, or someone in a similar capacity of command, is present and he has aviation and other forces with him, he should have top command and the responsibility.

---

* This was the evacuation of Hungnam. For Admiral Doyle's firsthand account, see "December 1950 at Hungnam," U.S. Naval Institute Proceedings, April 1979, pages 44-55.

I think we've kind of made two parts of this somewhat clear.

John T. Mason, Jr.: How long did you remain in the Inchon area before you turned your attention to the eastern coast?

Admiral Struble: Well, while this was going on and as we approached Seoul, it became obvious that the Army was going to want to push ahead as rapidly as they could. They were going to want to go through Seoul, because Seoul in itself really meant nothing. They were going to head right on for Wonsan. Wonsan was a big port on the east coast, just as Inchon was a far smaller port on the west coast. We were going to want to get in as quickly as we could and push the North Koreans out of Wonsan. As I told you previously, the railroad trains came down the east coast to Wonsan, went from Wonsan across to Seoul to Inchon.

John T. Mason, Jr.: Yes, Wonsan was a very strategic spot for the Army.

Admiral Struble: On the east coast. The Army wanted to get to Wonsan just as quick as they could. It was, therefore, determined to make a landing at Wonsan with a large number of troops that would be taken around by ship. Theoretically, we would have to maybe take Wonsan with a little military force.

John T. Mason, Jr.: It was being held by the North Koreans at that point.

Admiral Struble: At that point, it was under the control of North Korea, and that was one way of our getting in there. Now, it just happens that the operations of the troops going north were so much more successful than they had anticipated. Our own troops arrived at Wonsan a couple of days or so before the second landing that had been planned to go into Wonsan could get there.

John T. Mason, Jr.: You say our troops. They were the South Korean troops.

Admiral Struble: South Korean and American. The Army had been very vigorous in their attempt to get to Wonsan as quickly as they could, and they had gotten there frankly two or three or four or five days quicker than had been anticipated. But they were in Wonsan. They had taken Wonsan. They had taken over Wonsan about a day or two days at least before we were due to land troops there.

John T. Mason, Jr.: This was in October then.

Admiral Struble: This was in October.

John T. Mason, Jr.: Had you returned from Inchon to Tokyo for consultations before this operation?

Admiral Struble: Oh, no, no. I made up the plan to land at Wonsan while I was in Inchon, and we had sailed around and we were going to go in. When I realized that we had control of the harbor and it really wasn't a landing, I frankly was not interested in simply making the landing on the date planned so that the press could make a lot of big stories and we had made another invasion, because it wasn't.

I was also concerned that if they had mines over as far as Inchon, which they hadn't, they probably would have a hell of a lot of them there in Wonsan. They would be able to understand just as much as I or anybody else could that Wonsan was important. Therefore, if they had mines it was reasonable to suspect very strongly that we might have a pretty nasty mine problem there. I'm giving you my own views.

John T. Mason, Jr.: Yes, that's what you should.

Admiral Struble: So I was concerned about this landing. The necessity for making the landing on the specific day had no meaning other than simply face—we planned to go in on a certain date. As a matter of fact, our big armada had stopped at sea and not gone in. I could not agree with any such idea. I held the squadron at sea for a day. I turned them around, and I said, "Prunes," because I saw no reason until I felt pretty sure we had a good minesweeping operation completed in Wonsan before I took in a lot of heavily loaded ships with troops on board. I got criticized probably heavily for that because it's kind of a matter of face; we didn't go in on the date that we were supposed to.

John T. Mason, Jr.: The date selected had been the 20th.

Admiral Struble: I believe so. I think it was the 20th.

John T. Mason, Jr.: But you had begun minesweeping operations as early as the 10th.

Admiral Struble: That is right, but the minesweeping operations had not been under my command. This, in my opinion, was a bad command situation.

John T. Mason, Jr.: I see.

Admiral Struble: I think that the overall commander for an operation like that should have control of the minesweeping. I had asked Admiral Joy for that control and it had not been given to me.

John T. Mason, Jr.: Well, they soon discovered to their great surprise that there were many, many mines there.

Admiral Struble: Well, the mining that we got into was not at all under my command and I had nothing to do with it. It was handled by Joy in Tokyo and direct to Smith and to Captain Richard T. Spofford, the minesweeper man at Wonsan.[*] This is an example in my opinion of not good command.
    At Inchon I would have had control of that problem. I could have issued orders to the minesweeper man and could have handled it as I saw fit.

John T. Mason, Jr.: Well, why didn't it work out that way on the other side then?

---

[*] Rear Admiral Allan E. Smith, USN, Commander Task Force 95.

Admiral Struble: It was done the other way, that's all. It was not consistent with what we had done at Inchon.

John T. Mason, Jr.: In this particular book on the operations there, it mentions your conference on the 19th on board your flagship, the Missouri. Do you want to tell me about that? And it was after that, I think on the 21st, that you let your troops go in. You had your troops on board ship, but they didn't go into Wonsan itself. They reversed themselves and went back and forth along the coast for three or four days.

Admiral Struble: I don't think it was that long.

John T. Mason, Jr.: It wasn't?

Admiral Struble: No. My remembrance would be that I delayed the operation of landing about two days. I believe I delayed it about two days. My reasoning was what I told you previously, that we, the Americans and the South Koreans, were already in Wonsan and were conducting military operations to the north of Wonsan, that is, the troops were. And all we were going to do was make a peaceful naval landing.

John T. Mason, Jr.: Without opposition.

Admiral Struble: Without opposition. We were in control of the city. Now, if any doubt existed in my mind about how well the minesweeping had been done, I saw no reason why we had to go in on time with banners flying as if we were making an amphibious landing. I thought that I wanted to be sure that we went in safely, and that was why I made the decision.

John T. Mason, Jr.: You felt it wasn't justified to risk troops.

Admiral Struble: Unnecessarily, as long as it was not war. If we hadn't had control of Wonsan and the Northerners were still in there, I would have smashed in right on time, and we would have had to accept the casualties or results because it would have been a military wartime matter that determined that the landing ought to be pushed ahead. The necessity for the landing with that precision had disappeared, and I was not going to risk the ships because a few mines blowing up could have caused an awful lot of casualty and loss of life. So I just wasn't going to do it; it wasn't sensible. The people on the ships were mad as hell at me because they didn't come in with banners flying on the agreed date.

John T. Mason, Jr.: So when they did land, they did land without any—

Admiral Struble: They landed without any incident. Actually, I would say that they might very well have been able to have landed successfully two days earlier, but we went ahead with some mine checks that I thought were very desirable to accomplish before we entered.

John T. Mason, Jr.: Were you yourself surprised at the magnitude of the minefield at Wonsan, once it was determined that there was one?

Admiral Struble: Wonsan is a kind of a nice big open harbor—oh, boy! It was a miner's delight to plan the mining of it if you had plenty of mines. So the miner who planned and put stuff out there had an excellent opportunity to lay a big minefield and give you one hell of a lot of problems. That was why when I didn't have to face up to it, I didn't.

John T. Mason, Jr.: Were you surprised at the magnitude of the thing? The figure I have was 3,000 mines or something like that.

Admiral Struble: Oh, I don't believe that. I think there were a number of mines also at Wonsan that were on the beach like we had had at Inchon.

John T. Mason, Jr.: That hadn't been laid.

Admiral Struble: That hadn't been laid. I don't think the number is 3,000.

John T. Mason, Jr.: That's the number they give in this book, The Sea War in Korea.

Admiral Struble: I don't know where they got it from, but I don't think it was that much.

John T. Mason, Jr.: And also the variety of mines—magnetic mines and—

Admiral Struble: Well, if the Russians were helping out the North Koreans, they would have sent them a lot of mines of different types because the Russians are great mine men. They were probably the most mine-minded country in the world, much more than we were and much more than any other country that I know of. You could almost figure that if they were able to do it, they would have many more mines and a greater diversity of the kinds of mine than maybe anybody else would have had, in their position.

John T. Mason, Jr.: Then your position was accepted by the high command.

Admiral Struble: Well, I didn't ask for permission. I issued an order. Joy in Tokyo could have canceled my order if he wanted to and told me to do it.

John T. Mason, Jr.: But he didn't.

Admiral Struble: No, he didn't.

John T. Mason, Jr.: After Inchon, when you did discover that they had mines which they had intended to lay, why didn't Radford or some of the others make an effort to send more minesweepers out? You had so few.

Admiral Struble: Well, you see, you've asked me a question that's on the top administrative level. It's a question of what Joy asked for and what he tried to get and what he was given and so forth. If Radford turned Joy down, the chances are it was because he didn't have them or couldn't supply them for another month or two or something. Now, all of those things would come into that decision. Not having been in Tokyo, I'm not competent to comment on that part of it, really. I was only commenting on what I did out where I was in command.

John T. Mason, Jr.: Do you want to pursue your role in this campaign from that point on?

Admiral Struble: The Inchon operation was very successful, and actually the North Koreans were fleeing north. They were hardly even stopping in Inchon because they recognized that they had suffered quite a defeat. They didn't want to get flanked, and they were headed north because they were a little bit skinny. They were on the skinny side now.

John T. Mason, Jr.: It sounds like they were almost a house of cards here: when they got a solar plexus blow, they sort of collapsed.

Admiral Struble: Well, of course, they got in the same position that we on our side had gotten when they marched into Seoul. They marched into Seoul so quickly that our performance in getting the hell out of Seoul and finally holding on to the just little southern tip of the island was pretty close stuff.* They might very well have put us out of that peninsula at that time. We were down certainly in what you'd call the last ditch.

    Now, our Army—with a certain amount of South Korean help, but it was principally our Army—made a wonderful stand on the southern part of the peninsula, and we didn't get kicked out. Now, I think that in saying our forces did that, you must give considerable credit to the Army, but you must also give considerable credit to the left flank of our line, which was Marines. The Army man who was in command did not want

---

*This is a reference to the retreat to the south and establishment of the Pusan perimeter.

to give up the Marines for the Inchon operation and fought like hell to not take them out of the line when we wanted to start north. We wanted the Marines to be in the Inchon landing because they were more experienced in landing operations than the Army troops. That was one of the big fights that was not settled in Tokyo until almost the last minute before Inchon: would we have the Marines in the Inchon landing, or would they send us less-experienced Army troops instead to make the landing?

John T. Mason, Jr.: Certainly you were being heard on that issue, were you not?

Admiral Struble: I was being heard on that issue because I was in Tokyo. If I had not been in Tokyo, I would not necessarily have been the one involved. I mean, I would have been down planning, say, at Sasebo, but I wouldn't have been talking to the people in Tokyo. As a matter of fact, I think it was very desirable that we have the Marines in the Inchon landing.

John T. Mason, Jr.: Yes, the results prove the fact. Let's turn our attention to the east coast now again and your continued involvement in what was taking place above Wonsan.

Admiral Struble: Well, of course, above Wonsan I must give great credit to Doyle. He handled the operations of the landing and so forth very well as we went north. I think he did that part very fine. I was in command then of the naval aviation that we had afloat. We supported those operations going north the best we could and I think at times did very well.

One of our problems, of course, was that our method of handling aviation from carriers had its good points, but also it had its restricted points. So our aviation couldn't be just turned over to the Army aviation because they were different. While we could do some very fine aviation work, it had to be done a little differently than the Army and their aviation did it. So in the trip north, we were constantly trying to get along with the Army and work out a scheme for supporting with naval aviation the operation of the Air Force that was going on with the Army all the time on the way north.

Arthur D. Struble, Interview #11 (1/27/77) – Page 402

Now, as you know, we were very successful going north, and the North Koreans had gotten pushed right back up to the north and to the peninsula. Of course, at that time, after they had gotten pushed up from there, they were reinforced, so then they became stronger.

We were not able to take over all of Korea.

John T. Mason, Jr.: It was at that point that you got a very difficult assignment. You received word, I believe on the eighth of November, that your fliers from the fleet were to attempt to knock out the bridges over the Yalu and only on the Korean side, not on the other side.[*]

Admiral Struble: That's correct.

John T. Mason, Jr.: Do you want to talk about that?

Admiral Struble: All right. We were on the east side of the peninsula. It was a quite high, mountainous area between us and the western side and the Yalu River. So our aviation taking off in the morning, we'll say, for a flight, would have to go up to quite a height to get up over the mountains and then come down on the other side in the vicinity of the Yalu River. Now, of course, that took a certain amount of gasoline, and that meant that the amount of fighting time they had around the Yalu was limited. But even under those conditions, the boys were getting after the other fellow's aviation quite well. After the operations had gone on for a little while, the other man changed his tactics. He would wait until our planes had gotten up over the Yalu and were coming down, and then he would start attacking our planes but not coming too much over into North Korea. In other words, he'd dart over and maybe do a little fighting and dart back.

John T. Mason, Jr.: He was well aware of the fact that he was in a sanctuary when he was on the other side.

---

[*] The Yalu River separated North Korea from Communist China. President Truman was concerned that the United States not widen the war into Chinese territory.

Admiral Struble: That is the point. He knew he had a sanctuary that we were respecting. He knew that because we weren't crossing the line. The moment he knew that he could operate close, right up to the Yalu and nobody would come over to where he was, boy, he had about an 80-to-one advantage on us. So this was very difficult for our boys. A plane would come over from the other side, make a quick dash in, go after one of our planes, but then turn around and buzz out and in no time at all be back home where he couldn't be attacked.

So, of course, our aviators were up in the air. During that period I went over to the head carrier a number of times from the <u>Missouri</u>. I would go during the flight times, to see what was going on and to talk to the boys. Neither one of us, the carrier man and myself, nor any of the youngsters who were, of course, working on the problem just as much as we were, could figure out a reasonable solution to the problem.

John T. Mason, Jr.: Did you agree with the overall command that we should not violate the border across the way?

Admiral Struble: Well, I was just about to tell you. Finally, I came to the conclusion that the only thing we could do was be able to strike these people who were fighting us. The only way we could do it is if we went across the border and attacked them after they had attacked us. I realized we could not afford to send a flight up that would go right across the river and attack the other side because that was breaking the boundaries. But I decided that if we stayed on our side of the boundary line when we got there and one of their planes came over and attacked one of ours, we were at a disadvantage. He'd come over and maybe wouldn't be picked up right away and he'd make an attack on one of our planes. I then decided that what we should have was the right of hot pursuit.

John T. Mason, Jr.: This is a right under international law, is it not?

Admiral Struble: Well, it has always been a right. It was a right at the start of the Civil War, as I remember. If a ship of this type came in and attacked your forces, you could keep after him. Maybe you'd get out into international waters or something, but you could go after him and fight him as long as you had what was called hot pursuit.

John T. Mason, Jr.: That being a continuous operation.

Admiral Struble: That's right. That, of course, occurred between the north and the south and so forth. The aviators were very happy to have something done, so they were strongly behind me on that subject. I sent a message to Tokyo asking for the right of hot pursuit and explained the thing clearly.

I feel sure that it was shown to General MacArthur, and it went on to Washington, I believe, very promptly. But Washington turned me down on that one. So then it became apparent to me and I told Tokyo, that without hot pursuit, this tremendous up over the mountains and down on the other side to reach a little area where we could only afford to stay 20 minutes or so, was no good at all. We were risking altogether too much for a very uncertain amount of possible chance to really do some fighting. So I recommended that we discontinue the operation. We weren't getting anywhere.

John T. Mason, Jr.: Was it discontinued?

Admiral Struble: Yes, and then we came back south.

John T. Mason, Jr.: Let me ask you about while you were still operating against the bridges, how successful were you? It seems so impossible to pinpoint just the ends of the bridges that were in North Korea and ignore the other part.

Admiral Struble: Well, the whole burden of those operations was on us for doing something wrong almost if we did anything. That was why it was a no-good proposition. It wasn't that the boys were unwilling to make that long trip up over the mountain and down to do the fighting, if they could only do it when they got there.

John T. Mason, Jr.: It certainly had echoes in Vietnam, didn't it? The same kind of restrictions.

Admiral Struble: Well, sure. To my mind it was a very clear case of you had to do something to give the fighting man a chance, or it was no use asking him to do things like that. When I recommended that we didn't do it, there was nobody that was in the frame of mind to issue the order that it had to be done then.

John T. Mason, Jr.: What was the state of the morale of our fliers under those conditions?

Admiral Struble: Excellent, but it wasn't going to remain that way if we were going to continue this business. So we called that off; it was the only thing we could do.

Now, the aviation was ready and prepared and could have gone back the moment that the North Koreans put some troops over on the east side of the mountains headed down toward us. Boy, our aviation would have been very happy to get up there and do something about the troops. But that depended upon the enemy putting himself in a position where we could do something.

John T. Mason, Jr.: Were you involved in the efforts to break up the railroad system on the eastern side?

Admiral Struble: Well, yes. When we were getting pushed south, we engaged in it, and that did seem to be a suitable proposition to us for the air to take out the railroads. That would hurt the enemy coming south, and we were again being pushed south, as you realize. We had a tug-of-war a couple of times up there in the north. The only point I could say there is that, as events proved, it looked as if we were a little too optimistic after we got up north there on the ground because we didn't have enough Army troops behind us.

John T. Mason, Jr.: Had we really anticipated that the Chinese would come in in such force as they did?*

Admiral Struble: Well, of course, we hadn't anticipated that. Certainly it was always a possibility that was discussed, but on the whole I think most people didn't think they would come in.

John T. Mason, Jr.: Because that made quite a difference.

Admiral Struble: Oh, it made a lot of difference. When that drive happened, I guess you'd say we were again fortunate to hold on. Because each time a drive like that happened, the man that started the drive had the upper hand because he had control to some extent of the way things were going to go.

John T. Mason, Jr.: He had the impetus.

Admiral Struble: He had the impetus, and he had the choice of decision of when it was going to be started and how he'd do it. So he did have a big advantage.

John T. Mason, Jr.: Tell me more about those operations against the railroads. There were great problems, were there not? Do I not understand that there were lots of tunnels, and they would stay in the tunnels in the daytime and come out at night?

Admiral Struble: Well, that's true. That's just what was to be expected. They were going to develop, coming south, as many of these railroad lines as they could. If we retreated or were forced to retreat, they were obviously going to use the railroads to the greatest extent that could be done. The decision on our part, of course, had to be based on the practicality of the moment.

---

* On 25 November 1950 approximately 300,000 Chinese Communist troops entered North Korea to support the faltering North Korean forces.

If this was only going to be a temporary resurgence south that they were making, and if we were going to quickly get it under control and get them pushed back north again, it would have been to our interests to leave the railroads alone because we would be using them later. However, if this push on their part south was coming down pretty fast, we might as well take all of the advantages we could of disrupting the other fellow from coming south on the east side.

John T. Mason, Jr.: Was that the course of action?

Admiral Struble: Well, that, of course, is what happened, don't you see? That's logical. We had to make the decision ourselves. But I'm certainly not going to quarrel with those decisions because I was not sitting in Tokyo where I was party to making them. I think that knowing that things were bad on the western slopes and knowing that we weren't doing too well, I think I would have been inclined to try to break the railroads up on the east side.

John T. Mason, Jr.: By that time we had had a change in command, had we not? General Ridgway was there.[*]

Admiral Struble: Yes, I think Ridgway had come out by that time. Of course, Ridgway was an excellent man. I had known Ridgway previously in Washington. I think he was a very fine man, excellent.

John T. Mason, Jr.: The question of using the air for interdiction purposes and close support had been argued in terms of the Korean campaign. You had much experience with the use of naval air and so would you give your considered opinion as to the merits of one vis-à-vis the other?

---

[*] In December 1950 Lieutenant General Matthew B. Ridgway, USA, became commanding general of the Eighth Army following the death of General Walton H. Walker, USA.

Admiral Struble: Well, broadly speaking, I had become a firm believer of the idea that the use of naval air simply to bomb areas was not a very worthwhile operation. There was no doubt that occasionally such a specific bombing of a specific item might be worthwhile. But, in general, I felt very strongly that the naval air, if properly employed in support of troop movements, could be very damaging on the enemy and be very much better help to the Army troops.

This did involve, though, a means of communications between the naval pilot over the area and some ground Army arrangement so that the two could be kept in coordination with each other. In my opinion, *if* we had adopted that method, we would get greater effect favorable to the troops than we would get the other way.

John T. Mason, Jr.: Thank you very much. There are various dispatches of yours as carried in The Sea War in Korea which substantiate exactly what you said.

Admiral, this not in sequence in terms of what you've been saying, but there were a number of lessons that you deduced from the operations at Wonsan, and I think it would be worthwhile if you took them one by one as you listed them and elaborate on what you said. The first of these is you learned something about certain communication problems at Wonsan.

Admiral Struble: I think that the communications problem situation there was that there was no single Army command spot or person, let's say in Wonsan, to whom one naval person such as myself could maintain a regular communication with as the operations continued. I would say that the problem is that some Army unit tells the general something, and he communicates maybe with Tokyo about it. Well, that doesn't get me in the picture, nor does it permit me to help him.

It would be my opinion that under the conditions that existed in Wonsan that there should have been one senior Army man who was handling the Army side of the problem to whom I, at the time I was in Wonsan and apparently handling it for the Navy, could handle it rather than that all of the ideas we might have had be sent back to Tokyo and discussed in Tokyo and come back and not necessarily settle the problem properly for the ground.

John T. Mason, Jr.: A more organized approach then in terms of—

Admiral Struble: A more organized approach. I think that a more organized approach would have been much better.

John T. Mason, Jr.: In your experience now, was that peculiar to the situation in Wonsan, or had you experienced this elsewhere, the problem with communication and the Army?

Admiral Struble: Well, in general that situation existed in World War II often between the Army and the Navy.

John T. Mason, Jr.: Do you recall when you were in command of the amphibious forces from the Pacific Fleet in San Diego and you conducted a large-scale exercise with the Army—did you deal with this particular subject of communications?

Admiral Struble: I attempted at that time to persuade the Army senior people that this inter-communication was very important when you got down to offshore operations. It had been both in World War II and Korea, and it was going to be again the next time we got into it. The idea of going back to some home spot to have them take this up with the Navy and see if they can't persuade them to do something is, in my opinion, not a good way to do.

John T. Mason, Jr.: Not very expeditious, is it?

Admiral Struble: It is not expeditious, and it means that the people talking to each other really can't personally necessarily visualize the problem that is existing in the field.

John T. Mason, Jr.: A second lesson you've cited without elaborating was the map problems of the three services.

Admiral Struble: I think that maybe exists because we very rarely had joint actions, and therefore we have quite different maps and systems of employing them.

John T. Mason, Jr.: So again it's the coordination.

Admiral Struble: Then it's a question of is the Army in the United States going to go on doing things their way? Is the Navy on their part in the United States going to continue doing it their way? And both of them are not coordinated.

John T. Mason, Jr.: In latter years do you know whether this has been taken care of in terms of unified commands?

Admiral Struble: Well, of course, this subject we are talking about now isn't necessarily unified command. It's in having people use the same maps discussing the problem, as it were, rather than having their own approach to it. I'm inclined to believe that the Joint Chiefs of Staff arrangement is slowly making some progress toward improvement in these matters. But the desirable thing to have for operations like Korea would be for two local men to be authorized by their distant bosses who get together and try to solve problems locally.

I think that if the charts and/or arrangements of that character were exchanged, it would be desirable. In other words, if Tokyo had told Ridgway certain things and had a map connected with it, it might be well if Ridgway's Navy man who is coordinate with him out in the area got a copy of the Army order and the Army map. Maybe he could read it and understand it, and then he could coordinate better with Ridgway.

John T. Mason, Jr.: Another lesson you cite, the need for adequate intelligence teams operating on a theater level.

Admiral Struble: I don't believe that that occurred in the Korean business generally, and it could have very easily have happened. There should have been an attempt to have a joint intelligence thing, instead of the Army thrashing out their problem and then trying to confront the admiral with, "You're not doing us any good, you're on this thing thus and so." The admiral's knowledge is not at all the same as the Army man's knowledge. So, therefore, he can't be expected to be helpful.

John T. Mason, Jr.: I would gather from the accounts I have read at Wonsan in terms of the mining that we didn't really have that thorough an intelligence picture of what was there.

Admiral Struble: Well, of course, we didn't know, I believe, at the time we started the mining, what we had in Wonsan. I don't think we knew anything about it except that there had been some mines at Inchon and that therefore it was conceivable and almost sure that there were a large number of them in Wonsan and available to use.

John T. Mason, Jr.: In reading about this other operation in which you had no part up on the west coast at Chinnampo, that naval intelligence helped out greatly with that picture and facilitated the sweeping of mines by what they were able to glean from the people in the area.

Admiral Struble: I think we could have had better coordination, and I think that coordination between some of the lower echelons, between some of the higher echelons outside of Tokyo with each other would have been helpful. I say that the higher echelons outside of Tokyo, meaning the Army commander in the field and the Navy commander afloat out there, rather than too much of a tendency for the Army forces and the Navy forces to throw their problems back to Tokyo, where the Army and the Navy would thrash them out. It would have been more successful and better, I think, if the coordination had occurred in the field. Therefore the two commanders concerned would have had to have been able to talk to each other with some authority except to say, "That sounds good to me. I'll see if my boss back in Tokyo will let me." That's no way to solve problems. Do you see what I mean?

John T. Mason, Jr.: Yes.

Admiral Struble: Refer the problem then back to Tokyo later. The problem ought to be answered right out in the ground. Now if the Army and the Navy man out in the area are talking to each other and they can't reach a good conclusion, I think both should report to their senior in Tokyo, and Tokyo should come out with an answer.

John T. Mason, Jr.: Tokyo would be the arbiter really of two different viewpoints.

Admiral Struble: Tokyo would have become the arbiter, and the arbitration would be conducted in Tokyo between the top Navy man and the top Army man. If General MacArthur was the top Army man and the man in overall charge would say, "We'll try it this way," then go ahead and try to work it out that way. Don't continue to argue the problem. Get ahead trying a solution that has apparently been decided as the one to try first.

John T. Mason, Jr.: Now, you cited another lesson from Wonsan. The value of helicopters in minesweeping operations became very apparent, and you say that a suitably equipped vessel with helicopters should be considered as being available for such an operation.

Admiral Struble: I think that's obvious. I would think that that lesson had been learned and was probably accomplished. But in the future we would try to have that.

John T. Mason, Jr.: But you have to have a combination of helicopters and boats, too, don't you, for minesweeping operations? The helicopters by themselves can't achieve this.

Admiral Struble: Oh, no, the helicopter is simply an adjunct to the minesweeping problem and should be under the minesweeping commander, not under the admiral commanding the fleet. But it would be wise for the minesweeping man to have that type of assistance if he can.

When we first landed in the Philippines, I think it's clear that we needed good coordination between all the forces going into the Leyte landing. Now, on the whole, I think that we had pretty good coordination, but I'm not so sure that, even with MacArthur's headquarters and Kinkaid's headquarters, we had learned the importance of having the coordination work between the lower echelons once they get out in the field. I don't think I ever had a case where I felt that the Army let me down, but I'm not so sure that I always felt that we had mutual knowledge of what we were trying to accomplish. Therefore, our coordination wasn't necessarily as good as it might have been.

John T. Mason, Jr.: Then you have another point here. "We learned," you say, "that adequate mine countermeasure forces with trained personnel and equipment should be provided in each fleet."

Admiral Struble: I think that's important. In other words, when you say in each fleet, I meant that it would have been made available to the Navy element out in Japan and Korea. It would also have been a part of the Pacific Fleet at that time because probably that type of force which wasn't used necessarily too much should have been under, say, Radford in Honolulu. Now then, since he had this capability available, he should have dispatched it out to the head man in the Navy in Japan and Korea. He would be getting his orders not from Radford but properly getting them from MacArthur who was the theater commander there.

Therefore, the Pacific Fleet would temporarily lose that facility, but we in peacetime are not going to be able to afford anything like that more than maybe one outfit in the Pacific and one outfit in the Atlantic. But it should be made available then to the senior Navy man in the area involved. That would have put it under Joy. And then the responsibility for the employment of it should have been under Joy. If he had it and didn't use it with good coordination with the Army, then that's because he and the Army didn't handle it right.

John T. Mason, Jr.: You say that in peacetime we can't afford to have more extensive equipment in this area. But can't we afford trained personnel in peacetime?

Admiral Struble: I'm sure that the mine forces in peacetime are going to have to be small because they are going to be expensive, and you're not going to know where and when you'll need them and you can just have so much of them. I would think that if we had a fair outfit in the Pacific and a fair outfit in the Atlantic, that's all we can expect to have.

John T. Mason, Jr.: But my point is, can't we concentrate perhaps a little more on training personnel? Do we have to have trained personnel with given equipment that we might possess?

Admiral Struble: I see no reason why that the force we allow in each fleet area shouldn't be a properly trained group who knows what they are doing. But then it's important, like the case we're talking about, for Radford to send the whole thing out to Japan and not try to split it into two parts. If it's going to go somewhere or do something, it ought to go 100% as ready to do it as the size of it and the people that are capable of doing it.

They should immediately go under the appropriate command out in that area. They shouldn't necessarily, in other words, be under Joy in Tokyo. He should have an overall supervisory command of them, but he should send them to the area in which they are going to be used under the naval officer there, and he should be the one that tries to get the results out of them.

John T. Mason, Jr.: When you were in Korea on the latter half of your tour of duty your flagship was the battleship Missouri.

Admiral Struble: That's right.

John T. Mason, Jr.: How satisfactory was she as a flagship?

Admiral Struble: She was a fine, big ship and had excellent facilities on board; she was capable of being a very fine fleet flagship. She could make good speed and she could carry a lot of people. You could have had a big staff on board the Missouri. In other words, you could have been a commander of a large element at sea of many different types and have operated very successfully from the Missouri.

John T. Mason, Jr.: Am I right in understanding that her communication system was such that you could communicate directly with the U.S. if you wanted to?

Admiral Struble: Oh, I think so. But I don't think that's the big part involved. It was your ability to handle a very large fleet and get back. Normally, operating in the Missouri I'm sure you would have had excellent communications with Honolulu, which would be the point normally from which you should be operating. Except that in the case of this one specialty that we had in Japan, but I still think you could have undoubtedly communicated with Tokyo and could have handled that perfectly.

I don't mean to say that MacArthur and Radford were competing with each other. They weren't really. You had a specialized case in Japan. I think possibly the government's decision to have a special senior representative capable of doing business directly with Washington was possibly desirable to have in Japan, as well as another military officer in Honolulu who was basically responsible more for the Pacific than the man in Japan but who also could speak direct to Washington. It therefore became desirable that, having two people out in the Pacific with slightly overlapping problems, that you just had to expect that Radford and MacArthur would work with each other and keep each other informed in the handling of matters as they occurred.

It would have been better probably if it all could have been concentrated in one central spot, such as Honolulu. However, under the circumstances, politically it wasn't possible. The Japanese problem was so important that you had to have a military man in Tokyo who would talk direct to the Japanese and who would talk direct then to Washington. Do you understand?

John T. Mason, Jr.: Yes, I do. I'm projecting my mind into the Vietnam situation, where we had a Commander in Chief Pacific in Hawaii, but even there it was not possible

Arthur D. Struble, Interview #11 (1/27/77) – Page 416

always to have everything focused on him. We had General Maxwell Taylor in Vietnam who was doing things on his own.[*] And it didn't work out then either.

Admiral Struble: Well, I think that the element in Washington which is controlling those matters has got to make up its mind that it needs a local representative in a foreign country who will have direct communication with them, and they will issue orders direct to him. Then they have to live with it and fall with it. They should not try to make it, in my opinion, a three-ring-around-the-rosy thing, but it should be Washington's responsibility with a specific man such as MacArthur in Japan or somebody else in Vietnam. Then if and when and where it's important for the man in Honolulu to get into the picture, he should get orders from Washington to cooperate with MacArthur or cooperate with the man in Vietnam. That puts the man in Vietnam responsible, and that's where it's got to rest.

John T. Mason, Jr.: Well, of course, in the Korean War we hadn't come to the practice that we saw in Vietnam, orders going directly from the White House to the commander in the field and that sort of thing. That was a little later development.

Admiral Struble: Yes. That's not a desirable proposition. But if it's going to be done and if it is done, the man in the Pacific—while he should be kept informed of what's going on there—he should not be in the command channel. Washington is going to have to take its responsibility at that time. And that's what they had to take in connection with MacArthur and those operations which were getting pretty hot. The man in the field and the people in Washington disagreed, and there's only one way to settle it. In my opinion, that's in Washington, not out in Tokyo.

John T. Mason, Jr.: Do you lament the passing of the battleship, having had the Missouri as your flagship?

---

[*] General Maxwell Taylor, USA (Ret.), a former Army Chief of Staff and Chairman of the Joint Chiefs of Staff, served for a time as U.S. ambassador to South Vietnam. The position of Commander U.S. Military Assistance Command Vietnam was held by a succession of Army generals.

Admiral Struble: I think it's very unhappy that the battleship is over because it was such a fine ship and such a fine ship for the command ship. But I'm convinced in my own mind that in the future the intra-communication problem is going to be so much more complex and involved that no longer is the big battleship going to be the flagship at sea like it used to be. Therefore, the people who are going to issue some of these instructions are going to be ashore maybe, or in more distant spots. I felt like I had come home in one of the last times that the "Mo" was going to be quite as important as she had been.*

John T. Mason, Jr.: Tell me about the trip home.

Admiral Struble: It was a very pleasant trip home. We stopped in Honolulu, and I, of course, checked in with the boss there and talked to him. Then the Navy had decided to offer passage from Honolulu to Los Angeles for a number of important San Francisco people who were interested in the Navy. So I arranged a schedule for that trip—I suppose it was a five-day trip or something—and these prominent men were taken all over the "Mo" and shown the "Mo." I spoke to them once a day: views on Korea and everything that I thought it was desirable to try to give to people. I wanted to make them feel that they understood what the Navy and the government were trying to do, and they were probably a little better briefed than maybe people that read the newspapers. But if they were people who were important in the community, it was desirable for them to be able to talk to somebody who knew what was going on.

John T. Mason, Jr.: It was a public relations stint.

Admiral Struble: It was a public relations stint. I'm convinced that a man in that capacity has to recognize that public relations is a part of the problem. At that time, I surely didn't have any problems back in Japan that were mine, so there was no reason why I shouldn't have taken on some others temporarily.

---

* On 28 March 1951 Vice Admiral Harold Martin, USN, relieved Admiral Struble as Commander Seventh Fleet. At the same time, Struble relieved Martin as Commander First Fleet. Struble remained on board the Missouri for the ensuing trip back to the West Coast because the battleship was just coming to the end of her first deployment to the Korean War and was due to return to the United States.

John T. Mason, Jr.: Now, you were relieved as Commander of the Seventh Fleet by Admiral Beauty Martin.

Admiral Struble: He was an aviator, and I am convinced that it was probably better to have an aviator in that job because he would really know the aviation problem more thoroughly than I did. So I was glad to have an aviator relieve me for that reason. It was going to be much more aviation problems maybe, and he would be in a position maybe to handle them better than I would.

John T. Mason, Jr.: There is something you just told me off tape. There was a story that you want to tell me in connection with the air operations you conducted against the bridges on the Yalu on the North Korean side of the river.

Admiral Struble: It wasn't that I wanted to tell you the story, but I thought that in connection with those Yalu River operations it was interesting to know that I had proposed a solution; that was the idea that our pilots should be permitted to have the right of hot pursuit, which we previously discussed. Of course, hot pursuit immediately did become a rather important diplomatic matter because somebody in Washington had to make up their mind that they were willing to accept the dangers that were inherent in hot pursuit of causing problems between different countries.

John T. Mason, Jr.: Were there proponents of this policy in Washington?

Admiral Struble: I don't know that they had ever thought about it. So finding that our aviators were having this very terrible problem and that it was something that had to be done, I evolved the idea myself of the right of hot pursuit for this solution and then prepared a message to go from me to Tokyo. I recommended that if we were going to continue these operations that we be permitted the right of hot pursuit against the enemy who would dash across the Yalu, attack us, then turn and run. I thought otherwise we better discontinue the operations if we couldn't have the right of hot pursuit.

I hadn't necessarily expected to get permission because I could realize that there were a large number of diplomatic problems involved, but I thought I would ask. As expected, I'm sure that Tokyo communicated with Washington, and Washington vetoed any such right of hot pursuit, whereupon I promptly recommended to Tokyo that we close up shop and come south.

Now, there was a case where the right of hot pursuit, if we had decided to do it, could very easily have been considered as very bad for other nations. I mean other nations, not only China, Russia, but any number of nations could well have decided that they wouldn't agree with that idea.

John T. Mason, Jr.: Well, this was legally a United Nations operations you were engaged in, wasn't it?

Admiral Struble: It was legally a United Nations business, and the United Nations could easily have discussed it. I am sure that our best politicians decided that it was not good, that the U.N. wouldn't support us on it. Therefore, why antagonize the problem?

John T. Mason, Jr.: Was there a real concern also in Washington about involving China and Russia? Was there a real feeling here that they might jump in and then we'd be in a major war?

Admiral Struble: Well, of course, any time that you are conducting operations of this character as close as you are to these other countries, they are each going to have different views on it. In a way, both Russia and China were involved, as well as Korea. And a large number of countries in Europe would have probably questioned the advisability of this operation because of the chances that the gain would be so small and the risk of causing diplomatic problems would be so great. So I was not surprised when I was turned down.

John T. Mason, Jr.: But that didn't deter you from raising the issue?

Admiral Struble: No, I thought I might as well raise the issue because it was a legitimate issue. If raised, it was quite possible that the other fellow, even though we didn't get permission to do it, would maybe quit doing it himself.

John T. Mason, Jr.: That was being highly optimistic, wasn't it?

Admiral Struble: That was being a little optimistic. Actually, we decided to pack up shop on the matter so the question wasn't alive any more.

John T. Mason, Jr.: In retrospect, if such permission had been given, would it have changed the picture noticeably?

Admiral Struble: Well, I've got to say that's a gamble, and I see no reason for me to be sure of success on our part in that. It would have been one way of attempting to stop the matter, and whether it would have been successful or not, I think the only thing I can say is we would have had to try it out. I'm not so sure that it would have been successful in stopping it. He might have devised something then in return that would have made it no longer profitable from my point of view.

Interview Number 12 with Admiral Arthur D. Struble, U.S. Navy (Retired)
Place: Admiral Struble's Home, Chevy Chase, Maryland
Date: Thursday, 3 February 1977
Interviewer: John T. Mason, Jr.

John T. Mason, Jr.: Last time when you broke off, you were taking the battleship Missouri, which was your flagship, back from the Far East to the States. You stopped in Hawaii. Do you want to tell me about that?

Admiral Struble: Well, we stopped en route and I reported to the naval boss there.

John T. Mason, Jr.: That was Radford.

Admiral Struble: That was Radford. I told Radford what I had thought of things out in the Japanese area, and then there was a group of about 18 prominent businessmen from San Francisco that were there. So being able to do it, I brought them home with me to San Pedro and in that way was able to give them a certain amount of talk about Korea which I thought was desirable. As prominent individuals they would have some knowledge other than what they read in the papers. That was a very pleasant trip, and I think all the gentlemen from San Francisco were very pleased because they could ask questions then and get some answers to parts of this that they were interested in.

John T. Mason, Jr.: They had firsthand knowledge.

Admiral Struble: Fairly firsthand. Then in San Pedro-Long Beach area I debarked, and the flagship continued on around through the canal to the East Coast, which was where she was going for her repairs.

From San Pedro I went down to San Diego and reported in as Commander First Fleet. Commander First Fleet was an interesting assignment in that with the business going on out in Japan, I automatically took over what little training and so forth that we could conduct along the West Coast. Of course, a considerable amount of our forces were already out in Japan.

John T. Mason, Jr.: And actually in combat.

Admiral Struble: Actually out there in combat, but those that were left, we kept a certain amount of training exercises.

John T. Mason, Jr.: What was the nature of the training for them?

Admiral Struble: You'd send maybe the carrier and a certain amount of the surface ships out for two or three days and have some specific practices in which they would cooperate. All of the forces would get together rather than it just being individual aviation training for the carrier or individual destroyer training. It would be joint training of all the forces together in one training exercise.

It was maybe about a year later that I left that Com1stFlt job temporarily for a trip out to Singapore that I mentioned to you previously.

John T. Mason, Jr.: Were you engaged on this occasion in the training of any foreign contingents—Latin American?

Admiral Struble: No, I don't believe we had any foreign contingents during that period. We had had some in the earlier period that I was there when I was in the amphibious force. A couple of French ships and others that had gone through, but none at this time.

John T. Mason, Jr.: Inasmuch as you were engaged in training and inasmuch as you had had so much experience with amphibious operations, were you involved at all in the amphibious training in San Diego on this occasion?

Admiral Struble: No, there was a Commander Amphibious Force, and he conducted his own training things just as I had conducted them some years earlier when I had the amphibious force. Now, actually I think there was one big amphibious exercise while I was the Commander First Fleet. I believe that I assigned a carrier division and a cruiser division maybe to the amphibious forces for the exercise that they held. But I would not have taken charge of it.

John T. Mason, Jr.: Let me ask about the situation vis-à-vis the training schools, the Navy schools on the West Coast while you were with the First Fleet.

Admiral Struble: You mean my connection with them?

John T. Mason, Jr.: Yes. Were there a series of them on the West Coast?

Admiral Struble: Well, of course, the aviation training went on at the island right there in San Diego Bay—North Island. But that was under the Air Force man.* I, personally, as Com1stFlt didn't handle it. He handled that aviation training himself basically until we got up to the point where we had maybe a fleet exercise in which all of it would be tested and trained. That's when I would get into it. We had one exercise of that character, and I guess it must have been along about March that it happened, just before I left.

John T. Mason, Jr.: Did you make any trips to Pearl Harbor during the time you were there with the training fleet?

Admiral Struble: No. With the Japanese thing going on, our training was local. It was kind of cut short because a certain amount of the ships that would normally have been around were over in Japan.

John T. Mason, Jr.: You were constantly, I assume, getting demands from the Far East for units as they wanted them.

---

* This is a reference to the type commander, Commander Air Force Pacific Fleet. He was a Navy admiral, not part of the U.S. Air Force.

Admiral Struble: No, if the Far East wanted forces, they had to go either to Pearl Harbor or to Washington. Now, Pearl Harbor and Washington would have really made the decision. Then if they wanted my outfit or some other outfit to send something out there, then we'd get an order that would send them out. But that would have been started either on the Washington or the Honolulu level—I say Honolulu, meaning, of course, Radford.

John T. Mason, Jr.: What was the status in that time of new recruits coming into the fleet?

Admiral Struble: Well, of course, the Marines had quite a few new recruits coming in there in the San Diego training area. Then the amphibious forces on North Island—we had a considerable number of younger people coming in that were started in training.

John T. Mason, Jr.: Was there any problem in getting recruits for the Navy at that time?

Admiral Struble: Not that I remember. Usually, you know, the boys are more interested when something is going on. I mean they become more interested. Some of them become less interested.

John T. Mason, Jr.: Well, I guess the Korean War got a better press than the later war.

Admiral Struble: Of course, we had to stretch ourselves to supply everything that we could to help the Korean thing work. So while it wasn't like World War II in its extent, there was temporarily a fairly heavy call on the forces we had available because we were trying to fight Korea with just the normal naval force situation. We weren't approaching that at all to the extent we had World War II.

John T. Mason, Jr.: We are about to leave the First Fleet. According to the biography here you left in March of 1952, and you went back to Washington and were attached to the Joint Chiefs of Staff for a few months. Did you have any knowledge of what assignment you were going to get?

Admiral Struble: I think that was about the time when it was decided that I would go to the U.N. Now, I would have been willing, of course, and had hoped possibly to go to sea again, maybe in the Mediterranean. But that did not come to pass, and so therefore I went to the U.N. rather than one or two other jobs to which I might have gone.

John T. Mason, Jr.: Why did you aspire to the Mediterranean? Why would you have looked favorably upon an assignment there?

Admiral Struble: I had never been in the Mediterranean, really. I had been in the Mediterranean during the thing, but, of course, that's one of the big spots in the world. I had always been very much interested in its relationship to our overall strategy.

John T. Mason, Jr.: That's what I was getting at. The Mediterranean for the American Navy was getting to be a major spot.

Admiral Struble: It was getting to be a place with which we could well become thoroughly acquainted. We needed to have some thoughtful ideas on the different nations that are on the Mediterranean and of the effect of those nations on the bigger nations in Europe in which we were greatly interested. On our side were people such as the English and the French and those of whom we might not feel entirely happy. Maybe Germany and Russia and so forth. That is the center of the area where future trouble could come up. Not necessarily in Germany or in Russia, but Russia and/or Germany and/or a number of the European powers could be greatly interested in our future foreign relations.

At that time I did not foresee that we would get as heavily involved as we did later in Asia. Now, of course, Asia is always important, but I would think that relatively Europe was a little more important to us because of the presence of what for a time was Germany and her reactions and, of course, definitely in the case of Russia.

John T. Mason, Jr.: At that time also did you foresee the diminished stature of the Royal Navy?

Admiral Struble: Well, of course, we knew that the Royal Navy was never going to get larger under the circumstances that were existing. England was rather small, and there was no reason to believe that she could necessarily maintain as much of the Navy as she had. Therefore, I am sure we all recognized that we would have to take over some of the concern about areas of the world to which in considerable extent we previously depended upon England to provide knowledge of and maybe a few ships there.

John T. Mason, Jr.: As you reflect on it, what was the prevailing attitude in the upper echelons of the U.S. Navy at that time? Were we willing to take on those duties? Were we eager to do so?

Admiral Struble: I don't think I'd put it that way. I'd say that we recognized it was a matter of necessity. Without really an improved English position, we were probably the only one on our side that would do if it were done. So, in other words, we did need an increase in certain of our types of ships in order to have better knowledge and a more thorough understanding (a) in the Mediterranean and certainly (b) the other side of the Suez Canal up to the Pacific. We needed more knowledge, information, and ships under our own control if we were going to be able to handle what would be the world problem with Russia and other countries.

John T. Mason, Jr.: Well, now, just a few years before—immediately after World War II and the late '40s—we had taken great steps to cut down on our forces and diminish the size of the Navy. We looked forward to a long peacetime period when we wouldn't be so heavily involved. Now, just a few years later, we are beginning to think of taking on new responsibilities.

Admiral Struble: Well, those things kind of work as we go along. In the days when England, and to a reasonable extent France, had certain interests in foreign areas and were maintaining them within reason, there was no reason why the American Navy should demand more money just to have more ships, just to go to those areas. However, if those areas were starting on the wane as regards English and/or French participation, then it became a question of whether we were going to have to overtake it and handle that additional load. Certainly the Mediterranean was so important and still is, in my opinion. Egypt is a key spot. We've got to know what's going on in the Mediterranean and to the east of there or we don't know where we stand. That's why we would have had to increase our Navy when previously, at the end of World War II, we were ready to close down a little.

Now, the Australians were getting a little more capable of taking care of themselves, but they weren't any great shakes yet. But there was no reason probably why we had to worry too much about the Australian area. Australia was apparently able to take care of it adequately for what we needed.

John T. Mason, Jr.: Of course, you're talking about the breakdown of colonialism and the U.S. stepping into the breach where necessary.

Admiral Struble: I think that was the reason we started to realize that all this Mediterranean problem, which in general we had always counted on the English for, and should have—and they were pretty capable in that area. That was kind of going down the drain.

John T. Mason, Jr.: A mare nostrum.

Admiral Struble: Yes, sure.

John T. Mason, Jr.: Well, you spent a few months there in the Joint Chiefs.

Admiral Struble: I don't remember anything happening during that period that I could talk much about.

John T. Mason, Jr.: Was it more or less a preparation period, an educational period, a study period for you?

Admiral Struble: That's the size of it. It not having been determined where I was to go, it could have been a sea job in that area, which I would have been glad to take, or it could have been a shore job in the United States.

John T. Mason, Jr.: Why was it not determined because of the personnel matters?

Admiral Struble: Well, for instance, when you get to shifting the top people, it isn't a question of just picking somebody and saying, "I'm going to send him there," and then you order him there. You've got to move the fellow that was there somewhere. For instance, supposing you had a man who had just gone to the Mediterranean and had been there a year. He knew his business, then he would stay another year, fill out two years. So in a way that command would not be available.

Also, let's say you had a man up at New York in the United Nations. Well, actually that man was going to retire in about, let's say, four months. They're not going to kick him out right now, you see. You're not going to appoint anybody to his job for another four months. So therefore, you kind of stand around for a while.

John T. Mason, Jr.: You say you were offered a couple choices, and then you chose the United Nations assignment.

Admiral Struble: Yes. I wasn't offered a sea job, or I would have taken that one. But I also recognized that that was fairly logical in my case, so I took the U.N.

John T. Mason, Jr.: You went to the United Nations in May of 1952. Now tell me about the scope of that job.

Admiral Struble: There generally are three military representatives in New York who are military assistants to our ambassador to the U.N. The senior military member is the one that becomes the head working man that works with the ambassador.

John T. Mason, Jr.: All the military men are funneled through him, I take it.

Admiral Struble: Well, he's the one who advises the ambassador a little more than the other two. The other two had offices to keep track of their part—in other words, the Navy or the Air Force or the Army, as the case might be. And the senior one is the one that personally works more with the ambassador than the others. When I arrived, the Army man was the head man, but he was only there for about eight months. Then he left and I became the head military delegate.

At times the military job there was simply going and listening to a large amount of the debates on what happened and keeping your own department in Washington informed of anything that it appeared they ought to be familiar with and have your opinion on. In other words, I would communicate with the Navy Department on a certain amount of things about the U.N.

Certainly a part of your job was getting to know as many as possible of the foreign representatives and talking to them and being able to find out what their views were. And occasionally when some of the subjects came up, why, the ambassador would want to have a powwow on what was the military point of view on this matter. He generally would take that up with the senior man, but on occasion he'd have all the military men in to talk about it.

I personally attended practically all the meetings that I could, which was a very large amount. From the point of view of interest, I think when we had Vishinsky there was when we really had an interesting time because, of course, he was quite a talker, quite a powerful talker.* He was able to get press columns in newspapers that would have amazed you and photographs and press columns and, of course, nothing at all from the American side of the picture until the next day at the earliest.

John T. Mason, Jr.: He got the scoops then.

---

* Andrei Y. Vishinsky was first deputy foreign minister of the Soviet Union and U.S.S.R. permanent representative at the United Nations.

Arthur D. Struble, Interview #12 (2/3/77) -- Page 430

Admiral Struble: He got all the scoops, yes. And you can understand that. Now, not too long after I arrived, the head military man left. Even earlier than that, the man that was in charge left, so Cabot Lodge was really the one that was there during the interesting part of it and was the head man that I did business with.*

John T. Mason, Jr.: You came there when Warren Austin was still our ambassador.

Admiral Struble: Yes, and his term was going to be up, and that was when Cabot Lodge came. So my remembrance and relations with him were very minor because of that. Also, it was during the summer, and nothing happens at the U.N. during the summer. It's a dead spot from about May until generally October.

Now, to go on to the discussion of Vishinsky, which I think you might find a little interesting. By that time I was commencing to talk quite a bit to the ambassador. From the time Lodge came on, I talked to him quite a bit. Vishinsky was very interesting. For instance, there would be an afternoon meeting, let's say starting about 2:00 o'clock and generally lasting until about 5:00 o'clock. The head man for the U.N. conducting the meeting would always try to close up about 5:00 P.M. Occasionally, somebody would stand up and want to talk on what had been discussed, so the meetings might last until 6:00. By 6:00 o'clock, knowing the traffic problem and everything else, all the delegates wanted to get started home.

One thing Vishinsky did that Mr. Lodge and myself both noticed was that he would come to the afternoon meetings, and he'd make an arrangement with the speaker, which was perfectly proper, to speak at maybe 4:00 or 4:30. A lot of people would have made arrangements to speak, and the various speakers would speak. Then Vishinsky would come on to speak and he'd be the last one on the list. He would carry his talks up to about the time it was due for the meeting to finish. Then he would close off, and the meeting would generally be over.

In the meantime, the American press would be there in force. They had listened and heard everything that had happened. They would take pictures, and along about 5:30

---

* Henry Cabot Lodge, Jr., had been U.S. Senator from Massachusetts until his defeat by John F. Kennedy in 1952. Lodge then became U.S. ambassador to the United Nations when the Eisenhower Administration took office in 1953.

or 6:00 o'clock, the meeting was over and everybody would run. But all of that would get in the morning paper. Of course, there could not very well have been any reply until the next day after Vishinsky spoke. It's a practical fact.

John T. Mason, Jr.: This must have been irksome at times.

Admiral Struble: Well, this got very irksome because Vishinsky regularly had a big spread and no American reply to what he said because it was just too late. The speaker didn't want any Americans to get up then and prolong it unduly. So Mr. Lodge and I devised a method of keeping track very carefully of what Vishinsky said, and we would decide if there were any important things that he said that we could reduce quickly to a very brief reply. Do you understand what I mean? A minute, maybe two minutes, but at most three or four minutes.

John T. Mason, Jr.: And you could get recognition?

Admiral Struble: So Vishinsky would make his talk and would sit down, and then Lodge would get right on his feet and say, "Mr. Chairman, I ask your indulgence just for two or three minutes before adjournment." Well, it's pretty hard for the head man not to give it to you under those circumstances. In the meantime, Lodge had thought it over very carefully; I would be sitting behind him generally, and I would be maybe feeding him one or two points from time to time, what I thought might be good for two or three minutes' reply. Of course, Lodge would only pick one. And then he'd get up and he would make a reply to one he could reply to right off the cuff, very briefly.

So he'd get up and make a very brief reply and the press maybe would get it before adjournment. So at least the next day when all the press came out about Vishinsky, there would have at least been on the front page the American reply. Of course, that didn't suit Vishinsky; he didn't like that. But that getting a reply in did make a lot of difference. The big coverage that Vishinsky got became qualified a little by virtue of one well-stated but brief American reply. And Lodge did that beautifully.

John T. Mason, Jr.: That called for a great deal of skill to do that.

Admiral Struble: Yes, you first had to pick one that you were sure you could handle in two minutes to your own entire satisfaction, don't you see?

John T. Mason, Jr.: It also implies that it wasn't necessary for Lodge in making a rebuttal of this sort to check with the State Department in advance. He didn't have time.

Admiral Struble: Oh, of course not. No, and that was why if he had a big long rambling thing that was going to take a long time, then that was out of the question. He could afford to talk off the cuff on the matter without consultation with the State Department. He was very good at that sort of thing and he was willing to take the responsibility. Of course, he naturally on a number of things that might have been said by Vishinsky realized that they were too long to answer briefly. But if we could get in one good answer, that was all we needed. I thought Lodge made an excellent ambassador.

John T. Mason, Jr.: In getting to Lodge and his consultations with Washington, how frequently did he confer with Washington?

Admiral Struble: He was in constant contact with them by phone. There undoubtedly were fairly important representatives that came up from Washington, probably at least twice a week. A large number. When it wasn't good to talk about it on the phone, the Secretary of State could always call in a fairly important man and send him up.

Of course, when the U.N. was in session it wasn't good for Lodge to leave to go down to Washington for consultation if it could be avoided. And during those periods, I thought that he was a fine ambassador that way. He was constantly on the lookout to get a qualification of the initial press that Vishinsky was getting. Of course, Vishinsky was a capable talker.

John T. Mason, Jr.: Oh, yes, yes. And used it, obviously, as a propaganda vehicle.

Admiral Struble: Well, he used it to forward the interests of Russia, which was his country.

John T. Mason, Jr.: Tell me something about your meetings with the military delegations of the various countries.

Admiral Struble: I would say that I did more business with the foreign ambassadors than I did with the military delegations. However, we had excellent relations with most of the military delegations at the U.N., and most all of them were rather small. I deliberately made and arranged to see a number of the Russians regularly if I could and discussed matters with them. But actually no real business was ever settled by me with the Russian delegation because they were unable to take any real steps themselves.

John T. Mason, Jr.: That was all done in Moscow.

Admiral Struble: Well, it was all done either by Vishinsky or in Moscow, yes. They weren't able to get together too easily. For instance, in the case of when a plane was shot down in Korea or something once, the Russian delegation just said, "We can't talk to you about that." So any discussion that was had would either have to be Lodge or myself discussing it with the foreign office part of the delegation. Often Lodge would have me maybe discuss it, but it was then being discussed on the political level rather than on the military level. I think that's the point I'm trying to make.

John T. Mason, Jr.: Was that generally true with the foreign delegations? That it was done actually and ultimately on the political level?

Admiral Struble: It was as far as I was concerned because of Korea going on and because of that sort of thing. The military meetings were such that you found yourself having to do it with a political representative of the other country. The moment that became apparent, then, of course, I would always talk to Lodge immediately and determine whether he wanted me to pursue or whether he would pursue it himself. It being done on the political level rather than on the military level. I at all times tried to maintain good relations with the military delegations and I think I had them. But as regards doing business, if it got at all political, you usually had to talk it over on the political level.

Lodge had so much to talk over that he often preferred for me to do some of the political level work, maybe with some of his own political people because of my greater knowledge of the military aspects of the thing. He was willing to assume that I would handle the political part all right. I had had, of course, probably more political experience than most naval officers.

John T. Mason, Jr.: Yes, you had.

Admiral Struble: You understand that, having been in the Central Division twice in the Navy Department and doing business direct with the Navy Department from the Secretary of State down on two tours of duty in Washington, I did have probably as a military man a little more political experience than most naval officers would have had.

John T. Mason, Jr.: Also, in modesty you wouldn't, but I'll add, that in addition to all that experience and knowledge, you had the gray matter that was essential.

Admiral Struble: Well, I don't know about that. But that was the way it worked out. It made the job probably more interesting for me as an individual than it would be if I as only handling the military angle. I did it with Lodge's knowledge, and he was very happy to have me entertain a number of the foreign political delegates and talk to them than probably went on normally. I was able to do that because I had a nice set of quarters where I was located. I could entertain quite well there, and within reason I had a very small allowance for entertaining. If I was careful, it would stretch quite a bit. My having a couple of foreign ambassadors over for dinner, you could often discuss problems that could be handled smoother and easier.

John T. Mason, Jr.: This was an accepted thing. When they came to dinner they were perfectly willing to discuss serious diplomatic matters and issues?

Admiral Struble: Oh, I wouldn't say it that way; I wouldn't say it was understood. But, of course, if you had a couple of foreign ambassadors to a luncheon or a dinner, why, you would try to decide whether you could discuss a problem with both of them present at the same time. If you felt you could afford to do it, then you would open up the subject and say, "Well, you know, we feel this and we feel that." They would both hear you at the same time and everything, and you would not try to accomplish business. You would only try to maybe lay a background from which further good relations might ensue rather than attempting to do the business at that time. But you would try to point out why the hell couldn't the three of us get together and solve some of these problems. That would be the way to approach it.

John T. Mason, Jr.: Now, this implies a very, very careful selection of guests and the admixture of guests. How did you do this? Was this done on your own or did you have a chief of protocol who—

Admiral Struble: No, I did all that myself, except that when we found it was on some of these subjects, I might have discussed with Lodge or a member of the delegation, one of his political people, and say, "Do you think this would work out to discuss this problem with So-and-so and So-and-so?" I think that's the way you're going to improve conditions in these matters and if you had a reasonable point of view. For instance, let's take the Greeks and the Turks. I at times had the Greek and the Turk ambassadors to luncheon or to dinner at the same time.

John T. Mason, Jr.: With their ladies.

Admiral Struble: With their ladies. Then when the men went out after dinner to have a drink and so forth, the ladies retired, and I would talk to the men. But any choice of subject that I brought up was brought up in a way that you didn't force any issues or anything of that sort. But you said, "I wonder why in the hell you two fellows can't get together on this proposition so we'd all be better off in the Mediterranean?"

Maybe at that time we might discuss an island that was there. You wouldn't try to solve any problems, but you would say, "I wonder why in the hell we can't all get together on solving that island problem?" Well, then you might get some thought between the two of them where they would commence to see an area in which they maybe could forget some of their last 100 years of fighting with each other, and maybe the two of them could get together better. Well, then that would be progress.

That wouldn't mean that you wouldn't initiate any specific idea or endeavor to try to put it over. You would be just trying to see if you could get two people talking to each other in a reasonable way.

John T. Mason, Jr.: Very interesting. At that period, the membership of the United Nations was somewhat less than it is now. Do you recall how many nations were involved when you were there?

Admiral Struble: No, I don't remember exactly but I would think it was maybe 60 or more, maybe 80.

John T. Mason, Jr.: It was before the great contingent of third world—

Admiral Struble: Oh, yes, this was pretty much the original membership with maybe as many as five or ten additions that had been made but no large number of additions.

John T. Mason, Jr.: And the United States had a very powerful clout, did it not, in the United Nations at that point?

Admiral Struble: Well, I don't like that term clout because that wasn't the way we operated, and it wasn't the way we should have operated. The clout might apply to some of those situations where we just deliberately had to use our veto in order to prevent a very bad thing from happening. I wouldn't call that clout. Clout to me means that because we were bigger and stronger we would try to push these other people to doing things. I think we used our veto to try to prevent bad things from happening rather than forcing.

There were an awful lot of reasonable people at the U.N. I think at times we tried to get together, but then when some very old problem between two nations would get on the war path, you might say, then, of course, any attempt to try to bring those two people together for something that you felt would be a good thing was not very applicable. That's, of course, what politics is. It's diplomacy if you want to raise it a level in the words you use and in the handling of it. Of course, you get it at the government level and it is diplomacy rather than the other thing.

John T. Mason, Jr.: From what you say about the entertaining and discussing issues over dinner . . .

Admiral Struble: You weren't just making the man a sucker to agree with you by inviting him to dinner.

John T. Mason, Jr.: No. But is it fair to say that a great deal of business was accomplished in a social sense or under the guise of a social event?

Admiral Struble: No, I wouldn't put it that way. I would say that the social business got you and some other people talking, but I wouldn't say that the business was done. The ground for getting together and talking over one of these things slowly and sensibly but maybe with a long-range view of getting something done was what was accomplished rather than the accomplishment of the fact.

If you got people talking together, then you might reach something. As a matter of fact, I'm pretty sure we got the Greeks and the Turks on a better footing for talking for a while. But, of course, there were so many reasons in that Turkish and Greek thing for arousing troubles that you never really got it accomplished.

John T. Mason, Jr.: And would it not be true that when personnel changed, you fell back to the old position again?

Admiral Struble: Well, I don't know. As a matter of fact, when I was there we had a man that was the Turkish representative who left there. At that time we were getting along and talking very sensibly. He went back to be the new foreign minister so I don't know how you could have had—but the question was that thereafter then the Greeks and the Turks got at outs with each other on problems which I don't think we had a chance to discuss calmly among the number of people and maybe settled.

Cyprus I think was a problem that could have been settled if time had been taken and it had been handled very calmly. Of course, then again at the same time, you had the Egyptian problem coming into the Mediterranean problem. So it's a very intricate problem.

But I deplore the idea that it was our clout. I don't think we used the clout so much as we used the veto, which I think was not showing clout. It was just saying we were not getting anywhere and we didn't think this was going to prove anything. Let's stop and let's talk it all over again. That's the only sensible way to have the U.N. try to function.

John T. Mason, Jr.: Inasmuch as you were talking about the Greek and Turkish relations . . .

Admiral Struble: And the use of those two names in what you come up with has got to be very carefully considered and handled very carefully, or you antagonize one of the worst problems you have.

John T. Mason, Jr.: It brings to mind a question. How closely did you consult, as the chairman of the military delegation, with our NATO commander in the Mediterranean, who was more intimately involved with this on a day-to-day basis?

Admiral Struble: No, he wasn't really. He wasn't more intimately involved in that part of it. He would be trying simultaneously with what I was doing, for instance, to do the same thing over where he was. The only information that he would get would be when the Navy Department might brief him, or the State Department might brief the ambassador on what our mission or thoughts or ideas were commencing to be. We would not attempt to go direct to those people at all. That should be handled by the Navy and/or the State Department and their representative over there rather than us.

John T. Mason, Jr.: What was your relationship on a personal level and as a delegation with the Secretary General of the United Nations?

Admiral Struble: Very good. I'm sure Mr. Lodge got along with him very well. When a military problem came up—for instance, about the Korean business—the head man at the U.N. might ask Mr. Lodge to visit him, and he'd talk to Lodge about it. Lodge would often tell him what he thought politically. They'd have a discussion. Then Lodge would say, "You know, I've got a military man on my outfit who has been over there, and he is much more familiar with what I would call the military details and the military approach to handling the problem. Why don't I send him over to talk to you?" I'd go over and talk then to the head U.N. man.

John T. Mason, Jr.: I assume at that time that it was Trygve H. Lie, wasn't it?

Admiral Struble: Yes. All right, he would then decide after talking to me whether he could make a military proposal to the other side that then maybe I would sponsor at the next military staff meeting, and it would come to him through the military staff meeting at the U.N. Or maybe he would pick it up directly on the political level with the people involved, which, of course, might be China and/or other peoples. Then he would try to handle the problem, and he would say, "I feel pretty sure the Americans would be willing to do this." He would say that simply because I told him that I thought this would be a good solution and I thought we could probably do it.

In that way, you see, there is no question of these countries giving up their national rights or anything. They would take up with the head of the U.N. and say, "Well, if you can do this and do that, we'll be glad to have you come out here and so forth." Maybe we'd send a representative out to the Far East then who would be in a position to do some negotiation on it.

John T. Mason, Jr.: Did you get involved in traveling yourself?

Admiral Struble: Well, I didn't go out on any problems of this character. I, of course, went out to San Francisco about the big U.N. meeting when the President came out. We had a big U.N. meeting out in San Francisco about—I've forgotten the year it was now. I came out to that meeting in San Francisco, and Lodge had told me actually that "I don't think we'll need you in San Francisco. That's just going to be pure so-and-so." He says, "You can go ahead and go on to Canada if you're going up there."

I said, "Oh, I'm going up there this summer. I'll start as soon as you leave town then." Then about a week later he sent for me and said, "Oh, boy, listen. I've changed my mind. I think I'd better take you out to San Francisco with me."

So I said, "All right." And I went on out to San Francisco. As a matter of fact, we got in with the Filipinos, and, of course, I had known them from World War II and had Filipino people in there. And I think I was a considerable help to Lodge and Ike out in San Francisco.

John T. Mason, Jr.: And, of course, Korea was again . . .

Admiral Struble: Well, Korea and the Philippines were getting mixed up a little bit. That was where I think I was quite useful.

John T. Mason, Jr.: Looking at Korea, was there any degree of optimism in the United Nations circles and in the U.S. delegation that these interminable talks at Panmunjom would come to some solution?*

Admiral Struble: I guess I'd say I don't think too many people felt that the real solution would be reached. But I do believe they felt we could make a solution in which the talks at Panmunjom would be continued and that probably with more time lapsing maybe we could reach a solution. So I think there was a little optimism on the other side.

The trouble is that that was a situation that had its own problems in itself, which was the old Korean problem, the old Japanese-Korean-Russian-Chinese problem mixed up in it. That was a problem that instead of being a simple problem between North and South Korea, let's say, it often got into the Russian-Chinese, etc., problem. Do you realize that? Do you see what I mean?

John T. Mason, Jr.: Yes. And as a United Nations organization, you were operating with a broken wing, so to speak, in that Red China wasn't represented in any way.

Admiral Struble: One of the big problems was the Chinese-Russian problem that shouldn't have been mixed up in the local, let's say, Korean problem with some Japanese angle connected with it and some Chinese angle connected with it, with some Russian angle connected with it. If the thing had been held to a basic Korean problem as much as possible, with these other things coming in in not too prominent a way, then maybe we could have gotten it settled.

John T. Mason, Jr.: But in your experience with international relations, has it ever been true that there has been a problem so clear-cut that it didn't involve all sorts of ramifications?

---

* Panmunjom was a town on the border between North Korea and South Korea. It was the site of negotiating sessions that began during the Korean War and have continued to this day.

Admiral Struble: No, but the trouble was, could you get those ramifications ironed out and people being reasonable with each other? In other words, could we get anything to solve the Chinese-Russian border problem? And I will say that I felt at that time that probably we could get Japanese agreement almost easier than we could the other two. I felt the Japanese were going to be quite reasonable in the solution of that problem if we could get the other two to agree. Now, if the other two had agreed to quit supporting Korean problems and trouble, maybe we would have been better off.

John T. Mason, Jr.: You fall back to the intention of the nations involved then, don't you—whether they have a serious intention and an honest one to arrive at some solution or whether they have ulterior motives?

Admiral Struble: It isn't ulterior motives. Some of these motives they have had for 100 years, and they weren't entirely ulterior.

John T. Mason, Jr.: Well, I was thinking perhaps of Russian motives and the political philosophy that motivates some of their actions.

Admiral Struble: Well, I don't believe there was any possibility of the Russians giving up their ability to have a Pacific coast, in other words, the ability to go from Russia to the Pacific. I think that was something that we had to have accepted.

Now then, my opinion would be that we could have gotten Japanese acceptance of what the Russians already had provided they would, and in return make an agreement that they would bind themselves not to expand their Pacific area further. Do you understand what I mean?

John T. Mason, Jr.: I understand, but did you actually believe that the Russians had any point in negotiating that would desert their ideological premise that they were going to spread Communism throughout the world?

Admiral Struble: Well, of course, we wouldn't ask them for that to be a part of the treaty, but they would have to in effect agree to that if they agreed to maintain their status where they were. Now, I think in lots of ways they might have been willing to do that if they could have gotten China to agree to the same thing: that China would agree that they wouldn't invade this narrow little strip that Russia had. China would have been very happy to make that kind of agreement with Russia, but they wouldn't have gotten permitted to it. Then they would still have the opportunity technically available to them to try to cut in and cut off that Russian thing sometime. And the Chinese are great waiters. They'll wait until the time arrives to try to do it, and the Russians know that. So again at the moment when they were sitting a little high on the horse, why the hell should they agree to that? This is fundamental.

John T. Mason, Jr.: Let me ask, in your frequent discussions with the Russian delegation on this matter or that matter, and with the inevitable frustrations that came your way as a result of your discussions with them, did you or did our delegation ever seriously abandon the thought that the Russians basically were determined to spread Marxism throughout the world?

Admiral Struble: Well, what's the difference between spreading Marxism through the world and spreading your territories? It's almost one and the same thing except that you phrase it a little differently, isn't it? In other words, you're talking about Marxism in the case of Russia but you talk about Japanese desire for more territory, and you're saying the same thing about them.

John T. Mason, Jr.: Yes, but in your discussions with the Russians, did you ever idealistically think that you could arrive at some permanent solution of territorial problems with them?

Admiral Struble: Well, I think we might have if we had introduced it at Yalta.* We might have gotten somewhere better, but that would go way back to Yalta.

John T. Mason, Jr.: And, in effect, you're saying no to my question.

Admiral Struble: Well, yes. I don't believe the answer to your question could be anything but no from anybody that tends to be at all practical in the matter. Had we solved that problem before the Russians had completely solved their western area problem, it might have gone through. I think the Russians would basically be just as happy as they were when they changed things too much. I don't believe in the future they are going to expand too much because I don't think China will let them.

Now, if they want to jump on China when it's down and grab some Chinese territory, they might. But it isn't the Chinese territory that they want. They would take the northern section of China right now to amplify their area going out to the Pacific. But they would be taking it not for the purpose of increasing their area in Asia so much as improving their guaranteed area all the way out to the Pacific. It's the Pacific they're interested in.

John T. Mason, Jr.: Yes, the protection of their corridor.

Admiral Struble: It would protect their corridor better. So if the opportunity arose to take another 100- or so, 200-mile strip of north China to make their thing, they would take that and be very happy. They would say, "We won't have any fight with you. We won't fight at all. We don't have to fight each other." But the reason they would have taken it was not to get that stuff from China so much as to get the guaranteed corridor out to the Pacific. If you don't see the fundamental part of it, then you don't understand.

Now, the reason that the Chinese wouldn't want to consider anything like that is because their connection from south China up to northeast China has to be up going north

---

* The Allied leaders—Franklin Roosevelt, Winston Churchill, and Joseph Stalin—met at Yalta, a resort city on the Crimea, in February 1945. They negotiated objectives for the remainder of the war and for the postwar world.

and then coming out again to the northeastern part. And even to get down to China where their big part is, which as you know is north of Taiwan. Do you understand me?

John T. Mason, Jr.: Yes, and you're talking about the barrier which is the mountains.

Admiral Struble: So they have to go on a train to go inland and then go north and then come back down. China is never going to be willing to give up that northern territory there because it is their protection on the north side, and it guaranteed better their ability to keep the south and the north united.

You've got Shanghai down there sticking out like a sore thumb on the south side.

John T. Mason, Jr.: Wouldn't it also guarantee that if Russia attempted anything like that with a strip in northern China that it would be eternal enmity on the part of the Chinese toward Russia?

Admiral Struble: Oh, that's right. That's the point. The Chinese would unite under their own man, whoever he was at that time, to defend the thing very much.

John T. Mason, Jr.: Then would it be worth Russia's while to do this? Wouldn't that be a deterrent in itself?

Admiral Struble: No, I don't think Russia would worry about taking it over if they could have it permanently for a while and get it fixed up to suit themselves. They wouldn't be afraid to fight the Chinese on it. Because they would get it ready for it beforehand, and they could do a hell of a good job at it.

John T. Mason, Jr.: In your dealings with the Russians, both in a social sense and in political—

Admiral Struble: I never discussed this part of it with them because this wouldn't have been in the cards talking to them on the lines I've just talked to you.

John T. Mason, Jr.: No, but I was thinking now on a different level. In your personal dealings with the Russian delegation, whether it was in a social sense or whether it was discussing military or political matters, did you find in them a sense of freedom in what they could say or were they under wraps in terms of a political commissar in their presence and that sort of thing?

Admiral Struble: Oh, their military were entirely under the political part of the delegation. Their military had, I would say, no authority to talk and do the things that I did.

John T. Mason, Jr.: When they came to dinner, were they free, or did they have a commissar with them?

Admiral Struble: Oh, no, that was no good. I arranged that I had retained them differently so that I didn't get into this thing. For instance, I did talk to the Turk and the Greek in my own house—the top people. But that would not have worked in any way with the Russians. No, no, I had all the Russian military people to parties, but they were appropriate parties for that purpose. I wouldn't have thought of trying to have one of the Russians to one of these other private parties. That wouldn't have been a good business.

John T. Mason, Jr.: You mean perhaps they wouldn't have come anyway?

Admiral Struble: Well, I don't know whether they would have come or not. But it would not have been good business because that would have aroused an immediate suspicion on their part. It was no good. That just was no good; that wasn't the thing to do.

John T. Mason, Jr.: In your time there with the United Nations, there was the Indian/Pakistani problem.

Admiral Struble: Very much.

John T. Mason, Jr.: Did you have any involvement in that?

Admiral Struble: Well, yes. I had the number-one Indian woman who did come up from Washington to the U.N. when she was on a trip to Washington. I had her give an address to the assembled American delegation.

John T. Mason, Jr.: Was that Madam Pandit?*

Admiral Struble: Yes. I heard her talk in great privacy to the American delegation. Actually, it happened to be at a time when the captains and colonels were at this school in Washington. These were Army and Navy and Air Force people.

John T. Mason, Jr.: You mean the National War College.

Admiral Struble: The National War College. Those National War College captains and colonels—they were fairly senior officers. I had them at the U.N., and I had Madam Pandit make a speech to them about India. I think she spoke for approximately an hour. I had her talk 20 to 30 minutes, just her own talk, then I had a knock-off period for about 20 minutes while coffee was served. She and I were standing down below and they were all up in the chairs—you know how it is at the U.N. They had guards all around the place, but theoretically no one was in there but just Americans. She could talk pretty freely.

She gave one of the best talks that I had of that kind at the U.N. as compared to people from other countries. She did speak out very well and she spoke out much better than any other of the Indians that talked. She was quite frank in a lot of ways. However, while this was good information for these officers to hear and it was something for them to think about, I don't know if that particular thing in any way assisted in our solution of the Indian/Pakistan problem with India and Pakistan, except that it did give them some

---

* Vijaya Lakshmi Pandit was the sister of Indian Premier Jawaharlal Nehru. In September 1953 she was elected to serve as president of the eighth session of the U.N. General Assembly, the first woman to hold that post.

idea of her and her thought. She was a very capable talker, and she was much franker than any of the Indians who were on their own delegation by far. She made a very good talk and was pretty forthright.

John T. Mason, Jr.: Was the issue still undecided on the Kashmir Plebiscite? Was that laid to rest by that time?

Admiral Struble: No, the Pakistanis still felt that they hadn't quite solved the problem properly. I think Madam Pandit certainly felt that they had had this meeting. It had been settled and she wasn't going to change her position.

John T. Mason, Jr.: Do you recall that Admiral Nimitz had been named as our special envoy to conduct this plebiscite?

Admiral Struble: I have forgotten whether Nimitz had made his trip just before.

John T. Mason, Jr.: He never went to India because he cooled his heels at that United Nations for two years and it never was held.

Admiral Struble: Didn't he ever go over?

John T. Mason, Jr.: No.

Admiral Struble: Then I'm not sure. He still had that job, and it had not been settled.

John T. Mason, Jr.: You said off tape that you had a faint recollection that Nimitz was around New York at the time Madam Pandit came and talked to the group.

Admiral Struble: Yes, I think he was. I'm not sure of what happened too much after that because I am also inclined to believe that maybe this was just about the time that three or four months later or so maybe I retired in Washington. I talked to Nimitz a number of times in New York on this subject because generally, and at first he had been out on the West Coast. But when he was in New York he generally would send for me, and I would talk to him about the current course of events as I looked at it.

So I know Nimitz was not at this talk. Had he been in New York and immediately available, I might well have invited him to this talk, although he might not have thought it an appropriate place to come to anyway. I think the main point was that Madam Pandit was an excellent talker and made a fine talk. When it came to answering questions propounded by these captains and colonels, she was so far superior to the other Indian members of the delegation. We were impressed with her decision and willingness to answer a number of the tougher problems that some of their other people would have declined to even answer.

John T. Mason, Jr.: You were going to tell me about the, so to speak, emoluments of this job, the personal satisfactions that came your way because of this assignment.

Admiral Struble: Well, it was an interesting assignment because, of course, the U.N. was a big new thing that was a proposal to try to solve our biggest world problem almost, you might say. And whether it would work or not was going to be determined by the results that were achieved possibly in the first few years. It early became apparent that the progress, if we really made it, was going to take quite a long time. As has unfortunately been proven since, we have gotten now snarled down in a lot of situations that I think are no good at all. We have too many people voting and too many individual interests involved. I don't believe we'll ever be able to be a hardheaded, practical organization that will solve the problems. I hate to be this tough about it, but that's about the way I feel about it.

On the other hand, I would not discontinue it but would attempt to try to continue it holding on to every possible right that we have.

John T. Mason, Jr.: Now, the reasons for saying that it should be continued are what?

Admiral Struble: I think first to just throw the thing over would kind of create a type of chaos that isn't good in the world. Throwing over the U.N., even though it isn't useful and even though it is unsatisfactory—I wouldn't throw it over until the last minute, you might say. As long as there is any opportunity of keeping a certain amount of things lined up, I'd try to do it.

If the voting at some time in the future should prevent us from having the veto power that we have right now, if that gets modified as time goes on, I would then recommend we get out of it.

John T. Mason, Jr.: But, for the time being—

Admiral Struble: For the time being, as long as we have the veto power and it can function, I think maybe I would try to continue it and let it work.

John T. Mason, Jr.: You put a lot of credence then in the effectiveness of just being able to talk about an issue, air an issue.

Admiral Struble: I think airing issues is good, yes. And therefore, having a spot at which the people around the globe feel that issues can be aired even though they are from small little islands or something, well, that isn't bad. If it doesn't get too expensive and if it doesn't make the political thing prohibitive, why, then I think I'd keep it going.

John T. Mason, Jr.: You mentioned the word "expensive." It proved to be pretty expensive for America, did it not?

Admiral Struble: Yes, it's an expensive thing and I'm not sure that the money is well spent, but I don't know that but maybe it has aired a lot of these problems and it is useful because of that fact. I think that the fact that it permits the problems to be aired does have some value.

John T. Mason, Jr.: Now, would you comment and talk about the effectiveness of the United Nations military force being employed in a given situation?

Admiral Struble: I think the military force in the U.N. should only be provided after very careful thought. They should be limited, if possible, in the area and the scope of what they handle. Under such conditions, a U.N. force can be a good thing temporarily to let a problem cool off maybe and maybe then have some reasonable solution.

John T. Mason, Jr.: Was there a military force in your time there as the head of our military delegation?

Admiral Struble: Well, yes. You mean in Korea? It's a question of if you call Panmunjom an example, yes.

John T. Mason, Jr.: Well, it was not the kind of example I was thinking. I was thinking of an example such as we have seen in Africa or in the Middle East in Palestine.

Admiral Struble: Which one do you mean? I don't think I would remove these ideas of small forces used from time to time, where one or more countries may temporarily take over some sort of a neutral type of job. They will not be entirely satisfactory, I'm sure, from our point of view, but still they may be slightly useful. And if they cool off an area and a big problem in some spot—if they let it cool off, they will have at least been useful for that purpose.

I think, for instance, in the case of northeastern India, the solution wasn't satisfactory, but I don't know but what it was better to have had it than not to have had it. Do you understand what I mean?

John T. Mason, Jr.: Yes, under the aegis of the United Nations there is a greater acceptability among warring factors, isn't there?

Admiral Struble: You have an opportunity to temporarily stop something that way. Even though the results may not be satisfactory, if they actually stopped it and permitted time to take over before the solution was reached, I think it is generally a good thing. You remember that Burma stuff up there? I don't know that that did any harm, and I think maybe it did a little good. It cooled off a certain amount of stuff here and there and therefore was useful for that purpose.

John T. Mason, Jr.: Do you want to say something about the inner workings of the United Nations—the Security Council vis-à-vis the General Assembly?

Admiral Struble: Well, of course, the Security Council is very important, and it must continue pretty much with its present power and strength and the veto solution problem or I would say we don't belong in it anymore. Now, simply the veto power on the handling of the Security Council is not necessarily going to be entirely satisfactory for a minute or maybe for sometime is going to reach a fine, sound solution. But at the present, it's the one thing that makes the continuance of the U.N. at all suitable or useful.

Now, are we going to let all these nations get accustomed to being a part of the United Nations and are we then going to get back to a more stable situation and produce something? Who knows? I think that now that we've gone this far, we are almost committed to continue it until we have a really good case for calling it off.

John T. Mason, Jr.: What are your personal feelings? Are you optimistic about the ultimate effectiveness of the United Nations?

Admiral Struble: No, I'm not at all optimistic about the eventual solution of the problem. But until this current African enlarged thing is over and until we see how the number of nations now may join the U.N. and how the thing functions, I would not move to discontinue it.

John T. Mason, Jr.: In your time there, did you see the formation of so-called power blocs? I mean various delegations joining forces?

Admiral Struble: Oh, I don't think that was of great importance. I think as long as the Security Council maintains the veto power and ability to prevent too large a mistake to be made, I think I'd hold on. Is that clear? I don't think we can possibly reorganize it now. I don't think there's any method or reorganization unless some new idea comes in that decentralizes it into five areas and therefore makes each area smaller but with all five of the areas then being decentralized, let's say, still being under the Security Council with its power in one spot such as New York.

John T. Mason, Jr.: Is it not true there has been a great deviation from the original intention of the charter setting up the United Nations? Is it not true that it never anticipated that it would develop into the sort of thing it has in terms of vetoes and that sort of thing?

Admiral Struble: Well, of course, it was an optimistic thing at most when it was started. The question of whether such a thing could function was always questionable. I was offered a job when I left the U.N. to go around the country and talk for the U.N. and in favor of it, speaking all over the country of the United States. The reason I said no was that while it might have been an interesting trip for a year and all of that, I could not see at that time the sound, solid future that I felt the thing needed. I saw no way that by going around and making speeches could I help it out except to let it continue on and maybe get stronger. So therefore I wouldn't go. I'm not sure it's gotten stronger. The fact is I'm sure it has gotten weaker. We got a few bad points that have slipped in, and they are there now, but I'm not sure that I would discontinue it as of tomorrow.

John T. Mason, Jr.: I think we saw develop in the United States during that period when you were at the United Nations a kind of a policy—I don't know that it was ever proclaimed as a policy—which is termed massive retaliation. What were your feelings about that?

Admiral Struble: Well, I've got to mark the word massive out on my part because personally I think the moment somebody says that, they just don't understand. If after a lot of careful thought and everything a massive operation is necessary, then that's a different matter. When you start throwing out the words like "massive" right early in the game, that doesn't sound to me like good progress.

John T. Mason, Jr.: It didn't refer to conventional weaponry, did it? Wasn't it the ultimate weapon?

Admiral Struble: Well, the whole point is that the proposal in itself is going in for this threat kind of stuff and that's no good. The fellow that thinks he's going to solve some of these big important problems by making a big threat just doesn't understand it, and he's rarely going to solve it unless he's so big and the opposition is so little that there's no doubt he can put it over himself and there's little doubt that someone else will intervene and prevent him from doing it.

John T. Mason, Jr.: I wonder if we didn't by stressing this—as it was stressed by Secretary Dulles—I wonder if we didn't build up for ourselves a kind of a problem in terms of national defense and preparation.* I wonder if we didn't lull the general populace into thinking that this was the solution, this was the solution way out of any military effort.

Admiral Struble: Which action of his are you talking about?

John T. Mason, Jr.: This doctrine of massive retaliation, the idea of using in force atomic weapons in a great national emergency rather than to resort to conventional weapons.

Admiral Struble: I think frankly that if we got into a war, that we should have used everything we had to the extent that we felt it appropriate and to the extent that we felt it would eliminate and stop the war quickly. So to my mind, it's a hardheaded, practical

---

* John Foster Dulles was Secretary of State from 1953 to 1959, during the Eisenhower Administration.

problem. Again, I want to say it isn't the threat solution. I don't think the threat solution is a good one.

John T. Mason, Jr.: Well, then that applies to another term that was used quite frequently in connection with Secretary Dulles, brinkmanship.

Admiral Struble: Well, to me, you're talking almost the same kind of stuff. I think these kind of things have to be done on what I would call a little harder-headed and thoughtful basis. In my opinion, we should have taken very carefully the best possible steps to have tried to ensure that Egyptian situation remaining reasonably solid and in some sort of fair situation so that the use of the canal, no deprivation of the Egyptians of their normal rights and no problems that other nations could object to in the use of the canal as an all-world proposition. I think that was the strength of it. That the canal was open to everybody.

John T. Mason, Jr.: In your time at the United Nations there was another problem. In the Far East, the offshore islands Matsu and Quemoy. What kind of reaction was there in the United Nations to that issue?

[This is the end of the interview and the end of the oral history. Admiral Struble's interviews did not cover his final tour of active naval service nor his activities following retirement.]

Launched in 1969, the U.S. Naval Institute's award-winning oral history program is among the oldest in the country. Used in combination with documentary sources, oral histories offer a richer understanding of naval history through candid recollections and explanations rarely entered into contemporary records. In addition, they help depict the atmosphere of a particular event or era in a manner not available in official documents.

The nonprofit Naval Institute accomplishes its history projects solely through contributed funds and gratefully accepts tax-deductible gifts of all sizes for this purpose. This support allows the Institute to preserve the life experiences of today's service men and women so they may enlighten and inspire future generations.

For information about opportunities to underwrite Naval Institute oral history projects, please contact the Naval Institute Foundation at 291 Wood Road, Annapolis, Maryland 21402; by phone at (410) 295-1054; or by e-mail at foundation@usni.org.

Index to the Oral History of
Admiral Arthur Dewey Struble, U.S. Navy (Retired)

Abdill, Captain Everett W., USN (USNA, 1924)
Killed on board the light cruiser Nashville (CL-43) when she was hit by a kamikaze in December 1944, 237-241, 244

Air Force, U.S.
Conducted the Berlin Airlift in 1948-49, 335

Air Warfare
U.S./U.N. aviation operations in the early part of the Korean War, 1950-51, 369, 372, 376, 384-385, 401-404, 408, 418-420

Alaska
In the late 1940s Amphibious Force Pacific Fleet was looking into oil pipelines in Alaska, 297-299
Concern in the late 1940s about the status of U.S. military forces in Alaska, 299

Amphibious Warfare
Development of by the Army, Navy, and Marine Corps in the early 1930s, 64-66, 85-87
Planning and execution in 1943-44 of the Allied invasion of Normandy, France, 141-189
U.S. amphibious operations in 1944-45 to capture islands in the Philippine archipelago, 194-225, 229-260, 303-306, 309-310
Exercises and actions of Amphibious Force Pacific Fleet, 1946-48, 287-302, 306-307
U.S/U.N. amphibious landing at Inchon, South Korea, in September 1950, 301-302, 357-393
Landing at Wonsan, North Korea, in October 1950, 394-399, 401, 408-411

Antiair Warfare
Fire by U.S. ships at Japanese planes in the Philippine campaign in 1944, 233-234

Antisubmarine Warfare
Escort operations out of Queenstown, Ireland, in World War I, 35-40
In the Atlantic in World War II as protection against German submarines, 38, 190-192

Arizona, USS (BB-39)
Operations out of Hawaii in 1940-41, 128-130

Army, U.S.
In the early 1930s was involved in an amphibious landing exercise in San Francisco Bay, 64-66, 85-86

Established a base on the island of Bora-Bora early in World War II, 134-136
Part of the amphibious force that recaptured islands in the Philippines in 1944-45, 194-225, 229-260, 303-304
Role in amphibious warfare in the late 1940s, 288-302, 306-310
Operations in the early part of the Korean War, 376, 388-389, 394, 400-401

Army Air Forces, U.S.
Participation in the capture of the Philippines in 1944-45, 200, 205, 209, 213, 218-220, 222-223, 246-249, 255

Augusta, USS (CA-31)
Flagship for the U.S. naval aspects of the Allied invasion of Normandy in June 1944, 158, 161, 167, 170-173, 181, 185

Australia
Visited by U.S. warships in a fleet cruise in 1925, 45, 63-68, 109-110

Barbey, Rear Admiral Daniel E., USN (USNA, 1912)
Commanded the Seventh Amphibious Force in the Pacific in 1944-45, 194, 203-206, 254-255, 304, 310, 365

Battleship Division Three
Operations of the division in the early 1930s in the Pacific included early experiments in amphibious warfare, 64-65, 82-91

Berkey, Rear Admiral Russell S., USN (USNA, 1916)
Commanded Cruiser Division 15/Task Force 75 during amphibious operations in the Philippines in 1944-45, 230-231, 236, 248

Berlin Airlift
Conducted by the U.S. Air Force in 1948-49, 335

Bora-Bora, French Polynesia
The U.S. Army established a base on the island early in World War II, 134-136

Bradley, Lieutenant General Omar N., USA (USMA, 1915)
Command role in the Allied invasion of Normandy, France, in June 1944, 160-164, 172, 175, 180, 184, 264-266
Served 1949-53 as Chairman of the Joint Chiefs of Staff, 299, 337, 339, 363

Brazil
The stores ship Glacier (AF-4) was briefly the U.S. station ship in Rio de Janeiro during World War I, 31-33

Budgetary Considerations/Issues
Cutbacks in the Defense Department budget in 1949-50, 312-316, 328-329, 333-334

California, USS (BB-44)
    Operations in the Pacific in the mid-1920s, 56-63
    As part of the Battle Fleet, made a voyage to Australia in 1925, 63-68, 109-110
    Training cruise to the Caribbean and Atlantic in the late 1920s, 68-71, 76

Cebu, Philippine Islands
    Capture of by U.S. amphibious forces in 1945, 256-260

Chiang Kai-shek
    Relationship with Struble and the U.S. Seventh Fleet in the early 1950s, 344-349

China
    The gunboat Panay (PR-5) was sunk by the Japanese near Nanking in 1937, 117-118
    As a threat to Taiwan in the early 1950s, 344-349
    Red Chinese support of North Korea during the Korean War in the early 1950s, 352, 406
    Questions in the 1950s about the border with the Soviet Union, 442-445

Churchill, Sir Winston S.
    As British Prime Minister at the time of the Allied invasion of Normandy, France, in 1944, 148-149, 155-157

Coaling Ship
    Done by U.S. Navy ships circa 1915, 16

Coast Guard, U.S.
    Relationship with the Navy in the San Francisco area in the mid-1930s, 100

Collins, General J. Lawton, USA (USMA, 1917)
    As Army Chief of Staff, his involvement with the Korean War, 350-351, 358-361

Communications
    Work of the Office of Naval Communications in the late 1920s concerning codes, 78-82
    Role of the 12th Naval District communications office in the mid-1930s, 98-103

Coney, Captain Charles E., USN (USNA, 1919)
    Commanded the light cruiser Nashville (CL-43) when she was hit by a kamikaze in December 1944, 232-241

Congress, U.S.
    During World War II received testimony from officers in OpNav, 190-192

Convoys
    Escort operations out of Queenstown, Ireland, in World War I, 35-40
    Between Panama and the Western Pacific in 1941-42, 130-135

Use of in the Atlantic in World War II as protection against German submarines, 38

Cooper, Brigadier General Merian C., USAF (Ret.)
Went to fight in France with the Army in World War I and later the Pacific in World War II, 19

Corregidor, Philippine Islands
Recaptured by U.S. amphibious forces in 1945, 246-254

Cruisers
The U.S. Navy added a number of heavy cruisers to the fleet in the 1930s, 90-91

Cryptography
Concerns about the security of U.S. naval codes in the late 1920s, 78-82
U.S. Navy attempts in the late 1920s to break foreign codes, 82

Damage Control
Practices on board the heavy cruiser Portland (CA-33) in the mid-1930s, 103-108
Concern for on the part of Commander Cruisers Scouting Force in the mid-1930s, 111-113

De Gaulle, General Charles
Concern in 1943 about crew members of the battleship Richelieu being recruited by the Free French, 120-122, 139

Demobilization
Release from active duty of Mine Force Pacific Fleet personnel after World War II ended in 1945, 270-273

Denfeld, Admiral Louis E., USN (USNA, 1912)
Served as Chief of Naval Operations, 1947-49, 311-315, 331

Doyle, Rear Admiral James H., USN (USNA, 1920)
Served on Vice Admiral Richmond K. Turner's amphibious staff in World War II, 309
Commanded Amphibious Group One during the invasions of Inchon and Wonsan, Korea, and evacuation from Hungnam in 1950, 309, 363-365, 388, 393, 401

Dulles, John Foster
Served as Secretary of State, 1953-59, 454-455

Dunckel, Brigadier General William C., USA
Wounded on board the light cruiser Nashville (CL-43) when she was hit by a kamikaze in December 1944, 235-238

Eisenhower, President Dwight D., USA (USMA, 1915)
    Commanded the Allied invasion of Normandy, France, in June 1944, 142-149, 156-157, 159-162, 185, 263-265
    Service as President in the 1950s, 440

Fechteler, Rear Admiral William M., USN (USNA, 1916)
    Commanded amphibious operations in the Southwest Pacific in 1944-45, 194-197, 204-208, 256-257

First Fleet, U.S.
    In the early 1950s provided training to ships and aircraft headed for the Korean War, 421-424

France
    Allied invasion of Normandy in June 1944 and its aftermath, 146-189, 263-266
    Interests in Indo-China in the late 1940s, 318-319, 323-326

French Navy
    The New York Navy Yard repaired the battleship <u>Richelieu</u> in 1943, 119-122, 139

George VI, King
    British monarch who was briefed in 1944 about the coming Allied invasion of Normandy, France, 163

German Army
    Role in the defense against the Allied invasion of Normandy, France, in June 1944, 150-153, 162-163, 168-169, 172-176

German Navy
    Operations in the Atlantic during World War I, 31-40
    Sank merchant ships on the run from Panama to Australia in the early 1940s, 131-133
    U-boat sinkings off the U.S. East Coast early in World War II, 190-191

Germany
    The U.S. Air Force conducted the Berlin Airlift in 1948-49, 335

<u>**Glacier**</u>**, USS (AF-4)**
    Navy refrigerated stores ship that operated off the U.S. West Coast and down to Central and South America in the mid-1910s, 20-33

Great Britain
    Involvement in the Allied invasion of Normandy, France, in June 1944, 141-160, 176-179, 182, 185-189, 263-265
    Cutbacks in size and responsibility of the Royal Navy in the late 1940s, 317-318
    Interests in Singapore and the Malay Peninsula in the late 1940s, 320-326

Greece
   Interaction between Greek and Turkish representatives to the United Nations in the early 1950s, 437-438, 446

Greek Navy
   Purchased the U.S. battleship Idaho (BB-24) in the summer of 1914, 14-15

Gunnery-Naval
   Gunnery practice by the battleship New York (BB-34) in the early 1930s, 92-94

Haiti
   The U.S. destroyer Shubrick (DD-268) delivered money to Port-au-Prince during a crisis in 1919, 40-41

Hall, Rear Admiral John L., Jr., USN (USNA, 1913)
   Commanded U.S. naval forces during the invasion of Normandy, France, in June 1944, 159, 167, 181, 187, 263

Hawaii
   Pearl Harbor served as a base for fleet operations in 1940-41, 128-130
   Devastating effect on U.S. Navy ships by the Japanese air attack on Pearl Harbor in 1941, 46-49

Hornbeck, Dr. Stanley K.
   State Department official who was an expert in Far Eastern affairs in the 1930s and 1940s, 127-128

Hughes, Admiral Charles F., USN (USNA, 1888)
   Served 1927-30 as Chief of Naval Operations, 77

Hughes, USS (DD-410)
   Served as Struble's flagship during amphibious operations in the Philippine Islands in 1944, 201, 218-219

Hungnam, Korea
   U.S. evacuation from in December 1950, 393

Idaho, USS (BB-24)
   Battleship that was sold to Greece in 1914 while Naval Academy midshipmen were on board for a summer training cruise in the Mediterranean, 14-15

Inchon, South Korea
   Site of a United Nations amphibious landing in September 1950, 301-303, 357-393

India
Interaction between Pakistani and Indian representatives to the United Nations in the early 1950s, 447-448

Intelligence
Struble's belief that there should have been joint-service intelligence during the Korean War, 410-411

Ireland
Queenstown was a base for U.S. convoy escort operations in World War I, 35-40

Jackson, Captain Richard H., USN (USNA, 1887)
Commanded the Battle Fleet in 1926-27, 68, 71-77, 82-83

Japan
U.S. plans for invading the Japanese home islands, beginning in late 1945, 227-229
Attacked in August 1945 with atomic bombs, 228-229
Participated in the clearing of mines in the immediate aftermath of World War II, 1945-46, 267-282
As a base of operations for U.S. warships involved in the Korean War in the early 1950s, 350-351

Japanese Navy
Devastating effect on U.S. Navy ships by the Japanese air attack on Pearl Harbor in 1941, 46-49
After the battles around the Philippines in 1944, the Japanese were limited in their ability to wage naval warfare, 261-262

Johnson, Louis A.
Cutbacks in the Defense Department budget when he was the Secretary of Defense, 1949-50, 312-313, 328, 333-334
Meeting in the spring of 1950 about the Philippines, 339

Joy, Vice Admiral C. Turner, USN (USNA, 1916)
Served during the Korean War as Commander U.S. Naval Forces Far East, 342-343, 347-351, 358, 361-364, 396, 399-400, 414

Kamikazes
Struble's assessment of, 221
Attack on the destroyer Mahan (DD-364) at Ormoc Bay in December 1944, 216-217
Unsuccessful attack on the destroyer Hughes (DD-410) in December 1944, 219
Attack on the Nashville (CL-43) flagship of Struble, in the Mindoro operation in 1944, 232-241

Kessing, Ensign Oliver O., USN (USNA, 1914)
    Was held briefly as a hostage in Mazatlan, Mexico, during unrest in that city in 1916, 27-28

King, Admiral Ernest J., USN (USNA, 1901)
    In the 1920s was a latecomer to naval aviation, 59-60
    Concern about antisubmarine warfare in the Atlantic in World War II, 191
    As Commander in Chief U.S. Fleet, was involved in the planning and execution of the Allied invasion of Normandy, France, in 1944, 157-158, 188-189
    Received detailed information after the Normandy operation, 186-187, 193

Kinkaid, Vice Admiral Thomas C., USN (USNA, 1908)
    Commanded the U.S. Seventh Fleet during the capture of the Philippines in 1944-45, 200-202, 208-211, 221-222, 254, 262, 304, 413

Kirk, Rear Admiral Alan G., USN (USNA, 1909)
    Commanded the U.S. naval task force that invaded Normandy, France, in June 1944, 140-146. 159-162, 167, 170-174, 177-181, 185-189, 263-265

Korean War
    The beginning of the war in June 1950 came as a surprise, 333, 350-352
    U.S/U.N. amphibious landing at Inchon, South Korea, in September 1950, 301-302, 357-393
    Wonsan was the site of a U.S./U.N. amphibious landing in October 1950, 394-399, 401, 408-411
    Relationship of President Harry Truman and General Douglas MacArthur in 1950-51, 284-286
    Role of the Seventh Fleet in the war, 1950-51, 353-420
    U.S./U.N. aviation operations in the early part of the war, 1950-51, 369, 372, 376, 384-385, 401-404, 408, 418-420
    Negotiations between sides at Panmunjom, 441

Leahy, Fleet Admiral William D., USN (USNA, 1897)
    Served as chief of staff to President Harry Truman in the late 1940s, 336-337

Leave and Liberty
    In Queenstown, Ireland, during World War I, 39-40

Lee, Trygve H.
    In the early 1950s served as Secretary-General of the United Nations, 439

Leyte, Philippine Islands
    Capture of by U.S. amphibious forces in 1944, 194-206, 209-211

Lindbergh, Charles A.
    Solo flight from New York to Paris in 1927, 71-72

Lodge, Henry Cabot Jr.
In the early 1950s served as the U.S. representative to the United Nations, 430-435, 439-440

Long Beach, California
Site of an earthquake in March 1933, 94-95

Luzon, Philippine Islands
Capture of by U.S. amphibious forces in 1945, 245, 251-253

MacArthur, General of the Army Douglas, USA (USMA, 1903)
Commanded the Southwest Pacific Force during the capture of the Philippines in 1944-45, 193-196, 202-204, 209, 223-229, 247-248, 254-256, 259, 262, 303-306, 309-310, 341, 413
Role in Japan in the years shortly after the end of World War II, 268, 274-275, 282-284, 306, 341-343, 347-350
As United Nations commander in 1950-51, during the Korean War, 284-286, 302-303, 350-353, 358, 361, 364-367, 377-380, 386-388, 404, 412, 415-416

"Magic Carpet"
Once World War II ended, overseas personnel were brought back to the United States by ships collectively dubbed as the "Magic Carpet, 271-272

Mahan, USS (DD-364)
Badly damaged by a Japanese kamikaze in December 1944 and sunk by the U.S. Navy, 216-217

Malaya
British interests in Singapore and the Malay Peninsula in the late 1940s, 320-326

Marine Corps, U.S.
Development of amphibious warfare by the Navy and Marine Corps in the early 1930s, 64-65, 85-87
Role in amphibious warfare in the late 1940s, 288-296, 300, 306-307
Participation in the Inchon landing in 1950, in the early part of the Korean War, 363-365, 373, 376, 379-380, 384, 387-389, 400-401

Martin, Vice Admiral Harold M., USN (USNA, 1919)
Commanded the Seventh Fleet during the Korean War, 417-418

Massachusetts, USS (BB-2)
Used for training of Naval Academy midshipmen in the summer of 1912, 13-14

McCormick, Lieutenant Lynde D., USN (USNA, 1915)
Discussion in the early 1920s about assignment of officers to submarines, 53-54

Medals and Decorations
  Awarded in the immediate post-World War II period for wartime actions, 268-269

Mediterranean Sea
  Status of naval operations in the early 1950s, 425-427

Mexico
  The U.S. Navy established a presence off the coast during periods of unrest in the mid-1910s, 21-30

Mindanao, Philippine Islands
  Capture of by U.S. amphibious forces in 1945, 259

Mindoro, Philippine Islands
  Capture of by U.S. amphibious forces in 1944, 205-211, 220-224, 229-244

Mine Warfare
  German use of mines as part of the defense against the Allied invasion of France in June 1944, 176-177
  U.S. minesweeping around the island of Leyte in the Philippines in 1944, 199
  The Japanese were limited in their ability to mine the waters around the Philippines in 1944-45, 260-261
  Role of the Mine Force Pacific Fleet in clearing mines in the immediate aftermath of World War II, 1945-46, 267-282
  Use during the Korean War, 366-369, 381-383, 395-400, 411-414

Missiles
  U.S. development of in the late 1940s, 328-330

Missouri, USS (BB-63)
  Served as flagship of Commander Seventh Fleet during the Korean War, 397, 403, 414-417, 421

Moon, Rear Admiral Don P., USN (USNA, 1916)
  Commanded U.S. naval forces during the invasion of Normandy, France, in June 1944, 159-161, 164-167, 187

Nashville, USS (CL-43)
  Served as flagship for Struble during the invasion of Mindoro in the Philippines in 1944, 220-222, 229-241
  Hit by Japanese kamikaze on 13 December 1944, 232-241

Naval Academy, Annapolis, Maryland
  Hazing of midshipmen in the early 1910s, 6-10
  Summer sailing in 1914 on board the academy yacht Robert Setter, 11-12
  Academics in the 1911-15 period, 12-13, 18

Athletics in the 1911-15 period, 16-17
Summer training cruises, 13-14
Professional training of midshipmen, 17
Instructors in the early 1920s brought in fleet experience on engineering, 50-54

Naval Aviation
Competition with the Army aviation program for resources, 18-19

Naval Intelligence, Office of (ONI)
Role of in the late 1930s and relationship with the OpNav Central Division, 124-127

New York, USS (BB-34)
Operations in the Pacific in the early 1930s included gunnery practice, 92-98

New York Navy Yard
Repaired the French Battleship Richelieu in 1943, 119-122

Nimitz, Commander Chester W., USN (USNA, 1905)
In the late 1920s served on the staff of Commander Battle Fleet, 62, 76, 84
During World War II commanded the Pacific Fleet, 223-226, 261-262, 266, 268, 303-310
Involvement with the United Nations after World War II, 448-449

Normandy, France
Planning in 1943-44 for the invasion, 141-145, 148-150, 154-155, 161-165, 187-188, 263-266
Invasion in June 1944 and its aftermath, 146-189

Nuclear Weapons
Role of U.S. atomic bombs in compelling Japan to surrender in August 1945, 228-229
Residual effects in Japan after the war, 279
U.S. strategy in the 1950s called for massive retaliation with nuclear weapons in the event of attack, 454-455

Oil Fuel
Training at Philadelphia in 1917 concerning the use of oil, rather than coal, as a fuel in U.S. warships, 33-34
In the late 1940s Amphibious Force Pacific Fleet was looking into oil pipelines in Alaska, 297-299

Okinawa
Served as a base for minesweeping operations in the Western Pacific after the end of World War II, 267-269

OpNav
    In the late 1930s the Central Division of OpNav served as liaison between the Navy and State Department, 116-128
    Work of the Central Division in 1942-43, 119-125, 137-139, 190
    Role of OP-03, the DCNO (Operations), 1948-50. 311-338

Ormoc, Leyte, Philippine Islands
    Capture of by U.S. amphibious forces in 1944, 205-217, 222-223, 231-232, 258-260

Pakistan
    Interaction between Pakistani and Indian representatives to the United Nations in the early 1950s, 447-448

Panama
    The light cruiser Trenton (CL-11) operated around Panama in 1941, 130-137

Panama Canal
    Value of the canal to U.S. naval operations over the years, 42-43
    Protection against attack in World War II, 136-137

Panay, USS (PR-5)
    Sunk by the Japanese near Nanking, China, in 1937, 117-118

Pandit, Vijaya Lakshimi
    In the early 1950s served as India's representative to the United Nations, 447-449

Patton, Lieutenant General George S., Jr., U.S. Army (USMA, 1909)
    Command role in the Allied invasion of Normandy, France, in June 1944, and its aftermath, 164, 184

Pearl Harbor, Hawaii
    Served as a base for fleet operations in 1940-41, 128-130
    Devastating effect on U.S. Navy ships by the Japanese air attack in 1941, 46-49

Philadelphia, Pennsylvania
    Training at Philadelphia in 1917 concerning the use of oil, rather than coal, as a fuel in U.S. warships, 33-34

Philippine Islands
    U.S. amphibious operations in 1944-45 to capture islands in the Philippine archipelago, 194-225, 229-260, 303-306, 309-310

Planning
    In 1943-44 for the Allied invasion of Normandy, France, 141-145, 148-150, 154-155, 161-165, 187-189, 263-266
    In 1950 for the United Nations invasion of Inchon, Korea, 362-374

Portland, USS (CA-33)
    Damage control practices on board in the mid-1930s, 103-108
    Operations in the Pacific in the mid-1930s, 108-110

Pringle, Rear Admiral Joel R. P., USN (USNA, 1892)
    In the late 1920s was chief of staff to Commander Battle Fleet, Admiral Richard Jackson, 75-76, 82-83
    In the early 1930s served as Commander Battleship Division Three, 64-66, 82-88
    Death of in 1932, 83

Propulsion Plants
    Training at Philadelphia in 1917 concerning the use of oil, rather than coal, as a fuel in U.S. warships, 33-34

Public Relations
    In the spring of 1951, Struble hosted a number of businessmen on board his flagship, the battleship Missouri (BB-63), 417, 421

Puget Sound Navy Yard, Bremerton, Washington
    Did repair and overhaul work on heavy cruisers in the mid-1930s, 112-114

Queenstown, Ireland
    Base for U.S. convoy escort operations in World War I, 35-40

Radford, Vice Admiral Arthur W., USN (USNA, 1916)
    Served 1948-49 as Vice Chief of Naval Operations, 314-315
    From 1949 to 1953 was Commander in Chief Pacific Fleet, 342-344, 348-350, 399-400, 413-415, 421, 424

Ramsay, Admiral Sir Bertram H., RN
    British admiral who was in overall command of the naval elements of the invasion of Normandy, France, in 1944, 141-146, 159-161, 182, 188-189, 264

Reeves, Admiral Joseph M., USN (USNA, 1894)
    Developed the aviation capabilities of the fleet while in various billets in the 1930s, 88-89

Richelieu (French Battleship)
    Repaired at the New York Navy Yard in 1943, 119-122

Rio de Janeiro, Brazil
    The stores ship Glacier (AF-4) was briefly the U.S. station ship in Rio de Janeiro in 1917, 31-33

Rittenhouse, Commander Ellis B., USN (USNMA, 1934)
  Commanded the destroyer Hughes (DD-410) during the Philippine campaign in 1944, 219

Rommel, Field Marshal Erwin, German Army
  Role in the defense against the Allied invasion of Normandy, France, in June 1944, 150-153, 162-163, 169

Roosevelt, President Franklin D.
  Policy of keeping the U.S. Fleet forward based in Hawaii in 1940-41, 129-130

Royal Navy
  Cutbacks in size and responsibility in the late 1940s-early 1950s, 317-318, 425-427
  Participation in the Korean War in the early 1950s, 353-356

Rules of Engagement
  Prohibition against U.S. aviators flying over the Yalu River into Communist China in the early part of the Korean War, 401-405, 418-420

Sailing
  Summer sailing by midshipmen in 1914 on board the Naval Academy yacht Robert Setter, 11-12

San Francisco, California
  Operation of the Coast Guard station there in the mid-1930s, 100
  Role of the Twelfth Naval District communications office in the mid-1930s, 98-103

Seventh Fleet, U.S.
  Status of in the spring of 1950, 338-343
  Relationship with Chiang Kai-shek and Taiwan in the early 1950s, 344-349, 352
  Participation in the Korean War, 1950-51, 353-420

Sharp, Admiral Ulysses S. Grant, USN (USNA, 1927)
  Role in planning the invasion of Inchon, Korea, in 1950, 362

Sherman, Admiral Forrest P., USN (USNA, 1918)
  Suddenly became Chief of Naval Operations in late 1949, 331-332
  Involvement with the Korean War, 350-351, 358-362

Shubrick, USS (DD-268)
  Operations around Haiti in 1919, soon after the ship was commissioned, 40-42
  Operated out of San Diego in the early 1920s, 44-45, 49

Singapore
  British interests in Singapore and the Malay Peninsula in the late 1940s, 320-326

Sixth Fleet, U.S.
OpNav support of in the late 1940s, at the expense of the Pacific Fleet, 315-318

Soviet Union
In the early 1950s Andrei Y. Vishinsky served as the Soviet Union's representative to the United Nations, 429-433
Questions in the 1950s about the border with China, 442-445
Military delegation to the United Nations in the early 1950s, 446

Stark, Admiral Harold R., USN (USNA, 1903)
Commanded U.S. naval forces in Europe during World War II, 140-141, 186

State Department
In the late 1930s and early 1940s the Central Division of OpNav served as liaison between the Navy and State Department, 116-128, 137-139

Stevens, USS (DD-86)
Convoy duty in World War I, 35-38

Strategy
U.S. strategy in the Pacific in 1944-45 on which areas to invade, 223-228, 304-305
U.S. strategy in the 1950s called for massive retaliation with nuclear weapons in the event of attack, 454-455

Struble, Admiral Arthur D., USN (Ret.) (USNA, 1915)
Parents, 1-5, 12
Siblings, 2-3, 5
Wife Hazel, 35-36, 54-55, 74, 77, 94-95, 193, 266
Children, 55, 94-95
Boyhood and youth in Oregon at the beginning of the 20th century, 2-5
As a Naval Academy midshipman, 1911-15, 6-12
In the spring of 1915 Struble made his first airplane flight with an Army cavalry officer, 20
In the mid-1910s served in the Navy refrigerated stores ship Glacier (AF-4), 20-33
Served in the new destroyer Stevens (DD-86) in 1917-19, 35-40
In 1919-20 was executive officer and then commanding officer of the destroyer Shubrick (DD-268), 40-45, 49
Taught at the Naval Academy from 1921 to 1923, 50-54
Was in the crew of the battleship California (BB-44) from 1923 to 1925, 56-57, 60-68
Served 1925-27 as aide to Commander Battleships and then Commander Battle Force, 68-77
From 1927 to 1930 served in the Office of Naval Communications in Washington, 77-82
Served 1930-32 as flag secretary for Commander Battleship Division Three, 64-65, 82-91

In 1932-33 was gunnery officer of the battleship New York (BB-34), 91-98
Served 1933-35 as communications officer of the 12th Naval District, 98-103
In 1935-36 was first lieutenant and damage control officer of the heavy cruiser Portland (CA-33), 103-110
Served 1936-37 on the staff of Commander Cruisers Scouting Force, 111-115
From 1937 to 1940 was assigned to the Central Division of the OpNav staff, 116-128
As executive officer of the battleship Arizona (BB-39), 1940-41, 128-130
Commanded the light cruiser Trenton (CL-11) in 1941-42, 130-137
Headed the Central Division of OpNav in 1942-43, 119-125, 137-139, 190-192
In 1943-44 served as chief of staff to Commander Task Force 122 for the invasion of Normandy, France, 140-189
In 1944-45 commanded amphibious groups in the war against Japan, 193-266
In 1945-46 commanded Mine Force Pacific Fleet, 267-287
Served as Commander Amphibious Force Pacific Fleet, 1946-48, 287-300
Served 1948-50 as Deputy Chief of Naval Operations (Operations), 299, 311-338
In 1950-51 was Commander Seventh Fleet, 338-417
In 1951-52 served as Commander First Fleet, 421-424
From 1952 to 1955 was assigned as a U.S. representative to the United Nations, 428-455

Struble, Lieutenant (junior grade) George W., USN (USNA, 1908)
After serving an initial period of active duty, resigned from the Navy in 1914 and worked for Bethlehem Steel as a civilian, 5-6

Subic Bay, Philippine Islands
Capture of by U.S. forces in 1945, 245-246, 252-253

Taiwan
Relationship with the U.S. Seventh Fleet in the early 1950s, 343-349, 351

Tennessee, USS BB-43)
Involved in an amphibious warfare exercise in San Francisco Bay in the early 1930s, 64-66

Twelfth Naval District, San Francisco
Role of the communications office in the mid-1930s, 98-103

Training
Naval Academy summer training cruises in the early 1910s, 13-14

Trenton, USS (CL-11)
Operated around Panama in 1941, 130-133, 136-137
Convoyed ships to Bora-Bora in 1941-42, 134-136

Truman, President Harry S.
Attitude toward the armed forces in the late 1940s, 336-337
Relationship with General Douglas MacArthur during the Korean War, 284-286

Turkey
Interaction between Greek and Turkish representatives to the United Nations in the early 1950s, 437-438, 446

Turner, Vice Admiral Richmond K., USN (USNA, 1908)
Contributions as amphibious commander in the Pacific during World War II, 307-310, 364

United Nations
Was the overall organization fighting the Korean War against the Communists in the early 1950s, 353, 441
U.S. military representatives to the United Nations, 1952-55, 428-455
Value of national veto power in the Security Council, 452

Vishinsky, Andrei Y.
In the early 1950s served as the Soviet Union's representative to the United Nations, 429-433

Weather
A storm hit Normandy, France, shortly after the June 1944 Allied invasion, 180-185

West Virginia, USS (BB-48)
Departure from San Francisco in heavy weather in the late 1920s, 73

Wonsan, Korea
Site of a U.S./U.N. amphibious landing in October 1950, 394-399, 401, 408-411

World War I
German Navy operations in the Atlantic during 1917, 31-33
Convoy escort operations out of Queenstown, Ireland, in World War I, 35-40

www.ingramcontent.com/pod-product-compliance
Lightning Source LLC
Chambersburg PA
CBHW080626170426
43209CB00007B/1520